Augsburg Commentary on the New Testament
MATTHEW

Robert H. Smith

Augsburg Publishing House
Minneapolis, Minnesota

AUGSBURG COMMENTARY ON THE NEW TESTAMENT
Matthew

Copyright © 1989 Augsburg Publishing House

All rights reserved. Except for brief quotations in critical articles or reviews, no part of this book may be reproduced in any matter without prior written permission from the publisher. Write to: Permissions, Augsburg Publishing House, 426 S. Fifth St., Box 1209, Minneapolis MN 55440.

Scripture quotations, unless otherwise noted, are from the Revised Standard Version of the Bible, copyright 1946, 1952, and 1971 by the Division of Christian Education of the National Council of Churches.

Library of Congress Cataloging-in-Publication Data

Smith, Robert H., 1932–
  MATTHEW.

  (Augsburg commentary on the New Testament)
  Bibliography: p.
  1. Bible. N.T. Matthew—Commentaries.
I. Title. II. Series.
BS2575.3.S63   1988   226'.207   88-7767
ISBN 0-8066-8854-8

Manufactured in the U.S.A.   APH 10-9012

     2   3   4   5   6   7   8   9   0   1   2   3   4   5   6   7   8   9

For
Luther M. Doctor, Arnold H. Bringewatt,
and James W. Mayer†
Teachers of Righteousness

CONTENTS

FOREWORD

The AUGSBURG COMMENTARY ON THE NEW TESTA-
MENT is written for laypeople, students, and pastors. Laypeople
will use it as a resource for Bible study at home and at church.
Students and instructors will read it to probe the basic message
of the books of the New Testament. And pastors will find it to
be a valuable aid for sermon and lesson preparation.

The plan for each commentary is designed to enhance its usefulness. The Introduction presents a topical overview of the biblical book to be discussed and provides information on the historical circumstances in which that book was written. It also
contains a summary of the biblical writer's thought. In the body
of the commentary, the interpreter sets forth in brief compass
the meaning of the biblical text. The procedure is to explain the
text section by section. Attempts have been made to avoid scholarly jargon and the heavy use of technical terms. Because the
readers of the commentary will have their Bibles at hand, the
biblical text itself has not been printed out. In general, the editors
recommend the use of the Revised Standard Version of the Bible.

The authors of this commentary series are professors at sem-
inaries and universities and are themselves ordained. They have
been selected both because of their expertise and because they

worship in the same congregations as the people for whom they are writing. In elucidating the text of Scripture, therefore, they attest to their belief that central to the faith and life of the church of God is the Word of God.

The Editorial Committee
Roy A. Harrisville
Luther Northwestern Theological Seminary
St. Paul, Minnesota

Jack Dean Kingsbury
Union Theological Seminary
Richmond, Virginia

Gerhard A. Krodel
Lutheran Theological Seminary
Gettysburg, Pennsylvania

ACKNOWLEDGMENTS

I am grateful to Pacific Lutheran Theological Seminary and its Board of Directors for a study leave in 1985–1986 and to Lutheran Brotherhood for a sabbatical scholarship. My wife Meta and I were enabled to live and work in Athens, Greece, during the spring of 1986, and we remember very fondly the hospitality of Professor Savas Agourides and Professor Basil Tsakonas of the University of Athens. Here at PLTS several people assisted, always ably and cheerfully, in the typing of the manuscript: Jan Sheldon, Susan Nachtigal, and Laurel Alexander. I owe very much to the editorial staff of Augsburg Fortress for their friendship and patience over the past several years, as they shepherded this manuscript and other projects of mine. A special word of gratitude to John Nordin for countless detailed suggestions and to Jack Kingsbury, both for his encouragement and for his ever-friendly criticism. Finally, this volume is dedicated to three pioneering individuals who redefined the words "mission" and "ministry."

ABBREVIATIONS

ATR	*Anglican Theological Review*
BTB	*Biblical Theology Bulletin*
CBQ	*Catholic Biblical Quarterly*
ExpT	*Expository Times*
HTR	*Harvard Theological Review*
IBS	*Irish Biblical Studies*
IDB	*Interpreter's Dictionary of the Bible*
Interp.	*Interpretation*
JAAR	*Journal of the American Academy of Religion*
JBL	*Journal of Biblical Literature*
JSNT	*Journal for the Study of the New Testament*
NovT	*Novum Testamentum*
NTS	*New Testament Studies*
TDNT	*Theological Dictionary of the New Testament*, ed. Kittel
TS	*Theological Studies*
ZNW	*Zeitschrift für die neutestamentliche Wissenschaft*

INTRODUCTION

At one time "introductions" to biblical books in commentaries like this focused on the name of the author and on the time and place of writing. So arguments raged over the identity of Matthew. The titles to all four canonical Gospels were no part of the original documents and were probably added in the middle of the second century, around the year A.D. 150. Are those traditional titles reliable? Was this Gospel really written by a person named Matthew, and was this Matthew really a former tax collector called by Jesus as one of the original 12 disciples (Matt. 9:13; 10:3)?

And just where did the author live? Efforts to locate the place of writing have generally settled on Antioch of Syria, although some students have preferred other places: Tyre, Berytus (Beirut), Sidon, Caesarea Maritima, or some place in the Transjordan.

In an effort to answer these questions, biblical students pored over ancient Christian writings like the *Church History* of Eusebius, sifting early traditions in a search for clues. The centuries-long process has yielded a tremendous mass of information, pseudoinformation, and guesses about Matthew's Gospel and about the life of the early church.

Nevertheless, the quest for Matthew has taken in recent years a somewhat different tack. Many now believe that we must learn to live with this Gospel as an anonymous masterpiece. At least, the Gospel is anonymous in the sense that we may never know the author's precise name and address. And yet interesting things can be known of the author if we turn away from Eusebius and Irenaeus and Papias and concentrate instead on a close reading of the Gospel. The document itself reveals the author's public persona, and close attention to its details will tell us important things about what kind of person wrote it. We should be able to discover within the sentences of the Gospel itself the author's aims and assumptions.

I will continue to speak of the author as "Matthew," even though what most interests me is not the name but the author's message or spiritual vision. Each one of the evangelists received and gathered traditions about Jesus, lived by them, meditated upon them in the light of his own time and place, and then finally was moved to reformulate and reissue them. What we have in our four Gospels are four astonishing portraits of Jesus, shaped by the four evangelists under the pressure of the Spirit of God, published for the guidance and energizing of Christian communities.

1. Profiles of the Gospels

Over the centuries certain views of the Gospels have grown into stereotypes and, like all stereotypes, they are more or less true—and more or less helpful, depending on how true they really are.

So readers have returned ever and again to Luke's Gospel for its rich portrait of the humanity of Jesus or of Jesus as the great and gracious physician, and to John's Gospel for its lofty insistence on the deity of Jesus and his unique oneness with the Father. Until modern times the church has largely ignored Mark, with its picture of a powerful but persecuted Jesus moving swiftly through conflicts to terrible death.

Matthew's Gospel has been cherished as "the ecclesiastical Gospel" and as "the teaching Gospel." In support of this portrait of the Gospel, students have called attention to these features of Matthew's Gospel: the use of the word *church* (16:18; 18:17, the only one of the Gospels to use the word) and the ecclesiastical concerns of chap. 18; the liturgical ring to Matthew's version of the Lord's Prayer (6:9-13) and to the cry of the disciples in the boat (8:25); the detailed regulations regarding such matters as oaths and fasting, marriage and divorce and what appears to be a generally "conservative" attitude toward matters of law, including the Sabbath (24:20); the stress on the fulfillment of prophecy (cf. 1:22); the organization of the words of Jesus into five discourses and other signs of a systematic mind.

Matthew's Gospel certainly is a priceless treasury of the words of Jesus, and those words of Jesus, lovingly collected by Matthew, are marked by a stunning practicality and have proved to be perennially useful in the ordering of the life of the Christian community. What else can be said of the organization and substance of Matthew's Gospel?

2. Matthew's Plan

It is of course not possible to sum up the entirety of Matthew's Gospel (or any other) in any half-dozen words, no matter how artfully chosen. Matthew's Gospel is a complex affair, consisting of just over 18,000 words, making it roughly the same size as the Gospel of Luke and the book of Acts. Each of these three documents probably filled a standard length ancient scroll. The text was not divided into our now traditional 28 chapters and 1,068 verses until many centuries after the evangelists wrote. So the Gospel was published without all those handy numbers, and without the helpful paragraph headings provided by some modern translations.

Ancient writers did, however, provide some signals to help their readers catch the drift. And Matthew is no exception. It may be useful to mention three of Matthew's more obvious devices.

A. Matthew five times concludes collections of the words of Jesus with the phrase, "When Jesus had finished these sayings." Using that concluding formula as a clue has led to the observation that Matthew has organized many (not all) of Jesus' sayings into five great discourses:

I. The new community is called to practice a higher righteousness (the Sermon on the Mount): chaps. 5–7 (cf.
7:28);

II. The new community in its mission encounters hostility:
chap. 10 (cf. 11:1);

III. The new community brings forth things new and old in
its teaching (parables): chap. 13 (cf. 13:53);

IV. The new community practices forgiveness and reconciliation: chap. 18 (cf. 19:1);

V. The new community readies itself for the coming of the
Son of man: chaps. 24–25 (cf. 26:1).

Precisely because of these five discourses or sermons, Matthew
has the reputation for being the teaching Gospel, or the Gospel
that portrays Jesus as teacher. The fact that Matthew himself calls
attention to the discourses by means of the concluding formulas
has led many commentators to feature the discourses and to take
the alternation of discourse waith narrative sections as the basis
for their outlines of the Gospel.

B. Another formula occurs at 4:17 and 16:21 and suggests a
different kind of organization of the material: "From that time
Jesus began to preach" (4:17; "to show," 16:21). On the basis of
this repeated phrase, some tend to subordinate the discourses
and to understand the Gospel as developing along chronological
and geographical lines as follows:

I. Introduction of Jesus, 1:1-4:16;

II. Galilean ministry and first confrontations, 4:17—16:20;

III. Up to Jerusalem to death and resurrection, 16:21—28:20.

I tend to think that Matthew inherited the chronological and
geographical scheme that lies behind the transitions at 4:17 and
16:21. He accepted it as the foundation for his own presentation.
His basic modification of that traditional scheme does not consist
of any fundamental alterations of the framework by the addition
or subtraction of geographical or chronological data. Rather, it
consists of the insertion of the discourses into the framework so
that there emerges the portrait of Jesus as teacher. Those words
of Jesus had captured his own imagination and, by featuring the
discourses prominently and unforgettably, he hoped they might
also enthrall his readers.

C. A third device helps the reader to focus on Matthew's purpose. Commentators have not paid much attention to this device. It is obvious that Jesus is the protagonist in Matthew's narrative. What has gone largely unnoted is that authors will frequently take special care with their protagonist's first words and last words. The initial revelation of the protagonist's mind manipulates the readers' expectations and prepares them for the ensuing narrative. And authors take pains in the formulation of final words, because last words do more than summarize. They confirm correct readings of the preceding text and bring the narrative to rest.

Jesus' first and last words in Matthew's Gospel are unique, not paralleled in the other Gospels, and they have the look of words designed to guide readers to correct perceptions.

The first utterance out of the mouth of Jesus is in dialog with John the Baptist at the Jordan River. When the Baptist protests that Jesus is the one who should be doing the baptizing, Jesus' response reveals that God's righteousness is central to his existence: "It is fitting for us to fulfill all righteousness" (3:15). The first syllables from his lips focus on God's project, described as making the world "all right," and on Jesus' own commitment to that program.

As his final words (28:18-20), Jesus, now raised from the grave and exalted with authority over heaven and earth, utters an imperial proclamation. That final word has three parts: (a) Jesus begins with a declaration of his own supreme and unbounded authority, (b) centers on the task of creating a community of disciples utterly dedicated to performing "all that I have commanded," and (c) closes with the assurance of his own unending presence in the community.

Matthew's Gospel is especially rich in the words of Jesus, and all those words have been so arranged and so displayed that they march in order from that first word about righteousness (3:15) to that final declaration about his authority, about a community of disciples, and about his living presence (28:18-20).

That first word and that last word cast light on all the words and deeds and sufferings of Jesus reported in the body of the Gospel; they illumine the forces which propel the action from moment to moment and from place to place.

Matthew pictures Jesus as bringer and teacher of righteousness. He makes right, and he summons to a surpassing rightness.

Disciples and crowds (potential disciples) gather round him, as he calls into being a new community of doers of God's will. But powerful critics, scrambling to retain their own influence over the people, attempt to silence his words and halt his progress.

The tensions in Matthew's plot are not resolved in a typical happy ending, nor does the plot rest with the complete destruction of Jesus on the anvil of his enemies' power. Jesus does not escape crucifixion, but in the very act of crucifying him, his critics are exposed as standing in contradiction to God outside the community of the blessed. In fact, at the very moment of Jesus' death, God shook the earth and raised up "saints" of old, signaling that God intends through the crucified and resurrected Jesus to establish a new community, universal in time and in space, embracing both old saints and new disciples (27:51-53). Matthew's narrative comes to rest only when Jesus, crucified but now resurrected, appears with sovereign authority over the nucleus of a new community of disciples who will do all that he has commanded (28:16-20).

On the basis of all these indicators (formulaic verses, five discourses, first and last words of Jesus, discernment of plot) a narrative outline is offered at the close of these pages of introduction.

But first a few other issues need to be addressed.

3. Authority, Community, and Righteousness

Matthew has pondered the traditions about Jesus and reissued them as guidance for his own Christian community and especially for its leaders, facing difficult questions of authority and power, identity and life-style (ethos), as the community emerged from Judaism and struggled to find its place as a new religious movement in the wider Greco-Roman world.

Jesus is of course the most complex and rounded of the characters in Matthew's narrative, and he functions at many levels in the dialog between Matthew and Matthew's readers. He is a positive model of the use of authority, and all his opponents (and sometimes the disciples) in various ways exhibit abuses of power and authority. The conflict between Jesus' authority and other authorities propels the story toward its climax in Jerusalem.

From beginning to end Matthew makes it clear that Jesus represents God's own movement into history, fulfilling ancient promises and expectations, liberating from sin, acting with God's own authority to make all things all right.

That all-rightness is spelled out in terms of gift and vocation. The very name *Jesus* means "gift of salvation," "liberation," "all-rightness" (1:21). He travels the lowly path of service bringing forgiveness and life for many (20:28; 26:28).

The sign of the divine presence in the new community is a life of righteousness, of the doing of the will of God, of love for God and neighbor.

The crowds in Matthew's narrative seem at first to be favorably disposed toward Jesus, and they acclaim him almost to the end. They fail to see him as more than a prophet, however, and finally they abandon even that insight and clamor for his crucifixion. Through most of the Gospel they seem to be potential disciples, astonished by Jesus, more open than their leaders. But finally they represent all who let themselves be led astray by their leaders, by authorities other than the authority of God at work in Jesus.

The disciples are portrayed more positively by Matthew than by Mark. In Matthew's Gospel they understand Jesus, and at the end they are gathered in Jesus' presence on the mountain; readers have the sense that they are competent to accomplish the great task Jesus sets before them. Indeed, disciples are women and men who understand Jesus, acknowledge him as Lord, trust him unwaveringly in times of trial, give up the ordinary quest for power and all the usual trappings of authority, and single-mindedly seek to do the will of God as interpreted by Jesus.

At least the disciples should be all that. But as Matthew portrays them they are neither cardboard cutouts nor plaster saints. That is, they are neither one-dimensional nor consistently pious. Their transactions with Jesus are complex, and it is a fact that they frequently err under pressure and as often as not deserve the epithet "little faiths" (cf. 8:26). These 12 are not only the nucleus of the new community but are also a mirror of the complicated realities of the human situation within that new community.

4. Matthew and His Contemporaries

Matthew's portrait of political and religious leaders is particularly bleak. At times he seems to lump all leaders together without in any way differentiating among them in terms of their own special traditions or in terms of their attitudes toward Jesus. Pharisees, scribes (lawyers or theologians), Sadducees, rulers of the house of Herod the Great, elders of the people, members of priestly families (whether the poor priests of the villages or the aristocratic high priestly families resident in Jerusalem) usually seem to present a solid wall of unrelenting opposition to Jesus. What Matthew has to say about them seems negative, harsh, and condemnatory. His portrait of Pharisees in chap. 23 is notorious.

Very few Romans even figure in the narrative. Pontius Pilate tries to wash his hands of the matter but Matthew does not let him off so easily. Jesus was crucified, and crucifixion was a Roman form of execution carried out by a squad of Roman legionnaires.

The drama of the Gospel is dominated by sharp conflicts between Jesus and the authorities. They start early and continue to the end. And they have long intrigued interpreters. Why does Matthew, so much more than Mark or Luke, feature these conflicts, and why does he picture the Pharisees especially in such a negative fashion? He seems to be not only caricaturing but, some would say, slandering.

Surely Jesus did often find himself embroiled in controversy with the leaders and teachers among his people. His words and deeds were in various ways so strange and offensive that, while some people were astonished and transformed in their thinking and living, others were outraged and opposed him as a blasphemer.

But Matthew is not simply reporting what happened in a previous generation. He is highly selective in his presentation. He does not show how Pharisees historically differed among themselves, how some were gentle and lenient and pacifistic, while others were stricter and more unyielding in their teachings about the will of God. Many ancient Pharisees themselves condemned ostentation and hypocrisy, castigating the emptiness of outward deeds without a corresponding inwardness. Matthew reports none of that. And he speaks of the traditions or teachings of

Pharisees and Sadducees as though they were a single movement, brushing aside the deep differences separating these two parties and their mutual antagonisms.

Again, why is Matthew so selective, so negative? Various guesses have been ventured. (1) It has been suggested that Matthew and the other evangelists were at pains to exonerate the Romans for the death of Jesus and had to blame someone, so they blamed the Jewish leaders. The theory is that the Christian movement had broken out from Judaism and was making its way among Gentiles in the wider world dominated by Roman culture. As it did so, it tended to play down Jesus' conflicts with Roman governing authorities. Focusing on that part of the tradition seemed counterproductive for the church's missionary outreach among the inhabitants of the Roman empire. And so the church, needing to account somehow for Jesus' execution, began to exaggerate the opposition of Jewish leadership to Jesus. That is one theory.

(2) Another theory, perhaps the dominant view today, situates Matthew and his community in the 80s and 90s of the first century, locked in controversy with the Jewish Pharisaic leadership of Jamnia. The war of liberation fought by the Jews against the vastly superior power of Rome had ended disastrously in A.D. 70. Holy city and holy temple were reduced to rubble (compare Matt. 22:7 with Luke 14:16-24; cf. 21:43). Institutions basic to the life of the people were torn apart. When Vespasian and his son Titus jointly celebrated their triumph in Rome in A.D. 71, they displayed, among other spoils of victory, items plundered from Jerusalem's temple: the seven-branched candelabrum, the table of shewbread, the trumpets, and a copy of the Law.

The very life of Judaism was in jeopardy. The Essene communities, like the one at Qumran, had been destroyed. Defeat discredited the Zealots and other advocates of a holy war against Rome. The Sadducees and high priestly families once had enjoyed great prestige because of their control of the temple and its rituals, but with the destruction of the temple and the cessation of sacrifice they lost their mediating and priestly function and with it they lost their old power and influence.

The future of Judaism lay with the Pharisees. Even before the war they were identified with institutions (synagogue and school) outside the domain of temple and priests, and these institutions served as the basis for the renaissance of a devastated Judaism. A Pharisee named Johanan ben Zakkai gathered around himself at the town of Jamnia a council of Pharisaic sages and began the task of rebuilding Judaism. Practices formerly confined to the temple and the priests, like the blowing of the ram's horn or shofar, were shifted to the synagogue. The Jamnia council with its president began to assume functions formerly exercised by the Sanhedrin of Jerusalem under the leadership of the high priest.

In the aftermath of the war, with the virtual disappearance of the Essenes, the Zealots, and the Sadducees, two vigorous Jewish communities lived side by side: the Pharisaic synagogue community and the Christian congregation (consisting of Jews or of Jews mixed with Gentile converts). Pharisees and Christians survived the war and stood ready to lead the people. Both had deep convictions regarding Scripture and the will of God, the identity of the people of God, the meaning of the destruction of Jerusalem, and the direction to take into the future. And both communities enjoyed gifted teachers and leaders.

Many believe that Matthew's Gospel must be interpreted as a product of the dialog or polemical exchange between leaders of the two communities, as church and synagogue competed for the loyalties of the same people, offering divergent interpretations of the life of Jesus and events of the recent past.

On this theory, Matthew paints Jewish leaders with negative colors because he is retelling the narrative of Jesus for polemical purposes in a context of urgent controversy.

(3) The view taken in this commentary is rather different from the first two. I think of Matthew as a Christian sage disturbed primarily by developments inside the Christian community. He recalls harsh words of Jesus against Pharisees and other leaders, not because he is locked in combat with the Pharisaic leaders of Jamnia, but because he is probing the mind of Jesus regarding issues of authority and leadership. At the same time he addresses issues of discipleship and followership.

Matthew does what evangelists and teachers and preachers have always done. He remembers words of Jesus spoken in an older context, meditates upon them, turning them over and over, examining them from fresh angles, applying them to himself and then to his community.

In his own day Matthew sees Christian leaders displaying the very sorts of behavior and attitudes criticized by Jesus. If he had been a writer of epistles or essays, he would have named names and issued warnings and encouragements as clearly as Paul did in addressing the Corinthians. But Matthew is not a writer of letters, like Paul. He wrote a Gospel. His communication with his readers is more indirect and oblique and ironic. He trusted his first readers to catch the point of his retelling of Jesus' story and to make the appropriate applications to their lives. We modern readers are at a disadvantage. We live at a great distance (in time and space, in language and culture) from those first readers. We make guesses about the precise situation of Matthew and his community, and our guesses do not always agree. I am guessing that Matthew had a particular concern for inattention to righteousness and to doing God's will on the part of many in his community, and especially on the part of leaders.

Matthew reveals a concern for "false prophets in sheep's clothing" (7:15-23). These are Christian insiders, and not only that but they are leaders who confess Jesus with proper language, calling him "Lord" (7:21-22). And yet they are exposed as false by the fact that they do not bear good fruit but are "evildoers" or, literally, "workers of lawlessness" (7:23).

It is a sign of the last times that false prophets and leaders rise up in the community and lead many astray (24:10-11) so that lawlessness is multiplied and love (*agapē*) grows cold (24:12).

Jesus says that at the final judgment these false leaders will protest that they have done all things well, boasting of their gifts of prophecy and exorcism and wonder-working (7:22). That is to say, they will boast on the basis of spiritual gifts or charismatic endowments. These, they think, are infallible signs that God dwells in them and favors them.

Secure in their charismatic power, these prophets, visionaries, healers, and inspired leaders ride roughshod over the less impressively endowed members of the community. And those ordinary members of the community, the "little ones," make the mistake of being unduly impressed and follow those leaders.

Matthew was not simple-mindedly anticharismatic. Indeed, in

his view all Christians are endowed with the Spirit of God (3:11; 10:20). But for Matthew the one sure sign of the indwelling of God through Jesus Christ is a heart set on the will of God, a life yielding fruit to God. Where God is at work through Jesus, people display the surpassing righteousness of which Jesus speaks in his first and final utterances (3:15; 28:18-20) and in the Sermon on the Mount (5:17-20).

Matthew is sometimes thought to be "conservative" in his ethical teaching. But Matthew does not portray Jesus as a literalist or strict constructionist with regard to the Law. Jesus teaches a righteousness which surpasses that of scribe and Pharisee and not one which merely imitates theirs. Jesus is pictured as reacting against legalism or ethical rigorism on the one hand and against libertinism and carelessness on the other.

The first public teaching of Jesus, in the first of the five great discourses, is the Sermon on the Mount with its extraordinary explication of the will of God. The Sermon opens with the Beatitudes (5:3-12), those astonishing declarations of grace upon unlikely persons, sharply challenging all ordinary patterns of ethical thinking. And the final public teaching of Jesus, at the close of the fifth discourse, is the great vision of the Son of man seated on his throne judging all the nations and dividing them into sheep and goats (25:31-46). That paragraph caps all the public teachings with yet one more unforgettable description of the higher righteousness to which the members of the new community are called, whether they are leaders or little ones.

Leadership in the new community means traveling the way of Jesus and John the Baptist, walking the way of righteousness and encouraging others to do likewise even when the cost is as great as it was for John (14:1-12) or for Jesus (cf. 16:21).

Ordinary members are instructed by this Gospel how to discern true from false leaders and are warned not to be led astray. All are called to celebrate by means of their discipleship the grace of God in touching the world in Jesus to make it all right. All are summoned to live lives of all-rightness as members of the community indwelt by the exalted Jesus, who is Lord and Son and Emmanuel.

When students of Matthew's Gospel today describe their varied understandings of the environment in which the Gospel was produced, they are theorizing or guessing. If they are serious, then of course they have reasons for making their particular guesses. They can point to evidence and not simply to hunches. The kind of evidence they have tends to be elusive, since it consists of such things as nuances in phrasings or in the patternings of words and sentences in the text, in understandings of the histories of Judaism and Christianity late in the first century, in perceptions about the dynamics of new religious movements, and even in such things as our varied theories of literature and rhetoric.

It would be an enormous help if we knew Matthew's name and address, and if we had infallible information about his precise situation and the exact audience for which he was writing. But even lacking these, all can agree that Matthew's narrative of Jesus shines an especially brilliant light on issues of authority (of kings and priests and religious leaders in general and of Jesus in particular) and on the matter of righteousness (both as unfathomable gift and high calling). That these are central concerns of the Jesus of Matthew's Gospel is no theory or guess but plain fact. We are guessing only when we attempt an answer to the question: What was it in his environment (inside the church or outside it) that prompted Matthew to reword the traditions of the words and deeds and sufferings of Jesus in just this particular way? To attempt to say anything more at this point would only distract writer and reader from the immediate task at hand: to read the Gospel carefully.

OUTLINE OF MATTHEW

Jesus' Journey to Universal Authority

I. 1:1—4:25

The infancy narrative (1:1—2:23) is played out on the background of Bethlehem of Judea, the land of Egypt, and Nazareth of Galilee. After an undisclosed interval of time, Jesus is baptized at the Jordan River and tested in the Wilderness of Judea (3:1—4:11). Following the arrest of John the Baptist, Jesus launches into his public ministry in Galilee (4:12-16). Jesus announces the nearness of the kingdom of heaven (4:17). At the sea of Galilee he summons four fishermen to follow him as the nucleus of a new community (4:18-22). Crowds begin to gather, drawn from the populations of Syria and Galilee and the cities of the Decapolis, from Jerusalem and Judea, and from the districts beyond the Jordan (4:23-25).

II. 5:1—7:29

The first four chapters of the Gospel are all introduction. Identifying Jesus and stirring hope, they prepare readers for Matthew's first detailed report of Jesus' public work.

Jesus' mission begins on a mysterious mountain in Galilee as he sits (the posture of teachers), surrounded by disciples and crowds, and utters the Sermon on the Mount (First Discourse), announcing God's stunning blessing and calling to a higher righteousness (5:1—7:29).

III. 8:1—10:42

The same crowds that formed the audience of the Sermon on the Mount follow Jesus as he comes down from the mountain to perform 10 mighty acts, underscoring with awesome displays of compassion and power his summons to the life of discipleship and righteousness (8:1—9:34). Once he crosses the lake and casts out demons in "the country of the Gadarenes" (8:28). Except for that brief foray, all the acts of these chapters occur in Galilee by the lake. Matthew 9:35 repeats the phrase of 4:23, emphasizing how Jesus conducted a mission of authoritative proclamation and healing in all the cities and villages of Galilee.

After his own initial activity of proclamation (5:1—7:29) and action (8:1—9:34), Jesus calls the 12 disciples to him and makes them instruments of his mission, addressing them from the perspective of Galilee, sending them not to Gentiles, not to Samaritans, but only to "the lost sheep of the house of Israel" (Second Discourse, 10:1-42).

IV. 11:1—13:58

From his prison John the Baptist sends word of his doubts about Jesus (11:2-3), and that message from John opens three chapters highlighting the mystery of doubts about Jesus. In the course of his response to skeptics and opponents Jesus speaks of the Baptist's work in the wilderness (11:7) and of his own work in the towns of Galilee on the northern rim of the lake: Chorazin, Bethsaida, Capernaum (11:21, 23). In fact, during all these days Capernaum seems to be Jesus' "own city" (9:1), from which he tours surrounding towns and to which he continually returns. In the face of the mystery of rejection, Jesus speaks of his true family as all those who do the will of God (12:46-50). Jesus leaves the house (at Capernaum) and, preparing to teach, sits in a boat on the edge of the sea of Galilee (13:1-2). His parables (chap. 13, Third Discourse) speak of the difficulties he encounters in his mission, comment on the nature of the nay-sayers, and calls hearers to sharp self-criticism (Are they wheat or weeds?) and to renunciation of judgmental acts toward others. From the sea he travels a short distance to Nazareth, where people in his old boyhood home greet him with mingled astonishment and unbelief (13:53-58).

V. 14:1—15:39

Misunderstanding and opposition turn lethal, and confession to Jesus also is heightened. Herod the tetrarch executes John the Baptist (14:1-12), foreshadowing Jesus' own execution. Jesus still works in Galilee around the lake, but the names of Gentile territories and of Jerusalem begin to intrude into the narrative. Jesus feeds the 5000 (14:13-21) and comes to his disciples during the storm, treading the waters underfoot, so that they confess him as "Son of God" (14:22-33). At the shore of the lake at Gennesaret (14:34) officials from Jerusalem provoke Jesus to speak about purity (15:1-20), after which Jesus travels toward Tyre and Sidon, meets a Gentile (unclean) woman of astonishing faith, and cures her daughter (15:21-28). Returning to the sea of Galilee, Jesus heals many people on a mountain there and feeds 4000 (15:29-39), later crossing to Magadan.

VI. 16:1—18:35

At the seaside village of Magadan (15:39) Jesus rejects the request for a sign, put to him by some officials, and moves once more across the lake, warning his disciples against the leaven (teaching) of the Pharisees and Sadducees (16:1-12). Jesus travels with his disciples just beyond the northernmost limits of Galilee, to Caesarea Philippi. There Peter confesses Jesus as "the Christ, the Son of the living God," and Jesus declares his intention to found his church, the new community (16:13-20). For the first time Jesus talks of moving up to Jerusalem and of his suffering and resurrection there (16:21-28). At some unnamed and unknown mountain Jesus is transfigured gloriously, but his own next words speak of imminent suffering and of faithless and perverse hearers (17:1-21). During his last days in Galilee, he once again announces his passion and resurrection (17:22-23). At Capernaum

(17:24) he speaks (Fourth Discourse) of boundless forgiveness as the heart of the life of the new community (18:1-35).

VII. 19:1—20:34

Jesus abandons Galilee and crosses the Jordan, moving towards Judea and Jerusalem (19:1-2). Along the way he astonishes disciples by sharply contrasting the higher righteousness he proclaims with prevailing attitudes and practice (19:3—20:16). As they travel the way to Jerusalem, Jesus utters yet a third prediction of his passion and resurrection (20:17-19). The request of the mother of James and John on behalf of her sons shows how far the disciples are from understanding the path of Jesus at this late time (20:20-28). Leaving Jericho, just before the ascent to Jerusalem, Jesus heals two blind men (compare the two sons of Zebedee) who, upon receiving their sight, follow him (20:29-34).

VIII. 21:1—23:39

As meek and humble king, Jesus enters Jerusalem and the temple of God, where he scatters the merchants but heals the broken. For that he is criticized by officials but acclaimed by children (21:1-16). On his return to Jerusalem from Bethany the next day he causes the fruitless fig tree to wither and praises the power of faith and prayer (21:17-22). Jesus teaches in the temple, praising obedience to the will of God, faith in the power of God, wholehearted love of God and of neighbor, speaking with uncommon authority (21:23—22:46), calling into question the way traditional teachers exercise their authority, and summoning leaders of the new community to lives of service and humility (23:1-39).

IX. 24:1—25:46

Jesus quits the temple and sits facing the city from the Mount of Olives across the valley, speaking to his disciples privately (Fifth Discourse). The heart of his final instruction is a summons to readiness for the day of judgment. Readiness takes the form of fidelity to the unseen but returning Lord, and such fidelity is described as acts of love to the hungry, the thirsty, the stranger, the naked, the sick, the imprisoned (24:1—25:46).

X. 26:1—27:66

Having completed all his teaching, Jesus prophesies his crucifixion during the Passover (26:1-2). Immediately his enemies
begin to move (26:3-5, 14-16). Meanwhile, Jesus is anointed at
Bethany (26:6-13) and celebrates the Passover in Jerusalem
(26:17-29). After the supper he moves to the Mount of Olives to
pray (26:30-46) and is arrested there (26:47-56). After trials before
Caiaphas (26:57-68) and Pilate (27:11-26), after Peter's denial and
weeping, (26:69-75), after Judas's repentance (27:3-10), after the
crowds reject him (27:25) and the soldiers mock him (27:27-31),
Jesus is crucified and buried (27:32-66).

XI. 28:1-20

On the first day of the week Mary Magdalene and the other
Mary are confronted by the angel of the Lord at the tomb and
hear the news of Jesus' resurrection. They are instructed by the
angel and then by the resurrected Jesus himself to tell the disciples to travel to Galilee (28:1-10). In Galilee on a mysterious
and unnamed mountain Jesus comes to them, announcing his
universal authority, commissioning them to create a community
of disciples, and promising his enduring presence (28:16-20).

COMMENTARY

■ Light Has Dawned (1:1—4:16)

In his opening chapters Matthew presents unique material, found in no other Gospel. It includes the genealogy (1:2-17), the giving of the names *Jesus* and *Emmanuel* (1:18-25), the arrival of Eastern sages guided by a star (2:1-12), escape to Egypt (2:13-15), the wrath of Herod (2:16-18), settling in Nazareth (2:19-23), and the story of Jesus' moving to Capernaum as his ministry is about to begin (4:12-16).

In this same section he also frequently shares material with Mark or Luke: the preaching of John the Baptist (3:1-12), the baptism of Jesus (3:13-17), and temptation in the wilderness (4:1-11).

Matthew uses a number of devices to weave together materials, miscellaneous as they are, into an impressive unity. Seven times Matthew punctuates his material, calling readers' attention to great ancient prophecies fulfilled in Jesus (1:22-23; 2:5-6, 15, 17-18, 23; 3:3; 4:14-16). The advent of Jesus is marked by an explosion of fulfillments.

Furthermore, Matthew focuses in paragraph after paragraph on names and titles of Jesus, heaping them up (there are many, but highest of all is "Son of God"). And throughout these four chapters Matthew speaks of Jesus' geography (Jerusalem, Bethlehem, Egypt, Nazareth, Jordan, the wilderness, Capernaum, Galilee). These chapters begin to look like a sustained meditation on the titles of Jesus and the names of towns and territories designed to goad the religious imagination.

All these notes and narratives together begin to identify Jesus, establish his credentials, arouse the readers' curiosity, stir hope, provoke expectations.

In the comments at the start of the next large section (4:17), it will be argued that all the paragraphs and separate incidents of these opening chapters (1:1—4:16) finally serve to introduce the Jesus who sits on the mysterious mountain in Galilee and utters what we call the Sermon on the Mount (chaps. 5–7). Matthew 1:1—4:16 answers questions about who this teacher of the Sermon on the Mount is and by what authority he speaks as he does.

Who Is He? (1:1-25)

All the Generations (1:1-17)

Matthew launches into his Gospel differently from the other evangelists. He begins not with prophecy (Mark), history (Luke), or hymnody (John) but with a genealogy. Some readers, viewing genealogies as a crashing bore, simply skip right over them. But Matthew is sending important signals about Jesus to the readers.

1—**The book of the genealogy of Jesus Christ** is the way the RSV translates the opening Greek words (*biblos geneseōs*) of Matthew's Gospel, implying that these words are only an introduction to 1:1-17. However, alternatives suggest themselves. The phrase may introduce the entire infancy narrative (Matthew 1–2) and could be translated, "The Story of Jesus' Origins." Or perhaps the words stand over the introduction to Jesus' ministry, conceived as running all the way from 1:1 to 4:16. They should then be rendered, "The Story of Jesus' Beginning Days."

A fourth possibility, very intriguing, is that the words may have been designed to serve as title of the entire Gospel. In that case they should be translated, "The Book of the New Genesis Produced by Jesus Christ."

Each of these four renderings is possible, and no one of them should be rejected out of hand. Furthermore, Matthew is anything but simple-minded, and he is perfectly capable of intending more than a single meaning with this single phrase.

Throughout chap. 1 and into chap. 2 Matthew has heaped up a series of words sharing the same root (*gen-*). That common Greek root can be seen in the English words *genealogy* and *generation* but it lurks also behind "the father of," "was born," "birth," and "wife." The impressive repetition is a signal from the author that something new, bursting with fresh, generative possibilities, has entered human history with the advent of Jesus. He is not just one more name in a continuing series of fathers and sons.

Jesus climaxes a long list of significant names. This genealogy therefore differs in shape from the ones in Genesis 5, 10, and 11. Those old genealogies all record first the great ancestor (Adam or the sons of Noah) and then they list all the descendants who came after him. Matthew names first of all the one in whom all the prior generations climax and find their fulfillment. Then he names all the ancestors mounting up through the years towards the climactic epiphany of Jesus.

The genealogy begins not with Adam (as in Luke 3:38) but with **Abraham** who flourished about 2000 years before Jesus. Israel sprang physically from the loins of **Abraham** but, more importantly, God promised blessing for "all the families of the earth" through Abraham and his seed (Gen. 12:3). For Matthew the name **Abraham** (vv. 1, 2, 17) means source and founder, not of Israel only, but of a great inclusive community embracing Gentiles as well as Jews, sinners as well as saints, all who hear the call of God and walk in the way of righteousness (Matt. 3:9; 8:11; 22:32).

The other highly honored name in Matthew's list is **David** (vv. 1, 6, 17). His is the only name among all 46 in the genealogy to appear with a title: **David, the king.** In featuring **David** among the ancestors of Jesus, Matthew means to have the aura of royalty rub off onto Jesus. He is king, but the question is this: What manner of king is Jesus, and what exactly can we expect of him? (see notes on 3:17; 21:1-11; 22:41-46).

Matthew will wrestle throughout the Gospel with the Abrahamic and Davidic connections of Jesus, that is, with the boundaries of the people of God and with the meaning of the royalty of Jesus.

That Jesus is designated the **Christ** (1:1, 16-17) means that he is God's appointed agent for rescuing, gathering, and leading

God's people in these last times (see the notes on 3:17). The genealogy rests all the hopes and dreams of the people with this Jesus.

2—The genealogy offers still other clues to Matthew's interests. The bare list of names is twice broadened by the addition of the phrase **and his brothers** (1:2, 11). **Judah and his brothers** jogs our memories of the family of Jacob, the founders of the 12 tribes, the ancestors of the whole people. **Jechoniah and his brothers** (v. 11) reminds us of the tragedy of defeat by the Babylonians, the execution of the royal family, the exile of the people, crisis for the nation.

Matthew is getting set to narrate the story of "Jesus and his brothers and sisters," not just his physical kin but especially those connected to Jesus by bonds of faith out of "all nations" (25:32; 28:19). Disciples in Matthew are Jesus' true sisters and brothers (12:46-50; 18:21, 35; 23:8; 25:40; 28:10).

3-6—A further striking feature of Matthew's genealogy is the naming of women. Men fathered children **by Tamar** (v. 3), **by Rahab** (v. 5), **by Ruth** (v. 5), and **by the wife of Uriah** (= Bathsheba, v. 6).

What is Matthew's interest? Why precisely these four women? Why does Matthew not name instead the great and revered matriarchs Sarah, Rebekah, Rachel, Leah? (1) Pious readers have for a long time noted that three of the four are tainted with scandals of incest, prostitution, and adultery. Is Matthew thinking of God's grace in including even notorious sinners? Forgiveness is certainly a Matthean theme (see chap. 18). But by New Testament times these women had come to hold an honored place in Jewish lore and in Christian tradition. Rahab, for example, is praised as model of faith (Heb. 11:31) and of works (James 2:25). (2) What all four, including Ruth, have in common, however, is that they are Gentiles or, as in the case of Bathsheba, **the wife of Uriah** (v. 6), are united to a Gentile in marriage. Matthew may be calling them to mind in order to help define God's intentions regarding the nature and boundaries of God's true family. Perhaps they are included as expressing partial ancient fulfillment of God's promises to Abraham. Through Abraham blessing will come to all the nations, and "the children" of Abraham are not his biological descendants alone (cf. 3:9; 12:49-50).

(3) Or these women may be related not so much to **Abraham** at the beginning of the story as to **Mary** at its climax. **Mary of whom Jesus was born** (v. 16) is a fifth woman in the genealogy. God's sovereign and surprising use of those four ancient women foreshadowed the astonishing use of Mary (v. 20) in the fullness of time. All those women are signs that God has intervened and will do so yet again. History is wide open to God's fresh initiatives.

16—Matthew alters the basic formula of the genealogy when he gets to Jesus. He switches from the active to the passive voice, from "he gave birth to" or "he bore" to "he was born" (from *egennēsen* to *egennēthē*). It is the same verb and belongs to the same sequence but suddenly his birth breaks the pattern. It was different. The difference is to be described in 1:18-25.

17—Matthew compels readers to notice that the genealogy is carefully patterned and organized into 3 sets of 14 names: **from Abraham to David fourteen generations, from David to the deportation** or exile **to Babylon fourteen generations, and from the deportation . . . to the Christ fourteen generations.**

Actually it seems that only 13 names stand in the third section, from the exile to Christ. Perhaps Matthew counted some names twice: Abraham to David = 14, David (counted a second time) to Josiah = 14, Jehoiakim to Jesus = 14. Or perhaps Matthew counted "Jesus" (preresurrection name) as no. 13 and "Christ" (postresurrection name) as no. 14.

But in any case, why this neat pattern? What does it mean? (1) One popular suggestion is that **fourteen** is the numerical value of the Hebrew letters in the name **David.** So Matthew is saying by means of this patterning that Jesus is "great David's greater son" (cf. 22:41-45)

(2) Of course the moon waxes for 14 days and then wanes for 14, so it has been suggested that Matthew is talking about the ebb and flow of Israel's fortunes. The turning points focus on monarchy. So perhaps the genealogy declares that after 14 generations a glorious kingship was established under David. After 14 more generations the monarchy was crushed. Now the people of God stand at the end of another 14 generations, and kingship is about to be restored among God's people in a totally surprising fashion.

(3) We need to remember that mysterious numbers were a

popular feature of certain old religious books. The book of Daniel (9:24-27) speaks of "weeks of years" (periods of seven years each) as appointed by God in the governance of the world. **Fourteen** is twice seven, of course, and perhaps Matthew has in mind the passing of six weeks of years (or of generations) and the opening of the great seventh "week" in the advent of the Christ.

When we put it all together, what does the genealogy signal? What does Matthew proclaim by focusing on Abraham and David, by naming Tamar and Ruth and Rahab and Bathsheba, by organizing all the names into sets of 14 each, by opening the Gospel with this capsule history of 2000 years? The genealogy is an intriguing piece and only grudgingly yields up any of its secrets.

Because the genealogy is a highly compressed history of God's people it is useful to compare it with three other miniature histories recorded elsewhere in Matthew's Gospel: (1) the parable of the rebellious tenant farmers (21:33-43), (2) the parable of the marriage feast of the king's son (22:2-14), and (3) the seventh woe, reciting the shedding of innocent blood from Abel (many generations before Abraham) down to Zechariah (23:29-36).

These three capsule histories are largely negative histories, stories of rebellion, of petulance, and of violence. They present the past as the story, on the one hand, of God's wooing of the people through the prophets and, on the other, as the gloomy record of murderous efforts to still the voice of God and kill the messengers of God.

By contrast, the genealogy, so neatly patterned, omitting any hint of rebellion or disobedience, emphasizes God's own mysterious guiding and shaping and nurturing, leading the human story to its fulfillment.

God is nowhere named among all the names in the genealogy (contrast Luke 3:38). Nevertheless, this whole sequence of names is testimony to the presence of God. Without God there would be no genealogy, no patterning of generations, no sense, no direction, no meaning, no fulfillment of hope and promise, no deliverance, no movement toward the Messiah, not in that ancient history and not in our own.

From the time of the birth of the people in the days of Abraham, fathers and mothers bore children in hope. The word behind "the father of . . . the father of . . . the father of" or "bore . . . bore

. . . bore" (*egennēsen*) appears 39 times in vv. 2-16. But for all their mothering and fathering and for all their historical struggling the people were not able to bring salvation to birth.

Matthew reflects on the generations and declares that history is not just a tissue of broken promises, a record traced in spilt blood, a cry of agony lost in the howling hurricane. Matthew hears the promise of God and sees the finger of God leading events to the birth of Jesus. Through the genealogy, Matthew proclaims that in Jesus, the whole long history of Israel's hoping and struggling will reach surprising fulfillment. It is surprising because this lowly one, humble and persecuted from the beginning, is not easily recognizable as the Savior, the royal Son, the divine presence.

He Called His Name Jesus (1:18-25)

Mary and Jesus are named in this new paragraph, and yet it is Joseph who holds center stage. In fact Matthew has neatly plotted the material in 1:18—2:23 so that five successive scenes feature alternately Joseph and then Herod. (See commentary below on 1:25.)

One of the prime functions of this paragraph, following hard on the table of ancestors (1:2-17), is to show how Jesus can be both the culmination of the genealogy and at the same time be far more than the product of all those ancestors.

18—Matthew begins by pointing to the unique circumstances of **the birth** or origin (*genesis*) **of Jesus Christ. Before his mother** left her home and family, before **Mary** and **Joseph** ever **came together** in wedlock, she was somehow **found to be with child.** Matthew hastens to assure readers that the pregnancy resulted not from any human intercourse but from the creative energy **of the Holy Spirit** (3:16; 28:19).

19—The Law commanded severe penalties for sexual sins (Deut. 22:13-27). Matthew does not indulge in speculation about the hurt feelings of Joseph or tortured disclaimers of Mary but focuses entirely on the character of Joseph as **a just man** (*dikaios*, cf. 13:43, 49; 25:37, 46; 27:4, 19, 24), a man of righteousness, a quality lifted up and celebrated in this Gospel more than in any of the others (see commentary below on 3:15; 5:20).

35

As a man of righteousness, Joseph planned to follow the old law and put Mary aside. But mercy struggled in Joseph with his sense of right, and he resolved to divorce her **quietly** without exposing her to public shame.

20—While Joseph was considering his options, **an angel of the Lord appeared to him in a dream** with a fresh command, conflicting with the old law. Divine revelation comes via dreams or an angel especially at the beginning and end of Matthew's Gospel (cf. 1:20, 24; 2:12, 13, 19; 27:19; 28:2-5).

The angel's greeting, **Joseph, son of David,** echoes the genealogy and its assertion that Jesus stands in the line of the kings of Israel. The angel instructs Joseph that his fears about Mary are baseless. Her child is not the product of any human activity whatsoever. Jesus is pure gift, holy surprise, fresh act of God, a new creation. **The Holy Spirit,** God's own raw power in history, had touched Mary and generated that life within her. Mary **will bear a son,** and Joseph is instructed to **call his name Jesus** (cf. Luke 1:31), and so legally adopt Jesus as his own, thus including Jesus within a Davidic family.

Both law and biology are "real." Jesus is "really" Joseph's son by the legality of marriage, and Jesus is "really" God's miracle through Mary. He is Son of David and God's own presence.

21—The name **Jesus** (= "God's help" or "God's salvation") describes the future work of the unborn child. He comes from David's royal line to do a royal work: aiding and liberating God's people (cf. Luke 2:11). **He will save his people,** not just Israel but a new community of faith drawn from Israel and from among the Gentiles. And he will extricate them not only from disasters like the Babylonian exile (1:17) but **from their sins,** from all unrighteousness, from all that splits and severs them from God and neighbor and from the self intended by God (see commentary below on 9:1-8). Through Jesus, God will lay hands on the broken nations and on a broken creation, to heal, to give them "righteousness," to make them "all right."

The new king arrives at the end of generations with unique authority to generate a new universal people gathered from all the nations.

But how will Jesus **save his people from their sins?** By dying and gaining forgiveness for them, to be sure (6:12-13; 9:6; 20:28; 26:28). But Matthew specializes in showing how Jesus separates people from sin by calling them from sin, by summoning them to the way of righteousness, by inviting them to walk in the path of obedient discipleship (28:18-20).

22—The substance of the angel's announcement is repeated in words of scripture in the first of Mattthew's distinctive "formula quotations" or "fulfillment quotations." These passages are so named because the quotation of Scripture is introduced by a solemn formula of fulfillment: **this took place to fulfill what the Lord had spoken by the prophet** (cf. [2:5-6]; 2:15; 2:17-18; 2:23; [3:3]; 4:14-16; 8:17; 12:17-21; [13:14-15]; 13:35; 21:4-5; [26:56]; 27:9-10). Of all the quotations of Scripture found in Matthew's Gospel, these have been most thoroughly scrutinized. Those in square brackets are sometimes included in the list and sometimes excluded.

These formulas do not mean that Scripture rigidly predetermined the course of Jesus' life. Rather they invite lovers of Scripture to ponder this life, if they wish to see how God has brought ancient promises and age-old longings to present and astonishing fulfillment. In the process, readers are called to revise their old views of Scripture and their traditional expectations. The fulfillment in Jesus both fills up and exceeds old hopes.

Scriptural quotation and angelic announcement are perfectly parallel. Two divine messengers (angel, Scripture) focus on (1) a virginal conception, (2) the birth of a child, (3) a name to marvel at. And all three elements are then immediately echoed and so underscored in the report of Joseph's obedience (1:24-25). The whole paragraph (1:18-25), with parallel commands and formula quotation followed by a report of obedience, is identical in structure with 21:1-7 (the triumphal entry into Jerusalem).

It seems odd that Matthew did not select a scripture climaxing in a reference to salvation or liberation, playing on the name **Jesus.** Instead Matthew pounces on Isa. 7:14, mining that mighty scripture because of two treasures it contains: the promise of an astonishing birth and the reference to an equally astonishing name.

A virgin (*parthenos,* 25:1, 7, 11) **shall conceive and bear a son,** and that child will bear the name **Emmanuel** (Isa. 8:8, 10). That name carries one of Matthew's basic claims about Jesus. Whatever peaks and greatness mark the pocked landscape of human history, Matthew asserts that Jesus is more. He is more than saint or prophet, more than sage or hero, more than priest or king. In him resides more than human courage, more than the royal blue of kingly genes and chromosomes, more than a profound religious soul—not less but more.

Jesus is the unique welling up of God in human history (cf. 2:15). In this Jesus, the child and the adult, with the cross of his ministry and the power of his resurrection, we see God's face and hear God's final word. The presence of Jesus is the presence of God, and God's presence is saving.

24—If the heart of the paragraph is the revelation of the names of Jesus, the climax is the obedience of Joseph (cf. 21:6; 26:19). A troubled Joseph had fallen into fitful slumber but presently he **woke from sleep.** He **woke** from doubts, **woke** from fear, **woke** from calculating human possibilities, and with the new dawn of trust and the serenity of faith he began to count on the promises of God. This righteous man even **woke** from an old to a new obedience, responsive to the fresh speaking of God in these last times.

Joseph opened his eyes and **did as the angel of the Lord commanded** (*prostassō*, 8:4; 21:6; cf. *diatassō*, 11:1, *syntassō*, 26:19; 27:10; and *tassō*, 28:16). He **took** Mary instead of divorcing her, and instead of turning his back on the child he adopted him as his own, grafting the child into his own royal family tree. Joseph perfectly obeyed Scripture as interpreted by the angel, and expressed his new faith and obedience when **he called his name Jesus.**

This focus on Joseph's response is typical of Matthew. He loves stories which connect divine epiphany and human obedience. The story of Joseph is the first picture of discipleship that Matthew offers in his Gospel.

In 1:18—2:23 Matthew has composed five scenes. Three of them (1:18-25; 2:13-15; 2:19-23) focus on Joseph, and these three are separated by two scenes (2:1-12; 2:16-18) featuring Herod. Joseph and Herod respond in exactly opposite fashion to divine revelation and to the child Jesus. The advent of Jesus is God's direct and potent eruption into human history, and that intervention provokes two totally different reactions, as the thoughts and deeds of Herod and Joseph vividly reveal.

Where Is He? (2:1-23)

Chapter 1 is full of the names of people, listing the earthly ancestors of Jesus and meditating on Jesus' own names and title. But that first chapter is absolutely silent about cities and towns, not even identifying the place of Jesus' birth. Chapter 2, on the other hand, reveals Matthew's fascination with places. Matthew now spells them out, mulls them over, locates them not in any ordinary book of maps but in the atlas of prophecy, searching out their hidden meanings in the light of sacred Scripture. Throughout the chapter, as Matthew meditates on the geography of Jesus, he also focuses on the appalling struggle between Herod and Jesus, the mighty monarch and the powerless child.

In Bethlehem of Judea (2:1-12)

1—That **Jesus was born in Bethlehem of Judea** is a graphic way of repeating that he is "son of David" (1:1) and so king of Israel, and the fact that his first visitors were pagan astrologers shows him as "son of Abraham" (1:1) in whom blessing spills over to the nations.

Jesus not only was born during the reign of **Herod the king,** but **Jesus** and **Herod** defy and define one another. Herod bears the title **king,** but Jesus, born of the line of "David the king" (1:6) is also royalty. What is the difference between their majesties? Much!

Matthew assumes that Herod's reputation has preceded him. Matthew has no need to spell out for his readers that Herod was an Idumean usurper and no Jew. But Herod's lack of qualifications may be implied in the way Matthew stresses the correctness of Jesus' genealogy: Jesus is lineal descendant of David and Abraham.

Furthermore, the pages of Matthew's Gospel need not be cluttered with lurid details of Herod's multiple marriages and murders. In two short paragraphs of a few hundred words (2:1-12, 13-23), Matthew sketches an unforgettable portrait of the monarch of Judea as terrible contrast to king Jesus.

While Herod sat heavily on the throne, **wise men from the east** arrived in Jerusalem. Their brief speech to Herod (2:2) contains three elements which govern the rest of the paragraph: (1) **Where** is the newborn **king of the Jews?** (vv. 4-8); (2) we have seen **his star** (vv. 9-10); and (3) our purpose is **worship** (v. 11).

Naive and guileless, the magi arrived at Jerusalem with their pious intention and simple question: **Where** is the royal child, the newborn **king of the Jews** (21:5; 27:11)? They had read the announcement of his birth not in any earthly bulletin, not even in Scripture, but in the heavens. They had seen **his star in the East** or "at its first brilliant rising" (*en tē anatolē*).

Exactly what they saw has intrigued readers for centuries. Was it a nova, a comet, a conjunction of Jupiter and Saturn in the constellation Pisces—something any ancient observer might have seen? Was it perhaps a special star revealed to the wise men alone? Or should we search not the skies but instead the Scriptures for illumination? Balak, king of Moab, feared the invading Israelites and hired Balaam, a magician or astrologer of Mesopotamia, to come and curse them. However, Balaam was pressured by divine revelation so that he blessed and did not curse. In his oracle stand the famous words, "A star shall come forth out of Jacob, and a scepter shall arise out of Israel" (Num. 24:17). The oracle even speaks of Edom and of its being dispossessed, and Herod was an Edomite or Idumean.

Daniel 2 recounts how another monarch, Nebuchadnezzar, sought in vain for the meaning of his dreams among his magi, enchanters, sorcerers, and Chaldeans. He found truth and wisdom in Daniel. Josephus tells how an Egyptian priest predicted the birth of a Savior among Pharaoh's Hebrew slaves. Pharaoh immediately conferred with all the astrologers of Egypt (Josephus, *Ant.* 2.205-206). Persian king Tiridates traveled with astrologers to Rome in A.D. 66, and hailed Nero as king of the universe, because of revelations seen in the stars.

3—**Herod the king** acts like Pharaoh and Nebuchadnezzar. Dreams and portents troubled those rulers, and they turned for help to traditional sources: priests and wise men and astrologers. Herod assembled **all the chief priests and scribes of the people** (cf. Dan. 2:2) and, echoing the magi, raised the question **Where?** They had asked about **the king of the Jews** (2:2) and Herod paraphrases that title (cf. 27:11) as he inquires into the birthplace of **the Christ** (1:1, 16-17; 22:41-45). Indeed, the entire paragraph focuses on Jesus as legitimate king of God's people.

5—On the basis of Scripture, Herod's counselors and Jerusalem's religious leaders were able to to give a clear and unambiguous answer: **Bethlehem of Judea,** a rude village a mere five miles from the sophistication and splendors of Jerusalem. Here Matthew seems to contrast Jerusalem and Bethlehem, chief priests and magi, Scripture and star, just as he contrasts Herod and Jesus. And yet, while Matthew never has any good word for Herod, he can speak positively both here and elsewhere of Jerusalem (5:35) and priests (8:4). And Matthew's view of Scripture is incomparably high.

Herod hears absolute truth from priest and prophecy, and yet his own words are all a lie (2:8) and his deeds are a slaughter (2:16). Herod here at the beginning parallels Pilate at the end. Jesus lived and taught in the bright interval between that dark pair, and Herod's cruelty at the start is a gloomy premonition of Jesus' violent death. Both in the beginning and at the end Jesus' title **king of the Jews** is weighed, tested, disputed (2:2; 27:11, 29, 37, 42).

6—**The prophet** Micah had declared that in **Bethlehem in the land of Judah** there would arise a **ruler** who will, says the RSV, **govern.** But the word is not simply **govern.** It means "be their shepherd" (*poimainō/poimēn*, 9:36; 25:32; 26:31). The people are in disarray, badly led (9:36), but the king of promise will "feed his flock in the strength of the Lord, in the majesty of the name of the Lord his God" (Mic. 5:2-4). Bethlehem, the home of David, the first great shepherd-king, is home also of the final shepherd-king.

7-8—Dismissing the larger assembly, **Herod summoned the wise men secretly** to a private audience. He took care to discover from them **what time the star** had first **appeared.** Then he put them on the road south to Bethlehem, directing them to **search diligently for the child,** hypocritically announcing a desire to see and **worship** him.

9-10—No search was needed. As soon as the wise men set foot on the road, **the star** reappeared and **went before them till it came to rest over the place where the child was. They rejoiced**

exceedingly with great joy (contrast Herod's response, v. 3) to reach the goal of their pilgrimage.

11—Their goal was neither **Jerusalem** nor **Herod. Mary his mother** is named only in a prepositional phrase, and Joseph is not mentioned at all in this scene. The pilgrimage of the magi led only to **the child.** And they knew how to act when they got there. **They fell down and worshiped him** (*proskyneō*, cf. 8:2). On bended knee they touched foreheads to ground, offering Jesus all honor and allegiance. They came like subject kings rendering tribute (Ps. 72:9-10, 15), like royalty from afar streaming to a restored Zion laden with the wealth of nations (Isa. 60:1-7). **Opening their treasures, they offered him** gifts. **Gold and frankincense and myrrh** are gifts fit for kings and queens (Song of Sol. 3:6), offerings from royalty to royalty, and the three costly gifts have led to the notion that the magi were themselves kings and three in number. But Matthew focuses not on any royal status of these magi, certainly not on their number, but on their splendid gifts as a signal that in Jesus we see a kingship beyond all human kingship, just as promised in ancient Scripture for the last times.

12—Having completed their journey and having paid their homage, they slept the sleep of the innocent. **In a dream** God tipped them off to Herod's plotting, so that the magi **departed to their own country** not via Jerusalem but **by another way.**

Out of Egypt (2:13-15)

13—**Joseph** sleeps and dreams for a second time. In his dream **an angel of the Lord** (1:20) instructs him to take **the child and his mother** and **flee** from Bethlehem to **Egypt.**

That change in geography signals other changes: while "Bethlehem" means royal David and pictures Jesus as the promised shepherd-king, "Egypt" calls to mind Abraham and all the matriarchs and patriarchs at the dawn of Israel's history.

The narratives of Genesis 12–50 and of Exodus 1–15 repeatedly tell how individual children were born by God's gracious promise, then threatened by murdering kings and Pharaohs, and finally rescued by divine, almighty providence. Indeed those chapters tell how the people as a whole were the offspring of promise and how they were rescued at the Sea, when threatened with slavery and extinction. Egypt looms large in all those ancient stories, sometimes as land of oppression, often as place of sanctuary.

Herod, like ancient Pharaoh, fearing the threat posed by a nursing infant, roused himself—not to worship (v. 8), but to **search for the child** and, if possible, to **destroy** him (cf. Josephus, *Ant.* 2.205-206.

14—And just as the patriarch Joseph had summoned his whole clan to Egypt and so saved their lives in a time of famine, so the new Joseph, roused from sleeping and dreaming, **took the child and his mother** under cover of nightfall, and while the world and its rulers slumbered, they escaped to **Egypt.** There they remained, until **the death of Herod** (4 B.C.) ended the dark night of that monarch's plottings and murderings.

15—Matthew ponders the movements of Jesus, south to safety and then back again from foreign lands. He turns the light of Scripture on that journey. Jesus' return from Egypt means not merely that Herod has died and the coast is clear. Matthew sees in the death of Herod not Herod's end alone but the shifting of the aeons, the end of all our captivities and exiles. The one whom the Lord calls **my son** (see 3:17) has arrived. Day has dawned with healing in its wings (2:2; 4:16).

The formula quotation (cf. 1:22) exhibits Matthew's conviction that even powers as mighty and murderous as that of Herod pale before God's mightier and more awesome power to rescue and to grant life.

Weeping for Her Children (2:16-18)

16—**Herod,** like ancient Pharaoh (Exod. 1:16), lashed out in fury, pitting royal power against helpless infants in uneven contest. **Tricked by the wise men,** Herod dispatched his troops and **killed all the male children in Bethlehem and in all that region who were two years old or under,** that is, all unweaned infants.

17-18—If Jacob or Israel was the "father" of all Israelites, so his favorite wife **Rachel** was "mother" of all their generations. When the slaughter of the innocents at Bethlehem filled the land with their mothers' **wailing and loud lamentation,** Matthew heard the dirge chanted by Jeremiah (31:15) in a time of national disaster, at the moment of "the deportation to Babylon," one of the turning points in the genealogy (1:11-12, 17). Matthew's heart, like Jeremiah's, ached for all those slaughtered in times past and times present, for all the cruelties and senselessness of history. And yet here was a scripture. It does not say that the murders occurred "in order to fulfill" (1:22; 2:15, 23) what the prophets spoke but only that when these terrors happened, **then was fulfilled** the ancient word.

A Nazarene (2:19-23)

19-20—To keep his throne **Herod** had not hesitated to tell lies, practice deception, commit murder. But finally all his cruel power and eagerness to destroy were themselves destroyed when he himself **died.** That word **died** is a melancholy commentary on the pretensions of earthly rulers and stands in sharpest contrast to the final claim and promise of the exalted Jesus: "I am with you always" (28:20).

For yet a third time Joseph slept and dreamed and heard his marching orders. Word came to **Joseph in Egypt** that it was now safe to return to **the land of Israel,** for Herod was **dead.** This is the one place in the entire New Testament where the phrase **land of Israel** appears. Authors usually speak of the various districts: Galilee, Samaria, Judea.

21—Here again Joseph is a model of obedience (1:24; 2:14). **He rose** from his slumbers and with **the child and his mother,** Joseph returned to his old land but not to his same old home.

22—When Herod the Great died, his territories were divided among his sons and heirs. **Archelaus** ruled Judea together with Samaria to the north and Idumea to the south (4 B.C. till A.D. 6). **Joseph,** in spite of all the special guidance and protection he had enjoyed, was **afraid.** Archelaus shared his father's cruelty without inheriting his competence. What to do? Instructed in yet another **dream,** Joseph **withdrew to the district of Galilee,** ruled by Herod Antipas, another son of Herod the Great. Was **Galilee** really so much better than Judea? Was Herod Antipas any real improvement over his brother Archelaus? Manipulated by wife and stepdaughter, Herod Antipas would behead John the Baptist (14:1-12).

23—Better or not, Joseph went to **Galilee** (4:12) and settled there as an immigrant (*katoikeō*) **in a city called Nazareth** (4:13).

Matthew pondered that complex route full of twists and turns marked as much by fear as by faith.

All history seems opaque and clouded, full of chance and accident, meandering and crooked, but beyond the confusions of history Matthew sees the hand of God orchestrating events on earth, making them yield sense, guiding them to satisfying goals.

By God's design and not by human accident or human planning, Joseph settled in **Nazareth,** and therefore Jesus came to be called a **Nazarene.** Matthew had plain verses of scripture at hand to help readers meditate on Jesus' connections with Bethlehem and Egypt but did not so easily discover any scriptures about Nazareth. In fact, Nazareth is never mentioned in the Hebrew Scriptures, in Josephus, or in early rabbinic writings. Yet Matthew obviously traced the hand of God in the fact that Jesus was "from Nazareth" (21:11; cf. 26:69; Acts 10:38) and that he was called a **Nazarene** (2:23; 26:71; Luke 18:37; John 18:5, 7; 19:19; cf. Acts 24:5).

But what precisely does Matthew see in Jesus' nickname of **Nazarene?** Isaiah 11:1 promises the coming of a "shoot" (Hebrew: *netzer*) from the stump of Jesse. **Nazarene** might indicate that Jesus is that tiny and surprising shoot, springing from the royal line, destined to grow quickly into a mighty spirit-filled sovereign, bringing peace to Israel and to all the universe (cf. Isa. 11:1-9). Matthew has already spoken of Jesus' birth announced by the rising of a star (2:1-2). "Rising" (*anatolē*) can also mean growth or shoot, and in Isa. 11:1 "shoot" and "branch" are parallels (cf. Jer. 23:5; 33:15; Zech 3:8; 6:2). At Qumran the Messiah was called "Branch of David" (4QpIsa.1; 4QPat. Bl. 3.4; 4QFlor.10).

In Judg. 13:5 and 16:17 Samson is described as a "Nazirite," one set apart from everything unclean, consecrated wholly to God from birth till day of death, appointed to deliver the people out of the hand of their enemies (Judg. 13:2-7). Matthew certainly points to Jesus as dedicated to the will of God from first to last and as destined to bring liberty to God's people (1:21).

Perhaps Matthew deliberately avoids singling out one particular scripture, and we thwart his purpose in our search for one. This is the only one of the formula quotations to refer to prophets in the plural and to omit naming a particular prophet. Matthew has obviously traced the hand of God in the fact that Jesus was "from Nazareth" and that he was known as "a Nazarene." By God's mysterious will, something very good indeed has come out of Nazareth (cf. John 1:45).

The Prophet and the Son (3:1-17)

Even though a gap of some 30 years separates the end of chap. 2 and the beginning of chap. 3, these chapters belong together, and readers move easily across the gap.

Matthew's meditation on the names and titles of Jesus begins in the genealogy (1:1-17), continues through chap. 2 and climaxes in the declaration of the heavenly voice at Jesus' baptism: "This is my beloved Son" (3:17). And Matthew's mulling over the geography of Jesus, naming cities and towns (see on 2:1), continues until Jesus finally settles in "Capernaum by the sea in the territory of Zebulon and Naphtali" (4:12-16).

All the material in the first four chapters (1:1—4:16) is one long introduction, because all together it serves the single purpose of identifying Jesus, filling in his background, describing his connections, setting the stage for his public ministry. Further comments on the structure of these chapters stand at 4:16.

The Voice of One Crying (3:1-6)

John the Baptist comes bursting onto the scene all unannounced. When the paragraph introducing him opens, he is **preaching,** and as it closes, people are **confessing their sins.** In between, John's word is summarized, his credentials examined, his effectiveness recited. All in all, Matthew fixes our attention less on John's baptizing and more on his proclaiming, not at all on forgiveness (cf. 26:28), but entirely on John's aim to secure and seal his hearers' repentance.

Members of Matthew's community may have been finding their security before God in the ceremony of baptism and in spiritual endowments. They may have somehow disconnected baptism from any thought of the deadly power of sin, from the solemn call to repentance, and from the summons to the new life of righteousness. Some of Matthew's Christian contemporaries were fascinated with baptism as the magical moment of infusion with the Spirit, and they understood the Spirit primarily in terms of energy for prophecy and miracles and exorcism (7:15-23). Matthew on the other hand describes baptism as sealing repentance and as energizing people to walk the way of righteousness (cf. 21:32; 28:18-20). Matthew's report concerning John the Baptist amounts to a plea to his own community to rethink and reorder their lives.

1-2—**In those days,** after Jesus had been born in Bethlehem and had sojourned in Egypt and while he was growing to adulthood in Nazareth of Galilee, **John the Baptist** appeared in the wilderness of Judea (cf. Luke 1:80). As Bethlehem and Nazareth are fixed in the imagination as the places of Jesus, so John is forever linked to **the wilderness** and **the river Jordan** (v. 5).

Geographically, **the wilderness of Judea** is a lonely stretch of hills sloping down east and south of Jerusalem toward Jericho and the Dead Sea. Sere and hostile, those hills are able in their upper reaches to support a few fields of barley or scattered herds of goats and sheep. The wilderness was refuge to bands of robbers like those of the parable (Luke 10:30) and to ascetics like those of Qumran. Qumranites saw in Isa. 40:3, applied in all three Synoptic Gospels to John the Baptist, a reference to their own wilderness experience.

Spiritually, **the wilderness** is the place of Israel's origins, where God's people fled from the fleshpots of Egypt, where they were led by fire and cloud, fed by manna, uniquely close to God.

John **came preaching.** Even the unspoken activity of baptizing, which earned him his nickname, was an eloquent proclamation. A mere handful of words sums up the message of John: **Repent, for the kingdom of heaven is at hand.** The exact same words without a single addition or subtraction introduce the proclamation of Jesus in 4:17 (cf. 10:7). So these words, finely chiseled, not chosen lightly, bracket chaps. 3 and 4, unite the work of John and Jesus, and fix the minds of readers on two key themes: repentance and the kingdom.

The Kingdom of Heaven

The phrase, **the kingdom of heaven,** literally "the kingdom of the heavens" (*basileia tōn ouranōn*), occurs in no other writing of the New Testament but is used 33 times in Matthew's Gospel.

Kingdom of heaven means the same as "kingdom of God" (four times in Matthew, at 12:28; 19:24; 21:31, 43). It is a pious paraphrase designed to avoid speaking the awesome and holy name of "God" (cf. 6:9). Note also "thy kingdom" (6:10, 13; 20:21), "the kingdom of their (my) Father" (13:43; 26:29), and the simple "kingdom" (6:33; 25:34).

Among New Testament writers Matthew alone has "the gospel [or word] of the kingdom" (see commentary below on 4:23) and the phrase "sons (= citizens) of the kingdom" (8:12; 13:38; cf. 17:25). All these phrases (kingdom of heaven, kingdom of God, kingdom of their [or my] Father, or simply the kingdom) are very nearly interchangeable. The context may sometimes indicate why Matthew chose one wording over another (cf. 12:28).

In 13:41 and 16:28 "his kingdom" means the kingdom of the Son of man (cf. 8:20). In 13:41 the kingdom of the Son of man is a present reality in tension and continuity with the future kingdom of the Father (13:43).

To say that this kingdom or sovereign rule is "of heaven" or "of God" is not to locate it in the heavens above but to assert that it has its source in heaven or in God, that it comes as a gift from above, and that it is something wholly different from earthly kingdoms and sovereignties. Secular empires rest uneasily on the bones of slaughtered enemies and are sustained by violence and the threat of violence (cf. 4:1-11; 22:41-45; 26:52-53). The kingdom of heaven proclaimed by John (3:2) and Jesus (4:17) and the disciples (10:7) surpasses earthly imagining and earthly deserving. In what varied ways it is surpassing can be discovered best by continuing to read the Gospel, but here this much at least must be said: more than any other New Testament writer, Matthew stresses the vital connection between the kingdom and righteousness (cf. 6:10, 33).

John proclaims that the long-awaited kingdom is finally **at hand,** has drawn very close and is even now at the gates (cf. 4:17; 10:7; 26:45). As animals sense the nearness of earthquake or storm, John reads the signs and feels the shockwaves of the coming kingdom. John knows that he stands at the threshold to the kingdom. More on the time of the coming of the kingdom at 4:17. For the moment, Matthew focuses on the sudden appearing of John as proclaimer and trumpeter of the kingdom.

John shared the good hope of the kingdom with most of his contemporaries, but the exact contours of God's coming rule was not so much shared as fiercely debated. What shape will God's coming kingship take? Who will be the beneficiaries? And who should fear the coming of the Lord?

John called God's own people to **repent.** He summons not outsiders but insiders to radical reorientation, calling religious people in particular to stop insisting that they know best and to cease resisting God, God's judgment, God's sovereignty.

It would be serious enough if John called God's people to break with bits and pieces of generally recognized evil behavior. What makes John's summons so hard is that his call means smashing even hallowed assumptions about self and nation and God.

With his rough tongue and severe demands, John stands like a lion at the gate. Repentance is no option but is mandatory. It is necessary to pass through the tunnel of purgation before emerging into the light of the new age. And it is a hard passage, like a camel going through the eye of a needle (19:24). The beginning of living is drowning, and the price of liberty is unconditional surrender to God.

3—John was a prophet in a long line of prophets. Indeed, he not only utters prophecy but himself fulfills prophecy (cf. 11:9-14). The earliest Christians saw in John the prophesied **voice of one crying in the wilderness,** summoning people to **prepare the way of the Lord** and **make his paths straight.** Isaiah envisioned a fabulous road, paved not by civil but by divine engineering. The Lord was poised and ready to lead the captive people home from Babylon straight across the desert. John fulfills the promise of that vision as he works on hearts, cutting and filling the moral terrain, to make them ready for the appearing of the Lord Jesus. Josephus (*War* 3.118) describes how Vespasian sent detachments ahead of the main body of his army to straighten bends in the road, to level rough places, to widen the path by removing trees, in order to ease the Roman army's progress into Galilee. God wages spiritual warfare, sending prophets to the people. By his use of Scripture, Matthew wraps John in the cloak of finality and interprets John not as one more prophetic voice but as a cry at the end of the ages, at the turning of the eons. After John, the deluge—either the mighty waters of baptism or the storm of wrath, either the Holy Spirit or fire.

4—Matthew turns from John's prophetic geography and John's prophetic message to John's odd food and odder clothing. Certainly exotic, were they in any sense also prophetic? John wore **a garment of camel's hair** with a broad **leather** belt **around his waist.** To first-century eyes, that kind of outfit was a costume, signaling John's self-identification with Elijah (2 Kings 1:8; Zech. 13:4). Elijah had not died but had mounted up to heaven in a fiery chariot (2 Kings 2:11-12) and was therefore alive and ready to act for God, especially in times of crisis for the people (cf. 27:47, 49)

So by his strange dress John presents himself not simply as an ascetic renouncing the luxuries of the city, although that is part of it (11:8). He offers a sign that he is the expected prophet and that these are the expected times. Jesus later agrees, pointing to John as the fulfillment of the hopes clustering around the figure of Elijah, calling John a prophet and more than a prophet (11:9-14; 17:9-13).

John's diet was **locusts and wild honey,** food provided by the grace of the Creator, not produced by human labor or effort of cultivation, and that alone gives it special significance (cf. m. Berakoth 6:3). It may further signify John's standing as a Nazir (2:23), a holy man who had renounced meat and wine (Luke 1:15; cf. Josephus, *Life* 11-12, on the prophet Bannus and his food and clothing, and m. Hullin on locusts as clean food).

5—The Baptist's cry stirs hearts and people flock to him **from Jerusalem and all Judea and all the region about the Jordan.** Since Archelaus (2:22) had been deposed in A.D. 6, the Romans had governed **Jerusalem and all Judea** directly with Roman prefects like Pontius Pilate (A.D. 26–36). The **region about the Jordan** sounds like a vague description of Perea, a district lying to the east of the Jordan which together with Galilee was ruled from 4 B.C. till A.D. 39 by Herod Antipas, nemesis of John the Baptist (14:11-12). It might, however, mean the plain of the Jordan, which stretched nearly from the Dead Sea to the Sea of Galilee.

6—John lived with God in the beauty and terror of the wilderness, and he cried out on the edges of cities and settlements, drawing people to the Jordan, the ancient boundary between the desert where the people had been formed and the land of promise to which they crossed over.

John's voice moves the masses to confess their **sins** (cf. 1:21). **Sins** are not small infractions of ritual commands, ceremonial rubrics, traditional ordinances, or community rules. The crowds begin to own up to the fact that they have broken with God, broken faith with God, broken away from God, broken the bonds that tied them to God.

They confess their sins, and then they sign and seal their confession by submitting to being **baptized by him in the river Jordan.** Penitents do not wash themselves, but John administers the washing, perhaps assisted by close disciples (9:14), and so earns the nickname "Baptist" (cf. Josephus, *Ant.* 18.116-117).

The origins of John's baptism have been sought in ceremonial washings prescribed in the Torah, in proselyte baptism designed to purge Gentile converts to Judaism of their old uncleanness, in lustrations of Essenes questing after perfect purity, or in pagan rituals of initiation and purification.

Matthew focuses not at all on John's sources (except to insist that John is from God, 21:25) but entirely on John's goal: with his words and his baptizing he summons people to the way of righteousness as the one appropriate preparation for the day of the Lord's appearing.

Children for Abraham (3:7-10)

7—Many of the Pharisees and Sadducees come to John and come in for a tongue-lashing. Who are these **Pharisees and Sadducees?** It is easy enough to describe their histories and their doctrines and to do the same for those other factions, the Essenes and Zealots. With extreme brevity Josephus sketches the portraits of the "four philosophies" of the Pharisees, Sadducees, Essenes, and the followers of Judas the Galilean, who have "a passion for liberty that is almost unquenchable" (*Ant.* 18:11-25).

But what role do Pharisees and Sadducees play in Matthew's Gospel? Surely Matthew is doing something more than simply allowing readers to overhear old conversations between John and Jesus on the one hand and leaders of these religious factions on the other. But what more is happening here and in all those other places where Pharisees and Sadducees, priests and elders appear in Matthew?

By his retelling of the Gospel narrative, by depicting John and Jesus in dialog and conflict with religious and political leaders, with friends and foes, with crowds and disciples, Matthew is both recalling a history and proclaiming the kingdom. He is always criticizing or promoting certain kinds of thinking and behavior in his own contemporary Christian community.

Did many Pharisees and Sadducees really come **for baptism?** If so, why did John lash out at them? Perhaps they only came "to the baptizing" or "to the scene of baptism" (*epi to baptisma*) to see what was going on (cf. John 1:19). However, the paragraph itself lifts up a tension between **baptism** on the one hand and the **fruit** of repentance on the other. No tension is supposed to exist. Baptism in Matthew's Gospel means the moment of radical re-orientation of life and the beginning of walking in the way of righteousness. But for some it was apparently less than that or something different from that. At Corinth, baptism was the source of factionalism and of boasting about gifts of the Spirit (see commentary below on 5:3-4; cf. 1 Cor. 1:10-17).

To John those leaders for all their authority and respectability were no more than **a brood of vipers.** (12:34; 24:33). They are snakes or **vipers** because, instead of nurturing and guiding the people, they sting and poison them. With an equally unpleasant phrase Jesus attacks certain Christian leaders as "wolves" who snatch and tear at the flock of God (7:15).

Those leaders have been stirred, they have (perhaps) been baptized, but they are not yet safe from the dread day of **the wrath to come** (Zeph. 1:15; 1 Thess. 1:10). Escape is impossible, evasion hopeless, excuses vain. The choice is simple: repentance or wrath, John's water or the Lord's fire.

8—**Repentance** (*metanoia*) is neither casual resolution nor ritual washing lightly undertaken. What John demands is nothing magical, nothing institutional, nothing sectarian. His goal is deeply personal and moral, touching the bedrock of relations to God and neighbor. John calls for a shattering reorientation of life. If it is genuine, it will naturally and inevitably yield **fruit. Fruit** is different from works performed, efforts expended, deeds done on demand, actions coerced by a stick or coaxed by a carrot.

There is no way to force **fruit** to grow out of a dead tree, and good **fruit** is the infallible sign of the healthy tree (7:16-20; 12:33; 13:8; 21:19, 34, 41, 43; James 3:12, 17-18).

9—Why does John issue his summons to Israel and to Israel's leaders? And why does Matthew repeat that summons in his own time? **We have Abraham as our father,** they boast (cf. 1:1-2, 17). In effect they say, "We are privileged insiders; we are the people of God; we are all right" (cf. John 8:39-47). By that response, they imply that John should preach to others, to outsiders, to pagans, to those who need it. People regularly depend for security on pedigree or genealogy, on social class or citizenship, on religious affiliation or even certificate of baptism.

Is it all hyperbole or wordplay that **God is able from these stones to raise up children to Abraham?** In Hebrew and Aramaic the words for "sons" and "stones" are nearly identical. Perhaps John has in mind Isaiah's picture of Abraham as the rock and Sarah as the quarry from which Israel was hewn (cf. 16:18; Isa. 51:1-2). Or is John simply continuing to exploit the commonplaces of the desert: vipers, dead trees, stones? Living **children** from dead **stones.** Paul says that is how it was in the beginning, when by God's creative power a living child was granted to Abraham and Sarah, whose womb and body were as good as dead (Romans 4). In fact, God was about to work just such a miracle, as the proclamation of John and Jesus touched harlots, tax collectors, assorted outcasts, and Gentiles. Oddly enough, they all submitted in faith and obedience while pious religious leaders stood around debating, doubting and finally resisting (9:9-13; 15:21-28; 21:28-32). Thus many will come from east and west to sit at table with Abraham (8:11; Gal. 3:29).

10—John underscored the urgency of the call to repentance in a striking image. God as the world's ultimate critic stands poised like a farmer in his orchard, feet spread for balance, gripping an **axe,** sharp edge **laid to the root** of a tree, measuring the blow, set to lift the **axe** up and back and then to arc it forward and begin to hack **every tree that does not bear good fruit** and chop it into kindling (cf. Isa. 5:1-7; 10:33-34).

Wrath was expected to smash the heathen, but John does not warn that every Roman will be cut down, or every collaborator and traitor, or every thief and prostitute, or every pagan and foreigner, or even every Pharisee and Sadducee. **Every tree** of whatever race or religion or social class or nation **that does not bear good fruit** is worthless.

The Holy Spirit and Fire (3:11-12)

In a broad summary statement John now compares and contrasts his own work with that of the coming one. These sentences build a bridge from the work of John to the ministry of Jesus.

11—My baptism, says John, is **with water for repentance.** Some in Matthew's community severed the connection between baptism and repentance (cf. 3:2). The whole point of John's baptism is readiness for the **one who is coming after me.** By itself that last phrase could mean a successor, follower, disciple, a dependent. But John immediately calls him **mightier than I.** John describes himself as not even **worthy** to do a slave's job of carrying the sandals of that coming mightier one.

How worthy and how mighty is the coming one? **He will baptize you** not merely with water but **with the Holy Spirit and with fire.** John obviously means finality and ultimacy when he says **Holy Spirit** and **fire,** but how exactly are these two to be understood?

Are **Holy Spirit** and **fire** coordinated as two positive forces, working together for the final cleansing and refining of God's people (Zech 13:9; Mal. 3:2-3)? Or are they both destructive powers: the wind (*pneuma*) and fire of God's wrath breaking out against the chaff and consuming it (cf. Isa. 29:6; 30:27-28; Ezek. 1:4). Or should we understand **Spirit** and **fire** as the alternatives set before every human being by the fact of the coming of the mighty one: either come to the Lord in joy and be renewed by the cleansing and creative **Holy Spirit,** or turn your back on the Lord and then experience his appearing only as a consuming **fire** (cf. Joel 2:28-32)?

This last seems to fit Matthew's scheme. **Fire** in Matthew's Gospel is never associated with Pentecostal outpouring (cf. Acts 2:3) but is everywhere a symbol of judgment (3:10, 12; 5:22; 7:19; 13:40, 42, 50; 18:8-9; 25:41). And baptism with the **Holy Spirit** never suggests the wind that carries away chaff. At the conclusion of the Gospel, the **Holy Spirit** is associated with Father and Son in the work of gathering people lovingly into the family of God (28:19; cf. 3:16).

12—John has just spoken (v. 10) about the axe menacing the root of every fruitless tree and now repeats the warning, but with a different agricultural image: that of the wheat harvest. Harvest was a natural picture for judgment, coming at the climax of a long and often difficult season of growing (cf. 9:37-38; 13:39). And John fixes on the final stages of harvesting. The long stalks have already been cut from the fields and laid on the threshing floor. The heaps of stalks have been beaten to knock the grain from the stalks and the kernels of wheat from the chaff. Already the stalks have been bundled and laid aside for use as fuel in the ovens. Now the farmer has grasped **the winnowing fork** in his hand and is poised to toss the grain, letting the wind catch the lighter chaff and carry it a few feet away while the heavier kernels fall back in a heap onto the threshing floor, ready for the farmer to **gather his wheat into the granary.** So John pictures the fate of the penitent and of the impenitent at the hands of the mighty one.

Fulfill All Righteousness (3:13-15)

First words are as revealing as last words, even though the first words of Jesus in each Gospel have received far scantier attention than his "Farewell Discourse," "Seven Last Words from the Cross," or "Great Commission."

Matthew alone of the evangelists recollects a brief exchange between Jesus and John at the Jordan, and the response of Jesus to the objection of John is Jesus' first word in Matthew's Gospel. It is a striking and intriguing utterance. Matthew's Gospel is full of Jesus' words, many of them artfully composed into five great discourses. And in the Gospel's final scene (28:18-20) the resurrected Jesus surveys his own ministry and sums it up in terms of words, as he commissions the eleven to "teach" the nations everywhere to observe "all that I have commanded." Here at the beginning, in his initial utterance, Jesus points to the very core of all his commands, all his disclosures, all his teachings: **righteousness.**

13—**Then,** at the height of the Baptist's activity, Jesus makes a move. He strides forth from his own geography and steps onto

John's. **Jesus from Galilee** comes **to the Jordan to John,** not as
cool observer and even less as skeptic or critic, not to have anyone
carry his sandals and not to loose fire from heaven, but **to be
baptized by him.**

14—John is caught off guard by Jesus, not for the last time (cf.
11:2-3), and repeatedly resists the idea that he should baptize
Jesus. He protests that it should be the other way around: **I need
to be baptized by you.** John desires the baptism with Holy Spirit
and with fire which he himself had heralded as the work of the
coming mightier one. He longs to have his work of preparation
end and see the mightier one wield axe and winnowing fork,
judging the earth.

15—Others submitted to John's baptism "confessing their sins"
(v.6), as a sign of a clean break with their past and of a deep
resolve to walk the straight and narrow in the future, as preparation for the coming of the Lord. Some attached themselves to
John as his disciples (9:14; 11:2; 14:12; Acts 19:1-7). But what is
Jesus doing here? If he is the mighty coming one, why does he
wade out into the Jordan and submit to John's baptism?

The answer comes from Jesus' own mouth, the first words he
utters in this Gospel: **It is fitting for us to fulfil all righteousness.**
However much it may confound John and contradict his image
of the coming one, Jesus describes his submission as **fitting.** That
means that the path Jesus travels is in absolute harmony with
God's plan for the universe. Matthew can sum up the history of
God's ancient people as a turning of deaf ears to the prophets
(5:12; 23:27; cf. James 5:10). History was repeating itself when
chief priests and elders ignored John (21:25) and when Herod
butchered him (14:10). But Jesus hears in John's cry the authentic
voice of prophecy. Jesus has come to **fulfil,** to bring to fullest
flower the intent of God enshrined in law and prophecy. That
divine intention is here spelled out as **righteousness** (*dikaiosynē*,
see on 5:20; cf. *dikaios* in 1:19), a favorite theme of Jesus in
Matthew's Gospel.

At this point we seem to have two choices. This **righteousness**
is either a human work or it is God's gracious gift. Which is it?

Is **righteousness** an act of obedience produced by pious human
beings? Or is **righteousness** another name for salvation or deliverance, as so often in the psalms (22:31; 40:10; 98:2-3) and prophets (Isa. 11:4-5; 61:10-11; Mic. 6:5)? Is Jesus saying that he has

arrived on the scene to model perfect **righteousness,** yielding perfect obedience to God's ordinances, observing the law of God to the utmost, beginning with a joyous submission to the divine summons issued in John's call to be baptized? Or does Jesus mean that he will be the strange tool by which God will lay healing hands on a broken world and make it "all right"?

Does the one necessarily exclude the other? A phrase in 2 Peter (3:13) seems marvelously to summarize the expectation of Matthew and the Matthean Jesus: "We wait for new heavens and a new earth in which righteousness dwells." The fulfilling of that hope is the theme not of Jesus' baptism only but of the whole work upon which he launched out at baptism.

With a few quick strokes of the pen Matthew has hammered out a solid connection between righteousness and baptism, between being the sons and daughters of God and doing the will of God. Members of Matthew's community were almost certainly drawing different conclusions, celebrating different connections, enjoying baptism as the beginning of Christian freedom or as the moment of the first fine fling of ecstasy. Here at the start as later at the end (28:19-20), Matthew carefully defines baptism as the first step on the way of righteousness (cf. 21:32).

My Son (3:16-17)

16—As soon as Jesus is **baptized** and emerges from the **water** of Jordan, the solid and discouraging boundary between earth and heaven begins to dissolve, and the yearning for harmony between earth and heaven (6:10; 16:17) begins to be satisfied: "O that thou wouldst rend the heavens and come down, that the mountains might quake at thy presence!" (Isa. 64:1). The mountains do not quake, at least not yet (27:51; 28:2), but above the head of Jesus **the heavens were opened** (cf. Ezek. 1:1). Just as John had warned, the old order begins to crack and break up, but the way it happens is beyond the power of John to comprehend. The fulfillment contradicts and surpasses John's expectation.

Instead of striking like a woodsman's axe, raging like a fire, or destroying like a whirlwind, **the Spirit of God** descends gently as a **dove** (cf. 12:15-21). Matthew does not say that the Spirit is a dove or looks like a dove but that the Spirit's descent is dovelike.

Much ink has flowed but no consensus has been achieved over the exact meaning of the **dove.** Should we think of the Spirit's brooding over the waters of chaos (Gen. 1:2), hovering over Israel in the wilderness, inspiring prophets, embracing proselytes (cf. Luke 13:34)? The dove has been taken to symbolize not only the Spirit but also Israel, peace (Gen. 8:6-12), wisdom-sophia or reason-logos (Philo), sacrifice or poverty (Luke 2:24), or innocence (Matt. 10:16). The suggestion made here is that the dovelike descent signifies that the Holy Spirit contradicts John's vision of axe and fire (cf. 12:15-21). The ministry of the mightier one will not conform to the expectation of John.

17—A voice from heaven proclaims not to Jesus alone in quiet revelation (cf. Mark 1:11) but loudly and publicly: **This is my beloved Son, with whom I am well pleased.**

The story of Jesus as Matthew has told it so far is practically saturated with names and titles of Jesus: Jesus Christ, the Son of David, the Son of Abraham (1:1, 16-17), Jesus (1:21), Emmanuel (1:23), king of the Jews (2:2), my Son (2:15), a Nazarene (2:23).

Matthew's focus on names and titles climaxes in the narrative of Jesus' baptism. Here at the Jordan it is no human voice, not sages or even prophets, not just the evangelist Matthew, but God speaking from heaven who testifies to the identity of Jesus: **This is my beloved Son.**

This testimony climaxes the series of names and titles given thus far and is repeated and underscored immediately in the temptation narrative (4:3, 6). So here at the beginning of the Gospel, before the public ministry of Jesus gets under way, before the Sermon on the Mount or any of the miracles of Jesus, the evangelist narrates how God publicly applies to Jesus the highest name and profoundest title of them all: Son, God's Son (cf. 16:16; 17:5; 27:54; 28:19).

This climactic word is addressed not to Jesus only (cf. Mark 1:11) but to all, especially the readers! Therefore it is not adequate to label the narrative a call story, as though it focused on a private experience of Jesus, his own consciousness of being summoned from private life as a carpenter to public ministry, like one of the prophets (Jer. 4:1-10; Ezek. 1:1—3:27).

It is an epiphany, a revelation, a broadcasting of heaven's approval upon this one who has just declared (v. 15) that he will fulfill all righteousness. Readers are thus encouraged to believe that he will in fact make all things right. But how will it happen? Does the voice hint, or loudly shout, how Jesus will conduct his mission? It does offer clues, so many in fact that clarity is not easy.

The voice from heaven is powerful, mysterious, and full of tension. Similar confessions to Jesus as **Son** are uttered elsewhere in the Gospel, always in highly charged boundary situations: by demons near the tombs of Gadara (8:29), by the Twelve after Jesus trod the waters underfoot and stilled the howling wind (14:33), by Peter at a turning point at Caesarea Philippi (16:16), by the voice from the cloud on the mount of the Transfiguration (17:5), by Jesus himself, at least indirectly when he stood as a prisoner before his captors (26:63), and finally by a Roman army officer after Jesus yielded up his spirit and the earth trembled and shook (27:54).

This is my beloved Son (2:15), **with whom I am well pleased** is an extraordinary announcement, combining in provocative fashion elements of two great scriptural passages, Psalm 2 and Isaiah 42. Here are worlds in collision: a psalm of royalty and a song of a servant.

Psalm 2, composed to encourage king and people in a moment of crisis, quotes a formula pronounced on the day of the king's coronation: "You are my son; today I have begotten you" (Ps. 2:7). The coronation formula, used here as a promise, is rooted in Nathan's oracle to David. In it God pledged to establish and preserve David and Davidic kings forever: "I shall be his father, and he shall be my son" (2 Sam. 7:14).

With exile and the humiliation of Judah's royal house (1:11, 17), the oracle and the psalm were not thrown out onto the rubbish heap in a fit of bitterness or worldly realism. Pious interpreters, chastened by experience, came to understand them no longer as glorification of past kings or as encouragement of a present king but as a promise of a future king to be raised up by God and anointed by the Spirit of God to restore the lost fortunes of the people of God (Ps. 89:19-37; Isa. 9:1-7; 11:1-9).

So **this is my beloved son** means "This is the one chosen by God to rule." But in addition, the voice from heaven also loudly echoes the first of four great "Servant Songs" in Isaiah (42:1-4; 49:1-6; 50:4-11; 52:13—53:12).

The first of them begins, "Behold, my servant [or 'son,' *pais*] whom I have chosen, my beloved [*agapētos*, cf. 12:18] with whom my soul is well pleased." That first Servant Song and all of them together stand in tension with Psalm 2 and every other royal psalm. The Servant Songs portray the nation (or perhaps the prophet or some other individual) not as a powerful sovereign but as a magnificent servant, marked not by might but by meekness, with a passion not simply for victory but for justice, and a concern for enlightening the nations and not merely crushing them. The servant is mocked yet trusting, despised and afflicted yet uncomplaining and obedient (cf. 12:15-21).

Joining a royal psalm and a Servant Song is mixing oil and water. What has sovereignty to do with service, or majesty with meekness? Whatever difficulties the combination raises, the plain evidence of the Gospel itself is that Matthew really does understand Jesus' sonship along these two lines. In Peter's pious confession (16:16) and in the high priest's impious interrogation (26:63), "Son of God" is presented as a familiar synonym for "Christ," and "Christ" very clearly means the prophesied king of the last times.

"Christ" and "Messiah" are English transliterations of Greek and Hebrew words, both of which mean "anointed." The kings of ancient Israel and Judah were anointed with oil (1 Sam. 10:1; 16:13), but the Spirit of God would be the oil that would flow down over the head of the final future king, God's Messiah (cf. Isa. 61:15 and Luke 4:18; Ps. 2:1-2 and Acts 4:26). In Matthew's passion narrative at the trial (27:11-23), in the mock coronation (27:27-31), and at the cross, (27:32-54) "king of the Jews," "Christ," and "Son of God" are used interchangeably.

So the voice from heaven designates Jesus as Son of God, Messiah of Israel, king of the new age, beloved leader, restorer of lost fortunes, fulfiller of hopes, desire of nations, servant of God. Heaven had been shut, the Spirit had vanished, and there had been a famine of words from the Lord. But ever since Jesus came to the Jordan, nothing has been the same. Matthew celebrates the public anointing and presentation of Jesus and relishes that moment as the opening of a new age brimming with unimagined blessing. What Matthew fears is that pious people might so misconstrue baptism (Jesus' and their own), and sonship (Jesus' and their own standing as daughters and sons of God) that they might miss the blessings. More of that in what follows immediately.

Testing in the Wilderness and Beginnings in Galilee (4:1-25)

With the opening of chap. 4, the scene shifts from the sweet waters of the Jordan to the bleak wasteland of the desert, from the milling crowds to a lonely place, from converse with John to dialog with Satan. Pitiless testing (4:1-11) follows hard on the awesome presentation of Jesus as God's Son (3:17).

For all the breaks and changes between them, baptism and temptation belong together. Two of the three temptations begin where the baptism ended: **If you are the Son of God.** And the narrative of temptation speaks to tough questions raised by baptism: Has heaven really opened, the Spirit really descended, the new age of a new sovereign really dawned? Are we not still shut up in the prison house of the old age with demons as our jailers? Is not human history hopelessly stuck in all its old grooves, unredeemed and doomed? And if anyone dares whisper of cracks in the tough shell of the old world and of fresh life and a new world breaking in, then show us the cracks! What precisely are the signs of newness and of the kingdom's coming? What is the evidence of paradise regained?

How are kingdoms built? Caesar Augustus and his successors founded the Roman Empire and held it together by means that seem to correspond to the devil's three temptations: (1) by providing bread and circuses for the masses, (2) by outsmarting rivals on the inside and crushing hostile enemies on the outside through political intrigue and the power of the legions, and (3) by galvanizing the patriotism and religious fervor of the diverse peoples in a single cult devoted to the goddess Roma and to the genius of the divine emperor.

Dominating the Mediterranean world, Rome prided herself on extending to citizens and subjects alike the blessings of efficient administration, a system of justice, and, above all, the gift of peace and order. But the yoke lay heavy. Tacitus speaks of an ancient British king who complained of Rome's insatiable appetite for glory and wealth. As Roman legions cross land and sea devouring weaker nations, he said, "They create a desert and call it peace."

Rome gutted native political institutions, imposed a foreign culture, and shamelessly exploited the resources of subject nations by ruthless taxation.

In the East, dreams of freedom danced in Jewish heads, and from the start of direct Roman rule in the holy land (A.D. 6) bands of Jewish freedom fighters promoted armed rebellion. Full-scale war with Rome erupted in A.D. 66 and led finally to the destruction of Jerusalem and the temple, threatening the extinction of Judaism itself.

Many serious people today also have their lists of signs of the dawn of the new age, and some appear to correspond to the temptations: (1) a new economics based on a more equitable distribution of this world's bounty; (2) peaceful application of our awesome technology and dazzling feats of engineering yielding benefits to humankind and to the animal, vegetable, and mineral kingdoms as well; (3) the flourishing of music and dance, art and poetry, and the celebration of human genius and the invincibility of the human spirit.

Is Matthew describing how Jesus successfully resisted the temptation to equate **Son of God** with benevolent dictator, spellbinding demagogue, master of intrigue? Do the temptations deal with great public issues of economics and politics? Or with personal issues of trust, commitment, and style? Is the distinction between public and personal even helpful, or is it only misleading?

None of the above should be dismissed lightly. All embody great human hopes and human plans for handling the evils of history. Above all, it is an error to read the temptations merely as criticisms of old Jewish nationalism and as simple glorifications of routine Christian choices.

Pondering what directions he would travel and the means he would use to achieve his ends, Jesus clearly compares himself with Israel of old, freed from Egypt and dwelling in the wilderness. In these scenes of struggle, all who are called daughters and sons of God have discovered resources for their own journeys.

Son of God has royal overtones (3:17), so it is easy to understand that its bearer will bless God's people with powerful salvation (1:21). But also and more mysteriously it involves establishing righteousness (3:15) by means of selfless service (3:17), repudiating all the depressingly familiar behavior of ordinary earthly sovereigns (4:1-11). In fact, the one who is God's Son, God's own cherished offspring, the presence of God in the flesh (1:23), will collide head-on with earth's petty rulers, whether kings and governors or priests and teachers. How and why this will happen begins to be spelled out in the temptation narrative but will occupy Matthew all the way to the close of the Gospel.

If You Are the Son of God (4:1-11)

1—Jesus travels **up** from the Jordan **into the wilderness** (3:1), and so the traditional place of his fasting and of at least the first temptation is **up** in the cliffs and barren heights above Jericho. Yet he does not simply "go" there; he is **led up by the Spirit.** Jesus is **tempted** not by God but by **the devil** (*diabolos*) but **the Spirit** leads him to the fray (cf. 6:13).

The Spirit rapidly became Christian shorthand for "the Spirit of "God" (3:16) and "the Holy Spirit" (1:18, 20; 3:11). The longer titles remind us that not all spirits are "holy" or "of God." Furthermore biblical religion does not simply equate spirit with good, and matter or body with evil.

Christians were troubled from the beginning by the fact of their own struggles and fascinated by Jesus' temptations, by the knowledge not only of his victory but especially of his humanity and vulnerability (Heb. 2:18; 4:15; cf. 5:7). Matthew does not try to explain evil or temptation. He does not spin out theories balancing divine sovereignty and human freedom, with fine distinctions between God's permission and God's action. Nor does Matthew reflect on the history of Satan, on how Satan was once a member of the heavenly court (Job), or on how Satan in later tradition replaces God as source of temptation (compare 2 Sam. 24:1 and 1 Chron. 21:1; Gen. 22:1 and Jub. 17:16 [cf. Heb. 11:17]; and Exod. 4:24 and Jub. 48:2).

Nor does Matthew distinguish between God's testing and Satan's tempting. He simply tells how Jesus wrestled with Satan and conquered every temptation. What Matthew is doing is proclaiming Jesus as Savior from Satan's gloomy sovereignty (1:21; 12:28).

2—First, Jesus **fasted forty days and forty nights.** Mark and Luke say only "forty days." Perhaps Matthew by adding **and forty nights** wants to echo connections with Moses (Deut. 9:9; cf. Exod. 34:28) and Elijah (1 Kings 19:8), but probably Matthew is stressing the utter completeness of the fasting (cf. 12:40).

Jesus' fasting signifies total reliance upon God and sovereign freedom from every earthly security including the ordinary necessities of life. Matthew regards fasting as a useful exercise for the followers of Jesus (6:16-18; but see 9:15).

Afterward Jesus is **hungry.** What a marvel. God's beloved, the exalted Son, anointed with the Holy Spirit, experienced one of humanity's most mundane and nagging sensations: hunger pangs.

3—**And the tempter came.** In Jewish and Christian Scriptures and traditions the devil wears many hats: accuser, slanderer, adversary, ruler of the underworld, prince of demons, punisher of the wicked. But here Matthew focuses entirely on the devil as **tempter.**

The New Testament calls the devil **tempter** only here and in 1 Thess. 3:5. Matthew uses **devil** (*diabolos*) in 4:1, 5, 8, 11; 13:39; and 25:41. He has **Satan** (*satanas*) in 4:10; 12:26; and 16:23; "the evil one" (*ponēros*) in 13:19; cf. 6:13; "the enemy" (*echthros*) in 13:39; "prince of demons" (*archōn tōn daimoniōn*) in 9:34 and 12:24; and "Beelzebul" in 12:24, 27.

The devil tries to drive a wedge between Jesus and God, tries to draw Jesus away from holy reliance upon God to an unholy independence (cf. 24:10-12, 24).

The tempter seizes the word from heaven, proclaimed at Jesus' baptism: **Son of God.** What does that mean? What are the implications? The tempter proposes that Jesus **command these stones to become loaves of bread,** that he direct his powers to meeting his physical needs, that he devote his energy to satisfying his personal hunger, that he practice magic.

But Jesus, in the certainty that life is more than food (6:25), speaks not just for himself but for all: **Man** (RSV), every being worthy of the name "human" (*anthrōpos*), **shall not live by bread alone,** not by what is visible and edible, tangible and collectible, **but by every word** (*rhēma*) **that proceeds from the mouth of God.**

In this reply Jesus does not even bother to display any cleverness or originality but simply quotes Scripture (Deut. 8:3) in childlike submission and trust. In fact, in each of his responses Jesus applies to himself (and to his community) materials from the first chapters of Deuteronomy, describing how Israel ("God's son" or "God's child") was instructed to withstand temptation.

(On Israel as God's "child" or "son" see Exod. 4:22-23; Deut. 1:31; 8:5; Jer. 31:9,20; Hos. 11:1; 13:13; Mal. 1:6. For Israel as "sons and daughters" of God see Deut. 32:5,19; Isa. 43:6; 45:11; Hos. 2:1.)

5—For the second temptation the scene shifts to **the holy city** (27:53; cf. 5:35), an interesting name for Matthew to grant Jerusalem, since Matthew knew Jerusalem as the place of unholy plots and trumped-up charges, the center of opposition to Jesus (15:1).

The devil is pictured as setting Jesus on **the pinnacle of the temple.** A great basilica called the Royal Stoa ran the length of the southern edge of the temple platform. Some peak on the roof at the southeast corner of the basilica, high above the temple court, which itself was elevated by the great retaining wall, which in its turn sat on the crown of the hill, has often been identified as the **pinnacle.** Recent excavations at the foot of the southwest corner have uncovered a large stone inscribed, "To the House of Trumpeting." That probably means the place of the blowing of the shofar announcing the beginning and end of the Sabbath.

But southeast or southwest the point is the same: no longer in the solitude of the wilderness but in **the holy city** at the heart of **the temple** surrounded by reminders of God's promises and protection, the devil pressures Jesus for a public display of power (cf. 21:18-22). In response to the first temptation Jesus quoted Scripture and spoke of trust. In phrasing the second temptation, the devil turns the conversation with Jesus into a debate about Scripture and trust. **Throw yourself down.** You trust God, don't you, to send the angels promised in Psalm 91? Surely God will not let you **strike your foot against a stone.**

7—But Jesus refuses to test God and does not try to manipulate

God. He demands no proofs of God's care and again quotes Deuteronomy (6:16): **You,** and that means any people calling themselves God's people, **shall not tempt the Lord your God.**

8—For the third temptation the scene shifts once more, now to **a very high mountain** (cf. 5:1). Moses from Mount Nebo (or Pisgah) had looked "westward and northward and southward and eastward" and had seen all the land which the Lord would give to the people (Deut. 3:27) but Jesus saw **all the kingdoms of the world and the glory of them.** He was invited to become king over the whole vast realm without suffering. Had not the anointed ruler of Psalm 2 been promised universal dominion, the nations as his inheritance and the ends of the earth as his possession?

9—The devil boasted, **These I will give you if you will fall down and worship me.** How should Jesus become king of kings and Lord of the lords of earth? What path must Jesus travel to receive all authority in heaven and on earth (28:18)?

And what does it mean to **worship** Satan? In gross and literal form Israel in the wilderness fashioned a golden calf, sacrificing to it and dancing around it (Exodus 32; cf. 2 Thess. 2:4; Revelation 13).

10—But whatever swerves the people of God from the path of trust, obedience, and the service of God is satanic and idolatrous. Jesus says to blandishments of the tempter exactly what he will say to Peter, who also speaks of kingship without suffering and therefore without the necessity of trust: **Begone, Satan!** (16:23; 25:41).

Jesus' replies reach their climax: **You shall worship the Lord your God and him only shall you serve** (Deut. 6:13; cf. 5:6-7; 6:4-5). The attempt to serve two masters (Matt. 6:24) splits the personality, and is the death of integrity and wholeness (5:48).

Jesus is the only human being in this narrative. The devil fails to gain a foothold and is forced to leave the field. Surrounding Jesus and every struggling child of God (6:13) are the everlasting arms: In the beginning the Spirit led Jesus out, and in the end **angels came and ministered to him** (cf. 18:10; 26:53).

In his responses Jesus sounds as though he renounces power and will never perform a miracle. But Matthew will proceed to tell how Jesus stood in another wilderness and produced bread for the 5000 (14:13-21) and then for the 4000 (15:32-39). If Jesus did not throw himself off any towering temple height, he will step boldly out on the depths of the lake (14:22-33). What is the connection between temptation and miracle?

In some hostile quarters Jesus was denounced as a magician, practicing sleight of hand or, worse, working by the power of Satan (9:34; 12:24). In some friendly quarters followers of Jesus after his death and resurrection majored in miracles and at the same time neglected the weightier things of Jesus' program such as righteousness and the will of God, and they were leading many astray (7:15-23; 24:11, 24).

Matthew frequently touches these issues, arguing for example that Jesus has conquered the magicians (2:1-12; cf. Acts 8:9-13; 19:11-20), that he works by the Holy Spirit of God (12:28-32), that he refuses to perform miracles on demand in order to reap a harvest of popularity (12:38-39; 16:4) but does perform them out of compassion for broken and hungry people (9:36; 14:14; 15:32), and that the miracles erect in the midst of the old world eloquent signs of the wholeness and fullness of the coming kingdom (11:2-6; 16:2-3).

The temptation narrative reveals the inmost workings of the mind of Jesus. Standing as prolog to the entire ministry, this account declares that Jesus will wield speech and silence, power and weakness, action and passion with total disregard for self and in total harmony with the plain will of God.

The temptation narrative defines the whole work of Jesus not simply as an attack upon various illnesses or hypocrisy, greed or privilege, but as a frontal assault by the kingdom of heaven upon the whole power of Satan. Jesus, moved by the Holy Spirit and supported by God's holy angels, will press the attack against Satan and his evil empire, sweeping the world clean of demons (12:22-29). In and through Jesus, God touches the universe to cleanse and restore it, to make it "all right," freeing humanity from lawlessness and empowering lives of wholeness and righteousness (1:21).

Matthew expects readers to learn from this narrative the essentials of Christian existence and perhaps especially the basic qualifications of Christian leadership. The highest charismatic and pneumatic gifts are not miracles but trust and obedience, knowing God and doing God's bidding, as revealed in Scripture and interpreted by Jesus.

Biographers of heroes regularly recite, close to the beginning, a narrative of conflict that serves as a kind of qualifying test. The temptation is such a narrative. For a moment the veil is torn aside and the stuff of which Jesus is made is allowed to rise to the surface and to appear in plain view. He is revealed as he is tested, and he emerges from the testing tried, expert, ready.

A Great Light (4:12-16)

12—After the forerunner had been **arrested** or "handed over" (*paradidōmi*, cf. 10:4; 17:22), Jesus **withdrew** from the Jordan plain to **Galilee** (Mark 1:14a; Luke 4:14). But Jesus was not running to the security of home (cf. 10:37; 19:29). Of the evangelists, Matthew alone narrates how Jesus almost immediately abandoned **Nazareth** (2:23), cutting ties to family and old occupation (cf. 12:46-50; 13:55-56), and settled down (same word in 2:23) in **Capernaum** (8:5; 9:1; 17:24), which Matthew stresses is **by the sea, in the territory of Zebulun and Naphtali.**

The old tribal lands of **Zebulun** and **Naphtali** were the first chunks of Israelite territory to be swallowed by Tiglath-Pileser III and reorganized as Assyrian provinces (732 B.C.), 10 years before the rest of Israel was subjugated. Isaiah proclaimed that the first territories to feel God's wrath would also be the first to enjoy salvation at the birth of the messianic king (Isa. 9:1-7).

14-15—Throughout these opening chapters (1:1—4:16) Matthew has traced fulfillment of old hope in the geography of Jesus (see on 2:1). Here once again prophecy seems to provide a blueprint of Jesus' well-known movements away from the river, **across the Jordan into Galilee,** settling **by the sea** at the city of **Capernaum.** None of this is accidental. Nor would it be correct from Matthew's point of view to ascribe these moves to fear (4:2) or calculation on Jesus' part. All these movements lie deep in the mind of God, leading Jesus on his appointed path. Every inch of Jesus' way is in fulfillment of God's purpose.

Galilee was no isolated pocket of purely Jewish settlements. It lay astride international trade routes (also traditional paths of invaders) and had always been open to Damascus and Syria to the north, Egypt to the south, Phoenicia and the Mediterranean to the northwest and west. Jewish and pagan communities dwelled here, side by side, and precisely here in Galilee, not in Jerusalem, Jesus begins his ministry, silently prefiguring the universality he would later openly proclaim (28:19).

Jesus is no mere forerunner like John, as much as their ministries are linked. Nor does he come bearing the judgment John so eagerly desired. Matthew applies to Jesus stunning words from Isaiah (9:1-2). He is the prophesied **great light** rising and shining (2:2,9) upon people whose whole existence is described as sitting **in darkness** and **in the region and shadow of death** (Ps. 23:4). He is light and will give light, by his teaching and healing, by his suffering and his rising, and through the community of his disciples (5:14-16).

Jesus Began to Preach (4:17)

17—From that time, the time of the Baptist's arrest and of the move to Galilee, **Jesus began to preach.**

At 4:17 and 16:21 the identical phrase, **from that time Jesus began,** is followed by an infinitive: **to preach** (4:17), "to show" (16:21). Then comes a summary of the contents of the preaching or showing. Even though the phrase appears only twice in Matthew's Gospel, it has the look of a formula introducing a programmatic statement and, to some students of the Gospel, appears to be an important indicator of Matthew's view of the unfolding of Jesus' ministry (see the introduction).

Jesus began to preach. The public work of Jesus here is defined as preaching the kingdom's nearness. Preaching has a bad name in many circles today and often means the same as scolding, haranguing, or harping on moral platitudes. In the Bible, however, **to preach** (*kēryssō*) is not to deal in shopworn or secondhand goods but to stride forth as a herald (*kēryx*) with gut-wrenching news.

Exactly as John had, so Jesus also heralds, **Repent, for the kingdom of heaven is at hand** (cf. 3:2). It is surprising that Jesus does not utter here a brand-new word, different from the word of John (3:2). But John and Jesus belong together (11:11-19; 17:9-13) and the call to **repent** is the beginning of the good news of

the kingdom (13:14-15). **The kingdom of heaven** is present even in the Christian community as a countercultural force, untamed and raw, summoning away from all easy ruts to the new life of righteousness.

Ancient Jews and ancient Christians alike prayed that God might rule on earth as in heaven (6:10), that the enemies of God and the haters of the people of God might be cast down once and for all, that the new age might dawn speedily and soon, in our time and in our days.

Jesus, like John, announces the nearness of **the kingdom of heaven.** But how near is it? And in Matthew's view, when does the kingdom of heaven or the kingdom of God stop being near and actually arrive?

At Jesus' birth, climaxing that long history chronicled in the genealogy (1:18-25; 2:2)?

At Jesus' baptism, when the heavens split wide open and he was anointed with the Spirit and affirmed as God's Son by the voice from above (3:16-17)?

When he burst onto the scene in Galilee as the great light, heralding God's sovereignty (4:14-16)?

When he attacked Satan's power, healing the ill and freeing the possessed (12:28)?

At his crucifixion, when in the hour of his most awful weakness, the rocks split, the dead were raised, and Gentiles confessed him (27:51-53)?

At his resurrection, when the earth shook, opponents fell like dead men, and the angel declared his victory (28:2-4)?

No purpose is served by singling out any one of these and declaring that it alone is the moment of the dawning of the kingdom. It is rather in and through Jesus, in and through his birth and ministry, through his crucifixion and resurrection, in and through the undivided wholeness of his life that the kingdom begins to come, to dawn, to break in among us with God's own power.

Matthew insists that Jesus in the splendid entirety of his being is the approach of God, the epiphany of God. That is a central affirmation of Matthew's Gospel (1:23; 18:20; 28:20). In Jesus something new is already here. But Matthew also records sayings announcing the future sudden end, the close of the age, when

Jesus will come in power (10:23; 16:28; 26:64), when all the nations will be judged (25:31-46), when the kingdom of God will shine gloriously beyond all ambiguity and opportunity (13:43). That time is unknown, and the community is simply summoned to turn from calculation to vigilance of another sort altogether (see the introduction to chap. 24).

Christians today do not agree with one another about the time or the nature of **the kingdom.** And lines were sharply drawn between rival parties and movements also within first-century Judaism. Will **the kingdom** be an earthly or a heavenly rule? Reformation of this world and glorification of the present Jerusalem or the fresh creation of a new world and the divine gift of a new Jerusalem? Will it involve the slaughter of unrighteous and insolent nations or their conversion? Is it an inner, spiritual reality, triumphant wherever individual hearts are renewed? Or does it promise the rebirth of the entire universe (19:28), a new heaven and a new earth in which righteousness dwells?

Jesus' announcement of the approaching sovereignty of God prepares readers for the rest of the Gospel all the way down to the declaration of the universal authority of the resurrected Jesus in the final paragraph (28:18). Between this initial announcement and that climax of the Gospel, Jesus will everywhere steadily provoke audiences not only by proclaiming the nearness of the kingdom but especially by challenging dearly held definitions of the kingdom, by implying that the powers of the kingdom are at work in him, and by stubborn insistence that righteousness is the one indispensable and infallible sign of the presence of the kingdom. Ancient Jews and Christians alike envisioned the coming of the kingdom in terms of prodigious crops and astonishing fruitfulness of the earth. Matthew's Jesus steadfastly fixes his gaze on the fruit of obedience and love as the signs of the presence of the kingdom.

Fishers of Men (4:18-22)

18—The first recorded reaction to Jesus after he arrived in Capernaum is awesome. Walking **by the sea of Galilee** (vv. 13 and 15) Jesus saw **Simon who is called Peter** (16:18) and **Andrew his brother, casting a net into the sea, for they were fishermen.**

The sea, really a large freshwater lake 8 miles wide and 13 miles from north to south, ringed by settlements both ancient and recent, was the focus of life in Galilee.

19—Jesus issued a mysterious summons: **Follow me, and I will make you fishers of men.** Jesus is often pictured as a rabbi surrounded by pupils or as a wise man with students at his feet. But rabbinical students sought out their teachers and attached themselves to them. Here Jesus takes the initiative, calling the brothers. And he does not invite them to master Torah, to learn intricacies of biblical scholarship, to memorize a tradition, to meditate on texts. Nor does Jesus insist on a curriculum of study leading to a future as independent scholars. Instead Jesus holds before their eyes a startling picture of life as following him on his path.

Follow me (*akoloutheō*, 8:19, 22; 9:9; 10:38; 16:24; 19:21; 27:55). Is there any analogy for this kind of authoritative summons to unconditional obedience? Jesus calls disciples as God had called prophets in more ancient biblical times.

He summons disciples to follow him and promises that he will make them **fishers of men.** That picture of netting or fishing out human beings has a sinister ring. Fish are dragged from sea to shore, from water to dry land, from their life to their death. In the ancient world fishing was a metaphor for two distinct activities: judgment and teaching. Fishing for people meant bringing them to justice by dragging them out of their hiding places and setting them before the judge at the end of the world (cf. 13:47). And fishing was also used of teaching people, of the process of leading them from ignorance to wisdom. Both cases involve a radical change of environment, a break with a former way of life and entrance upon a new.

20—Without hesitation or lengthy consultation, as though it were the most obvious thing in the world, **they left their nets** (cf.4:13; 19:21,27) and **followed him.**

21—Immediately Jesus spotted another pair, **James the son of Zebedee and John his brother** (cf. 10:34-39) **in the boat with Zebedee mending their nets.** The unnecessary repetition in **son of Zebedee** and **Zebedee their father** underscores the sacred character of the bond about to be severed and the poignancy of the moment.

Just as Peter and Andrew had done, so these two also **left the boat and father and followed him.** They dropped what they were and what they were doing. They simply turned their backs on family and occupation, on social and economic entanglements, on old identities and old securities, and placed themselves at the service of the kingdom as disciples of Jesus.

Two pairs of brothers, all four of them fishermen, are the first to be called by Jesus into discipleship. Jesus uttered the cry, **I will make you fishers of men.** That call sets fishing at the head of Jesus' ministry as a kind of theme. That means that his words and deeds and sufferings have to do with the final judgment or the teaching of ultimate wisdom.

Great Crowds Followed Him (4:23-25)

23—Jesus walked through **Galilee,** not aimlessly wandering but conducting a deliberate campaign of words and deeds. Matthew here describes the work of Jesus in a programmatic statement as **teaching in their synagogues, preaching the gospel of the kingdom, and healing every disease and every infirmity among the people.**

When Matthew speaks in this context of "their" synagogues (4:23; 9:35; 10:17; 12:9; 13:54; 23:34), and elsewhere of "their" scribes (7:29) and "their" cities (11:1), he indicates that a break has occurred between Jewish institutions on the one hand and his own community on the other.

Does Matthew's language hint at other divisions as well? It is possible to set **preaching** and **teaching** against one another as opposites or at least as quite different activities. **Teaching** can be defined as measured, calculated, crafted discourse aiming to persuade or conquer ignorance by argument and evidence. **Preaching** can be defined as revelatory, urgent, absolute, and lapidary heralding. But Matthew connects the herald's work of **preaching** as closely as possible to **teaching.** He pictures Jesus both as heralding (preaching) the nearness of the kingdom and the urgency of decision and also as defining (teaching) his own royal interpretation of the kingdom's nearness in terms of the practice of the will of God (chaps. 5–7).

While three participles (**teaching, preaching, healing**) suggest three separate actions with three distinct contents, the immediately succeeding chapters cluster Jesus' activities into two broad categories: words (chaps. 5–7) and deeds (chaps. 8–9). In 9:35 a sentence nearly identical to 4:23 closes the subsection, bracketing everything between as a unit. Matthew would have readers ponder and find the unity in Jesus' words and Jesus' actions. Finally, all Jesus' words, whether uttered within the walls of a synagogue or outdoors under the open sky, whether described as **teaching** or as **preaching,** together with all his **healing,** have not three contents or even two but only one: **the gospel of the kingdom.**

Matthew, unlike the other evangelists, specifies that Jesus proclaimed **the gospel of the kingdom** (4:23; 9:35; 24:14; cf. 13:19). Mark's vocabulary is a bit different. He speaks of "the gospel" (1:15; 8:35; 10:29; 13:10; 14:9), "the gospel of Jesus Christ" (1:1) and "the gospel of God" (1:14), stressing its character as the good news of liberation for a world long held in the thrall of evil.

For Matthew the good news is both a word of freedom and a word of new allegiance. Matthew stresses the fact that the good news has the **kingdom** as its content. He thereby declares that the misrule of all the tired old sovereignties is now being replaced by God's own kingship of mercy and righteousness. The **gospel** (*euangelion*) invites people to cast off an old yoke and to take up the easy yoke of Christ (11:28-30). The kingdom is near, at the gates. Its powers are already present in Jesus, blessing and healing, but also disturbing the old order, shaking its foundations, reordering all of life.

24—Jesus' **fame** spread through the entire region. People had streamed to John for baptism. Now there moved toward Jesus a startling procession of **the sick: those afflicted with various diseases and pains, demoniacs, epileptics, and paralytics.** People trembled at the voice of John but found mercy in the presence of Jesus. **And he healed them.**

Matthew notes that crowds have gathered about Jesus not only from **Galilee** and **Judea,** from **Jerusalem** and from **beyond the Jordan,** but also from **the Decapolis** and indeed from **all Syria.**

The Decapolis was a scattering of ten Greek cities founded by the successors of Alexander the Great and organized into a federation by Pompey in 63 B.C. at the same time that he established the territories and kingdoms of the eastern Mediterranean into the large Roman province of **Syria.** Matthew and his community are usually reckoned as inhabitants of **Syria** (perhaps Antioch) and that may account for his naming the province here. However, all the individual places named in v. 25 were subordinate to **Syria,** and Matthew's basic point is that the whole region was stirred by Jesus' appearing. **Great crowds** both of Jews and of Gentiles, crowds of sheep without a shepherd, crowds with myriads of needs, crowds thirsting for life and wholeness, gathered about him and **followed him** (8:1).

Summary (1:1—4:25)

From the opening verse of the Gospel, Matthew steadily and deliberately has been building up to his narrative of Jesus' public ministry. Throughout these early chapters Matthew has raised readers' expectations. He has done that by revealing bit by careful bit Jesus' awesome credentials, rehearsing Jesus' ancestry, his names and titles, his geographical movements, his fulfillments of prophecy, his choice by God, his hard testing, his bursting on the scene in Galilee.

Matthew's opening chapters are full of materials at once familiar and strange. They contain puzzles, like the real meaning of the number *14* (1:17), pathos as in the sensitive portrait of Joseph struggling to balance the demands of justice and mercy (1:18-25), marvels like "the star of wonder" with its startings and stoppings (2:1-12), memorable portraits of cruel and scheming Herod, of naive and trusting magi, of ascetic and prophetic John. Matthew has probed the mind of Joseph (1:19), of Herod (2:3-8, 16), of Satan and the wholly other mind of Jesus (4:1-11) and even lets us hear the voice of God expressing the mind of God (3:17). Then Matthew brings the introduction to swift close as Jesus moves from Nazareth and life in his hometown among his family and settles in the heart of Galilee of the Gentiles (4:12-16), proclaiming the nearness of the kingdom, summoning disciples and attracting great crowds.

All that astonishing material—the genealogy, seven detailed fulfillments of the sacred writings, evidence of star and dreams, the testimony of the Baptist and of the voice from heaven, Jesus' success in the contest with the devil, and his provocative travelings through geographical spaces—all these are preliminary and introductory.

In his opening chapters, Matthew solemnly presents Jesus as God's own movement into the world, God's own interfering presence, God's counterattack upon Satan and all things devilish and twisted. Jesus' arrival on the scene is freighted and laden with awesome and terrible possibilities.

So far in his Gospel, Matthew has refrained from recording the details of any specific piece of Jesus' teaching and he has offered no particulars regarding any individual healing. So far in these opening verses on the public ministry of Jesus, Matthew carefully has been setting the stage for the centerpiece of his presentation of Jesus: the Sermon on the Mount.

The Sermon on the Mount will be Matthew's first detailed report on Jesus' public ministry. Matthew permits nothing to overshadow it or even compete with it. For the moment he mentions Jesus' proclamation of God's kingship (4:17) only in order to announce the great theme of the sermon. And he speaks of Jesus' healings only to establish the generosity and authority of the one who speaks the sermon (4:23-24). Then there is the question of an audience for the sermon. Jesus has now called the nucleus of his community of disciples (4:18-22), and a great international crowd has been attracted to Jesus (4:24-25). Finally everything is ready for the sermon.

■ FIRST DISCOURSE: The Sermon on the Mount. The New Community Is Called to Practice a Higher Righteousness (5:1—7:27)

The Sermon on the Mount sets its stamp on the whole of Matthew's Gospel. Everything so far has been leading up to it. Jesus' first word about fulfilling righteousness (3:15) pointed toward it. The entire rest of the Gospel will flow out from it, and the resurrected Jesus will underscore its centrality, its primacy, its foundational character, in his solemn charge to his disciples at the end (28:19).

The sermon has been hotly debated over the years, and generations of serious readers have come to widely divergent conclusions concerning its meaning, its use, its intent.

The sermon is sometimes considered an impossible demand,

designed to drive readers to their knees in repentance. Or perhaps it is a set of emergency rules valid not for all times but only for the brief interval before the full dawn of the kingdom. Or it has been read as a body of regulations meant not for all believers but only for an elite corps of especially dedicated believers within the larger whole.

Still others have tried to shift the focus by suggesting that the sermon, for all its legal language of command and ordinance, is fundamentally liberating. It is Jesus' vision of fresh possibilities opening before us with the advent of the renewing powers of the kingdom at work in his ministry.

However it is interpreted, it has usually been praised. Nevertheless, some have protested that its content seems one-sidedly individualistic and inward-oriented, devoid of real help for facing hard issues of economy and politics and society. In response it has been declared that the sermon is a revelation of the life of a new community, offered to the world as a sign of God's larger intentions for all creation. What God intends is a world, not just assorted individuals, but a whole universe freed from the bondage of sin and made "all right" by the experience of God's presence in Jesus. The life of the new community is salt and light, not for itself, but for the world (5:13-16).

The Structure of the Sermon

Matthew clearly signals the opening (5:1-2) and close (7:28-29) of the sermon. Following are a few comments on the structure of chap. 5.

Transitions inside chap. 5 are plainly marked. (1) The sermon opens in solemn fashion with the Beatitudes (5:3-12), capsule summaries of Jesus' vision. (2) Passing from the Beatitudes, Jesus in 5:13-20 states his theme, showing how the kingship of God, operating according to a new and strange dynamic, is a counter-cultural force and yet is good for the world (5:13-16). He has come at the end of a long time of expectation and preparation to fulfill the old thirst for a world that is "all right" and to summon the new community to lives of surpassing righteousness (5:17-20). (3) That new righteousness is then spelled out in a series of breathtaking "Antitheses" designed to stretch the moral imagination

(5:21-48). That series climaxes in the hard words, "love" and "be perfect."

Further comments on the structure of the sermon are offered at 6:1 and 6:19.

Blessing and Righteousness (5:1-20)

He Taught Them (5:1-2)

1—By his preaching tour of Galilee and by his acts of healing and exorcism, Jesus has fired the imagination of the crowds. He has their eye and ear. Now what will he do? What will he offer them? Onto what path will he lead them? Everything has been leading up to this moment, to the teaching we call "the Sermon on the Mount."

He went up on the mountain where **he sat down,** assuming the traditional posture of the teacher (23:2; cf. Luke 4:20). **His disciples came to him** and great crowds (7:28) surround him. What images would Matthew have dance in our heads? Moses on the mount receiving the tablets of the Law? Yes, but on this unnamed and mysterious **mountain** (cf. 17:1; 28:16) it is the disciples who are like Moses, and Jesus who speaks in the place of God, engraving words on their minds and hearts.

Jesus' teaching is not for the disciples only but also for the crowds (7:28-29) and not for those particular crowds alone. By the end of the Gospel, Matthew will have made it plain that what Jesus said is what the exalted Jesus says in the passing generations to new crowds and new disciples. The exalted Jesus, resurrected from the dead, is the community's one Teacher and one Master, and the centerpiece of his teaching is the Sermon on the Mount (23:8-10; 28:18-20).

2—Seated, surrounded by disciples and crowds, by the committed and the curious, Jesus **opened his mouth and taught them.**

The Beatitudes

Poetry and symmetry are not the least marks of Matthew's nine Beatitudes, organized into two stanzas of four each (5:3-6, 7-10) with the ninth (5:11-12) in a somewhat different form sounding a powerful crescendo.

Each of the two opening stanzas of four contains exactly 36 words (in Greek). The recipients of blessing in the first set are all persons described by Greek words beginning with the letter *pi.* Something of the effect may be gathered in this paraphrase: "Blessed are the poor . . . the penitent . . . the powerless . . . those who pant after righteousness." In the second set, the letters *epsilon, kappa,* and *delta* are repeated, and so shorter bursts of alliteration continue. The Beatitudes are carefully crafted and composed.

Matthew has opened and closed the entire series of eight with the same solemn promise: **theirs is the kingdom of heaven** (vv. 3, 10). **The kingdom of heaven** is the theme of Jesus' proclamation (4:17, 23), and the Beatitudes begin to flesh out what Jesus means by God's rule. Each Beatitude reveals some aspect of God's astonishing seizure of power.

Kingdom opens and closes the series, and in the center at the heart of the Beatitudes are the words **righteousness** and **mercy** (vv. 6, 7). These mighty realities are basic to everything Jesus has to say in Matthew's Gospel about the character of God's rule.

In all these respects the Beatitudes, the first paragraph of Jesus' public teaching, are a perfect counterpart to the last paragraph of his public teaching in 25:31-46. Both are visionary. Both speak of blessing (and curse). Both focus on great surprises as the kingdom dawns. Both underscore the centrality of righteousness and mercy.

The Beatitudes are like proverbs: brief, dense, memorable. They encapsulate Jesus' fundamental vision.

Jesus' Beatitudes are not theories presented for discussion, not mere wishes for a better world, not nuggets of advice drawn from some ancient version of *Poor Richard's* almanac, not rules for right living with the promise of high wages to be paid into the hands of the virtuous, not a call to arms in a spiritual warfare. They have certainly provoked dreams, stiffened backbones, stimulated discussion, sharpened resolve, and have served as exhortations. But they are not identical with any of these.

They stand at the head of the Sermon on the Mount like fabulous carved lions at the entrance of a sanctuary. They send shudders up the spine, fill the heart with a sense of dread, mark the line between the sacred and the profane.

Jesus' Beatitudes are bolts of lightning splitting the skies. They crack open the heavens, astonish eye and ear, and carry with them the smell of burning ozone. They are ecstatic, inspired declarations trumpeted from the mouth of the revealer, and they are brimming with infinite grace.

The Beatitudes usher the reader into a new world, and its inbreaking is marked by a royal distribution of gifts, by the announcement of amnesty, by surprising and surpassing generosity.

But where exactly is the surprise? All the reasonably good and religious people of that day looked for the kingdom of God, and they knew by heart the promises of psalms and prophets about inheriting the land, seeing God, and being children of God.

Each Beatitude consists of two parts. One surprises and the other does not. The second half of each Beatitude is couched in traditional language. Real surprises come in the first half of each, where Jesus names the beneficiaries of the promised blessings.

Who will benefit from the inbreaking kingdom proclaimed by Jesus? Who will enter the kingdom? Inherit the earth? Have all wants supplied? Be ushered into God's presence, stand at God's right hand, see God face to face, count as God's own dear children? To whom will the Lord say, "Come, O blessed of my Father, inherit the kingdom prepared for you from the foundation of the world" (25:34)?

In Jesus' day, the Essenes of Qumran taught that the pure will benefit; they prayed for a kingdom of the perfectly clean. Pharisees said the law-observant will benefit; they looked for a kingdom of energetically good people. Zealots promoted the way of religious patriotism; they expected God to suppport their efforts to establish a kingdom of free people.

Frequently, interpreters focus on the Beatitudes and succeeding portions of the sermon as revelations of Jesus' surpassing compassion and inwardness, as opposed to the alleged legalism of the Pharisees with sidelong glances at the revolutionary program of the Zealots, the ascetic platform of the Essenes, and the superstitious practice of the Gentiles.

But other comparisons are at least equally important. Even a quick reading of Luke 6:17-49 reveals that Matthew and Luke issued Jesus' Beatitudes (and other portions of the sermon) in slightly different wordings. Those differences show that Matthew and Luke made somewhat different use of Jesus' teaching as they applied it to their own particular times and places.

Matthew no doubt struggled on several fronts. One of his more important struggles was with Christian insiders. Matthew reports Jesus' criticisms of bluster and displays of piety (6:1-18). Jesus failed to be impressed by people with all the right slogans, the gift of healing, the power of exorcism, the ability to see in dream or vision and speak a word of prophecy (7:15-23). In Matthew's day, Christian prophets and leaders said that the Spirit-filled will inherit; they envisioned a kingdom of inspired people.

Matthew himself heard the voice of Jesus invoking heaven's blessings, not upon the spiritual virtuosos, but upon those who were inspired to seek God's rule of righteousness.

The one indispensable fruit of the Spirit desired by Jesus is righteousness. Righteousness may be defined for now as hearts set on the will of God, on love toward God and toward the neighbor, and even toward the enemy. But the reality of righteousness surpasses easy definition. Matthew spends 28 chapters describing its contours and singing its praise.

Blessed (5:3-12)

3—Blessed are the poor in spirit. Centuries before Jesus, **poor** in the vocabulary of Israel had come to mean something deeper than lacking in wealth. As **rich** easily became a synonym for "self-sufficient" and then "arrogant," so **poor** came to signify "humble" and "trusting." It was proverbial to speak of those **poor** in the goods of this world as rich in faith and heirs of the kingdom of heaven (Ps. 34:19; 37:14; Isa. 61:1; James 2:5).

But Matthew stresses poverty **in spirit.** He sees in this beatitude special encouragement for people who seem to themselves and to others to be deficient in spiritual gifts, lacking charismatic endowments. Others in the community, because they were rich in shining gifts of the spirit—prophecy, exorcism, healing—were full of pride, puffed up, and acting as though their gifts were achievements (7:21-23; cf. 1 Cor. 4:6-7, 18-19; 13:4-5).

Jesus opens his inaugural sermon with extravagant praise for those whose boast is in the Lord, whose one resource is God, whose prime gift is their emptiness, who rely without flinching on the inexhaustible grace of God. **Blessed** (*makarioi*) are they! This is a word of heartiest congratulations, of ultimate approval. And it is the very opposite of "cursed" or "condemned" (see commentary below on 11:6; 13:16; 16:17; 24:46; cf. *eulogēmenos* in 21:9; 23:39; 25:34).

4—Blessed are those who mourn. What do they **mourn?** The humiliation of God's people under Roman occupation? The daily reality of pitiful wages and cruel taxes, of crushing illness and untimely death? Certainly all that.

But to **mourn** means also to grieve over sin. Even good people adopt all kinds of other attitudes toward sin: they have been known to gloat over ills suffered by enemies, to smirk at the news of a pillar of the community nabbed red-handed in an unlawful act, to feel fascination as much as revulsion at reports of atrocities or heinous crimes, to view the sins of society with massive indifference.

But this beatitude may have in mind that peculiar temptation of godly people to place "religion" and "the will of God" (or morality) into separate watertight compartments. Any century can supply examples of people who equated the heart of religion with the contemplation of esoteric knowledge or revealed truths, or with the practice of a ritual whether intricate or utterly simple, or with the cultivation of spiritual experiences. This last was an issue in Matthew's community, where some prophets and wonderworkers felt they were above the demands of the law (7:21-23).

Corinth provides a parallel and a clue. A member of the Corinthian congregation lived in an incestuous relationship with his stepmother, a liaison forbidden both by Jewish and Roman law. Paul was shocked not simply at that man's sin but by the fact that some Corinthians were celebrating that man's daring as a sign of his spiritual liberation, an act by which he was demonstrating that in Christ and the Spirit he was free from the law. The law with its restraints belonged, they thought, entirely to the passing eon. He had become a culture hero and the congregation struck an arrogant pose. Paul shot back that they should rather have gone into mourning (1 Cor. 5:2; cf. James 4:9).

Blessed are those, who because they love the will of God, deeply **mourn** their own sin and then also the whole terrible reality of sin hanging like a weight on the neck of the world. In effect, **blessed** are those who pray, "Deliver us from evil" (6:13). **They shall be comforted.** God is poised to grant the comfort of final deliverance, the consolation of the new age, the joyous liberty of the children of God (Isa. 61:1-2; Rev. 7:17; Luke 2:25).

5—Blessed are the meek. The same Greek word (*praüs*) here translates as **meek** is also behind RSV's "gentle" (11:29) and "humble" (21:5). Jesus himself sits for the portrait of meekness in Matthew's Gospel. He enters Jerusalem as a king unlike any earthly sovereign: "meek and mounted on an ass" (21:5). He depends neither on bribes nor cruelty, neither on coins nor scourgings. He comes to serve and refuses to ride high or live high at the expense of others. With his yoke he seeks not to oppress and burden but to give God's full and final relief (11:28-30).

In the New Testament meekness or gentleness is a fruit of the Spirit (Gal. 5:23) and the opposite of jealousy and selfish ambition (James 3:13-18). It is openness to the word from above (James 1:21) and to erring sisters and brothers below (Gal. 6:1). It means renouncing all boasting of our imagined goodness or spirituality as we contemplate the wayward, and it means commitment to restoring them gently (Gal. 6:4).

In one sense meekness is the renunciation of power in human relations. In another, it is the weaponry of God's kingdom, powerful to destroy obstacles to the knowledge of God, able to take every thought captive to Christ (2 Cor. 10:1-6).

It is a perennial temptation for leaders, especially the most impressively gifted, to assert their authority and issue orders in the congregation (23:8-10; 1 Cor. 4:21). They particularly need the reminder: **Blessed are the meek! They shall inherit the earth.** Israel of old was promised a land (2:21). Here Jesus dusts off that ancient promise and transforms it. God is preparing a new heaven and a new earth, and the meek are first in line to inherit that fresh creation.

6—Blessed are those who hunger. Luke takes the beatitude only that far (Luke 6:21). Luke has meditated profoundly on how precious in the eyes of the Lord are the world's poor and hungry.

Matthew does not disagree, but he remembers the word of Jesus in slightly expanded form. God's favor leaps upon those whose deepest **hunger and thirst** is for **righteousness** (cf. 21:18). Not for personal gain or even personal growth. Not even for astonishing gifts of the Spirit like tongues, prophecy, healing, miracles, or the utterance of knowledge.

Blessed are those who absolutely ache for the high and excellent gift of **righteousness** (cf. 1 Corinthians 12–13), whose yearning is all for the coming world wherein righteousness dwells (3:15; 5:20; 6:33; cf. 2 Pet. 3:13). **They will be satisfied,** filled, vindicated, saved (Isa. 61:3) in that day when God will richly supply every need.

7—**Blessed are the merciful.** "Have mercy" is the cry of the blind and of wounded parents (9:27; 15:22; 17:15; 20:30-31) as it is of the debtor (18:33; cf. 6:12-15). And because mercy is the prime necessity of the poor and the broken, the words "mercy" (*eleos*) and "alms" (= deeds of mercy, *eleēmosynē*) are cousins (6:2, 3, 4).

So to be **merciful** is to major in the compassionate actions of almsgiving, healing, and forgiveness. For some these are only electives.

How easy it is for religious communities, without ever intending to be cool or condemning, to exalt some doctrine, some ritual, some tradition, some ecstatic experience above God's simple desire for that marvelous trio of "justice, fidelity, and mercy" (23:23; cf. 9:13; 12:7; James 2:13; 1 Clem. 13:2).

Matthew here recalls every reader to the passionate and compassionate core of Jesus' own concerns. And to the promise: those who live by mercy will at the end be astonished by mercy (25:37).

8—**Blessed are the pure in heart.** The acme of religious experience is often described as stepping into the presence of God, enjoying familiar access to God, seeing God not dimly but face to face (1 Cor. 13:12; 1 John 3:2; Rev. 22:4). Matthew's Gospel from beginning to end celebrates the altogether astonishing presence of God in Jesus (1:23; 18:20; 28:20).

But is the experience of seeing God open to the many or only to the few? To whom is it given? To the first generation of Christians who saw Jesus in the flesh? To apostles to whom Jesus appeared after resurrection? To prophets and prophetesses and other ecstatics who dream dreams and see God and Christ in trance and vision? And do all these constitute elite ranks of the spiritually privileged, completely outclassing ordinary believers? And in the end at the Lord's coming to judge the quick and the dead will all those seers be given the nod to enter the kingdom, leaving ordinary Christians to bring up the rear?

Jesus takes an old prophetic coin and restrikes it: **Blessed are the pure in heart** (see Deut. 10:16; 1 Sam. 15:22; Isa. 1:10-17; Jer. 4:4; 7:3-7; Ps. 24:3-6; 51:6, 10). It is, of course, easier to scrape dirt off the body than to purge the heart, that deep wellspring of thought and intention (15:19). But Jesus exalts purity of heart, which is a will and a mind neither divided nor confused in its affection, devotion, commitment (6:24; James 1:6-8; 4:8). The **pure in heart** have turned to God (3:2; 4:17) and they will **see God.** And God will see them, acknowledge them, lift up the divine face upon them.

9—**Blessed are the peacemakers.** The Prince of Peace (Isa. 9:6) is not blind to conflicts in the world or in the church. Later in this same chapter (5:21-48) Jesus reveals a keen eye for the sad fact of enmity: brothers and sisters divided by insults (5:21-24), women as objects of lust and sexual exploitation (5:27-30), the old warfare of husbands and wives (5:31-33), neighbors taking one another to court (5:33-37), occupation troops oppressing the natives (5:38-42), insiders unresponsive to outsiders (5:43-48).

The Gospel elsewhere echoes all these divisions and more: Jew and Roman, devout and careless, patriot and collaborator, rich and poor, Israel and the nations, church and synagogue, nation against nation. Factions and rifts are sad in any case. But how much more melancholy when they erupt in the heart of the new community itself.

Jesus in Matthew's Gospel pays particular attention to two threats to the peace of the community: some of the leaders are in love with their own titles and status, forgetting that all are sisters and brothers (23:8-10); apparently the same leaders are dishing out rough justice to straying "little ones," cutting them out of the community without a second thought (chap. 18).

By divine decree the sun shines and rain falls both on God's enemies and on God's friends. By crossing boundaries carefully drawn by culture and tradition, by including and befriending, by loving rather than hating their enemies (5:44), communities practice the peace of God.

Blessed are they, **for they shall be called** daughters and **sons of God** (see commentary on 4:4; 5:43-48; cf. James 3:18).

10—Blessed are those who are persecuted for righteousness' sake. Persecution is hardly what disciples expect when they sign on with a leader bristling with power. But the pious, the prophets, the wise who have in every age placed their lives at the feet of the Lord of the universe always have been strangely vulnerable, never immune to contradiction and rejection.

Righteous sufferers are almost stock figures, but they are still profoundly moving. The perfect tense of the verb in Greek indicates that these blessed ones have been persecuted and are still being oppressed. Or they have been persecuted and now bear the marks of persecution. They bear their wounds like badges of authority, provided their suffering is really **for righteousness' sake** (Psalm 22; Isaiah 53; Wisdom 5; 1 Pet. 3:14; 4:13-14).

The first generations of Jesus' followers were no more exempt from the fire of persecution than Jesus himself was (10:16-23; 24:9). Jesus foretold heightened conflict, worlds in collision, as the old and fallen world gathered its forces to resist the inbreaking of the new world of **righteousness** (3:15; 5:20).

But **blessed are those persecuted,** for the new world of God's righteous and sovereign Son shall come and it will be theirs.

11-12—A ninth beatitude, different in form, expands on the eighth, concludes the series, and prepares for what follows.

Jesus switches from the third person ("those who") to the second person ("you"; see further at 5:17). **Blessed are you.** That **you** includes the reader. The reader is not simply learning what Jesus said once long ago, but is directly addressed in the present.

Furthermore, Jesus here abandons the extreme brevity of the preceding beatitudes to dwell on the sad fact of persecution. He knows that people will **revile you** and **utter all kinds of evil against you,** misunderstanding and resenting, hurling insults in public and accusations in court.

Most intriguing is the way this beatitude encourages those persecuted **on my account** (cf. 10:18), where the preceding reads **for righteousness' sake.** Jesus and righteousness are simply inseparable here and throughout the Gospel.

12—Jesus never advises anyone to seek sufferings, but when they come, disciples may still **rejoice and be glad.** Persecutions are signs that the disciples are not citizens of the old world but of the new and that they are fellow citizens with those servants of God, **the prophets,** who hailed the new world from afar (cf. 7:22; 10:41; 23:34, 35; 21:11).

Salt of the Earth, Light of the World (5:13-16)

The Beatitudes are full of paradox and contradiction. They dethrone ordinary values and customary expectations. No woes have been uttered, no curses spoken (cf. Luke 6:24-26; Matt. 23:13-36), but obviously strong lines have been drawn between the blessed heirs of the coming kingdom and all other people. Every beatitude implies tension, but the series climaxes on a note of downright hostility and dwells on the grim prospect of persecution.

Now what? May disciples hate the world? May they retreat from a hostile environment to nourish the sacred flame in splendid peaceful isolation? Instead of this, Jesus utters a "great commission" paralleling his words at the end (28:18-20).

13—Disciples are **salt** for the earth. Salt, omnipresent seasoning and essential preservative, was a necessity also for sacrifice and for binding parties to a covenant (Mark 9:49-50; Exodus 30–35; Lev. 2:13). No wonder ancient sages praised Torah and Wisdom as the salt of the world. But Jesus has high expectations of his disciples, tempered by a shocking realism.

You are the salt of the earth, he says, but immediately warns that people, like salt, can become contaminated and useless, fit only to be **thrown out** of the house onto the street to be **trodden underfoot** (cf. 7:6).

14—Jesus' birth was signaled by the rising of "his star" (2:2), and by his settling at Capernaum by the sea he fulfilled the prophecy of the dawning of "a great light" (4:12-16). Poets and sages sang of the Lord God as light (Ps. 27:1; Isa. 60:1-3), and praised both the Law of God and teachers of that Law as lamps and lights for the human path (Ps. 119:105; Rom. 2:19). But here Jesus speaks not of God, nor the Law, nor learned scribes, nor even of himself. He utters no awesome "I am" (cf. John 8:12) but an even more astonishing **you are. You** disciples, insignificant and reviled, **are the light of the world** (Phil. 2:15).

And **light** is as difficult to hide as **a city set on a hill.**

15—Once people have gone to the trouble **to light a lamp,** they do not then immediately snuff it out under a measuring bowl. Naturally they set it **on a stand** so it may illumine **all in the house.** Just as obviously Jesus has not created a community of disciples to sequester them.

16—**Let your light shine.** But what flashes of light are the sure mark of the intimates of Jesus and the friends of God? The fire and thunder of John the Baptist? The deadly lightning bolts of Zealot and rebel? The white-hot brilliance of desert monks? The dazzling pyrotechnics of ecstatic seer or miracle worker? Jesus defines **light** as **good works. Good works?** Good grief! That sounds so flat. Jesus will devote the entire sermon to defining these **works** but here simply names them as theme and as challenge.

Stern warnings are reserved for disciples who show off their piety to gain human compliments (6:1-6, 16-18). Here, however, disciples are cautioned against withdrawing into the inner sanctum of self or the hothouse of the group.

Finally the vision of the speaker of the Sermon on the Mount is that the earth (v. 13), the world (v. 14), all in the house (v. 15), all people (v. 16), may **give glory to your Father who is in heaven** (6:9). When that vision is realized, when people's hearts have been captured by the love of God for the will of God, then the kingdom will have come in all its splendid newness.

To Fulfill the Law and the Prophets (5:17-20)

This paragraph packs into a handful of dense phrases the entire point of the Sermon. All the preceding is prolog. The Beatitudes are stirring revelations of a grand vision. Announced—not argued—they are awesome and provocative. They bind a spell, lift spirits, capture hearts. Now Jesus is ready for the work at hand. He compresses into this paragraph of four sentences the proposition he will be defending throughout the remainder of the sermon.

Jesus began by speaking in the third person (5:3-10) and then switched to the second person (5:11-16). He now adds the first person singular: **I have come** (5:17) and **I say to you** (5:18). Jesus directly confronts the reader from this point to the end of the sermon, although the concluding challenges are phrased again in the third person (7:11-27).

Each sentence in the paragraph focuses on the will of God: **the law and the prophets** (v. 17), **the law** (v. 18), **these commandments** (v. 19), **righteousness** (v. 20). Jesus defends or praises the will of God in all four sentences, and in the first three of them does so by means of vividly contrasting sets of positive and negative phrases.

17—Think not that I have come (cf. 10:34) **to abolish** (*katalyō*; cf. *lyō* in v. 19) **the law and the prophets. The law and the prophets** was a common designation for the Hebrew Scriptures as a whole (7:12; 22:40), the singular but complex revelation of the mind and will of God, a treasury of learning and lore, wisdom and commitment. As the context indicates, here it is the commanding function or moral content of **the law and the prophets** which comes to the fore. Sometimes the sequence is reversed and then "all the prophets and the law" stresses the promising character of Scripture (11:13).

What is the attitude of Jesus toward the commanding content of Scripture? That question arose not only in the years 27–30 as an issue between Jesus and the Pharisees, but also after Easter, and then not only between church and synagogue but also within the church among a welter of movements and factions. What is the heart of discipleship? Where is the primal and most authentic experience of God? In the adoration of cult? In the ecstasy of vision and prophecy? In the prudence of wisdom? In devotion to the law? In the freedom of the Spirit? Where do we hear God, see God, meet God? In Scripture or in Jesus or in the fresh winds of prophecy? In all three? But first things first. What is the attitude of Jesus to **the law and the prophets?**

Jesus was accused by some enemies and perhaps praised by some friends as a destroyer. Didn't he put himself forward as destroyer both of law and of temple? A single Greek word (*katalyō*) is behind "abolish" in 5:17 and "destroy" in 26:61 and 27:40, and the same word is behind "will be thrown down" in 24:2. Does not the coming of the Messiah and the age of the Spirit mean that need for the law has ceased, its usefulness ended, its rule terminated, and from now on freedom is the only rule?

Jesus solemnly declares that he has come **not to abolish but to fulfill** (*plērōsai*, cf. 3:15), not to undermine but to establish, not to diminish but to bring to fullest expression. Jesus is fulfiller of **the law and the prophets,** not of the prophets only (see commentary above on 1:22) but of **law and prophets** in their indivisible unity. He is the bringer of the promised new world, and it is a world marked indelibly by a new and higher righteousness. He came not to shatter the Law and the Prophets but to affirm their fundamental intention and carry it forward in his life, in his teaching, in his death and resurrection, and above all in his disciples' life of love (7:12; 22:40; 28:19). Already in his struggle with Satan in the wilderness Jesus announced his loyalty to the Scriptures, declaring God's word to be his bread (4:4).

18—Here in vv. 18-20 (unlike v. 17) Jesus speaks not of "law and prophets" but of "law" alone, and here it means God's will as he now is interpreting it—not the same as Pharisees and Scribes and Sadducees taught (5:21-48; 15:4; 19:3-9; 22:31, 37-40; 24:35; 28:18-20). "Law" here means the will of God as Jesus authoritatively declares it.

Jesus takes the **truly** or "amen" ordinarily used to close a prayer to God and makes it the opening of his own oracular utterance. What can be more solid and enduring than **heaven and earth?** They abide age after age as generations come and go, as nations rise and fall, and so also the law abides. Not the smallest letter in the whole alphabet of the law (Hebrew *yod*, Greek *iota*) nor the tiniest curlicue or flourish of the pen (a **dot**) **will pass** away or disappear **from the law.** Enduring earth, enduring law.

In every age the authority of **the law** suffers both quiet erosion and noisy assaults, and pessimists view history as a rising tide of immorality. Jesus separates himself from all who ignore the law, attack it, or bemoan its decline. He declares that, far from vanishing, not the smallest bits will disappear and indeed that **all,** namely, the law in the complex totality of its breadth and height and depth, **will be accomplished.** God's will shall be done on earth as it is in heaven (6:10), by Jesus (26:42), and by the new community (28:19).

19—A third pair of contrasting statements repeats the themes of abolishing and fulfilling (v. 17), of passing away and being accomplished (v. 18).

Jesus draws a conclusion for the community of his followers, and in particular he puts the finger on teachers. Anyone who **relaxes** or annuls (*lyō*, cf. v. 17) **one of the least of these commandments** and does it deliberately as part of a program and then also **teaches** others to do the same **will be called least in the kingdom of heaven. And whoever does** or observes them **and teaches them will be called great in the kingdom of heaven.**

20—Surely voices would rise in protest: the new age and new community are new wine, new coins, a new creation and have no traffic with the old! No more legalism, no more Pharisaism, no more childish subjection to traditions, customs, laws! In their place new energies, a new Spirit, new visions! But Jesus disappoints all who desire some blanket condemnation of law and **the scribes and Pharisees.** However he may disagree with the latter, with their spirit, achievement, or tactics (see esp. chap. 23), Jesus credits them with the right concern: **righteousness.**

Others might argue: all disciples from the Gentiles must be circumcised and taught the entire Law, every jot and dot, exactly as it has been handed down generation to generation. To them Jesus says: **exceed** (*perisseuō*, cf. 5:47, "more"). **Unless your righteousness exceeds that of the scribe and Pharisee, you will never enter the kingdom of heaven.** From here to the end of the chapter Jesus will spell out the meaning of **righteousness** which "exceeds" or is "more." Here he contrasts his position with that of a scribe and a Pharisee. At the end (5:47) he will contrast his posture with that of the Gentiles.

Readers find it easy to disagree with one another regarding 5:17-20. On the surface Jesus appears to defend the abiding validity of the entire Law. He does that here and elsewhere in the Gospel, sending the leper to the priest (8:1-4), commending the Law to the rich young man (19:16-22), praising the weightier things of the Law (23:23), fearing flight on the Sabbath (24:20). But Jesus also seems to contradict the Law and break it. He appears to attack the Law in the Antitheses (5:21-48). And he will soon offend strict observers of the Law by forgiving sins (9:2-9), eating with tax collectors and sinners (9:10-13), not fasting (9:14-17, 11:19), working and healing on the Sabbath and teaching others to do likewise (12:1-8, 9-14), dining with unwashed hands (15:1-20), speaking with a Gentile woman and healing her daughter (15:21-28), disagreeing with Moses over divorce (19:3-9). After the resurrection Jesus commands his disciples to gather Gentiles and says not a word about teaching them Moses or requiring circumcision (28:18-20).

Jesus in Matthew's Gospel seems to break the Law not carelessly but deliberately and simultaneously to demand strictest observance of the Law.

This tension or contradiction is interpreted in several ways.

1. Perhaps Jesus declares the temporary validity of the Law up to the time of his death and resurrection. That might be the moment when heaven and earth pass away and all things are accomplished (v. 18). Only after that time is the Law abolished, and only in that new time are the Gentiles invited into the community. So apparent contradictions are handled as diverse material valid for different times. History to the rescue. But it does not account for all cases.

2. It has been suggested that the Gospel is a patchwork of sayings derived from different sources with differing attitudes toward the Law, and that Matthew incorporated them with little or no editing into his Gospel. Source theory to the rescue.

3. Jesus in Matthew's Gospel everywhere praises the Law but never says that everything in the Law carries equal weight. In fact, Jesus designates some things weightier than others (23:23-24) and assigns priority to some things (22:38-39) over others. He clearly distinguishes between human legal tradition and divine commandment (15:3-6) as well as between external observance and inward devotion (15:8-9). But from every page of Matthew's Gospel a consistent picture emerges. Jesus pursues the divine intention in the Law (whether written or oral), and not only pursues it but practices it, and not only practices it but teaches it, and teaches it not only in his earthly ministry but also as the resurrected one (28:19).

Matthew sees no contradiction in the varied expressions of Jesus' passion for the will of God. Nor does he see any contradiction between the picture of Jesus as Savior and as teacher of righteousness. Jesus saves (1:21) and ransoms (20:28) and freely bestows forgiveness through his dying on the cross (chaps. 26–28). The saved, the ransomed, the redeemed are empowered to practice righteousness and are summoned to it. Matthew's portrait of Jesus will disappoint anyone who imagines that discipleship should mean escape from morality into spiritual experience.

But I Say to You (5:21-48)

This summary statement of Jesus' program announced in somewhat abstract terms as centered on surpassing righteousness (5:17-20) is now followed immediately by an abundance of concrete and shocking detail organized in a series of six paragraphs (5:21-48) dominated by six statements usually called "Antitheses." They bear that label since contradiction is the chief mark of their form and substance.

All six follow roughly the same pattern, opposing traditional teaching (A) and Jesus' teaching (B). (A) **You have heard that it was said to the men of old**. . . . (B) **But I say to you.** . . .

Teachings are set in opposition, but are all six statements really antitheses? Rather, is it not true that Jesus in some cases contradicts the tradition but in others he deepens or radicalizes it? Most interpreters nowadays agree that the list contains both genuine antitheses and also radicalizations. But they argue about which fall into each category.

It is commonly agreed that the first two intensify and that the third and fifth involve cancellation and replacement. The force of the fourth and sixth is debated.

And what precisely is Jesus canceling or deepening? Scribal and Pharisaic interpretations of the Law? Or is Jesus setting himself against the Law spoken by God to the wilderness generation? Of course, one hardly exists without the other. The Law is always an interpreted law; the commandments are always "the commandments as commonly understood" or "as taught by our authorities."

The full impact of the "Antitheses" can only be felt if we see that Jesus is opposing permissions, arrangements, and institutions sanctioned by Law and vital to the well-being of society. He attacks provisions dealing with such basic matters as worship, marriage, courts, politics, and business. The commentary below will attempt to show that those provisions were both respected and reasonable.

What is Jesus doing? Whatever else he may be up to, he is putting flesh on the bare bones of the propositions of the preceding paragraph (5:17-20). He is illustrating what it means not to cancel but to fulfill the Law and the Prophets (5:17). He is offering concrete examples of the higher righteousness (5:20). He is spelling out how people saved from sin (1:21) think and behave.

It is vital to recognize that the higher righteousness does not (cannot!) exist by itself but is the mark of the dawning kingdom, the new age. Kingdom is inseparable from righteousness, and righteousness from the gift of the kingdom (cf. 6:33).

The labels "antitheses" and "radicalizations" are both too narrow, if they rest on the assumption that Jesus' work can be summarized by saying that he is issuing a new set of rules for human behavior. Jesus is involved in something broader than an assault on the old rules. His language is revealing: "It *was* said to people **of old** . . . but **I now say**." He is declaring the passing not just of old rules but of the old time, the time of hardness of heart (19:8). The new time of the new creation with its new wine and new energies is now breaking in. Jesus in the "Antitheses" is tolling the passing of the entire old age and heralding the dawn of the kingdom.

The basis of Jesus' radicality and freedom is not simply that God's judgment is coming, and that God in the divine court can be counted on to right all present wrongs. That would mean that we have not yet broken clear of the iron framework of laws and regulations with their attendant rewards and punishments. Jesus in Matthew's Gospel often uses the traditional language of law and reward and punishment but always in the effort to set readers in the presence of the power of the new world as the power of righteousness. But it is a surpassing righteousness, surpassing all ordinary thinking about laws and calculations of rewards and punishments.

This is, after all, chapter 5 of the Gospel. Matthew has carefully paved the way for the Sermon on the Mount, announcing Jesus' coming as the advent of the virgin-born Savior from sin (1:21), who is the presence of God (1:23), who is God's anointed Son

(3:17), who cast down Satan (4:1-11), fulfills the hope for the dawn of a new day (4:13-16), heralds the nearness of the kingdom (4:17, 23), gathers a new community (4:18-22), heals the sick, and casts out demons (4:23-24).

He is the one who speaks with incomparable authority (7:28-29) in the magisterial phrase, **But I say to you.** This is the speech neither of prophet nor of rabbi. They quoted the Lord whom they had seen in vision or the tradition which they had memorized in schooling. Jesus grounds his utterances neither on vision nor Scripture, neither on legal precedent nor scholarly tradition. He introduces his words with the boldest, baldest assertion of his personal authority. He is the one to whom "all authority in heaven and on earth has been given" (28:20; cf. 11:25-27). Matthew may lack the great "I AM" sayings of John's Gospel, but Matthew is rich in "I came" and "I say" statements. (On "I came" see 5:17; 9:13; 10:34-35).

Matthew's Gospel reproduces many sayings of Jesus introduced by some kind of "I say" formula: "Truly (*amēn*) I say," "Again I say," "Nevertheless I say." Jesus is himself the Amen, the seal of the words of the Lord (Rev. 3:14; cf. Deut. 27:14-26; Justin Martyr, *First Apology* 65.4).

So the six statements are more than antitheses and more than radicalizations, because they are more than demands. More than a set of rules. They are in their own way, however indirect and veiled, joyous announcements that the old world is passing and the new age of righteousness is breaking in.

In view of that dawning new world, Jesus utters these words, these radical demands, couched in phrases that seem sharp, intense, unyielding, harsh. It is a mistake to read these statements as though they were ordinances passed by majority vote in some legislative assembly, designed to be enforced by police power and courts of law. Jesus speaks of anger, lust, and hate. All these move in the secret depths. They cannot always be detected, let alone regulated. This is rather the language of the visionary or poet, brimming with passion and exaggeration, at once imaginative and shocking.

At least one other feature of those sayings must be mentioned. They are not broad ethical principles from which teachers in a community might deduce a system of enforceable rules. Far from being broad and general, they are shockingly narrow and specific. So much so, that many readers find them foreign, impossible to understand, let alone apply.

They are indeed specific: a particular insult (**You fool!**); being led to sin by your right eye; swearing by your head; being slapped on the right cheek; being sued for your coat. These cases do not come up very often!

And the images Jesus uses are severe, extreme. Insults lead to hellfire; a lustful glance is as deadly as adultery; chop off your right hand and throw it away; give away all your clothes!

Specific and extreme, drawn from the outer edge of the possible, barely imaginable, the sayings are shocking, and deliberately so. They assault normal patterns of thought and behavior. Every action Jesus recommends is the polar opposite of our natural tendency.

The sayings are heaped up, arranged in series. Three in 5:22 are supported by two parallel scenes in 5:23-26; a single extreme saying in 5:28 is reinforced by two parallel sayings in 5:29-30; an extreme point in 5:34a is backed up with specific cases in 5:34b-36; a series of five fills up 5:38-42.

Not isolated but ordered in series, they constitute a pattern and establish a dynamic. They are designed to propel readers out of ruts and get them moving in a fresh direction. The pattern is open-ended, and the meaning of the sayings cannot be restricted to their simple literal sense. The reader is being impelled to extend the sense to new times and new situations.

What new time? What new situation? The Antitheses are a blow to our ordinary calculations, conditioned by our own acceptance of the old world of darkness and the shadow of death (4:16) as the ultimately real world. They would send us reeling in the direction of the new world in which light shines and righteousness dwells.

First Be Reconciled (5:21-26)

21—You shall not kill; and whoever kills shall be liable to judgment (Exod. 20:13; Deut. 5:17). Murder stirs primal passions and cannot be ignored or left to the kin of the murdered individual. The community must deal with it or be torn apart.

22—Jesus finds no fault with the old command, but refuses to rest on the surface of these words. He penetrates to the will behind them. Launching out from the prohibition on murder, Jesus condemns sins so insignificant that ordinary courts must ignore them: **Everyone who is** (a) **angry,** or (b) **insults** (says "*rhaka*"), or (c) says, **"You fool!"** (*mōre*) to sister or brother **shall be liable:** (a) **to judgment,** (b) **to the council,** (c) **to the hell of fire.**

Jesus here parodies the moral casuistry which weighs sins and then assigns matching punishments. These verses seem to describe escalating offenses and an escalation of judgments, moving from a verdict rendered by a local court (**judgment**), to the verdict of a higher human court of appeal (**the council** = the regional or Jerusalem Sanhedrin) to the highest verdict of God's own court (**hell of fire**). Or "judgment" might correspond to the inauguration of a suit (cf. on the way to court, 5:25a), "council" to the trial itself (cf. handed over to the judge, 5:25b), and "the hell of fire" to a verdict (cf. handed over to the guard and to prison, 5:25c). "Hell of fire" is literally "Gehenna," the Valley of Hinnom south of Jerusalem (Josh. 15:8), notorious as the place where children were burned as an offering in the pagan cult of Molech (2 Kings 23:10; Jer. 7:31; 32:35). By Jesus' time, Gehenna had come to signify the place of fiery torment reserved for the punishment of the wicked (5:22, 29-30; 10:28; 18:9; 23:15, 33).

At any rate, the threefold repetition hammers the point, keeps up the pressure on ordinary ways of thinking. Anger, insults, verbal assaults are in the same bag as murder! All these divide and cut people off from one another. They are all the terrible antitheses of brotherhood and sisterhood, of reconciliation and righteousness.

The word **brother** (*adelphos*), meaning both the female and male members of the community, punctuates the sermon (5:22, 23, 24, 47; 7:3, 4, 5) as do frequent references to God as "Father" (5:16, 45, 48; 6:1, 4, 6, 8, 9, 14, 15, 18, 26, 32; 7:11, 21). Jesus is unfolding his vision of a new world and the birth of a new family under God (12:46-50).

23-24—The first of two brief parables of reconciliation continues Jesus' probe of the old commandment against killing. The picture shifts from law to cult. Imagine standing **at the altar** in the temple's sacred precincts, half-way through a liturgy, **gift** held in uplifted hands, and all unbidden the memory presses in that you have hurt a sister or brother. Stop everything! Break off in the middle of the liturgy! **Go, first be reconciled!** Why can't it wait? It is inconvenient and impractical to stop. Worse, interruption will ruin the sacrifice! The ritual act will come unglued and lose its force. But nothing is more urgent than the call to peace among brothers and sisters (cf. 9:13; 12:7).

According to the Mishnah, *Yoma* 8:9, the rabbis taught, "If a man said . . . 'I will sin and the Day of Atonement will effect atonement', then the Day of Atonement effects no atonement . . . For transgressions that are between a man and his fellow, the Day of Atonement effects atonement only if he has appeased his fellow."

25-26—Or, to return from liturgy to law, picture a fellow being hauled off to court at the insistence of an accuser (cf. Luke 12:57-59). Is this the same fellow as in 5:23-24? Had the brothers gone unreconciled, and has the dispute reached the stage of legal proceedings? In any case, earthly wisdom suggests the stupidity of letting pride lock oneself out of reconciliation and into prison.

Just so, the children of God should seek peace with their sisters and brothers, and so fulfill the will of God who forbids the spilling of blood and the destruction of life.

So Jesus urges thinking in a new direction: away from anger, insults, murder; away from vengeance, prisons, punishments, and pride; and towards reconciliation and life, towards peace and righteousness.

Pluck It Out (5:27-30)

27-28—**You shall not commit adultery.** Every society has surrounded sex with rules in an effort to harness its mysterious power and prevent it from turning hurtful. Adultery means breaking into another person's marriage and is sharply condemned in the Ten Commandments (Exod. 20:14; Deut. 5:18).

Jesus again presses beyond the letter and sharpens the command. The tendency of Jesus' day was to place the guilt for sexual sins at the woman's door. With her sexuality, she is dangerous! But Jesus here addresses men: **Everyone who looks at a woman lustfully has already committed adultery with her in his heart.**

29-30—He follows one extreme statement with two more, urging unthinkable action: **Pluck out your right eye, cut off your right hand,** if that is what it takes to keep you from coveting (**eye**) or seizing (**hand**) another man's wife, and so injuring her and her husband and also ruining your own life with God. This harsh saying is used in another context in 18:8-9.

Except on the Ground of Unchastity (5:31-32)

31-32—Talk of marital relations continues. A legal procedure laid down in Deut. 24:1-4 permitted men to divorce their wives (but not vice versa in ancient Judaism), requiring only that they provide their former wives with a certificate. That paper removed any ambiguity about her status, declaring her legally free to remarry.

That arrangement seemed not only practical but downright humane. Nevertheless, Jesus objected, **Every one who divorces his wife** and so sends her forth, certificate in hand, to a second relationship or more, **makes her an adulteress; and whoever marries a divorced woman commits adultery.**

With procedures for divorce and rules about certificates, serious citizens of an old world had devised serious ways of dealing with the ills of the world. It is sensible, they say, to trade greater evils for lesser. But Jesus says it is not a lesser evil that results after all. It is **adultery.** Even our most serious efforts fall short of God's intention that one man and one woman live in lifelong union. And Jesus will score all such serious and practical arrangements and accommodations to the hardness of human hearts (19:8).

So again Jesus does not cancel but radicalizes an old commandment. But what are we to make of the phrase, **except on the ground of unchastity?** That exception seems to dilute the radicality of Jesus' position and to involve him in the very compromising and calculating which he condemns.

1. Perhaps Jesus here is rejecting the trivial reasons for divorce recognized among more liberal Pharisees of Hillel's school; for example, the inability to cook to a husband's satisfaction. Could Jesus be siding with the stricter school of Shammai, recognizing only **unchastity** or impurity as a valid ground for divorce? (In fact,

Jewish law in New Testament times demanded—not just permitted—divorce in cases of impurity; cf. 1:19.)

While this explanation places Jesus on the side of strictness, it is a far cry from the shattering radicality of the higher righteousness.

2. Perhaps **unchastity** here means not adultery or just any kind of uncleanness but is a technical term for marriage within forbidden degrees of kinship, outlawed by most Jews but tolerated among many of their pagan neighbors. People who enter the new community from the Gentile world must not live together within the forbidden degrees (Lev. 18:16-18; Acts 15:20-29; 21:25). That is an illicit sexual liaison and no real marriage. Break it off!

The Greek word for adultery is *moicheia*. That word (or its cognates) stands in 5:27; 15:19; 19:18. On the other hand, the word translated as "unchastity" in 5:32 is *porneia*. It and its cognates appear in 15:19 and 19:9. It is used of a broad range of sexual immorality, and it is a technical term for marriage within the forbidden degrees (Acts 15:20, 29; 21:25).

This interpretation moves closer than the first suggestion to the radical character of the Antitheses, and may reflect the conditions in Matthew's community. In either case, however, Jesus declares that where an illicit union already exists, divorce will obviously not produce one.

Jesus' sayings on divorce are reported in slightly different versions and contexts in the New Testament: (1) Matt. 5:31-32; cf. Luke 16:18; (2) Matt. 19:9, cf. Mark 10:11-12; (3) 1 Cor. 7:10-11. Only in Matt. 5:32 and 19:9 is there any mention of the exception, but 1 Cor. 5:1 looks like the application of an assumed exception.

Again, Jesus deals in specifics but it is a mistake to take them as rules. He is not merely fine-tuning our grosser adjustments to this old world. Neither does he promulgate a more stringent or a more lax code of conduct. He shocks and shatters in order to lift eyes to behold a new world where everything is all right.

Simply Yes or No! (5:33-37)

33—You shall not swear falsely but shall perform to the Lord what you have sworn (Exod. 20:7; Lev. 19:12; Num. 30:2-3; Deut. 23:21-24; Ps. 49:14).

Precisely because talk is cheap, memories self-serving, and promises often broken, people resort to oaths, dressing up their poor words by throwing over them a cloak of divinity, thinking to use God to make their words impressive.

Flawed people in a flawed world attempt to safeguard personal, economic, and political transactions by attaching oaths to them, and then they back up their oaths with sanctions, punishing perjurers and oath-breakers. An entire tractate of the Mishnah (*Shebuoth*) is devoted to the complex issue of oaths.

Jesus does not introduce a new set of simpler or stricter oaths or suggest more stringent sanctions. He shakes his head at the pious effort to avoid directly naming the name of God, as he alludes to the swearing of oaths **by heaven, by the earth, by Jerusalem, by your hand.**

The variety of oaths is one sign of the fertility of the human imagination, but again Jesus tries to kick the imagination up to an altogether new plane: **Do not swear at all** (James 5:12). Instead, let what you say be an unadorned **Yes** or **No. Anything more than this** is simply an admission that you are bogged down in an old and **evil** world.

Josephus says of the Essenes that "every word of theirs is stronger than an oath; they avoid swearing, thinking it worse than perjury" (*War* 2.135; cf. *Ant.* 15.371). Josephus says, however, that on entrance to the order they swore "tremendous oaths" (*War* 2.139). In their own Damascus Document the Essenes picture themselves as rather less reluctant to use oaths (CD 15:1-5; cf. 1QS 5:8-23).

Do Not Resist (5:38-42)

38—An eye for an eye and a tooth for a tooth. And Jesus could have continued as Exod. 21:24-25 does, "Hand for hand, foot for foot, burn for burn, wound for wound, stripe for stripe" (cf. Lev. 24:20; Deut. 19:21). The original intention has very nearly been lost from sight: to set reasonable, even humane, limits to retaliation. Ancient Assyrian law has earned a reputation for being especially brutal, punishing crimes against property by the mutilation of the offender's body (cutting off ears, nose, fingers, tongue.) The Babylonian Code of Hammurabi (late 18th c. B.C.)

expresses the principle of "a tooth for a tooth" in the case of peers. If a lord knocked out a commoner's tooth, however, the lord needed only to make a cash payment.

An eye for an eye meant that the punishment should fit the crime and that vengeance must be controlled. Injustice and revenge are explosive forces, and unless they are confronted and dealt with they will erupt. Laws, courts, police, punishments are a social necessity, whatever their imperfections.

But Jesus does not call for their perfecting. He glimpses a totally other world, one of disproportionate generosity, odd and unbalanced giving, lopsided, careless, and irrepressible sharing (see Gen. 4:23 and Matt. 18:21-22).

39—In contrast to the good old principle of social equilibrium, Jesus utters the stunning command, **Do not resist one who is evil.** What? No police, no self-defense, no precautions, no locks on the door, no evasive actions? Does this saying make any sense?

The meaning is actually very close to Paul's, "Repay no one evil for evil" (Rom. 12:17). Instead of forever keeping score and striving to stay even (or to get the upper hand) with our sisters and brothers, Jesus says, "Do not thirst for revenge, do not take sister or brother to court, do not try to ruin your adversary! To do that is to follow the easy path of enmity and killing." Jesus summons followers to the higher and more difficult art of peace, to the science of righteousness.

The Essenes of Qumran also could write, "I will repay no one with evil; I shall pursue him with goodness, for with God is the judgment of all living" (1QS 10:18; CD 8:5-6).

Four extreme cases follow in rapid succession. (1) If you are grossly insulted by a slap with the back of the hand **on your right cheek,** what is the natural tendency? Hit back! But Jesus goes against nature's stream: **Turn to** that insulter **the other** cheek as well.

40—(2) **If anyone would sue you and take your coat** (*chiton*), your long undergarment, far from fighting the case, Jesus says, **let him have your cloak** (*himation*) **as well.** The Law recognized that the **cloak** (21:7-8; 27:31-35) served the poor as clothing by day and blanket by night and so required that it be returned by nightfall if it was ever taken as security on a loan (Exod. 22:26-27; Deut. 24:12-13).

But Jesus announces the strange logic of the kingdom: "Let yourself be stripped naked rather than get involved in a fight with sister or brother. Do not trade blow for blow, insult for insult, or injury for injury."

41—(3) **And if any** Roman soldier exercises his rights under the laws of military occupation and **forces you** (*aggareuō*, "press into service" cf. 27:32; Didache 1:4) **to go one mile,** lugging his gear all that way, volunteer to **go with him two miles!** The words of this third example are galling and offensive. Patriotic Jews chafed under Roman rule, and Zealots fanned the flames of rebellion. But Jesus looks beyond the kingdoms of this world and their agony, beyond the warfare of the Roman and Jew to the struggle between good and evil, beyond all the complex mechanisms of tips and favors, shares and payments, with litigation and courts to arbitrate smaller disputes and rebellion or warfare to settle larger ones. Jesus points beyond all that to a new world and its righteousness.

42—(4) The series of four cases concludes with a summary sentence of two parallel clauses, both touching the subject of loans. **Give to him who begs** a loan **from you, and do not refuse him who would borrow from you.** Jesus brushes aside as of no consequence all such matters as credit checks, references, co-signers, security, contracts, and interest rates, all the devices invented to protect ourselves in a chancy world. Instead he demands what again appears to be a ruinous self-giving, reckless and exuberant sharing.

Be Perfect (5:43-48)

43—**You shall love your neighbor** (Lev. 19:18). It is not difficult to get human beings to salute that old rule, as long as they are free to define **neighbor** (Luke 10:39). It is apparently inborn instinct for most people to restrict the scope of **love** to some in-group, permitting themselves leeway to **hate** nonmembers or anyone who qualifies as the **enemy.** That is standard operating procedure, quickly defended as prudent, realistic, and wise.

Spirited new movements, especially if they are unpopular, resented or persecuted, can be as vigorous in their hates as in their loves, particularly when the hated object can be defined in abstract terms: hate sin, hate evil, hate godlessness, hate greed. But Jesus is unfailing in summoning to the banner of love.

The Manual of Discipline required the members of the Qumran community to "love all children of light" but to "hate all the children of darkness" (1QS 1:4-10; 9:21-22). In writing to his followers, the elder warns, "Do not love the world or the things of the world" (1 John 2:15). Hostility toward "the world" is a strong element in all the documents of the Johannine circle.

44—Jesus is not blind. He sees that some people really are **enemies,** and he knows how cruel and sadistic **enemies** can be. But still he says, **Love your enemies, and pray for those who persecute you.**

Love (*agapē, agapaō*) here enters the vocabulary of the sermon and the Gospel for the first time (cf. 6:24; 16:19; 22:37, 39; 24:12). The word would have fit earlier but Matthew has been holding it back so that it now forms the climax for all six antitheses.

Not only is the word **love** new here, but the form of the sayings in this final paragraph also is new, abandoning the pattern of the preceding. Here at the end Jesus supports his demands with arguments, reasons, rhetorical questions, and references to motives.

45—Why love? **So that** you may be daughters and sons **of your Father who is in heaven** (cf. 5:9). Here is the first reason for loving: so that you may be like God, reflect the essential being of God, display kinship with God. Like parent, like child. God would have people stamped with the divine likeness, just as human parents would have their children replicate their values and their style or achieve a higher level!

The essential likeness is captured in the word **love,** pouring forth, overflowing, embracing friend and foe, even as God **makes his sun rise on the evil and on the good,** and sends rain **on the just and on the unjust.**

46—Even **tax collectors,** hated for their unbridled greed, love those who love them. If that is the best you can manage, **what reward** (see commentary below on 6:4) **have you?** What good is it? What praise can such a withered love expect from a boundlessly loving God?

47—And even **Gentiles salute** their friends and wish them well. If your greetings and good wishes, prayers and benedictions are restricted to your narrow band of **friends,** the members of your circle, your religious community, **what more are you doing than others?**

Indeed what **more?** What is there for you, about you, from you that **exceeds?** Jesus began the series by calling for a righteousness which **exceeds** that of the **scribes and Pharisees,** paragons of virtue (5:20). The series comes full circle now with his call to do **more** than **tax collectors** and **Gentiles,** on the bottom rung of the accepted ladder of virtue. Exceed the best, do more than the worst! He neither legislates a new strictness nor suggests a new laxity. He envisions a new world.

48—In a final cry wrapping up the entire series (5:21-48) a powerful new word steps into place alongside **righteousness** (5:20) and **love** (5:43): **You must be perfect** (*teleioi*), **as your heavenly Father is perfect** (*teleios*).

Parallels to this saying have the words *holy* (Lev. 19:2; 1 Peter 1:16) or *merciful* (Luke 6:36) where Matthew's Jesus says **perfect.** *Holy* has about it an air of mystery and cult, of total separation from everything profane. *Merciful* conjures up warm pictures of the Lord as shepherd, tenderly caring for the least and the lost. For better or for worse the word **perfect** struggles under impressions of mathematical correctness, moral rectitude, flawless virtue, and tight-lipped severity.

Nevertheless, the underlying word is related to goals and targets, to growth and ripening and maturity, to coming of age. *Teleios* ("perfect," "mature") is a cognate of *telos* ("goal"). To be **perfect** (19:21) means to grow up into full stature as a woman or man of God (cf. 5:9, 45). It is to reach the high goal of a rich, deep sharing in the life of God, the nature of God, known in Jesus as love, holy and astonishing, beyond the old calculus of "mine" and "ours," shattering even the careful frameworks of justice and merit, springing up and pouring forth in giddy abundance, embracing the just and the unjust, the friend and the enemy. This "perfection" is related to the wholeness of heart and soul and mind that Jesus lauds in 22:37-40 (cf. 13:44-46), and it is the very opposite of the fatally flawed piety called by the name "hypocrisy" (see commentary below on 6:2).

Practicing Your Righteousness (6:1-18)

It is widely agreed that the Beatitudes (5:3-12) trumpet the indispensable introduction to the Sermon on the Mount, and that the paragraphs on salt and light (5:3-16) and the higher righteousness (5:17-20) announce the theme. Then follow three expositions of that surpassing righteousness. First come the Antitheses (5:21-48), defining it in situations involving family, neighbor, and enemies. Now in 6:1-18 comes a second exposition, defining the higher righteousness in terms of traditional acts of religious devotion: almsgiving, prayer, and fasting (cf. Tobit 12:8-10). The third exposition begins at 6:19 and carries over into the next chapter.

Shabby concern for self intruding into the moral arena gets people twitching so that with great ingenuity they manipulate the commandments to their own benefit. The same energetic egotism contaminates devotional acts, destroying their purity. No longer are they simple, direct cries from the hearts of women and men to the heart of God. Instead, the self makes a grab for the center of the stage, elbowing neighbor and God off to the wings.

When You Give Alms (6:1-4)

1—First, the heading for the section (6:1-18) as a whole: **Beware of practicing your piety,** literally "your righteousness" (*dikaiosynē*), cf. 3:15; 5:20, out in public with the intent **to be seen.** The need to catch human eyes and provoke human admiration is symptomatic of lack of faith and is curiously inappropriate in an act designed as an expression of faith. Such persons are not even looking for a **reward** from their **Father in heaven,** and so should not be surprised when they receive none. All they are really doing is laying up treasure on earth (6:19).

The teaching on almsgiving (6:2-4), on prayer (6:5-6), and on fasting (6:16-18)—all follows exactly the same pattern. Each brief paragraph sharply contrasts the behavior of hypocrites with the behavior of disciples.

2—**When you give alms you must not be like the hypocrites.** In the Greek world, *hypocrite* was the ordinary word for an actor, but in the New Testament the word has the larger sense of a moral or spiritual pretender, one who merely plays the part of righteousness without possessing the inner reality. The word is much used in Matthew (6:2, 5, 16; 7:5; 15:7; 22:18; 23:13, 14, 15, 23, 25, 27, 29; 24:51; cf. 23:28).

In Matthew's Gospel hypocrisy is ranged against righteousness (5:20), perfection (5:48), and wholeness (22:37-40). Those other terms speak of integrity and soundness, while hypocrisy describes a fateful rift or split.

No doubt people do not set out in the morning deliberately planning hypocrisy. But people easily accept a role assigned to them by society or government or business or religion, and they perform all kinds of acts in the name of duty or tradition. When people accept a split between their own deepest sense of right and their external or public behavior, they are maskers or hypocrites.

Only **hypocrites** will need to **give alms** out in public **in the synagogue and in the streets** to the accompaniment of **trumpet** fanfare.

3—Jesus urges the opposite extreme: far from calculating when and where an offer of alms will make the greatest public splash, give in such unself-conscious fashion that **your left hand** does not even **know what your right hand is doing.**

4—Do it **in secret,** hiding the deed not only from the public but even from yourself. Give **your alms** not to impress crowds, not to win gratitude from recipients (that only patronizes and uses them), but simply from being God's partner in the divine generosity toward all, especially toward the poor and defenseless.

Your Father who sees in secret will reward you. It is simplistic and misleading to latch onto this word **reward** and to describe Jesus in Matthew's Gospel as teaching a system of rewards and punishments based on merits and demerits. Jesus' language is concrete and colorful. He happily combines traditional religious images and phrases from home and market, and never fails to produce fresh results, cracking through tired old systems.

Many find the language of **Father** even more distressing than images of reward. But Jesus plunges along. God is already your **Father** (10 times in 6:1-18; cf. 5:16) God does not first become fatherly or first turn motherly, receptive and loving, as some kind of payment only after a disciple has piled up a sufficient heap of deeds well done.

In homely fashion Jesus makes the point that God likes good deeds better than evil, that God rejoices at spontaneous and unfeigned generosity, is repelled by ostentation and posturing, disappointed at hypocrisy, angry when human beings use other human beings only to showcase their own religious standing (cf. chap. 23).

When You Pray (6:5-6)

5-6—Hypocrites are consistent. They **pray** the same way they give alms. **They love to stand** (the ordinary posture of prayer, just as sitting was the posture of teaching, 5:1) **and pray,** putting themselves on display **in the synagogues and at the street corners, that they may be seen.**

Set prayers and fixed hours of prayers were observed by Jews and Christians. The Shema (a creedal statement combining Deut. 6:4-9; 11:13-21; Num. 15:37-41) was prayed twice daily. The chief ancient Jewish prayer was the Eighteen Benedictions (*Shemoneh Esreh*). Called simply "The Prayer," it was prayed three times a day. An entire tract of the Mishnah (*Berakoth*) deals with the times and the manner for praying the Shema and the Eighteen Benedictions as well as table prayers and free prayers. According to Acts 3:1 and 10:9, early Christians observed traditional prayer hours at traditional places. Later it became the custom to recite the Lord's Prayer three times daily (Didache 8:3).

Would Jesus sweep away all public devotion, the chanting of the Psalms, together with all their poetic supplements ancient and modern? Does he set his face against public liturgy and all set prayers? Or does he crusade against common prayers, liturgical piety, gathering in throngs to enthrone God on the praises of the community? Would he banish therefore not only public worship but also liturgical architecture?

What Jesus is doing is setting one extreme against another: prayer on street corners versus prayer in the tool shed or broom closet (cf. 2 Kings 4:33). Ostentation versus secrecy. Pathetic grubbing about for applause from neighbors versus single-minded communion with God.

Our Father (6:7-13)

It is easy to slip into the mistake of thinking that Jesus is spending his energy in the sermon primarily in criticism of Pharisaic habits. The mention of **Gentiles** or pagans (6:7; cf. 5:47) opens the door only a crack, but it may be enough to let in a welcome light. Throughout the Gospel, Jesus is the exalted Lord teaching his own community of post-Easter disciples. Often Jesus is portrayed in his earthly ministry as castigating some habit, some tendency, some practice of Jews or Gentiles. But he always is really addressing his own community about its practice and present habits.

7—**In praying do not heap up empty phrases,** vainly imagining that you will be heard for your **many words.** Outside the New Testament community, pagan incantations heaped up names of the gods in the hope that one of the names would claim the attention of the proper deity (cf. Acts 17:33; 19:11-20). Or devotees chanted the name of their deity repeatedly and hypnotically (1 Kings 18:26-29; Acts 19:24; cf. "the Jesus Prayer").

On the other hand, Jesus himself is pictured spending hours at prayer, sometimes the entire night (14:22-25; Mark 1:35) and early Christians remember Jesus' insistence on stubbornness in petition to God (Luke 18:1-7; cf. 1 Thess. 5:17; Rom. 12:12; Eph. 6:18).

What is Jesus criticizing? Paul opens a window onto a piece of early Christian life which bears examining in this context. The apostle criticizes a certain form of Christian prayer at Corinth. Meetings bordered on the chaotic when members insisted on praying in tongues, without provision for interpretation, without waiting for others to finish, eager to display at great length their spiritual gifts. Gatherings were degenerating into a cacophony of indistinct sounds, a Babel of tongues, nearer madness than sense.

For his part, Paul declared that he would rather speak five sensible words (one handful) than 10,000 (literally a myriad, the largest Greek number) in a tongue (1 Cor. 14:18-19).

Matthew's Gospel contains scattered bits and pieces hinting at a situation in Matthew's community akin to that at Corinth. Discipleship was being measured in terms of spiritual endowments and manifestations like prophecy, miracles, exorcisms, inspired utterance, and perhaps tongues (see commentary below on 7:15-23). But it is vain, a pagan hope, to imagine that prayers will be heard if you **heap up empty phrases** and use **many words.**

8—Disciples are summoned to simplicity and brevity, secure in the trust that **your Father knows what you need before you ask.** Prayer is no uncertain negotiation, with results contingent on discovering the right phrase or the correct number of syllables. The disciple is invited to the free and intimate conversation of child with loving parent. Aimless, carefree chatter belongs by nature to such exchange, but here at the very heart of the sermon, almost exactly the midpoint, Jesus offers a model for serious talk with God.

9—Praying **like this** does not mean pedantic repetition of these formulas barring all others. Many prayers have circulated in the church from the beginning, and the Lord's Prayer itself has been transmitted in multiple versions, the result of free use and adaptation in different communities of believers (Luke 11:2-4; Didache 8:2).

Ancient Greek manuscripts reveal that the prayer circulated in several versions: with and without a concluding doxology, and with alternative clauses to those that finally won the day. For example, some manuscripts of Luke 11:2 read, "Let your Holy Spirit come upon us and cleanse us."

Jesus talks as one on most intimate terms with God, speaking easily of "my Father" (10:32, 33; 12:50; 15:31; 16:17; 18:10, 14, 19, 35; 20:23; 25:34, 41; 26:29, 39, 42, 53). What is almost more startling, he invites his disciples to break with the formality of liturgical phrasing and abandon quasi-royal salutations. Draw near, he says, as trusting children to loving Parent and say, **Father.** If current surmises are correct, Jesus encouraged the use even of the most intimate, most informal address: *Abba* (cf. Rom. 8:15; Gal. 4:6; Mark 14:36). The first words Jewish children learned in Jesus' day were *abba* and *imma* = "dadda," "mamma." That way of addressing God is unique, nowhere paralleled in the prayer literature of the ancient world, and it must have sounded irreverent.

Where Luke's version has the simpler **Father,** Matthew has **Our Father** and further qualifies that address with the phrase **in heaven** (cf. 5:16, 45, 48; 6:1, 14, 15, 26, 32; 7:11, 21). The language of earthly parenting points to heavenly realities. God is neither male nor female, but language of the family circle expresses the conviction that God is personal and caring as opposed to some unfeeling, impersonal force like gravity or electricity.

Three petitions with **thy** (vv. 9b-10) are balanced by three with **us** and **our** (vv. 11-13).

The three **thy** petitions are parallel to one another, and so reinforce one another, stepping around the same awesome reality to view it from three distinct angles. God's **name** is hallowed and God's **kingdom** comes when God's **will** is done on earth.

Pious hearts had long desired that God would burst out from behind the ambiguities of daily events and the cruel triumphs of Israel's enemies: display the holiness of your **name** with irresistible power, and stop the mouths of mockers (Ezek. 36:23; 39:7; Isa. 24:14-16; 29:23), that all nations may give God glory (5:16)! That prayer is the equivalent of praying for the advent of God's **kingdom,** God's sovereign rule no longer under pressure from rival sovereignties both great and small (cf. 3:2; 4:17).

The third petition, lacking in Luke's version, tells how the first two petitions are realized: **thy will be done on earth.** God's **name** is not necessarily **hallowed** when people cry, "Lord, Lord" (7:21; 25:37), nor are exorcisms an infallible sign that the kingdom is at work (7:22). What better signs are there? Is it absolutely characteristic of Matthew's Jesus to focus on the **will** of God, a term that takes its place alongside "love" and "perfection" in Matthew's rich vocabulary of "righteousness."

These first three petitions invite disciples to pray for God's new world, a world healed of all fractures and rifts, a world that is all right, comprehensively and in every detail right and healthy. The newness of the new world is not pictured in terms of golden streets and shining prosperity, or speaking in tongues and raptures of visions, or doing miracles and transcending old limits. But in terms of doing God's will, freshly interpreted as an exceeding righteousness, exuberant love, single-minded devotion to God and neighbor. That alone is the hallmark of the family of God (12:50). As the **will** of God is done **on earth** (by people) as it is done **in heaven** (by angels), God's name is hallowed, God's sovereignty comes.

The doing of the will of God is not presented here as a mandate or a goal. The power to perform God's will is a gift sought in prayer: **Thy will be done.**

11—The community is taught to fix its heart and mind on God's name and sovereignty and will. Then the second stanza opens with a petition for **bread.** But what **bread** is this? **Daily bread?** Or, as a footnote in the RSV has it, **Our bread for the morrow?** The Greek adjective (*epiousios*) with bread is a rare word and its meaning is elusive. It may indicate ordinary **bread** of wheat or barley, often in extraordinarily short supply in an unrighteous world. **Bread** is the staff of life and symbol of the full range of physical necessities: food, clothing, shelter, and the fundamental conditions for getting them, namely, health and job and peace.

Jesus ponders all these. He targets anxiety over bread as a sign of unbelief (6:25-34), and yet he has compassion on the crowds and multiplies loaves (14:13-21; 15:32-39).

It would be just like him to teach his disciples the simplicity of this petition: Do not nervously demand the guarantee of a full pantry nor beg for the clutter of luxuries, but seek bread for a single day (this day or tomorrow), secure under God in the confidence that it will suffice.

And yet this may be a petition for spiritual **bread** for the presence of Jesus himself, Wisdom incarnate, who issues the invitation to come and take his yoke (11:28-30), to enter his presence (18:20), to receive him as food and drink (26:26-28). Or, as a variant of this view, **bread** may stand for the messianic banquet, powerful symbol of the entire bounty of the coming kingdom, when many will stream from east and west to sit at table with Abraham and Isaac and Jacob, in the presence of the exalted Christ (8:11-12; 22:1-10; 26:29).

Or is it an error to pose physical and spiritual as alternatives? Eating bread may be a physical act, but sharing bread is a spiritual act (25:31-46). Jesus hungers and thirsts for the new world of righteousness (3:15; 5:6), and he acts ahead of time in the power of the coming world, eating with tax collectors and sinners (9:10-11), multiplying loaves for the hungry (14:13-21; 15:32-39).

Give us today the **bread** we most desperately need: the reality of the new world, the divine presence, the gift of nourishment from the hand of God and the power to nourish, to feed, to clothe, to house.

The petition is not easy; the difficulty is usually located in the rare word translated **daily** (*epiousios*). But the problem may lie in the little word **us.** The petition is bent out of shape when we pretend it says, "Give me my bread." This is rather a prayer for **us,** for **our bread,** for the community, for brothers and sisters. And then where is the limit, the boundary? Jesus bids disciples pray for **our bread,** for a world where all share bread and eat together, and that is indeed a new world.

12—**And forgive us our debts.** In Jesus, people met something greater than a teacher of peculiar warmth and understanding. They experienced the last word, the final judgment, God's own verdict, spoken ahead of time. It was a word neither of hot wrath nor of cool justice and deserving. In the event of Jesus, God as judge erupted into the old world, dispensing grace and forgiveness.

Jesus met shock and resistance. Precisely because he insisted on enacting forgiveness he was derided as "friend of sinners" (11:19) and accused of blasphemy (9:3; cf. 26:65). Yet even at the point of death Jesus declared his outpoured blood to be a strong tide able to destroy every barrier to the presence of God, washing clean the entire slate of debts, purging away accumulated pollution. In short, his blood was "for the forgiveness of sins" (26:28).

Forgiveness undermines the foundations of the old world and brings into being a new community (chap. 18). But the new community still inhabits the old world, and the old world still inhabits the new people. Forgiveness, like bread, must be received day by day. And, like bread, it is given to be shared. Sharing can never diminish love or forgiveness. Only hoarding can spoil the gift and destroy its power. That alone is the meaning of the reminder: **as we also forgive.** Forgiveness is the power of the new world both in relation to God and in relation to sister and brother.

13—**Lead us not into temptation** (cf. 4:3) is the opposite of any ecstatic boast of spiritual renewal, any enthusiastic cry for a chance to prove one's power over evil. It is full of realism about the vulnerability of the disciple, in spite of the inbreaking of the new world, in spite of membership in the new community.

Temptation is understood variously as (1) seduction to wrongdoing felt every day in the most mundane social transactions, as (2) persecution with its cruel power to kill faith and to plunge into apostasy (26:41; 24:9-13), as (3) the dread energy of this world's final agony, labor pains gripping the universe as the new world struggles to be born (24:2-28).

In the previous petition we beg to be drawn wholly into the new world energized by forgiveness; in the present petition we ask that we be kept from sinking back into the old world dominated by evil.

Deliver us from evil (2 Tim. 4:18; Didache 10:5) or **from the evil one** (13:19, 38). Jesus has bound Satan, swept demons out and the kingdom of God in. Liberated from the strong man's house, disciples pray that they may be preserved in the liberty of the children of God (12:22-29, 43-45), and that they may do God's will in freedom.

If You Forgive (6:14-15)

14-15—A solemn statement on forgiveness concludes the Lord's Prayer like some great exclamation point. The prayer envisions God's new world and begs that it become a reality now on earth in a new community. It is God's, it is a gift, it is powerful, and yet its approach hangs by a thread. **If you forgive,** it comes. **If you do not forgive,** it withdraws.

Forgiveness has peculiar power to mirror the heart of God. Like righteousness, it is both gift of God, prior to all the acting and praying of disciples, and it is the disciple's high calling (cf. ch. 18).

When You Fast (6:16-18)

16-18—The triptych on pious deeds, interrupted by the Lord's Prayer, continues now with a panel on fasting. **When you fast,** again do the opposite of the **hypocrites. They disfigure their faces that their fasting may be seen.** They deliberately cease bathing and anointing their bodies and combing their hair. They sprinkle ashes on their heads and don a garment of course material (cf. 3:4). In a word, they advertise their piety.

But fasting by definition means abstaining from food as a way of afflicting the soul and humbling oneself before God. Fasting was (1) as expression of penitence over sin. The Day of Atonement was and is the most solemn fast day among Jews (Leviticus 16).

(2) Fasting was undertaken as a means of strengthening prayer (cf. Jer. 14:12; Neh. 1:4; Acts 13:3; 14:23). (3) Fasting was an expression of sorrow at personal or national loss; thus the destruction of Jerusalem, for example, was commemorated with fasting (2 Kings 25:8; Jer. 52:12). (4) Fasting was practiced as preparation for entering God's presence (Exod. 34:28; Dan. 9:3; 10:2-3).

Jesus does not forbid fasting (cf. 9:14-15), even though some prophets declared that God preferred justice to fasting (Isa. 58:3-9; Joel 2:12-13; Zech. 7:5). Jesus urges those who fast to go to extremes the exact opposite of the **hypocrites: anoint your head, wash your face.** In other words, the piety of disciples is for God's eyes only.

Seek His Kingdom and Righteousness (6:19—7:12)

It is far from easy to lay bare the structure of this section of the sermon in any satisfactory manner. After a first (5:21-48) and a second (6:1-18) exposition, this new section (6:19—7:12) is a third exposition of the theme of the surpassing righteousness (5:20). In chap. 6 the loosely organized material consists of sayings on treasure in heaven (6:19-24) and on anxiety (6:35-34).

Treasure in Heaven (6:19-21)

19—**Treasures on earth** in the ancient world typically included expensive cloth and finely woven garments, easily ruined by moths (James 5:2). And if the treasure was a hoard of coins (Sirach 29:10), or an exquisitely carved box or piece of paneling, or an entire barn full of wheat, then it was vulnerable to eating away (*brōsis*) by **rust** or **worm.**

Or thieves **break in,** by digging through the mud-brick walls of a home or by digging up a family treasure from its hiding place, and **steal** (24:43; cf. 13:44).

20—The answer to human insecurity is not to hire extra guards or to invest in more durable goods, but to turn with utter finality away from **treasure on earth** to treasures in heaven, to security beyond the reach of **moth, rust, thieves** who **break in and steal.** The rapid repetition of these destructive forces (cf. 7:24-27) drives home the vulnerability of earthly treasures and the inevitable insecurity of life fixed on them.

21—Jesus challenges disciples to cut the chain linking their joy, their peace, their security to the ebb and flow of markets and fortune. If **your treasure** is in heaven, if what really counts with you is the name of God, the sovereignty of God, the will of God (6:9-10), then **your heart,** your life and joy, will rest on a foundation as firm as heaven itself.

The Lamp of the Body (6:22-23)

But people do not see God (6:18) or heavenly treasure (6:19-21) as clearly as they see treasure of silver and bolts of cloth. Everything depends on correct, sharp vision (cf. 7:2-5).

22-23—**The eye is the lamp of the body.** It captures light on behalf of the body and directs all its functioning. **So if your eye is sound, your whole body will be full of light.** Your members will have the information they require to act with confidence. **But if your eye is not sound,** if you have blurred and double vision, then not just your eye suffers but **your whole body will be full of darkness,** and you will be condemned to guessing and groping.

Disciples summoned to be the light of the world (5:14-16) might be stung by the suggestion that they could be in the dark or blind (cf. 15:14; 23:16, 17, 19, 24, 26). They would naturally defend themselves by saying, "We see perfectly!" (cf. John 9:40-41).

But precisely here in a context bracketed by talk of treasures on earth (6:19) and by the call to seek first the kingdom (6:33), Jesus asks disciples to consider the terrible possibility: What **if the light in you is darkness,** what if you are fundamentally wrong in allegiance and orientation, what if your eye is evil (marked by greed) and not sound (generous) at all (cf. 20:15), what if you have one eye on mammon and only one on God (6:24)? In such a case, how great is the darkness!

God and Mammon (6:24)

24—From two kinds of eyes (vv. 22.-23) Jesus moves to talk of two kinds of masters. **No one can serve two masters.** Being a slave of two masters would be like serving simultaneously in two armies, carrying two passports, saluting two flags, being married to two wives or two husbands. That style is schizophrenic, and a divided individual will in the end **hate the one and love the other.** Decision for the one involves decision against the other. Just so, **you cannot serve both God and mammon.**

Mammon derives from a Semitic root meaning "that which is firm and solid." (The word *amen* is related.) It was in common use as an ethically neutral term for physical property or money. Jesus does not here demand relinquishing all possessions but does issue a sharp call not to fall down in front of them, nor even to fix a greedy eye on them (19:16-25; 20:15).

This saying climaxes the series of three brief paragraphs, all focused on the single topic of allegiance toward God. Talk here of **mammon** or possessions leads naturally to the following section on anxiety over material things (6:25-34).

Do Not Be Anxious (6:25-34)

The preceding section (6:19-24) corresponds in some respects to the opening stanza of the Lord's Prayer (6:9-10), and this new section seems to parallel the fouth petition on daily bread (6:11).

25—Jesus already has spoken about greed for luxury items (6:19). Here he utters an authoritative instruction about anxiety over basics. **Do not be anxious** (vv. 25, 31, 34) about fundamentals: **life, what you shall eat** or **drink,** and **body, what you shall put on.**

He would woo people from insecurity and help them see that **life** and **body** are **more than food** and **more than clothing** (4:4). If God has provided the **more** (life, body), can we not depend on receiving also the lesser (food, clothing)? It is a hard lesson to learn. Jesus points for support in successive verses to **birds** and their food, then to **flowers** and their surpassing finery.

26—Think hard about the **birds.** Since one God has made both them and us, perhaps we can learn something about ourselves from them. They know nothing about methods of cultivation or crop rotation, fertilizers or irrigation, the latest equipment or threats to harvest, going to market or storing in barns.

All these activities may be undertaken in anxiety or in joy. Nevertheless, compared with the intricacies of human activities,

birds for all their restless quest for food live simply. And yet they
do live from the hand of **your heavenly Father.** And you are **of
more value:** God lavishes **more** care on you.

27—A sudden afterthought interrupts the flow. A **cubit** is a unit
of length measuring about 18 inches (elbow to tip of the fingers)
but here is used casually of time. Being anxious adds no inches
to the length of your life. Worry is a useless emotion.

28-30—These items parallel the example of the birds (v. 26),
repeating the pattern with fresh emphasis, pressing the point
more urgently. The imagery shifts from birds and food to flowers
and clothing, from men's work in the fields to women's work at
the loom.

Take a good look at **the lilies of the field. They neither toil nor
spin, yet I tell you, even Solomon in all his glory was not arrayed
like one of these.** Extravagant phrases compel a fresh look at
common wildflowers and their really extraordinary beauty. God
pays marvelous attention to insignificant flowers, useless plants,
grass of the field. Today those lilies are splendid and alive, and
tomorrow, lifeless and tied in little bundles, they are **thrown into
the oven** as kindling.

If God is so lavish with birds and flowers, so small and short
of life, how much more will he care for those he calls children?

Jesus concludes with a rebuke, calling his disciples for the first
time by a title he regularly employs in Matthew's Gospel: **men
of little faith,** people of small trust (cf. 8:26; 14:31; 16:8; 17:20).
They are not unbelievers but disciples whose faith wavers in
moments of crisis, rendering them incapable of fulfilling the will
of God.

31—The section closes with a restatement of the opening instruction (v. 25): **Therefore do not be anxious!** The same basic
anxieties are named once more: **What shall we eat** or **drink** or
wear?

32—Leave anxiety to **the Gentiles,** the pagans (6:7)! It is their
hallmark. Disciples may rest secure in the knowledge that they
have a **heavenly Father,** maker of all creatures great and small.

33—If Gentiles anxiously **seek** food and clothing (6:31-32), what
do disciples **seek?** What is the nature of their quest? What do
they imagine will perfect their lives, ripen them, fill and fulfill
them? In John's Gospel disciples are pictured as seeking Jesus

himself, seeking to abide with him and finally in him and he in them (1:38; 20:15; 17:20-24). The members of the Qumran community devoted themselves to seeking God with their whole heart by devoting themselves to every commandment of the Law of Moses (1QS 1:1-2; 5:8-11).

Here in the Sermon on the Mount, Jesus cries, **Seek first,** above all and singlemindedly, God's **kingdom and his righteousness** (cf. 3:15; 5:20; 22:38). **Seek first** the hallowing of God's name, the coming of God's kingdom, the doing of God's will (6:9-10). Then **all these** other **things** like bread (6:11) **will be yours as well.**

Anxiety and grasping confine rich and poor alike, as prisoners in narrow cells, secure for a while but ever unfree, with multitudes of neighbors but few sisters and brothers.

Negatively, to **seek his kingdom and his righteousness** means breaking from that kind of life. Positively, as the very words suggest, it means pursuing in daily life the surpassing vision of the Lord's Prayer.

Seek his kingdom: pray and press daily for the coming of God's sovereign rule not in some other, distant time or space but here and now in the midst of our communities. **Seek his righteousness:** life wholly in accord with the will of God. Is this **righteousness** human performance or divine gift? The question arises almost every time the word appears. Our right conduct or God's own salvation?

Must it be either-or? As God lays healing hands on the universe and makes it "all right" again, human beings are freed and made whole to live anew as trusting children in a family of love.

All these things, enjoyed by birds and flowers, nervously sought by Gentiles, **shall be yours as well,** gifts of the one who moment by moment upholds all things visible and invisible. Hearty fullness, not pale diminution, mark those who trust. Gift upon gift shall be added unto them.

34—Let the day's own trouble be sufficient for the day. This homely proverb is the strongest evidence that "daily" in "daily bread" means nothing more subtle than a literal span of one day's sunshine. To try to see beyond the coming night or to forfeit sleep to anxiety and scheming is a sign not of prudence but of unbelief. It means playing God, acting as though all times are after all not in God's hands but in our own, as though we and not God are sovereign.

Judge Not (7:1-5)

1—The new paragraph, perhaps expanding on the fifth petition of the Lord's Prayer ("forgive us . . . as we forgive," 6:12), opens with a prophetic exhortation and warning: **Judge not, that you be not judged.** All the talk of perfection, righteousness, serving God, doing the will of God, seeking the kingdom of God is given a demonic twist if it sets disciples to galloping on crusades against imperfection or unrighteousness in others.

2—Disciples may indeed be tempted to establish a critical environment and turn the community of the forgiven (6:12, 14-15; 18:21-35) into a house of judgment. If so, they need to remember what strict justice implies: **With the judgment you pronounce you will be judged.** The truth of that maxim should give them pause. And Jesus presses on.

3-4—All campaigns of judgment rest on a simple but perverse foundation: the conceit that my faults are smaller than your faults. Jesus assaults that foundation with a bizarre image, contrasting **the speck in your brother's eye** with **the log in your own eye.** A log in my eye? Jesus repeats the crude phrase three times in three verses. The image is not just bizarre. It is disturbing, and it is meant to be.

5—Disciples are warned (and must have needed the warning) that judging others is just one more way of playing the *hypocrite* (cf. 6:2). Far from increasing righteousness and so building the new world, it frustrates righteousness. Jesus concludes with irony: When disciples have completely eliminated all their ills (that is, never), then they can **see clearly to take the speck out of** their **brother's eye.**

Pearls before Swine (7:6)

6—**Do not give dogs what is holy; and do not throw your pearls before swine.** So begins an obscure little parable full (once more!) of bizarre and shocking imagery. It is no help to treat it as an allegory and imagine that it will suddenly become clear if only we discover the proper equivalent for each of the major terms: **dogs, holy, pearls, swine.** It has only misled to note that in other passages a *pearl* stands for the priceless treasure of the kingdom (13:45-46), and Gentiles are compared with **dogs** (15:27). Working along these lines, some early Christians took this saying to mean that the **holy** things of eucharistic bread and wine were to be withheld from outsiders (**dogs**) and offered only to the baptized (Didache 9:5).

However, this is a parable and not an allegory. Who would ever take sacrificial food set on an altar (**holy** things) and throw it like ordinary table scraps to **dogs**? Or who would reach into a jewelry box, grasp a handful of costly **pearls** and throw them like corn before **swine**? Unthinkable!

In fact, such behavior could even be life-threatening: taunted and provoked, **swine** have been known to **trample** tormentors **under foot** (cf. 5:13), and **dogs** to attack and **kill**.

For all their limitations, human beings instinctly recoil at the thought of feeding **holy** things to **dogs** or **pearls** to **swine**. With the same sure instinct they should know how inappropriate and how dangerous it is to judge others (7:1-5). Judging others is a monstrous profaning of the **holy** things, all the vast treasures, entrusted to them in the coming of Jesus, in the dawning of the kingdom, in the opening up of the new world and the new community with its life of righteousness. In a way this parable is a counterpart to the last petition of the Lord's Prayer: "Deliver us from evil" (6:19).

Ask (7:7-11)

The entire section beginning with the Lord's Prayer has been describing the disciples' life as a life of prayer, of trusting and childlike communion with God. Now Jesus concludes this section with direct encouragement to pray.

7-10—Ask, and it will be given you; seek, and you will find; knock, and it will be opened to you. Too good to be true? Jesus repeats all three imperatives, gently prodding towards trust that will break out in asking (7:8). **Ask** is the dominant word, appearing five times in these five verses (cf. James 1:5), while **seek** and **knock** connect these phrases to Jesus' saying about aiming to enter the kingdom and questing after righteousness (6:33).

11—Earthly parents **know how to give good gifts to their children.** They do not give a **stone** instead of a **loaf** or a **serpent** instead of a **fish** (cf. Luke 11:12). These terms may have been chosen in part because of the superficial resemblance between some flat round stones and ordinary Palestinian loaves, between some serpents and some fish.

How much more will your Father who is in heaven give good things to those who ask him. The parallel in Luke 11:13 has "the Holy Spirit" where Matthew has **good things.** For Luke the Spirit is the ultimate sign of the coming kingdom (cf. Matt. 6:10), but for Matthew the ultimately good things are the exceeding righteousness, perfection, the will of God, sharing the life of forgiveness. These **good things** are not mere demands, imperatives, achievements. They are gifts freely lavished on those who **ask,** those who **seek,** those who **knock** on the gates of the kingdom opening up to humankind in the ministry of Jesus.

Do So to Them (7:12)

12—The "golden rule" is both climax and conclusion. It begins with **so** or "therefore," recapitulates the specific teachings of the foregoing paragraphs in broadest terms (**whatever**), and echoes here at the end the topic announced way back at the beginning (**the law and the prophets,** 5:17): **So whatever you wish that others would do to you, do so to them. This,** all these maxims, warnings, proverbs, urgings, and instructions in 5:17—7:11, summarized now in the golden rule, **is the law and the prophets.** Later, in 22:34-40, Jesus will even more briefly describe the essential content of the law and the prophets as love toward God and neighbor (cf. also 9:13).

Other forms of the golden rule appeared in Judaism before and after Jesus. "What you hate, do not do to anyone" (Tobit 4:15). A Gentile seeking to know Judaism asked Shammai to expound to him the law and the prophets "while standing on one foot" (that is, briefly). Shammai drove him away with his carpenter's rule. When the Gentile put the same request to Hillel, he was told: "What is hateful to you, do not do to anyone. That is the whole law; all the rest is commentary" (Tosephta *Sabbath* 31a). See also Didache 1:2; the Western text of Acts 15:20, 29; Rom. 13:10.

Beware (7:13-29)

Jesus has now offered three expositions (5:21-48; 6:1-18; 6:19—7:12) of the life of surpassing righteousness. He has described how the law and the prophets are fulfilled. Now he brings the sermon to an end in four paragraphs full of sharp alternatives: two ways and two gates lead to two opposite destinations, two kinds of trees yield two different kinds of fruit, two houses on two different foundations suffer two fates. The wrong choice leads to destruction, to the fire, to expulsion, to a great fall.

Two Ways (7:13-14)

13-14—The theme of Jesus' proclamation has been the kingdom of heaven, and Jesus has spoken of its nearness (4:17) and of seeking it (6:33) or entering it (5:20) or simply having it (5:3, 10).

Now as a synonym for *kingdom* Jesus speaks of finding and entering **life** and of avoiding **destruction.** A **narrow gate** and a **hard way** lead to **life,** while a **wide gate** and an **easy way** lead to **destruction.**

The imagery is wonderfully simple: life is a daily progress toward one of two goals (not more) along one of two paths (not more). The scheme denies that there are as many ways as there are nations or races or tongues or generations. Two paths alone are set before all, and the features of each path are painted simply in bold strokes and primary colors. It would be easy to add details to the basic picture. For example, Sirach 21:10 describes "the way of sinners (as) smoothly paved with stones but at its end is the pit of Hades." In 4 Ezra 7:1-19, the narrow way is only wide enough for one person at a time. Furthermore, that narrow path is steep and lies between fire on the right and deep water on the left.

Jesus here practices a striking economy. It is impossible to tell whether with the word **gate** he is picturing the gate of a city, the entrance to a temple, or the door to a banquet hall. Such details can safely be omitted for in any case he is talking about access to **life,** to joy, to God.

The imagery of two ways leading to two diametrically opposed goals has a long history. (1) Jeremiah 21:8 and Didache 1:1 contrast the way of life and the way of death (cf. Deut. 30:19-20, life and death, blessing and curse). (2) Psalm 1:6 contrasts the way of the righteous and the way of the wicked (cf. Prov. 14:2; Test. Asher 1:3-5, good and evil ways, inclinations, kinds of actions, and endings; Mishnah *Pirke Aboth* 2:9, the good way [and good eye, good companion, good neighbor, good heart] and the evil way). (3) The Essenes of Qumran (1QS 3:20-21) and Barnabas 18:1 contrast the way of light and the way of darkness.

Few travel the **hard way** and enter the **narrow gate** to **life.** That is neither realism nor pessimism. It is a challenge to make an unpopular but infinitely wise choice.

False Prophets (7:15-20)

15—In Matthew's day the Christian community certainly included prophets (10:41; 23:34). In handing on Jesus' warnings about **false prophets,** Matthew seems to have some of these Christian leaders in view. Matthew's community seems to have been agitated or even led by charismatic leaders, richly endowed with gifts of the Spirit. But in their enthusiasm they were apparently careless about the will of God and righteousness (cf. 24:4-12, 24).

They wear **sheep's clothing** and so have the trappings of real disciples but inwardly they are **ravenous wolves,** an old epithet for predatory leaders within the flock of God (Ezek. 22:27; Zeph. 3:3; Acts 20:29; cf. John 10:12; Matt. 10:16). Reference to false teachers here in the conclusion to the sermon echoes the reference near the beginning, in the statement of the theme (5:19). Both times the falsity has to do with the will of God.

16-20—Talk switches from sheep and wolves to trees and vines. **False prophets** can be recognized **by their fruits** (cf. 3:8). No one gathers **grapes** from thornbushes or **figs from thistles.** Nor does a **sound tree** yield **evil fruit** or a dead or **bad tree** bear **good fruit.** And everyone knows what to do with dead trees (3:10)!

21-23—Some in the community, both **false prophets** (7:15-20) and those whom they have misled (7:21-23), will be shocked **on that day,** the **day** of reckoning, when they stand before the Judge (10:15; 11:22, 24; 12:36; 24:36; Mal. 3:17—4:5). Denied entry to the kingdom, to life, to the presence of God, they will plead with Jesus, pointing to their record. They catalog not just any deeds but specifically Christian deeds performed, they say to Jesus, **in your name.** They know Jesus' true name, and they shout it aloud, **Lord, Lord!** (8:2; 21:3; 22:43-45).

Nor is their record mere knowledge or words. Spiritual energy has overflowed in spiritual deeds, and they recite their deeds in threefold fullness: prophecy, exorcism, miracles. To each of those inspired working in turn they attach the formula **in your name.** They claim that they are his own and have acted in his **name** and by his authority, and they seek his approval.

23—But in spite of everything they claim, Jesus disowns them: **I never knew you, depart from me!** Why? They may be members of the community, even prophetic leaders and spiritually gifted followers, and yet they are branded as **evildoers,** "workers of iniquity" (KJV), doers of "lawlessness." The Greek word for "lawlessness" is *anomia,* and it appears here in 7:23, echoing Ps. 6:8, and in 13:41; 23:28; and 24:12. For Matthew it, like hypocrisy, is opposed to righteousness, the will of God, and love.

Jesus in Matthew's Gospel connects God's inbreaking kingdom with two bodies of evidence: on the one hand prophecy, exorcisms, miracles (cf. 10:7-8; 11:2-5; 12:15-32), and on the other hand righteousness, doing God's will, loving God and the neighbor. The one set of signs is often labeled spiritual or charismatic; the other is called moral or ethical. Whatever the labels, the distinction is not merely modern but is present in Matthew's Gospel. What is even more intriguing is the evidence of 7:15-23 that Jesus writes off as utterly useless any "spiritual" activities severed from "moral" action.

Early Christian communities were ablaze with spiritual energy. One Christian community after another was forced to deal with the question of how to distinquish false Christian prophets from true, false signs from genuine (cf. 1 Corinthians, 1 John, the Didache).

For the sake of his community Matthew has collected traditions about Jesus and sayings of Jesus accentuating the indissoluble connection between God's new world and righteousness. Matthew proposes that God's prophets—and in fact all God's people—measure their discipleship and test their lives by the standard of righteousness (3:15).

Two Houses (7:24-27)

24—Who are the few who will walk the hard way and pass through the narrow gate (7:13-14)? Who are the sound trees bearing good fruit (7:15-20)? Who will hear words of welcome on the last day as doers of God's will (7:21-23)? Jesus removes any lingering ambiguity: **Every one who hears these words of mine and does them.**

That one will be **like a wise man who built his house upon the rock.** Luke in his version of the parable (Luke 6:47-49) has more to say about the process of building, but Matthew moves quickly to details of the storm.

25—Blow after blow beats upon that house: **rain fell, floods came, winds blew and beat upon it.** Yet **it did not fall, because it had been founded on the rock** (cf. 16:18).

26-27—However, others are hearers only and not doers (James 1:22-25). They are **like a foolish man** (cf. 25:1-13) **who built his house upon the sand.** The same three blows strike, violently, insistently, shock upon shock. That house **fell, and great was the fall of it.**

Perhaps Jesus derives the imagery from observations of the damage actually wrought by literal storms. But he also has in view the biblical picture of God's judgment as storm and flood (cf. 24:37-39; 13:10-16; Sirach 22:16-18). The sermon begins with Beatitudes and here concludes with ominous rumblings of final judgment.

This last paragraph of the Sermon on the Mount is paralleled by the final paragraph of all of Jesus' public teaching, the vision of the sheep and the goats in 25:31-46. Each is climax or conclusion (one concludes the sermon and the other concludes the entirety of Jesus' teaching), each is an unforgettable portrait of judgment or separation, and each describes righteousness or observing the teaching of Jesus—and nothing else—as the basis of judgment.

He Taught with Authority (7:28-29)

Five times in his Gospel Matthew concludes a sermon of Jesus with the formula, **When Jesus finished these sayings** (7:28; 11:1; 13:53; 19:1; 26:1; see the notes on structure in the introduction).

The first sermon of Jesus has focused on the surpassing righteousness (5:17-20) of the new commmunity, created by God's surprising blessing (5:3-12). **The crowds** (cf. 5:1) **were astonished** (cf. 9:33) **at his teaching, for he taught them as one who had authority** (cf. 28:18).

■ Jesus' Mighty Acts and the Mission of the Twelve (8:1—10:42)

In accord with his basic plan of alternating narrative and discourse (sermon) sections, Matthew follows the great discourse we call the Sermon on the Mount (chaps. 5–7) with a narrative section consisting primarily of miracle stories (chaps. 8–9).

More than simply standing them back to back, Matthew connects these two large blocks of material root and branch (see commentary below on 8:1). Some linking devices are obvious. Immediately before the sermon (at 4:23) and immediately after the miracles (at 9:35), Matthew has set the identical summary statement: Jesus "went about . . . teaching in their synagogues and preaching the gospel of the kingdom and healing every disease and every infirmity among the people."

Later, Matthew pictures Jesus looking back on these chapters in his reply to John the Baptist, who has raised questions about Jesus' identity and authority: "Tell John what you see (the miracles of chaps. 8–9) and hear (the sermon of chaps. 5–7)." These two, sermon (word) and miracles (deeds) together, identify the one Jesus (see 11:2-5).

But why is Matthew so anxious that the miracles be viewed as much as possible in company with the Sermon on the Mount? Partly because the ancient world knew many miracle workers: pagan, Jewish, and Christian. Miracles give an unclear signal. The evidence of Matthew's Gospel alone shows that miracles were seen variously (1) as signs of their doers' favored status as children of God (7:22), (2) as displays of demonic energy and of partnership with the prince of demons (9:34; 12:24), (3) as proofs or "signs" (*sēmeia*) eliminating the need for the risk of faith (12:38-39; 16:1), (4) as part of the insidious apparatus of false Christs and false prophets leading many astray by their signs and wonders (*sēmeia kai terata*, 24:24). Jesus' mighty acts (*dynameis*, 11:20-23; 13:54, 58) are expressions of God's own saving might. They are powerful incursions into a world "in darkness and the shadow of death," moving out from God who is power (*dynamis*, 22:29; 26:64), aiming to reclaim and renew creation (cf. 6:13).

The mighty acts of Jesus are not displays of raw energy designed to cow opposition, to gain great throngs of adherents, or to separate the masses from their money (cf. 4:1-11). The power of Jesus enacted in miracles is the power of the speaker of the Sermon on the Mount. His mighty deeds (chaps. 8–9) begin to enact the world of righteousness envisioned in the sermon. His energy yields bodily health but, surpassing that, it presses toward a comprehensive righteousness, towards shifts in social relations, reordering of priorities, kindling of great expectations, fresh visions of God and humankind, toward a new community of women and men in harmony with God and with one another. His words and his deeds are earthquake and storm, shaking foundations, flattening old assumptions, rousing to new life.

Both in word (chaps. 5–7) and work (chaps. 8–9) Jesus opens doors for those locked out of real life by hopeless illness or by anemic moral vision. The miracles show that Jesus' eloquent and stunning words are more than grim demand, more than impossible dream, more than sweet vision. He comes armed with God's own power to cleanse dread impurity, to give power to the powerless, to subdue the roar of primal chaos, to bring to fruition half-forgotten dreams, to cast out demons, to open blind eyes, to renew the power of speech, to raise the dead, or, summing it all up, to save from sins (1:21).

The miracles of Jesus are so astonishing that it is easy to forget that he performed other signs, other significant and provocative deeds, such as eating with tax collectors and sinners, breaking the Sabbath, feasting and not fasting, calling twelve, receiving children, giving names, conversing publicly with women, riding an ass, cleansing the temple, breaking bread. Matthew 8–9 reports some of these other signs but focuses especially on what we call "miracles."

What Jesus did *not* do is also revealing. He did not galvanize the masses into a popular political movement; he did not train bands of guerrilla warriors to attack Roman troops or Roman sympathizers; he did not abandon village and town to establish a religious retreat in splendid isolation, teaching meditation techniques to a circle of devoted disciples; he did not demand stricter adherence to ancient laws or extend the sway of the law with fresh and more vigorous rules; he did not stand in the temple at the altar and offer a more perfect sacrifice. He did not define himself in terms of existing Zealotic, Essenic, Pharisaic, or priestly options.

Jesus' miracles of healing and rescuing flesh out aspects of his authority and his vision. They capture the imagination and provoke some people (not all) to serious consideration of his call to discipleship.

The reaction to his deeds is mixed. Chapters 8–9 present a kaleidoscope of images of Jesus: healer, exorcist, master (teacher), physician, bridegroom, lord, servant, son of David, Son of man, Son of God. Note, however, a terrible progression. These chapters open (8:1-4) with awesome power and promise, but they come hissing and crashing to an ominous close: he is called a blasphemer, in league with the prince of demons (9:34).

The miracles in chaps. 8–9 are narrated in language designed to encourage the post-Easter community to pray. The language of early Christian liturgy is everywhere. People solemnly approach Jesus and cast themselves humbly at his feet whether prostrating themselves or kneeling. They address him as "Lord," at once owning their weakness and his authority. They set before him their needs, begging his almighty help. The responses of Jesus sometimes mirror the very contours of their request, so that his authority meets and matches their need.

He hearkens to the cry of faith and lavishly praises faith, but even when he rebukes littleness of faith, he does not fail to rescue. In all this Matthew is celebrating not only the Jesus who lived in Galilee in a generation past but especially the Jesus who still lives in the midst of the community mediating God's own presence.

Matthew 8:1—9:34 contains nine miracle stories (reciting 10 miracles, since 9:18-26 is a single complex narrative reporting two miracles). They are arranged in three clusters of three miracle-stories each. The three clusters are stitched together by reports dealing with issues of discipleship (8:18-22 and 9:9-17):

1. He Took Our Infirmities (8:1-17)
   A Leper (8:1-4)
   A Paralyzed Servant (8:5-13)
   Peter's Mother-in-Law (8:14-15)
   He Bore Our Diseases (8:16-17)
2. Follow Me (8:18-22)
3. What Sort of Man? (8:23—9:8)
   Storm at Sea (8:23-27)
   Two Demoniacs (8:28-34)
   Sins of the Paralytic (9:1-8)
4. Follow Me (9:9-17)
5. Never Anything Like This (9:18-34)
   Jairus' Daughter and the Hemorrhaging Woman (9:18-26)
   Two Blind Men (9:27-31)
   A Dumb Demoniac (9:32-34)

Matthew reports many other miracles of Jesus besides those in chaps. 8 and 9. A second cluster occurs in chap. 12 and a third in chaps. 14–17.

He Took Our Infirmities (8:1-17)

1—The scene shifts but Jesus still moves in the company of the same **great crowds** which had heard the sermon (5:1). And the first of the miracles looks like a comment on the higher righteousness which appears to cancel the law but really fulfills it.

Make Me Clean (8:1-4)

2—**A leper came to him.** The Law forbade that. For the good of the community, lepers were condemned to wear torn clothing, let their hair grow down in tangles, live perpetually quarantined in camps beyond the villages of the healthy, and they were required to warn people off with cries of "unclean, unclean" (Lev. 13:45-46). Not only in cases of leprosy but from beginning to end it was the function of the Law to maintain intact a wall of separation between clean and unclean, lest the unclean pollute and contaminate the clean. But this leper recognized in Jesus an authority (7:29) greater than the Law. Like a beggar before a king or a worshiper before God, he came and threw himself at Jesus' feet (*prosekynei*, see commentary on 2:2).

The leper addressed Jesus as only disciples do in Matthew's Gospel: **Lord** (21:3; 22:43-45). And he spoke in faith: **If you will, you can make me clean.**

3—Jesus **stretched out his hand** across the barrier separating clean from unclean and **touched** that leper. The word of Jesus perfectly mirrors the leper's cry: **I will; be clean.**

Is Jesus insensitive to the distinction between clean and unclean? Does he feel contempt for the Law and its guardians? The relationship between Jesus and the Law is not simple cancellation but complex fulfillment. Jesus (like the leper) looks beyond efforts to define boundaries. He has come with the authority of God neither to build a better wall nor to bow before the power of uncleanness. Acting in the place of God, Jesus begins to roll back polluting powers and to restore God's creation to primal purity and wholeness.

Then Jesus sent the leper, freshly cleansed, **to the priest to offer the gift that Moses** commanded (Leviticus 14). Do it, he said, **as a proof,** as testimony. Of what? Of Jesus' authority to produce a new reality beyond the competence of the law.

Only Say the Word (8:5-13)

5—Jesus had touched the leper, crossing the boundary between clean and unclean in the interest of healing. Does his touch know any bounds? A pagan (v. 10) **centurion** approached Jesus when he entered **Capernaum** (4:13). Luke in his version of this narrative (7:1-10) carefully documents the extraordinary piety of this centurion. Jewish elders intercede for him with Jesus, calling the centurion "worthy" of the boon, pleading his love of Israel demonstrated in generous donations for the construction of the local synagogue. Matthew omits all that as irrelevant and concentrates on one thing only: his faith.

6—The centurion addressed Jesus exactly as the leper had: **Lord.** He laid before Jesus not his own need but the case of his **servant lying paralyzed at home.**

7-9—When Jesus volunteered to cross the boundary separating Jews and Gentiles, the centurion first of all offered a sober self-assessment. He boasts neither lineage (3:9) nor innocence (25:37) nor spiritual capacity (7:22). **I am not worthy** (cf. Luke 7:4). But he has trust: **You need not enter my house or touch the lad; only say the word, and my servant will be healed.** He calls himself a man **under authority;** yet his word is strong. How much stronger, he implies, must be the word of Jesus, who is not **under** any authority but is set over all authorities in heaven and on earth (28:18).

10-11—That declaration had such power that **Jesus marveled.** And he praised **such faith** (contrast 6:30) in extravagant terms: **many** who lack personal merit or correct genealogy or high spirituality **will come from east and west,** from totally unexpected quarters beyond the boundaries of the in-group. Those outsiders **will sit at table** in the great banquet (6:11; 22:1-14; 26:26-29; Isa. 25:6-8) of **the kingdom of heaven** in the company of **Abraham** (1:1) **Isaac,** and **Jacob.**

12—Meanwhile, **the sons of the kingdom,** and that means both Christian and Jewish insiders (13:38), may find that complacency has landed them in **outer darkness** (cf. 13:42, 50; 22:13; 24:51; 25:30), the absolute darkness farthest from the house, farthest from the kingdom, farthest from God, who is source of all light.

13—Responding to the centurion's faith Jesus sent forth his all-powerful word: **Be it done for you as you have believed.** And healing occurred at that very moment (9:22, 29; 15:28; 17:18).

Sick with a Fever (8:14-15)

Some pray to Jesus for healing (8:5-13), and sometimes Jesus seizes the initiative (8:14-15). He **entered Peter's house** at Capernaum (8:5), apparently all by himself (contrast Mark 1:29). He saw Peter's **mother-in-law lying sick with a fever,** and without hesitation or invitation **he touched her hand** so that **the fever left her.**

Jesus served her (v. 17) by healing her. Matthew says that she then rose and served him (see Mark 1:31). Jesus and the unnamed woman are thus pictured as sitting at table together (v. 11), mirroring the life of mutual service in the new community.

He Bore Our Diseases (8:16-17)

16—As **evening** came, concluding the long day which began with the Sermon on the Mount, **many** sick were brought to Jesus and he **healed** them **all** (cf. 4:23-24; contrast Mark 1:32-34). Behind **healed** is the verb *therapeuō*, which means both to heal and to serve (4:23-24; 8:7, 16; 9:35; 10:1, 8; 12:10, 15, 22; 14:14; 15:30; 17:16, 18; 19:2; 21:14).

17—The task of interpreting his exorcisms and cures is not entrusted to demons, as in Mark (1:24, 34) and Luke (4:34, 41). In Matthew the demons remain silent but Scripture speaks. Jesus exercised his authority not for personal benefit nor to reward especially pious people but to fulfill the servant's role. Matthew quotes Isa. 53:4, **He took our infirmities and bore our diseases.** He used his power as one who serves. He used it and used it up, finally using also his weakness and his death on behalf of others (20:28; 26:28).

I Will Follow You (8:18-22)

18—**Great crowds** (8:1) surround Jesus, and he **gave orders** to break away from them and from Capernaum in favor of **the other side** of the Sea of Galilee. These breaks seem to signal a desire to break readers away from the fascination of the masses with the power of Jesus (4:5-7; 7:20; cf. John 6:15) and to provoke them to follow Jesus into unknown places.

19-22—The following record of two conversations on discipleship is highly condensed and the rhetoric is extreme. As a result, the exchanges border on the cryptic.

A scribe, a recognized teacher of the Law, moved by the words and deeds of Jesus, blurts out his feelings in language at once extreme and dangerous. **Master, I will follow you wherever you go. Master** (*didaskalos*) means teacher or rabbi, and we could jump on the use of that term as evidence of the scribe's inadequate comprehension of Jesus.

Teacher

Because outsiders address Jesus as a "teacher" (9:11; 12:38; 17:24; 19:16; 22:16, 24; 24:36), and especially because Judas calls him "rabbi" (26:25, 48), the use of *Master, Rabbi,* or *Teacher* is frequently said to mark the speaker as an unbeliever. That theory seems incorrect, since Jesus speaks of himself as a teacher (10:24-25; 23:8-10; 26:18; cf. 26:55) and Matthew describes Jesus as teaching (4:23; 5:2; 7:29; 9:35; 11:1; 13:54; 21:23; 22:16).

Son of Man

In this context Jesus refers to himself for the first of 30 times in Matthew's Gospel by the enigmatic title "Son of man." In recent scholarly discussion it has been suggested that the phrase might best be translated as "the human one" or "this human being" (picturing Jesus in the latter case as pointing a finger at himself as he uses the phrase). The title is found in Matthew only on Jesus' lips. Disciples never use the title to identify or confess him, even though they repeatedly hear Jesus use the title of himself in private moments with them (10:23; 16:13, 27-28; 17:9, 12, 22; 19:28; 20:18, 28; seven times in the discourse of chaps. 24–25 and four times in the beginning of the passion narrative in chap. 26). Nor does the high priest use it in examining Jesus about his identity and authority (26:63), even though Jesus has used it previously in the hearing of the crowds and of Jewish leaders (8:20; 9:6; 11:19; 12:8, 32, 40; 13:37, 41) and uses it again in his response to the high priest's questions (26:64). The title is never found in the New Testament outside of the Gospels except in Acts 7:56 (cf. Rev. 1:13).

Efforts are made to understand it (1) by looking for its roots in ancient Jewish literature and (2) by examing its use in the Gospels. In the Psalms and Ezekiel "son of man" means something like "mere mortal" in contrast to God. In Daniel God's people are represented by "one like a son of man," that is, by "a great human figure" as contrasted with the inhuman beasts representing a succession of powerful pagan empires. In some later Jewish apocalyptic literature (1 Enoch), the Son of man is an agent of God in the last times who comes to judge and to rule. It appears that the equivalent Aramaic phrase could mean something like "this person" or "yours truly."

It has become traditional to say that the earthly Jesus is pictured as using the title in connection with three moments: his experience during his ministry, his future suffering and resurrection, and his final coming in glory.

At first that assertion seems to say very little. Jesus simply used the title in talking about the successive phases of his existence: his presence, his passion, and his parousia. However, the title binds these successive periods together into a unity. The title warns readers that this Jesus with his homelessness, with his offensive words and deeds, with all the abuse and betrayal he suffered, with his vulnerability and cross, at last will be vindicated and will come at the end as God's agent in the final judgment. And the norm or criterion of judgment will be nothing other than the righteousness which the Son of man offered and taught. The use of the title therefore underscores the authority of his action, the grandeur of his teaching, the seriousness of his call. And the title reveals what a hideous mistake it is to deny or distrust him, and what a monstrosity it is to condemn and crucify him.

In view of all this, it is true that the word *teacher* (v. 19) does not say everything there is to be said about Jesus. But addressing Jesus as teacher is not by itself sufficient to brand the speaker as an unbeliever. What certainly is inadequate is the scribe's grasp of where it is that Jesus is going. For him and for all volunteers Jesus has a hard word about the cost of discipleship. **The Son of man,** the one who has all authority and heals all diseases and commands all demons, actually possesses less than **foxes** and **birds** (cf. 6:26-30). He has no easy welcome in the world, no home, no permanent place of abiding, **no place to lay his head** (John 1:11). Not exactly **no place.** He most definitely is heading toward one **place** in particular, and the crucifixion narrative will reveal that goal. This exchange with the scribe is one in a series of hard sayings about the fate awaiting Jesus and his disciples (cf. 10:38; 6:21-23; 20:20-28). Of course, the Son of man is heading toward glory but only via crucifixion.

21—Yet, paradoxically, the way Jesus travels is the path to life, and he joyfully issues the call to follow on that narrowest of ways.

Another of the disciples made a request both reasonable and pious, at least so it seems. Jesus has ordered a move to the other side (8:18) but this disciple asks, **Lord** (8:2), **let me first go and bury my father** (Gen. 50:5-6; 1 Kings 19:20). Elsewhere Jesus castigates any who would shirk duties toward mother or father. Honoring parents is a command of God (15:4-6). But what is **first?** Are family responsibilities **first** or is the kingdom with its righteousness **first** (6:33)? The fellow who requests release from the call to discipleship, pleading family obligations, sounds like those invited to the wedding banquet who begin to make excuses (22:3-6). They prefer the old and familiar world to the new world of

God. Jesus' reply seems clipped, harsh, and shocking: **Leave the dead to bury their own dead.** This response by Jesus is not advice for handling social and familial obligations. It is a cry, embodying a vision, of an old world passing away and a new world in the process of being born. It summons hearers to open their eyes and hearts to God's new world.

The present paragraph (vv. 18-22) is closely connected to the following (vv. 23-27). Both deal with disciples and discipleship, and in fact it seems that the scribe (v. 19) and the bereaved disciple (v. 21) both get into the boat with Jesus.

What Sort of Man? (8:23—9:8)

The second cluster of miracles is in some ways even more astonishing than the first, as Jesus demonstrates mastery over forces of nature, over demons in Gentile territory, and over sin and paralysis in his own city.

Winds and Sea Obey Him (8:23-27)

The stilling of the storm (cf. 14:22-33) is a shining revelation of Jesus' power. This miracle describes Jesus' omnipotent care for every follower. It stands as encouragement to disciples, who may be dismayed by the hardships and severe demands, which are so dramatically portrayed in the preceding paragraph.

Matthew alerts readers that he is still talking about discipleship. First, Jesus climbed into **the boat** and then his disciples followed him. How differently Mark pictures the scene, declaring that the disciples left the crowds and took Jesus with them (Mark 4:36).

24—Exactly as Jesus had warned (8:18-22) those who follow him need not expect smooth sailing. **There arose a great storm on the sea so that the boat was being swamped.** The **storm** (literally, "a great shaking," *seismos*) is a terrible convulsion signaling the breakup of everything stable and secure (24:7; 27:51; 28:2; Rev. 6:12; cf. Matt. 7:24-27).

Meanwhile Jesus was **asleep.** Facing powers more terrible than individual illness or fever, threatened by raging chaos, the disciples voice the cry of the church: **Save, Lord; we are perishing.**

26—They call him **Lord** and look to him for salvation (1:21), and yet he rebukes them as people of **little faith** (6:30; 14:31). Not unfaith, not all out of faith, but wavering because of the fury of the storm. They forget his presence (1:23; 18:20; 28:20) or imagine he might be present but uncaring or powerless. He rebukes their panic. Only then does he rise and rebuke **the winds and the sea,** as though they were demons. He stilled their rage, and there was a **great calm.**

The whole narrative raises the question: **What sort of man is this?** If he has such authority that **even winds and sea obey him,** then why do readers hesitate to embark with him?

28—Jesus comes to **the other side** (8:18) and invades Gentile territory, **the country of the Gadarenes.**

Two Demoniacs (8:28-34)

Two demoniacs (not just one, as in Mark 5:2; cf. Matt. 9:27; 20:20) emerge from **the tombs,** their unclean and makeshift home beyond the circle of ordinary human habitation. They challenge Jesus. They control the road, and they try to block Jesus' progress there at his entrance to Gentile lands.

29—What business does Jesus have outside Jewish territory? Some in the early church seriously raised that question. What was Jesus doing among the Gentiles? Jesus was Jewish, as were all 12 of the original disciples. Furthermore, Jesus in the days of his flesh confined his attention entirely to Jews (10:5-6; 15:24). Even from the point of view of Matthew, who obviously favors the mission to the Gentiles (28:18-20), Jesus' visit to the land of the Gadarenes and confrontation with the demons there occurred **before the time.** This event is an anticipation, a sign of things to come beyond his death and resurrection.

29-31—Attempting to master one another by means of names or titles and verbal bargaining are standard elements in exorcisms. The demons are about to be overpowered and cast out of the human bodies they inhabit. And they must know it, since they call Jesus **Son of God** (3:17). Still, they scheme to carry on through other bodies: **Send us away into the herd of swine.**

32—Jesus said, **Go.** But when they entered the swine, **the whole herd rushed down the steep bank into the sea.** And so the demons **perished in the waters.** Jesus stilled the storm and established his authority over the sea. Now he consigns pigs and demons to the deep, putting them also under his feet, signaling (1) that the way is clear for the future Gentile mission, and (2) that inclusion of the Gentiles will be accompanied by exorcisms and rejection of things unclean.

33-34—The herdsmen fled and reported Jesus' actions, rousing **all the city** (21:10) to emerge in ceremonial procession to meet Jesus. Yet they did not come to welcome him but begged him to leave their region.

Your Sins Are Forgiven (9:1-8)

1—Jesus granted their request, as he had the requests of leper, centurion, and disciples (8:1-27). Once again he crossed the sea, southeast to northwest, back to Capernaum (8:5-17), described as **his own city,** where he had settled down (4:13), and where he appears to have had his own house (9:10).

2—There in Capernaum people brought to him a **paralytic,** lying helpless on his bed. Matthew omits the picturesque details narrated by Mark: four good friends, the crowds barring access at the door of the house, businesslike digging through the roof, lowering the paralytic at Jesus' feet. Matthew concentrates on this one thing: **Jesus saw their faith** (cf. 8:5), and his words are therefore full of promise and power: **Take heart, my son** (cf. 9:22; 14:27), **your sins are forgiven.**

3—The scribes do not see as Jesus does. They fail to see the dawning of God's new world in Jesus. In their eyes Jesus is simply guilty of **blaspheming,** of speaking arrogantly, insulting God's majesty by usurping a privilege that belongs to God alone (26:65; 27:39; cf. 12:31; 15:19).

4-6—But the new world promised for the end is already breaking the chains of the old world of sin and death through Jesus' miracles of healing and forgiveness. Therefore, that people may know that Jesus as **Son of man** (8:20) **has authority on earth** even now **to forgive sins,** he commands the paralytic, **Rise, take up your bed and go home.** His call is a call to new life.

8—Faced with his word and deed, so far surpassing all their prior experience of teachers and leaders, they felt awe and shuddering (17:6; 28:5, 10). **And they glorified God, who had given**

such authority (7:29) not just to Jesus but **to men** (RSV). Human beings have it in their power to be vehicles of death or life, chains or liberty, healing or misery. It is not enough merely to define and condemn sin; Jesus forgives it. And he calls disciples to be a community of healers and forgivers (chap. 18), agents of God's sovereignty.

Follow Me (9:9-17)

A Man Called Matthew (9:9-13)

9—Jesus passed on from Capernaum and **saw a man called Matthew sitting at the tax office.** Near Capernaum was the border between the territories of Philip and of Herod Antipas. Where the road crossed the border, customs officials set up their booth and collected a duty on goods in transit. So Matthew was probably collecting import and export duties for Herod, not poll taxes or property taxes for the Romans. In any cases Matthew was in a despised profession (v. 11).

The name *Levi* (Mark 2:14; Luke 5:27) does not appear here, and the tax official bears the name of **Matthew,** one of the Twelve (10:3; cf. Mark 6:18). It was once thought that the author of this Gospel was here subtly introducing himself. It is possible that he is here honoring the memory of one of the great past founders of his community. But certainly the author here presents a powerful parable of discipleship in the new age. Jesus calls to himself people totally lacking in all ordinary qualifications of piety, rectitude, or spirituality. The new world is a miracle beyond human expecting or deserving, based on Jesus' gracious call: **Follow me.** And Matthew **rose and followed him** (cf. 4:18-22).

10-13—Strange kingdom, strange new world, strange righteousness. **Jesus and his disciples** reclined at a festive meal with **many tax collectors** (like Matthew) **and sinners** (like the paralytic, 9:2). Some **Pharisees,** worshiping God as holy, concerned to defend God's people from pollution, grateful for the Law as a dike against the flood, saw nothing but impiety, carelessness, and danger in Jesus' conduct (cf. Mishnah, *Tohoroth* 7:6). **Why** does he defile himself? **Why** does he touch lepers? **Why** does he go to Gentiles? **Why** is he so careless about the line dividing pure from impure, righteous from unrighteous?

12—In response, Jesus describes himself as a **physician,** a healer, come to rescue the **sick.** He does not romanticize and say that the **sick** are really well. They are **sick,** but he will neither write them off nor build a wall to isolate or contain them. Instead, true to his name and vocation (1:21), he heals them.

13—His behavior is not impiety or blasphemy (9:3) but **mercy,** precisely that **mercy** for which God called through the prophets (Hos. 6:6; cf. Matt. 12:7; 1 Tim, 1:15). **Mercy,** said the prophets, is better than **sacrifice.** In this context **sacrifice** is a code word standing for any device, procedure, arrangement, tradition, or teaching of pious people which somehow manages to obscure **mercy.** And **mercy** is another word for the love that reaches out even to enemies (5:44).

I came, says Jesus (see commentary above on 5:17, 22), **not to call the righteous,** not to confirm standard definitions of righteousness, not to undergird standard strategies for dealing with unrighteousness. **I came** to announce and to enact a surpassing righteousness (5:20). **I came** to summon sinners out of their old life into newness of life.

New Wine (9:14-17)

14—First scribes (9:3), then Pharisees (9:11), and now **disciples of John** question Jesus' practices. The Pharisees ask why Jesus feasts with sinners; John's disciples ask why Jesus feasts at all. Why do John's disciples and the Pharisees **fast** but Jesus and his disciples do not?

15—Jesus responds with a little parable: **Can the wedding guests mourn as long as the bridegroom is with them?** The presence of Jesus spells a totally new situation, the advent of fulfillment and joy, the dawning of the kingdom (5:3-12). His presence banishes sadness, just as it overcomes illness, cancels sin, and stills the storm. Nevertheless, the days will come **when the bridegroom is taken away** by crucifixion. The disciples may well sorrow at that deed arising from unbelief, misunderstanding, and downright perversity. That will be a moment for fasting.

Perhaps the saying looks beyond crucifixion and resurrection to the time of the church, when the presence of Jesus, affirmed in faith (1:23; 18:20; 28:20) is sometimes also obscured by the cloud of unknowing and by littleness of faith. As a sign of sorrow over their own sin (5:4) and as a means of undergirding their prayer for the full and final revelation of the kingdom (6:9-10), disciples may then fast. But it will still be a new thing (6:16-18), for the new day really is dawning.

16-17—Therefore, to continue old religious practices would be as silly as patching **an old garment** with **a piece of unshrunk cloth.** Everyone knows **a worse tear is made.** Or it would be like putting **new wine into old wineskins. The skins** will inevitably **burst** and then **the wine is spilled and the skins are destroyed.** Everyone agrees: **fresh wineskins for new wine.**

The Crowds Marveled (9:18-34)

The third and final cluster reports four miracles in three narratives, and brings the whole section to a close.

Take Heart, My Daughter (9:18-26)

18—While Jesus was still at table conversing (v. 10), **a ruler came in.** Mark and Luke describe the man as a ruler of the synagogue and give his name as Jairus, but Matthew again economizes (cf. 8:5). The ruler **knelt before** Jesus (cf. 8:2) with a cry of anguish and a confession of trust: **My daughter has just died** (contrast Mark 5:23); **but come and lay your hand on her, and she will live.** Jesus immediately **rose** (8:26) and **followed with his disciples.**

20-21—On the way **a woman who had suffered a hemorrhage for twelve years came up behind him.** Reaching out in faith, **she touched the fringe of his garment** (cf. 14:36; 23:5).

22—Jesus turned. He viewed the woman the way the ruler viewed his child. Jesus said, **Take heart** (9:2), **my daughter** (9:18); **your faith has made you well.** Instantly, as soon as Jesus spoke the word (8:8), she was **made well.** For all his abbreviating, Matthew lets that word **made well** (from *sōzō,* "save") resound three times in two verses. The woman trusted Jesus and was made well, made whole, saved (1:21) by his word.

23—Jesus continued on his healing path. He **came to the ruler's house** and found the professional mourners and **flute players** leading a **crowd making a tumult** in premature lamentation. Of the evangelists only Matthew mentions hired flute players. Jesus commanded: **Depart; for the girl is not dead but sleeping.** Those realists **laughed at him.** The mourners and mockers model un-belief just as the woman now healed is a model of faith. She believed and was saved; these laugh and are **cast out.** Jesus entered the house of death, took the girl by the hand, and the girl arose.

In this context Matthew lacks Mark's "talitha cumi" (Mark 5:41), as he elsewhere lacks "corban" (Mark 7:11; Matt. 15:5) and "eph-phatha" (Mark 7:34). Matthew's community may have been more Greek and farther from the Aramaic language than Mark's.

With her hand in his, the gates of death could not prevail against her (16:18).

The two miracles in 9:18-26 are neatly interwoven. The healing of the woman serves to give a sense of time passing and also of spatial movement from the banquet hall to the ruler's house. But the two miracles are linked also in other ways. Mark in fact says that the woman had been ill 12 years and that the dead girl was 12 years old (5:42). The ruler calls his child "daughter," and Jesus uses the same word when he addresses the sick woman. The ruler wants Jesus to touch his daughter, and the woman believes that her touching Jesus will be her salvation.

The two stories complement one another. The woman exem-plifies profound but simple faith. The dead girl, of course, cannot serve as a model of faith. But her story shows that the authority of Jesus extends beyond illness, even a 12-year illness, into the kingdom of death itself (16:18). He has all authority. Throughout chaps. 8 and 9 Matthew has featured the limitless authority of Jesus and the absolute necessity of faith, and here a single complex narrative develops both themes.

He Touched Their Eyes (9:27-31)

27—Mark (8:22-26) has the story of the one blind man of Beth-saida, a stone's throw from Capernaum, but Matthew offers an account of **two blind men** (cf. 8:28). They **followed him, crying aloud, Have mercy on us, Son of David.** That title often is on the lips of suppliants (15:22; 20:30-31; 21:9, 15; cf. 12:23).

Son of David

Jesus, adopted by "Joseph, son of David" (1:20), is himself not simply one more male in David's continuing line but the one in whom all the brightest hopes of that line find their crown and fulfillment (1:1). He is the promised "son of David" (1:1), "the Christ" or "Messiah' (1:16-17), the true "king of Israel" (2:2). These titles basically are equivalents of one another, variations on a single theme (2:5; 27:11).

Jesus' birth in David's town was hailed as royal by visitors from afar (2:1), and from the moment of his baptism and first public activity his eye was fixed on Jerusalem, royal David's city. The fact that the title "son of David" so often appears in contexts with miracles can be understood as part of the royal imagery. As Jesus goes his way toward Jerusalem, he hears petitions and distributes gifts, like a king mounting up to coronation (Psalm 68).

Jesus really is "royal David's royal son," and yet it is vital to see that Jesus surpasses expectation, alters hopes, breaks the mold. The old traditional titles are strained to the breaking point in the effort to define him (cf. 22:41-45).

28-29—Jesus entered a house, and the blind men came to him there. He posed a question, focusing once more on faith: **Do you believe that I am able to do this?** In their reply they speak the title used only by disciples: **Yes, Lord** (8:21). At that, he touched their eyes and declared, **According to your faith** (8:13) **be it done to you. And their eyes were opened.**

30-31—Jesus healed in a house, in private, and commanded silence, but word spread **through all that district** (cf. 9:26). So the prophecy of Isaiah quoted at 4:16 keeps coming true: throughout the land, Galilee of the Gentiles, Jesus shines as great light, light of fresh dawn, for all who sit in darkness (9:27-30) and in the shadow of death (9:18-26).

The Dumb Man Spoke (9:32-34)

Matthew concludes the series of miracle stories by reporting with extreme brevity that Jesus exorcised a **demon,** so that a **dumb man spoke.** Matthew has told this story precisely here to ensure that he has presented at least one example of each kind of miracle named in Jesus' reply to the Baptist in 11:5. The word translated **dumb man** (*kōphos*) can mean mute, deaf-mute, or deaf. Here it obviously means "mute" (v. 33). It appears again in 11:5 and there is translated as "deaf."

33-34—The deeds of Jesus, products of his matchless authority, compel no one to believe. In fact they provoked wildly diverging responses. The crowds marveled at the newness of Jesus' authority: **Never was anything like this seen in Israel** (cf. 7:28-29). The response of the **Pharisees** is the diametrical opposite. They evaluate Jesus on the basis of old standards and old assumptions: **He casts out demons by the prince of demons** (cf. 10:25; 12:22-27).

The main theme of the next narrative section (11:2—16:20) is stated right here: diverging responses to Jesus and especially mounting opposition to his ministry. But before that narrative section unfolds, Matthew will describe Jesus' missionary charge to the disciples (9:35—11:1).

Shepherd of the Sheep, Lord of the Harvest (9:35-38)

Matthew now has concluded his initial presentation of Jesus' words and deeds. Matthew 9:35 is practically identical to 4:23, and between these two summary verses Matthew has narrated Jesus' giving of the Sermon on the Mount and has introduced Jesus' healing ministry. Those summaries (4:23 and 9:35) trumpet the great themes of the ministry of Jesus: he teaches and heralds **the gospel of the kingdom,** and he heals every **disease** and **infirmity.** Matthew 9:35 differs from 4:23 only in that it speaks of Jesus' activity in **all the cities and villages.** These words look not backwards but forward to 10:5, 11, 14, 15, 23; 11:1.

36—Crowds throng about Jesus ever since he first emerged in public (4:25), drawn by his authoritative presence. At the same time, Matthew offers glimpses of the hostility of the leaders (shepherds) towards him. That hostility will become a major theme of 11:2—16:20. Jesus had **compassion** on those crowds (14:14; 20:24), seeing them as neglected, straying, preyed upon, like **sheep without a shepherd** (Num. 27:17; Ezek. 34:5; Matt. 2:6; 10:6).

37—Suddenly Jesus switches from a pastoral to an agricultural figure of speech. **Harvest** symbolizes ripeness, fullness of time, and also judgment (3:12; 13:30, 39; John 4:35; Rev. 14:15; cf. Isa. 27:12; Jer. 51:33; Hos. 6:11; Joel 3:13; 4 Ezra 4:28-32). It is high time to gather the **harvest** (cf. catching fish, 4:18-22; gathering the sheep and separating them from the goats, 25:31-46).

38—Jesus is not launched on some solitary, heroic venture. So he gathers disciples and gives them a share in his mission to Israel and the nations. They stand with Jesus on the threshold of a new time, a new community, the new heaven and the new earth in which righteousness dwells. That new world is not humanity's achievement but God's awesome and shattering gift. It differs from every merely human project, and from the start it requires something higher than human resources. Therefore the first order of business is not to act but simply to **pray** to **the Lord of the harvest.**

■ SECOND DISCOURSE: The New Community in Its Mission Encounters Hostility (10:1-42)

Why is Jesus' second discourse, featuring his missionary charge to the Twelve, located exactly here, following the chapters on Jesus' authoritative words (chaps. 5–7) and powerful deeds (chaps. 8–9)? The answer is that chaps. 5–10 taken together describe the work of Jesus in two phases: Jesus' own ministry (chaps. 5–9) and his ministry through his disciples (chap. 10). See the further remarks on 11:2. Matthew has just described Jesus as Lord of the harvest (9:36-38) and will now tell what awaits disciples as harvesters (chap. 10). In spite of Jesus' strange and stunning authority (7:28-29; 9:33-34), to be shared with his disciples (10:1), both he and his disciples may expect opposition and persecution.

The second of Jesus' five discourses in Matthew's Gospel focuses on the mission of the new community. The first part seems to be aimed narrowly and specifically at the Twelve (10:1-15). Readers naturally expect that it will be followed by an account of the actual mission of the Twelve and then a report of their return to Jesus (as in Mark 6:7-13, 30 or Luke 9:1-6, 10). Instead, Jesus' opening charge to the Twelve continues with additional words on the life and mission of the community in a hostile world. And these further words are more general than the opening commission, and they appear to be directed no longer to the Twelve alone but to the later community and its missionary existence all the way to the end of time. That is especially true of vv. 24-42, but it also applies to vv. 16-23.

It has been suggested that each of the five discourses of Jesus in Matthew's Gospel begins with words meant for the Twelve and then eventually turns to the needs of their descendants in the church. I would like to propose a slightly different reading of the situation. Matthew's procedure resembles that of storytellers and preachers of all ages. First he shares a well-known tradition about Jesus and Jesus' contemporaries, setting it forth as would a preacher announcing a text. Matthew then follows up on that familiar tradition with a selection of further sayings of Jesus, designed to show how the tradition connects with the lives of the readers in the generations after Jesus and the Twelve. So in the discourses of Jesus we have an arrangement like that of "text" and "sermon," composed by Matthew out of the larger body of the sayings of Jesus.

Following is a simplified (perhaps oversimplified) outline and summary of chap. 10:

(1) The Twelve (vv. 2-4), nucleus and mirror of the entire new community of all times and places, are (2) equipped with Jesus' own astonishing powers and commissioned (vv. 1, 7-8). (3) They are instructed to travel light, as befits those whose trust is in God (vv. 8-10). (4) Jesus offers no glib promise of easy harvest but instead announces that his agents and envoys may expect the same reception Jesus himself has received, namely, more abuse than welcome (vv. 11-25). (5) Nevertheless, they may live without fear, knowing that they enjoy the Father's watchful care, and with the invincible faith that they will find their own true lives (vv. 26-42).

He Called Twelve (10:1-4)

1—First **he called to him his twelve disciples,** drawing them into tight orbits circling his own person. And he shared with them his own radiant **authority over unclean spirits,** not to work with those spirits (cf. 9:34), **but to cast them out, and to heal every disease and every infirmity.** Plainly, that charismatic authority, grounded in his own, is solely for the sake of mission to the world.

In rapid succession, Matthew calls these missionaries the **twelve disciples** (10:1), and the **twelve apostles** (10:2). They follow Jesus as apprentices (**disciples**) and they act as his envoys (**apostles**). Previously Matthew has named only five of them, but here he lists all twelve (10:2-5). As **the twelve,** no fewer and no more, they are a sign of Jesus' summons to the twelve tribes of Israel, and that summons and its reception or rejection is the theme of the chapter. Indeed this chapter is full of the language of tribe and family and nation and community. In describing Judas (v. 4) as the one who **betrayed** him, Matthew again speaks of opposition (2:13; 9:3, 34).

To the Lost Sheep (10:5-15)

5—After naming the Twelve, Matthew repeats the mission charge to them in direct speech of Jesus, beginning with the astonishing statement that they must go not to **Gentiles** and not to **Samaritans** but only to the **lost sheep of the house of Israel.** This statement is often misinterpreted as narrow and particularistic, an astonishing contradiction of the universalism of 28:19.

One thing it means is that Israel, contrary to expectation, is a mission field. The tradition viewed Israel in the last times as destined to be a light for the Gentiles, but Jesus is saying that Israel needs enlightening, needs a shepherd (9:36). John preached to Israel (3:2-9). So did Jesus (4:12-16), and so will the disciples (v. 5). Israel will be offered the gospel of the kingdom not once but three times, fully and comprehensively.

7-8—The activity of the Twelve mirrors both the geography of Jesus and the very words and works of Jesus. They are to preach, **The kingdom of heaven is at hand** (4:17). As signs of that inbreaking kingdom they are to **heal the sick** (8:1-17; 9:1-8, 27-31), **raise the dead** (9:18-26), **cleanse lepers** (8:2-4), **cast out demons** (8:28-34; 9:32-33). Of the miracles of Jesus narrated in chaps. 8–9, only the stilling of the storm is not paralleled in the charge to the disciples.

8b-9—The Twelve had received their call to life, their place in the new community, their share in the mission freely, as a gift, without pay (Isa. 55:1-2). And they are to give as freely as they have received, neither peddling their services like so many wandering teachers nor anxiously calculating the cost of the mission. They are free to travel light: no **purses** weighted with coins, no **bag** stocked with provisions, no extra **tunics** for their comfort (cf. 5:40; 6:25), no **sandals** for their feet, for they are slaves of God, no **staff** to ward off snakes or wild dogs or robbers on the way, for God is their defense and they have Jesus as their shepherd (9:36).

All these shocking phrases are parables of a radical break with the kind of planning associated with human projects. They are parables of radical trust in God and in God's promise to build a new community. **The laborer deserves food** (1 Cor. 9:14; Luke 10:7), and God will see that these workers are sustained. By their unburdened style they signal that they trust God and not mammon (6:24), that they are free from anxiety (6:25-34), and that they themselves seek the kingdom and the righteousness they proclaim (6:33).

11-12—In each village or city (9:35) the missionaries will find hospitality in homes of the **worthy.** The worthy are defined as having one qualification only: they listen to the apostles' words and perceive in them the message of God's own **peace.** The unworthy are marked by resistance to message and messengers. The apostles should break from them: **Shake off the dust from your feet** (18:17; cf. Acts 13:51). **It will be more tolerable on the day of judgment** for the notoriously sinful land of **Sodom and Gomorrah** than for that unreceptive house or town (11:23-24; Genesis 19).

Sheep in the Midst of Wolves (10:16-25)

16—The crowds have just been described as lost sheep (9:36; 10:6), but now suddenly only the disciples, those who respond to the shepherd's call, are **sheep,** and the others, unworthy and unresponsive, will turn on them like **wolves** (7:15; Luke 10:3). In the face of mortal danger disciples are to be as **wise as serpents,** not courting martyrdom by senseless provocations. And they must be as **innocent as doves,** not evading persecution by duplicity.

17-18—A dreadful prospect of resistance looms whichever way they turn: trials before Jewish **councils and synagogues** on the one hand, and before Gentile **governors and kings** on the other. But Jesus calls them to redeem those dark hours by their **testimony.**

19-20—Their witness needs no anxious rehearsal, for the **Spirit**

of their Father will provide words. Indeed, they should be free of any anxiety whatsoever, perfectly secure in God alone (6:19-34). John and Luke in their Gospels have extensive material on the **Spirit,** and Mark has a little. But this is the solitary reference in Matthew to the work of the **Spirit** in the life of Jesus' disciples (cf. 3:11; 28:19).

21-22—You will be hated by all for my name's sake. What Jesus sets in motion is radically new, an unexpected wonder, and it will meet with commitment from the few but will provoke resistance in the many. It comes with explosive force, dividing the indivisible, **brother** against **brother, father** against **child, children** against **parents,** dread sign of the final breaking up of the old world in the time before the full revelation of the new (Mic. 7:6).

23—Hated by all, persecuted from town to town, they still need not despair. Before they have run out of places to hide, **the Son of man** (8:20) will come (cf. 26:64). Here for the first time in this Gospel, **the Son of man** is assigned a role in connection with the future end of the age. His advent will be good news for disciples (cf. 25:31-46).

24-25—Disciples of all times and places have the privilege of sharing the authority of Jesus and the mission of Jesus. Inevitably that entails sharing the suffering of Jesus. But the consolation of every **disciple** and **servant** is precisely this: rejection and persecution mean that they are **like** their **teacher, like** their **master** (cf. John 13:16; 15:20; 1 Pet. 4:1; 1 Cor. 4:12). The sufferings of the disciples are linked to the sufferings of Jesus and to their own fidelity to their mission. Those linkings prepare readers to view the mounting opposition to Jesus as the inevitable consequence of his fidelity to his mission.

If people call **the master of the house Beelzebul, how much more will they malign those of his household.** Both here and at 12:24, 27 **Beelzebul** is a name for Satan, and in both contexts Jesus and prince of devils are characterized as **master of the house.** If people slander the true **master of the house,** and call him and his works demonic, **how much more will** they slander also the disciples.

149

Have No Fear (10:26-33)

Jesus has warned of terrible opposition (17:25) but now encourages with a threefold **Fear not!** (vv. 26, 28, 31).

26-27—(1) **Fear** must not stop the disciples' mouths. God's gracious sovereignty, at first **covered** and **hidden,** will at the last be **revealed** and **known** (cf. 11:25). Wheels are turning and no earthly power can stay their revolution. Yet the unveiling of the kingdom is almost unnoticed. Almost. Jesus has whispered to his disciples the secret of the kingdom. He calls them not only to live by that secret but to share it as heralds amplifying his quiet voice.

28—(2) In speaking of **fear** a second time, Jesus echoes familiar themes from the literature of martyrdom and the suffering of the righteous (cf. Wisdom 16:13-15; 4 Macc. 13:13-15; 14:6). Human tyranny at its absolute worst is limited to hurting the **body,** the physical and material self. Why **fear** that? The one great tragedy, the only one to be feared, is the destruction of the **soul,** cutting the bond that connects the disciple with God. That deep and secret connection with God, eternal and altogether glorious, can be destroyed only by unfaith and disobedience.

29-30—(3) For yet a third time Jesus addresses the disciples' **fear. Two sparrows are sold for a penny.** The poor buy them for food or to offer at the temple. But cheap as they are, sparrows neither live nor die outside God's knowledge and will. God's care extends to the smallest creatures. (**Even the hairs of your head are numbered!**) Persecution can stir up doubt about God's care or power to provide, but Jesus declares that God is there for the disciples beyond all good and evil, beyond living and dying. **Fear not, therefore; you are of more value than many sparrows.**

32-33—The section began in vv. 17-22 with dread warnings regarding human courts and comes full circle here with talk of heaven's court. Beyond all human verdicts Jesus pictures God's own final judgment: **my Father who is in heaven** (7:21; cf. 6:9) is poised to assign each one to the bliss of enduring joy or to the agony of outermost darkness. Jesus portrays himself both as advocate and prosecutor (cf. 7:23). In the parallels Jesus speaks of the testimony of "the Son of man" (Mark 8:38; Luke 12:8-9), but here says simply **I. I will acknowledge** and **I will deny** (cf. 16:13).

150

He will acknowledge those who now acknowledge, and he will deny those who now deny him.

Not Peace but a Sword (10:34-42)

This new section is a further meditation on the theme of acknowledging or denying Jesus. A striking topic sentence (10:34) is backed by quotation of prophecy (10:35-36). Then follow two parallel sections. The first focuses on the natural family of biology and law (10:37-39) and the second on the new family, the community of faith (10:40-42).

34—Do not think that I have come to bring peace on earth; I have not come to bring peace but a sword. Sword means pain and warfare, worlds in collision. Because the new world from God really is new, it confounds and contradicts the old world with its old arrangements. So the coming of the kingdom is never smooth or easy. The advent of the Prince of Peace provokes old kingdoms and old powers, and the people comfortable with them, and they mount stiff opposition (11:12). Jesus mounts a kind of holy war against the evil powers of the old eon (cf. Joel 3:9-12).

35—How new is the coming kingdom? How deeply will it cut? How hard will it shake the old foundations? In a daring parable, designed to shock, the prophet Micah had pictured the dawning of the new world as shattering even the dearest, deepest connections of all: **man against father, daughter against mother, daughter-in-law against mother-in-law.** Micah climaxed his words with a dreadful picture of unnatural conflict: **a man's foes will be the members of his own household** (cf. 4:21).

Jesus quotes Mic. 7:6 (cf. Matt. 10:21) to prepare his disciples ahead of time for the ferocity of opposition they are bound to meet, precisely because they are heralds of a new world.

37—Jesus extends Micah's figure of speech. When he goes on to talk of loving **father or mother, son or daughter, more than me,** he is in effect saying: "Whoever loves the old world more than the new world of God" **is not worthy of me** (10:11-13) or of the miracle of the inbreaking kingdom of God.

38-39—Exactly because the old world resists the new world, there is the **cross.** That word **cross** appears here for the first time in the Gospel (cf. 16:24). To **take his cross** means to affirm the

wonder and the glory of the new world and to accept the consequence of the scorn of the old. All who shoulder the cross and
willingly lose their own life (and that is the most shocking thing
of all) for the sake of Jesus and the kingdom will find life, their
own true and indestructible life with God (16:24-27).

40-42—Does the approach of the kingdom do nothing but shatter and divide? Does its coming stir only resentment? No. Some
receive the kingdom in its envoys and welcome it with open arms.
And that openness, that hospitality has its **reward** (6:1-2). Those
who receive the envoy receive **me,** says Jesus, and those who
receive **me** receive God **who sent me.**

Who are the envoys of the envoy of God? (cf. 23:34) The **prophet,** endowed with authority to heal and cast out demons, and yet
persecuted (5:11-12) and sometimes going astray (7:15)? **Righteous** ones, disciples whose lives are obedience and who both
practice and teach the higher righteousness (5:20) of the kingdom?
Little ones (18:6, 10), the seemingly quite ordinary, even ungifted
members of the community? All these are fathers and mothers,
brothers and sisters in the community. The smallest act of encouragement or love (cf. 25:35-36) done to any one of them in
support of their lives as prophet or righteous or disciple has its
reward.

Jesus' **instructing** (*diatassō,* cf. 1:24) of the Twelve in chap. 10
has completely ignored questions of organization, administration,
church offices, liturgy, and doctrine. All attention is riveted to
the singular authority of the Twelve to bear witness to Jesus and
the inbreaking kingdom among the peoples of earth.

■ Jesus' True Family (11:1—13:58)

Come to Me (11:1-30)

This section of the Gospel (4:17—16:20) opened when Jesus
burst upon Galilee like a great light, proclaiming the nearness of
the kingdom (see the notes at 4:17). That kingdom, expounded
in words (chaps. 5–7), signaled in deeds of power (chaps. 8–9),
proclaimed by the Twelve (chap. 10), is radically new. Prophesied
in Scripture, it yet remains unexpected and catches peo-

ple off guard. The mouths of the crowds drop open and they gape awestruck. But leaders of the old order mount fateful resistance to the new, and the noise of conflict clangs loudly through the following chapters of the Gospel (11:1—16:20), even as these same chapters with ever greater clarity and insistence reveal the true nature of Jesus' authority as meek and lowly servant (11:25-30; 12:18-21), yet greater than temple or Sabbath (12:1-14), stronger than Satan (12:22-29), Son of God and Lord over wind and wave (14:33; 16:16).

The Deeds of the Christ (11:1-6)

1—When he had **finished instructing** (cf. 7:28) his disciples regarding the mission of the new community and obstacles lying in the way, Jesus himself marched out to teach and herald the news of the nearness of the kingdom in the cities and towns of Galilee.

2—It is not easy to see in Jesus the dawning kingdom. **John,** arrested and imprisoned (4:12; 14:3-12), is himself stunned by the contrast between the strong deliverance of his own apocalyptic vision (3:11) and the irksome weakness of his chains. He has received reports concerning **the deeds of the Christ** (cf. 11:19) and fires off a question to Jesus: **Are you he who is to come?** (3:11). In effect he asks, "If you are the irresistible liberator, why am I cooped up like a bird in a cage?"

3-5—To that poignant question Jesus responds: **Tell John what you hear** (= my words) **and see** (= my deeds): **The blind receive their sight and the lame walk, lepers are cleansed and the deaf hear, and the dead are raised up, and the poor have good news preached to them.** It is not difficult to find a paragraph in the preceding chapters to match each phrase in this sentence.

If this reply had come one chapter earlier, then Jesus would be talking exclusively about his own words and deeds. But this grand summary stands not only after chaps. 5–7 (= Jesus' words in the Sermon on the Mount) and after chaps. 8–9 (= Jesus' mighty deeds) but also and deliberately after the gift of authority and mission to the Twelve (chap. 10)—and for good reason. The words and deeds of the new community are an integral part of Jesus' reply to John and to all troubled doubters. The activities of Jesus plus the activities of the community add up to **the deeds of the Christ** (11:2), the signs of the new age. Matthew pictures the life of Jesus (words, deeds, suffering, vindication) and the life of the new community as together fulfilling the ancient hope voiced by the prophet Isaiah (Isa. 35:3-6). But it is not the mighty judgment pictured by John (3:11-12). The work of Jesus continued in the community inaugurates the new world envisioned by the prophet and, prophesied or not, is easily misunderstood (cf. 9:14-17).

6—Fully and finally **blessed** (5:3-11) are all who take **no offense** (cf. 15:12) at Jesus or his envoys. And the disciples of John **went away,** presumably satisfied. The awful tension between faith and offense will dominate this section of Matthew's narrative, and will continue in the world and in the church as long as both endure.

More Than a Prophet (11:7-15)

7—John had raised a question, and now Jesus uses John as he asks the crowd three times, **What did you go out into the wilderness** (3:1) **to behold?** What was it that began to stir and quicken hope within them? **A reed shaken by the wind,** bending to every shifting breeze?

8—**A man clothed in soft raiment,** his rich attire the badge of his wealth and status (Luke 16:19; James 2:2)? No, that is not what fascinated the multitudes. It was the way John stood, hard as granite, despising the whirlwind. It was precisely because his garment was not silken but rough camel's hair (3:9) and because he did not lounge as guest at the king's table but ate locusts in the desert and ended up in the king's dungeon. Precisely because of his simplicity and independence and fearlessness the crowds loved him.

9—**Why then did you go out? To see a prophet?** The crowds suspected that much about John (14:5; 21:26) and would later say the same of Jesus (21:11,46). But Jesus does more than confirm their hunches and congratulate them on their admiration of John and openness to him (10:41). He begins to challenge them to draw conclusions for their own lives and well being. **Yes, I tell you,** John is even **more than a prophet,** more than one additional voice in the illustrious chorus of prophetic and countercultural voices. He is the seal of the prophets, himself the fulfillment of prophecy, sent by God to prepare Messiah's way (see commentary on 3:3; 17:9-13; cf. Mal. 3:1).

11—The crowds had high expectations, yet John exceeds all that. Jesus heaps on John the most extravagant praise, inviting comparison not with prophets only but with emperors and kings, poets and priests, builders and sages. He draws a stunning conclusion: Of all human beings who ever saw the light of day, **no one** is **greater than John the Baptist.**

But Jesus is not teaching a doctrine about John. Suddenly he declares that for all John's incomparable greatness, any one in the crowd could be **greater than he.** John was great because he had looked at the face of Jesus and knew what he was seeing: the drawing near of the kingdom (see on 3:2). Yet John stood only on the threshold. The kingdom dawns only after John's ministry, with the ministry and death and resurrection of Jesus. The new world is now beginning to crack open and **the least** who steps across the threshold and dwells **in the kingdom of heaven** under the authority of the crucified and resurrected Jesus is **greater than John,** who heralded the kingdom but did not know the resurrection and the presence of the exalted Jesus.

12—**The kingdom of heaven** does not creep into the old world quietly like the dawn of a peaceful day. From the moment John first announced it (3:2), it has **suffered violence.** It has collided head-on with the old world. Before John's name ever appeared in this Gospel, worldly power had already unleashed its violence to subdue, if possible, the threat posed by the coming king (2:16-18). John will feel the full weight of the old world's wrath (14:3-12), as will Jesus also. The kingdom makes its way neither automatically nor easily but only in the midst of agony and struggle (10:16-23). That is one reason the crowds hold back, admiring John's courage but fearful themselves. **Men of violence,** people like the Herods and Pilate who are committed to tactics of power, and other guardians of the old order who may not think of themselves as violent types, **take it by force,** lay seige to it, oppose it actively.

13-14—The theme of vv. 10-11 is repeated. Before John the whole world lived in a state of anticipation, straining toward the future. **All the prophets and the law** (13:17; cf. 5:17) **prophesied,** sighing and groaning for the new world. But after John, the kingdom. John is the great hinge of history, the end of the old, the beginning of the new. He is the long awaited **Elijah** (16:14; 17:3-4, 10-13; 27:47, **36**—49), immediate forerunner of the Lord (3:4).

15—Therefore the only adequate response to John is not admiration but a venture of faith into the kingdom he heralded. **He who has ears to hear, let him hear** (13:9).

Children in the Market Place (11:16-19)

16-17—The crowds were stirred, but as a whole, **this generation** does not really **hear** (v. 15) what John announces and does **take offense** (v. 6). Jesus utters a parable. **This generation is like children,** all moody and fickle, **calling to their playmates:** If we say, Let's play wedding games, you refuse. If we say, Then let's do the opposite and play funeral games, you still refuse. Or, closer to the original: **We piped** a wedding tune, **and you did not dance. We wailed** a funeral dirge, **and you did not mourn.**

18-19—John and Jesus came yoked as heralds of the one kingdom, but as different in style as funerals and weddings. John came fasting with a call to repentance (9:14), and they thought him mad, possessed by a demon, obsessed with discipline, impossibly ascetic.

The Son of man (8:20) **came eating and drinking.** In fact, he came feasting, inviting to joy (9:14-15), and they recoiled as from a **glutton and drunkard,** a keeper of bad company, definitely not spiritual. As a whole, **this generation** finds fault with both, takes offense at both, and so evades the call of both.

But public opinion is no reliable guide. The crowds (and the readers) are summoned to ponder Jesus' **deeds** in the light of prophecy. Seen in that light, they are **the deeds of the Christ** (v. 2), and they are the **deeds** of **wisdom** (v. 19). His deeds testify that Jesus is **Christ,** agent of God for establishing the kingdom of God, and they point to him as the incarnation of heavenly **wisdom** (*Sophia*, cf. 11:28-30; 23:34-39). As **Christ** (11:2), **Son of man** (11:19) and **wisdom** (11:19), Jesus inaugurates the new age, speaks God's verdicts of blessing and woe, and reveals mysteries long hidden.

Woe to You, Chorazin (11:20-24)

The words and deeds of Jesus (and of the new community) are the thunder and lightning of the promised age (11:2-5). That world has come as final blessing (11:6). But what if ears do not hear (11:15)? Jesus turns from beatitude and wooing to stern warning and woe (11:20-24).

20—First, the announcement of the theme: Jesus began to scold **the cities where most of his mighty works had been done, because they did not repent.** What cities? Three are named: **Chorazin and Bethsaida** in a first woe, and then **Capernaum** in a second and parallel woe. All three are thoroughly Jewish settlements of the Galilee, and are contrasted in what follows with despised and notorious Gentile cities. In the immediately preceding chapter Jesus focused the mission of his disciples on Israel, even commanding them to avoid Gentile territory (10:5-6), but now his own mission efforts are leading him to reword the contrast between Israel and the nations.

21-22—**Chorazin and Bethsaida** examined themselves and found only life. They knew the prophets, they had rushed into the wilderness to see John, and Jesus had walked in their streets and done miracles there. How privileged they were. How different from pagan cities headed for destruction, cities like **Tyre and Sidon** (Isaiah 23; Ezekiel 26–28; but see Matt. 15:21-28). They felt blessed but Jesus cried, **Woe.** Woe is a dirge, a lament for the dead. Precisely because **Chorazin and Bethsaida** were so highly privileged, their failure to repent will count heavily against them **on the day of judgment** (cf. 10:15).

23-24—**Capernaum** could boast that it was Jesus' own city, place of his dwelling and hub of his work reaching into all Galilee and the surrounding region (4:13; 8:5). Surely this city will be **exalted to heaven,** but Jesus warns, **You shall be brought down to Hades.** Again, not blessing but woe (cf. Isa. 14:13-15). People of that generation spat out the name **Sodom,** emblem of everything evil and perverse. Heaven's wrath came down hard on Sodom (Genesis 19; Isa. 1:9-10) but **it will be more tolerable** for Sodom than for Capernaum **on the day of judgment.** Those cities of Galilee, smug and secure (11:23; contrast 9:36), admired Jesus' deeds but felt no call to repent (cf. 3:9).

Come to Me (11:25-30)

Here at the end of the chapter, all brooding over opposition is banished, woes cease, and ecstatic joy holds the field. For the sake of the readers, puzzled at the rejection Jesus met and still meets, Matthew paints a picture of Jesus in the intimacy of private prayer (cf. 26:39, 42).

25-26—At that time, in the very teeth of rejection, Jesus neither complains nor despairs but instead voices high thanksgiving, praising God as **Father** (6:9) and **Lord of heaven and earth** (6:10), caring sovereign of the universe of all things and all beings, seen and unseen.

Jesus discerns the divine plan in the way God has **hidden these things,** concealing them from the wise and understanding, from rulers and leaders of that generation and their counterparts in succeeding generations. What are **these things?** The glory of the kingdom coming through the speech and action, through the passion and exaltation of Jesus (4:17).

What is **hidden** has also been **revealed,** but mysteriously and paradoxically to **babes,** to the poor and the meek, to tax collector and sinner, to those lacking the blinders of expertise and power, to the little ones.

The theme of God's hiding and revealing of mysteries is dealt with also in other passages (10:26-27; 13:1-23, especially vv. 10-17; 13:35, 51-52; 16:17). The mysteries cannot be mastered like some problem in mathematics. The revelation has an elusive character, calling for wholehearted trust, with the result that the **wise** and self-sufficient easily miss it. God creates an astonishing constituency out of what this age counts for nothing. It pleases God to act in ways that upset hallowed human calculations. Exactly because God's plan cuts across ordinary expectations, it often gives the appearance of no plan at all.

27—What has God revealed to babes? And what has been hidden from the worldly wise? The content of the revelation is here spelled out in words extraordinarily like those of the so-called Great Commission (28:18-20). **All things have been delivered to me by my Father,** says Jesus. He boldly declares that the incomparable intimacy of human parent with human child is a parable of his own relation with God. Elsewhere Jesus' theme is the kingdom of heaven (4:17) but here the theme is the deep, mutual, shared connection between God as **Father** and Jesus as **Son.** And that intimacy, that connectedness, that familial relationship, that sharing in divine life, is mediated to others by Jesus as Christ (v. 2) and wisdom (v. 19) and Son (v. 27).

28—Jesus has spoken of Father and Son, and we might expect as climax a word about the Spirit in the church, but instead Jesus cries, **Come to me.** This **me** is the Jesus of the Galilean ministry, but even more the crucified and resurrected Jesus now wearing the mantle of all authority in heaven and earth.

Jesus issues his summons to **all who labor and are heavy laden.** These are the **babes,** innocent of education in matters legal and religious (v. 25), the people named unexpectedly as God's beneficiaries in the Beatitudes (5:3-9), the sheep left defenseless by the shepherds (9:36), women and men upon whom political and religious leaders have heaped burdens without lifting a finger to help bear the load (23:4), people held prisoner in the house of the strong man Beelzebul (12:22-29).

John foresaw axe and fire (3:10) and Jesus himself had spoken of sword (10:34), but here Jesus invites to God's own **rest** or refreshing. The weekly Sabbath was a joyous parable of the final **rest,** when the universe will lay aside its aching burdens to enjoy God's unveiled presence, refreshing and enlivening creation (12:43; Rev. 14:13). Jesus' summons to enjoy God's **rest** will be followed in chap. 12 by two healings on the Sabbath, the day of rest. Those healings underscore the truth of Jesus' extravagant promise. He has come to bestow God's **rest,** nothing less than new life in God's new world.

29—But what does it mean to **come** to Jesus? Jesus restates the invitation in two fresh images: **Take my yoke** and **learn from me.** What **yoke** is this? Actual yokes of wood and iron were laid on the necks and shoulders of oxen and other draft animals, on prisoners of war and on slaves. The **yoke** was a familiar symbol for subjugation, slavery, bondage, oppression, burden bearing. In some contexts, however, the **yoke** carries the positive sense of being harnessed to God in the joy of obedient life. So Torah personified as Lady Wisdom (cf. 11:19) invites the people of Israel to take her yoke upon their necks (Sirach 51:23-27; 6:24-31; 24:33). Rabbis spoke of reciting the Shema and of performing God's ordinances as the act of taking upon oneself the yoke of God, the yoke of Torah, the yoke of the kingdom of heaven (Mishnah, *Berakoth* 2:2).

The image of the yoke is followed by another: **Learn from me,** be schooled by me, be apprenticed to me (cf. 13:52). The word behind **learn** (*mathete*) is a cousin of the Greek words for "disciple" (*mathētēs*) and "make disciples" (*mathēteusate*, 28:19). And so Jesus in effect is summoning women and men to **come** and **take** up the **yoke** of discipleship, trusting that he is neither tyrant nor oppressor. Indeed he says, **I am gentle and lowly in heart.** The word behind **gentle** (*praüs*) is in its two other appearances in Matthew translated as "meek" (5:5) and "humble" (21:5; cf. 2 Cor. 10:4). The three passages illumine one another. Jesus approached Jerusalem mounted on an ass and on a colt, the foal of an ass, entering the city not with the arrogance of the conqueror but with the humility of the servant, ready to **take** his cross and suffer in his body the almighty indifference of tyrants. All who **take** his yoke will find **rest** and renewal. They may worry that they will lose their lives but he assures them that they will find their lives (10:38-39) and will inherit the earth (5:5).

30—Discipleship is both **yoke** and **burden,** yet it neither oppresses nor crushes. Because it means being yoked to God's Son (v. 27), to his indestructible life, to his majestic and surpassing authority, to Jesus once crushed under foot but now highly exalted, it is **easy** and it is **light.**

The Kingdom Has Come upon You (12:1-50)

Matthew 12 is full of terrible conflicts: opposition to Jesus intensifies as Pharisees begin to debate with Jesus directly (12:1-8). Previously, scribes and Pharisees have criticized Jesus among themselves (9:3-4), questioned Jesus' disciples (9:10-11), or rebuked the crowds (9:32-34). Now they speak to Jesus directly and begin to rebuke him for offending their convictions about the will of God, and they depart to plot his death (12:14). By the end of the chapter they are painted as representatives of "this evil generation" (vv. 39, 41, 42, 45).

Greater Than the Temple (12:1-8)

1—**At that time** connects what follows with Jesus' promise of rest and his assurance that the burden of discipleship is light (11:28-30). Jesus walked through fields of grain **on the sabbath,** the day of rest. His disciples **were hungry and began to pluck ears of grain,** rub them in their palms, puff on them to blow away the chaff and to **eat.** They were breaking the law by doing what amounted to reaping, threshing and winnowing, 3 of the 39 classes of works (40 minus 1) expressly forbidden on the Sabbath (Mishnah, *Shabbath* 7:2).

2-3—Pharisees rebuke Jesus for tolerating unlawful behavior in his disciples, but Jesus defends their action with three arguments. In the first, **David** and **those who were with him** parallel **Jesus** and **his disciples.** The disciples **were hungry** as David had been **hungry.** David entered the house of God, the old sanctuary at Nob before even the temple stood in Jerusalem, and he **ate the bread of the Presence.** Strictly speaking, that was **not lawful** for David **nor for those who were with him but only for the priests.** Scripture in telling David's story (1 Sam. 21:1-6) says nothing of his incurring guilt before God. If he remains blameless, how much more may great David's greater Son, the Messiah (1:1), eat together with his companions!

Here Matthew differs slightly from Mark in two respects. Mark names Abiathar as priest of the sanctuary. According to 1 Samuel, it was Ahimelech. Matthew simply omits the priest's name altogether. Furthermore, Matthew stresses that the disciples were hungry, not simply to make more explicit the parallel with David, but to name a circumstance that begs for more than mere conformity to old rules.

5-6—Jesus' second argument builds on the mention of priests and sanctuary in the first. **Priests in the temple** actually **profane the sabbath** every week as they continue their appointed works in the temple without interruption even on the Sabbath. Priests exchange old loaves of the Presence for new (Lev. 24:8), and they actually offer double the usual daily amount of lambs and flour on the Sabbath (Num. 28:9-10).

Priests continue their services because the greatness of the temple overrides the law against working on the Sabbath. Temple is greater than law, and **something greater than the temple is here.** What is this **something?** God and the kingdom of God are present in Jesus, in his mission, in his community (1:23; 12; 28; cf. 4:17; 10:7). If priests serving the temple may break the Law, how much more may the disciples of Jesus!

7—Finally and fundamentally, Jesus' critics fail to understand **mercy,** its excellence, its incomparable greatness, dearer to the heart of God even than the law of **sacrifice** (9:13; cf. Hos. 6:6). Lacking this key to Scripture and God's will, they are doomed to misunderstand Jesus and to condemn his **guiltless** disciples. They remain experts only in binding burdens, not in lifting them (23:4; cf. 11:28-30).

8—If only they understood the prophets, they would also know that **the Son of man** (8:20) with his gentle yoke of mercy is greater than the rules governing the sabbath. He is **Lord of the sabbath,** both in the sense that he has authority to break through the old Sabbath rules but even more in the sense that he opens wide the door to the final sabbath of God, the promised rest (11:28-29).

Stretch Out Your Hand (12:9-14)

9-10—That same Sabbath Jesus **entered their synagogue** (see the comments on 4:23), where both Jesus and his critics are confronted with conflicting demands. The **sabbath** presses on them its hallowed obligations of the Law, and the body of **a man with a withered hand** cries silently for an act of healing. **Phariseess** (12:2) already have revealed a failure to embrace mercy as their guiding principle (12:7). For them the obligation to sanctify the Sabbath weighs more heavily. Again they do not lift burdens. Mercy must wait for another day. They press Jesus for his decision, suspecting they will be rewarded with confirmation of his carelessness toward the Sabbath in particular and the Law in general. They pose a terrible question: **Is it lawful to heal on the sabbath?**

11—Jesus replies with a homely observation. What does a man do if his **one sheep falls into a pit?** Sabbath or not, the farmer seizes that sheep and hauls it out, and he does so without incurring guilt. The Law as interpreted by rabbis permitted doing something to help an animal help itself, while the stricter Essenes allowed no aid on the Sabbath (Zadokite Document 11:13-14). But whatever the Law says, instinctively the farmer rushes to help his stricken animal. If they pity a sheep, **how much more** should they show mercy to a human being (cf. 6:26; 10:31). **So it is lawful,** not offensive to God, but pleasing not to do just any kind of work but **to do good on the sabbath.**

13-14—So Jesus celebrates the gift of the Sabbath by healing the man, so that his hand was **restored, whole like the other.** And, terrible irony, the opponents of Jesus on that festival of rest and wholeness, on that day devoted to celebrating the gift of life, **took counsel against him how to destroy him** (cf. 2:13), how to kill the one whose very name means life and wholeness and salvation (1:21; cf. Acts 3:14-15). In denying the priority of mercy, they make themselves instruments of death and destruction, in spite of their piety.

He Will Not Cry Aloud (12:15-21)

This paragraph, featuring the longest of Matthew's special quotations (see the comments on 1:22), sums up several themes of chaps. 10–12. In his mission to God's ancient people in villages and towns of Galilee, in synagogues and on the Sabbath, Jesus provokes stubborn opposition, and he begins to speak generously of infamous pagan cities. God's incursion into the world is hidden from the wise and revealed to babes (10:26-27; 11:25). Insiders (like his family and the leaders of Israel) misunderstand, while outsiders (like the cities of Tyre and Sidon and Sodom) begin to enter the discussion as more likely to repent and believe (11:21-23). The downward movement of Jesus, opposed by his own people, and his quietly turning in blessing to the Gentiles (cf. 4:14-16) is all foreseen in Scripture.

15-16—In the face of stony opposition, **Jesus withdrew** quietly. **Many followed him,** namely, the ill and the broken, the laboring and heavy laden, **and he healed them all** (see the comments on 8:16). And then he solemnly commanded them that they **not make him known.**

His withdrawal and silence are emblems not of fear or weakness but of spiritual power (cf. 26:63; 27:14). Again Matthew uses Scripture to interpret events in Jesus' ministry.

17-18—The quotation is an odd translation of Isa. 42:1-4, designed to echo the narratives of Jesus' baptism in chap. 3 and of Jesus' prayer in chap. 11: (1) Jesus is God's **servant** or child (cf. 8:5-13), equivalent of "beloved son" (3:17; cf. 11:25). (2) God has **chosen** him and is **pleased** with him (3:17; 11:26). (3) The **Spirit** of the Lord rests upon him (3:16; cf. 10:20; 12:28).

His inspired task is to **proclaim justice to the Gentiles** (contrast 10:5-6) and that does not mean subduing them with force of arms but bringing them the grace of God's salvation.

19-20—**He will not wrangle or cry aloud,** will not lapse into debating nor trade insults. He moves forward on the path ordained for him, not snapping but healing the **bruised reed,** not quenching but rekindling the **smoldering wick.** For broken bodies and battered spirits his gentle presence (11:28-30) is mercy and life.

He will work on the Sabbath and on other days, with opposition or without, **till he brings justice to victory. Justice** (*krisis*) elsewhere is praised by Jesus as one member of a precious trio (justice, mercy, and fidelity) neglected by his critics (23:23). **Justice** is also closely allied with righteousness and as such is a hallmark of the new age (6:33).

21—Jesus' own family and his own cities may be offended at him (11:6; 12:46-50) but **in his name will the Gentiles hope** (v. 17; 10:18; 28:19). Jesus in meekness (11:29) lifts burdens and heals brokenness and therefore is hope of all peoples, desire of nations.

The Kingdom of God Has Come upon You (12:22-32)

22—Matthew compresses the most astonishing day of a man's entire life into a single sentence: **A blind and dumb demoniac was brought to him, and he healed him, so that the dumb man spoke and saw.**

Not one extra word, no lingering on the poignancy of the moment of confrontation between Jesus and this poor wretch locked in the prison of his double or triple illness. No reading of his mind, or of the hopes of family or friends. Matthew races through the healing and then his real story begins. The miracle of Jesus sends sparks flying.

23-24—The crowds of people around Jesus **were amazed** and found themselves wondering, **Can this be the Son of David?** (9:27). **But,** and that is a strong word and a sad word, **but the Pharisees** (12:2, 14), presented as leaders of the people, viewed the matter in an altogether different light. Not Son of David, not Messiah, not fulfiller of the hopes of God's burdened people, not servant of the Lord (12:17-21), not God's agent at all but the lackey and servant of Satan. To the people they say, **It is only by Beelzebul, the prince of demons, that this man casts out demons** (9:34; 10:25).

25-26—**Knowing their thoughts,** Jesus responds with argument and warning. First a simple parable. **Every kingdom divided against itself** by civil war or internal strife is easy prey to external enemies and is soon **laid waste.** Likewise, **no city or house divided against itself will stand.** It is patently ridiculous to imagine that Jesus' war on the demons has the backing of the prince of demons. The Pharisees should know that, and they should be rejoicing that Jesus by his exorcisms is striking the foundations of the evil empire.

27—Disciples of the Pharisees, whom Jesus calls their **sons,** the members of their spiritual family (cf. 12:46-50), practice exorcisms (cf. Acts 19:13; Tobit 8:1-5; Josephus, *Ant.* 8:45-49; *War* 7:185).

28—Jesus puts to his critics the hard question of the source of his authority (cf. 21:23). What if it is not by Beelzebul? What **if it is by the Spirit of God** (v. 18) **that I cast out demons?** If the kingdom of Satan is suffering defeat, only one power can be credited: **the kingdom of God** (cf. 19:24; 21:31,43). Here it is quite fitting that the usual "kingdom of the heavens" (3:2) is replaced by **the kingdom of God,** since the latter makes clear that the choice is between Beelzebul and God.

The kingdom is not simply nearing the gates (3:2; 4:17; 10:7), but it **has come upon you,** has arrived and is active in your midst. This is the strongest statement in Matthew's Gospel that the kingdom is not just a future hope but in some sense already is a present fact.

29—Another parable. Anyone planning to rob **a strong man's house** better be sure he **binds the strong man.** Then he can move from room to room and plunder his goods. Jesus by his exorcisms is freeing people from Satan's rule. He is plundering Satan's goods, and that implies that Jesus has already tied up Satan in knots. Jesus really is the one prophesied by John: the stronger one (3:11), not Satan's servant but Satan's conquerer (4:11).

30—The final battle is joined, and as in any total war, with two kingdoms locked in mortal combat, whoever is **not with me is against me.** Or, changing the image, whoever does not work with Jesus to **gather** the sheep and **gather** the harvest (9:36-38) is guilty of **scattering** (cf. John 11:52).

31-32—If those Pharisees had merely scratched their heads and fixed on Jesus an uncomprehending stare, their situation would not have been so grave. But in their conceit they believed they had penetrated his cover and grasped his secret. They pointed to the power welling up in Jesus and called it evil. That, said Jesus, is **blasphemy against the Spirit** and **will not be forgiven.** Jesus has come to rescue from sin (1:21; 26:28) and the new community is called to be endlessly forgiving (chap. 18). Indeed, **every sin and blasphemy** (9:3), even speaking **against the Son of man** (8:20), **will be forgiven.** But to storm against the Holy Spirit and rage against the power of the coming age means bricking oneself up in a terrible prison of one's own making.

The Tree and Its Fruit (12:33-37)

33-34—Negative verdicts on Jesus lead to a paragraph of sharp warning. The words of the Pharisees are **bad fruit** from a **bad tree** (cf. 7:16-20). Or, to change the image, those critics are a **brood of vipers** (3:7; 23:33), and their mouths drip venom.

35—Words proceed from the **heart** and lay bare the secret of the inner being (15:17-20). The **heart,** and here now is a third image in rapid succession, is like a treasury. **The good man out of his good treasure brings forth good** (cf. 13:52), **and the evil man out of his evil treasure brings forth evil.**

36-37—**On the day of judgment** (10:15) people will be called to account for their speech, their good and evil words, those revelations of the heart, their denials or confessions of God and of Jesus as agent of the power and Spirit of God (cf. 10:32-33).

Confessors will be **justified,** embraced by the heavenly judge, while blasphemers (v. 31) will be **condemned.**

The Sign of Jonah (12:38-42).

38-39—Some of the scribes and Pharisees (19:2; 5:20) requested a **sign** (16:1), some bit of unambiguous proof that Jesus really is the agent of the Holy Spirit of God and not the tool of the unholy spirit of Beelzebul. What exactly would satisfy their requirement is not specified. People inside the church as well as those outside have been fascinated with miracles from the beginning, impressed with them as signs of the presence of God. But Jesus rejects their demand as a symptom of an evil and adulterous generation (11:16), actively impious and void of simple trust in God.

The only **sign** they will be given is **the sign of the prophet Jonah. As Jonah was three days and three nights in the belly of the whale, so will the Son of man** (8:20; 12:32) **be three days and three nights in the heart of the earth.** The **sign** is either Jesus' passion and weakness, bringing him down to the grave, or perhaps the mute and ambiguous evidence of his empty tomb. In any case, Jesus will not provide the kind of powerful and overwhelming signal which skeptics demand.

41-42—Confronted with the wisdom and **preaching of Jonah,** fresh from his watery tomb, the people of **Nineveh repented** (cf. 4:17). The cities of Galilee have not repented (11:20), even though **something greater than Jonah is here.** Days are coming when God will rip the stone from Jesus' grave and lift Jesus to unparalleled authority. And then the same leaders who here demand a sign will, once it is granted, try to suppress it and will spread the story that grave-robbing emptied his tomb (28:11-15).

Chapter 12 is full of comparisons. John is a prophet and more. He is greatest of humans, yet any child in the kingdom is greater than he. Jesus and the kingdom are greater than the temple (12:6), greater than Jonah (12:41), greater than Solomon (12:42). And the critics of Jesus and the cities of Galilee are less. Less responsive than pagan Nineveh, less faithful than **the queen of the south** who **came from the ends of the earth to hear the wisdom of Solomon** (1 Kings 10:1-13).

The Last State Worse Than the First (12:43-45)

43-45—When the unclean spirit has gone out of a man, it seeks new quarters (8:31). Finding none, it returns to its old dwelling delighted to discover it clean, orderly, and above all, unoccupied. It moves right back in with a horde of evil cronies and **the last state of that man becomes worse than the first.** These things are a parable of **this evil generation** (cf. v. 39). Jesus' march through Galilee has broken the grip of demons and signaled the presence of the kingdom of God. But if people of this generation do not take him to heart, bend to his yoke, follow him, enter the new community, become filled with new energies, they will not merely miss an opportunity. They will put themselves in terrible jeopardy.

That word stands as sober warning, not to cities of Galilee only, but to the new community. Readers are challenged to thrust hands into their bosoms and make sure they are alive and filled with the powers of the new age.

Brother, Sister, Mother (12:46-50)

46—Jesus is told that **his mother and his brothers stood outside,** wishing to speak with him.

48-50—But the coming of the kingdom redefines insiders and outsiders and the meaning of family (10:34-39). Jesus stetches his hand toward his disciples and says, **Here are my mother and my brothers! Whoever does the will of my Father in heaven** (7:21) is my family. In this context the **will** of God means being a disciple, grasping in simple trust the secret of the Father and the Son (11:25-27), acting on the great invitation and accepting Jesus' yoke (11:28-30).

At this point in the narrative only the disciples are clearly on Jesus' side. The position of the crowds (12:46) remains ambiguous, and their final verdict on Jesus is in doubt. Will they join the disciples? Or will they be persuaded by the old religious authorities and go away? They gather about Jesus to hear his parables (13:2; 14:13).

■ THIRD DISCOURSE: The New Community Brings Forth Things New and Old in Its Teaching (13:1-58)

Preceding chapters have announced two conflicting truths about Jesus. (1) He is the unique Son of God (3:17; 11:25-27) and agent of God chosen to establish the kingdom of God (12:28). (2) However, powerful enemies oppose him and will not be satisfied with anything less than his death (9:34; 11:12; 12:24).

Divine affirmation and human opposition stand in awful contrast, Jesus and his very imperfect disciples on the one side, religious leaders on the other. The crowds are caught in the middle. What will they do? How can the question even arise? If Jesus really is the Son of God, how can it happen that he is not always and everywhere persuasive? How is it that he does not easily take every heart captive under his authority?

Furthermore, chap. 13 is the third of Jesus' five discourses, and it is not unrelated to the one preceding it (chap. 10). That earlier discourse is outspoken and grim in its forecast of hostility lying in wait for the new community as it pursues its mission in the world. In fact, rejection and persecution, abuse and division seem to be very nearly the sole results of the mission. That reaction of the world is dismaying and puzzling.

Chapter 13 replies to questions and puzzles posed by preceding chapters, and part of the response may be sketched here: Jesus really is the fulfiller of prophecy, and his appearing renders his disciples more blessed than ancient prophets and righteous ones (vv. 16-17), even though his identity remains hidden and his authority may fail to impress. His followers must banish the notion that God's plan is in any way deficient, even when the present working and future climax of that plan remain veiled from sight. Jesus summons hearers to seize the kingdom, despising tribulation or persecution, ignoring ridicule or any other cost, for the kingdom is supremely worth possessing.

One reason disciples or crowds are puzzled by the course of history is the failure to understand that Satan also sows bad seeds in the world.

All those who receive the good seed of the word of the kingdom proclaimed by Jesus and understand it are described as citizens of the kingdom (v. 38) and righteous (vv. 43, 49). On the other hand, weeds also spring up and flourish alongside the wheat in the kingdom. They closely resemble the righteous and live in the community with them but are in reality citizens of an evil empire (v. 38), and they are described as causing others to stumble (11:6) and as doing deeds of lawlessness (v. 41; cf. 7:23).

At the close of the age the righteous will shine like the sun in the kingdom of their Father (v. 43), while the evil will weep and gnash their teeth (vv. 42, 50).

So the parables focus relentlessly on what God is doing in the world through the ministry of Jesus and on the choices set before people right now.

A Sower Went Out (13:1-9)

1—The opening phrase, **that same day,** links the parables of chap. 13 with the immediately preceding chapters, full of conflict. So it is with the smoke of controversy hanging in the air that **Jesus went out.**

2—In spite of the mounting opposition on the part of the leaders, great crowds continue to press about Jesus, hanging on his words. He stepped from the shore to a **boat,** and signaling his intention to teach, he **sat** (5:1) and began to speak **in parables** (cf. v. 10).

3—**A sower went out to sow** (cf. Mark 4:1-9; Luke 8:4-8; Gospel of Thomas 19; John 12:24). The repetition of the verb **went out** (13:1, 3) draws attention to parallels between Jesus in his ministry and the sower in the parable.

Three kinds of loss are balanced against three forms of abundance, as a result of the sower's work: **some seeds** are devoured by birds (v. 4), some are scorched by the sun (vv. 5-6) and some are choked by thorns (v. 7). **But other seeds fell on good soil and brought forth grain** not merely abundantly (tenfold) but downright spectacularly: **a hundredfold,** and **sixty,** and **thirty** (v. 8)!

The sower **went out,** and sowers continue to go out, knowing full well that much seed will be destroyed by one hazard or another. That sowers persist in going out, season after season, is a tribute not to their ignorance nor to sheer stubbornness but to their confidence in the processes of nature and in nature's Lord.

By speaking of a harvest of such astonishing proportions, Jesus shares his confidence in God's eventual total triumph over all opposition, of victory beyond all present loss, of glory on the far side of pain. The parable is thus a response to the misunderstanding and plain rejection Jesus has been suffering at the hands of crowds (11:12, 16-19), Galilean cities (11:20-24), and religious leaders (12:24). At the same time the parable raises questions: Are some people good soil and others not? Does the sower share any blame for the differing results? Is the sower using good seed? (See the comments on 13:24-30.)

9—He who has ears, let him hear! is a phrase similar to those used to call for careful study of Scripture in ancient times. Jesus applies the phrase to his own words, marking them as at once difficult and vital.

Blessed Are Your Eyes (13:10-17)

10—Privately the **disciples** put a hard question: **Why do you speak to them,** to the crowds, **in parables?** Why not use plain unvarnished speech? And they get a hard answer. Everything seems to hinge on the fact that **parable** can mean either an extended comparison or a riddle.

11—**To you** disciples, says Jesus, **it has been given** (namely, by God, 11:25; 16:17) **to know the secrets** (*ta mystēria*) **of the kingdom of heaven,** to understand God's puzzling strategy, to see that the kingdom of God is breaking into the world through this Jesus, who contradicts expectations every bit as much as he fulfills them. But **to them,** to many people of privilege and power and piety, **it has not been given.** God simply has not gotten through to them. They have been offended or disappointed or puzzled rather than gladdened and satisfied (5:6) at the appearing of Jesus.

And what are the puzzles, the **secrets?** That the kingdom comes with such meekness and weakness, that Jesus who breaks the Law is agent of God's ruling, that Gentiles and outcasts are included.

12—Jesus has addressed the crowds in the Sermon on the Mount (chaps. 5–7) and has displayed deeds of power and mercy in their cities (chaps. 8–9). All these words and acts were plain and public, and yet the response was mixed (ch. 11-12).

If at this time the crowds shake off the influence of their leaders

171

and recognize Jesus as God's Son and giver of ultimate rest (11:25-30), then from now on to them **will more be given.** But if the deep truth of Jesus' words and deeds so far has eluded them, then even what they have **will be taken away,** as they find themselves increasingly at odds with him. The saying is repeated in 25:29 where it stands as a spur to the faithful to use their privilege wisely.

13-15—Talking in **parables,** on top of words and deeds that already strike many hearers as a thicket of riddles, is Jesus' way of warning the masses that they are playing with fire. If they do not **see** or **hear** or **understand** the meaning of the presence of Jesus, if all his words and deeds seem dark, then his parables are warning and accusation: the crowds will turn out to be the generation pictured by the prophet Isaiah (6:9-10), people whose **heart has grown dull,** whose **ears are heavy of hearing,** whose **eyes** are **closed,** so that there is scarcely a chance that they will **perceive** or **hear** or **understand** and **turn** for God **to heal them.**

The use of this particular prophecy accomplishes two other things: it reminds readers that the word of the Lord always wages an uphill battle in the world, and it shows that God's purpose is fulfilled even in people's resistance.

16—Upon disciples, however, Jesus utters a beatitude (5:3; 11:4-6), **Blessed are your eyes, for they see, and your ears, for they hear** (cf. Luke 10:23-24). The disciples are the ones who have, in the words of Isaiah's prophecy, seen and heard and understood. They have turned or repented and have been touched by God's healing. Beginning in this chapter, Matthew portrays the disciples as those who **understand** Jesus (13:23, 51; 16:12; 17:13). At times they have only little faith (8:26), but in contrast to Mark's far less flattering portrait, the disciples in Matthew are never totally without faith. For example, note how Mark in 4:13 and especially 8:18 lumps the disciples together with the crowds as lacking in faith and sight; also compare Matt. 14:33 with Mark 6:51-52.

17—Jesus underscores his words with a solemn introduction: **Truly, I say to you** (5:18; cf. 5:22), **many prophets and righteous** ones yearned to see and hear what has been granted to the disciples: the experience of the nearness of the kingdom in the ministry of Jesus. The description of the ancient community of hope as consisting of **prophets and righteous** (not "prophets and kings," as in Luke 10:24; but cf. Luke 1:6; 2:25; 23:50-51) has a parallel in 12:41-42, where Jesus speaks of the "prophet" Jonah and of the "wisdom" of Solomon, since biblical wisdom is the teaching of righteousness. In Matthew's view, the gifts of prophecy and righteousness are marks of the new community as of the old. Indeed, Matthew everywhere warns against prophecy that has broken the vital connection with righteousness (7:15-23).

Hear the Parable (13:18-23)

The word of the kingdom is proclaimed openly to all. But as **the parable of the sower** indicates, that word experiences both total failure and astonishing success. Some people lose it immediately (v. 19), like seed **along the path** trodden under foot. Others fall away **when tribulation or persecution** arises (cf. 10:23-24; 24:9). Others begin well enough, but **cares of the world** (worries of the poor, 6:25-32) or **delight in riches** (the worries of the wealthy, 6:19-21) eventually choke the word, so that it proves unfruitful and bears nothing.

23—Nevertheless, some seed falls on **good soil.** Here now is a thumbnail sketch of a disciple: one who **hears the word** of the kingdom and **understands** it (13:13, 19, 51). One who holds fast the word (v. 19; cf. 4:4), trusts God and lives joyfully in spite of tribulation (v. 21; 4:6-7), caring more for God than all earthly treasures (v. 22; 4:8-10; 6:19-32). One who with the prophets and the righteous longs for the full unveiling of the sweet mysteries of the kingdom (13:17; 6:33). Such a one is blessed (v. 16) and **bears fruit** (7:16-20; 12:33).

Or should we see in the parable a portrait of Jesus? Called and chosen by the word from heaven, he holds fast that word, living with simple trust and joy under pressure of rejection, obeying God all the way to the cross, caring nothing for his own security, thus bearing much fruit (cf. John 12:24).

Is the parable so hard? Is it really an enigma? Every word is plain, the entire matter simple, provided only that people hear in Jesus' words the voice of God and see in Jesus' deeds the dawning of the kingship of God (11:2-6). If that is missing, then his Sabbath-breaking is irresponsible, his claim of sonship blasphemy, his death deserved, his resurrection a hoax, and the call to discipleship in the post-Easter church is a summons to masochism or suicide.

His Enemy Sowed Weeds (13:24-30)

24—Jesus put to them **another parable** of sower, seeds, and soil. At first it appears to differ sharply from the Markan parallel, and yet the parable of the seed growing automatically (Mark 4:26-29) and the parable of the wheat and weeds (Matt. 13:24-30) have much in common, even as they differ:

1. They stand in the same relative position, after the parable of the sower and before that of the mustard seed.

2. Both focus on sowing, seed, and growth (as do the parables of sower and mustard seed).

3. They share a significant number of words beyond the words either shares with the other two seed parables:

   sleep: Mark 4:27; Matt. 13:25.

   sprout: Mark 4:27; Matt. 13:26.

   green shoot or blade: Mark 4:28; Matt. 13:26.

   wheat: Mark 4:28; Matt. 13:25,29,30.

   harvest: Mark 4:29; Matt. 13:30.

4. Both parables also are emphatic that the farmer or the servants do nothing. They take no action before the harvest.

This second seed parable addresses questions raised by the first. How can it be that any seed fails to yield? After all, is not the Son of man the sower, and is not his working invincible?

Jesus said, **The kingdom of heaven may be compared to a man who sowed good seed in his field.** Indeed, both sower and seed are **good** (cf. 19:17; 20:15).

25-26—**But his enemy came** in the still of the night and **sowed weeds,** darnel or cheat, a noxious weed, **among the wheat.** When the first blades of **wheat** pierced the soil, **weeds** at the same time raised their ugly heads.

27-28—Immediately **the man's servants** (standing for Jesus' disciples, cf. 10:24-25), betrayed a loss of confidence in the owner by questioning the quality of his seed. In Matthew's day and in every generation it takes little talent to finger members of the community who look like bad seed. Where do they come from? It is easy to lose confidence in the way God runs the universe. Why does God permit evil to grow and flourish?

The owner calmed the servants and fixed the blame squarely on **an enemy** (cf. v. 39). Then the servants wanted to rush out into the field and eradicate every last weed.

29-30—The owner restrained the servants, and again his serenity stands in sharp contrast to their confusion and nervous agitation. He commanded them to let weeds and wheat **grow together until the harvest** (v. 39). At that time, the day of judgment and division, and not before, he will direct that the weeds be bound **in bundles to be burned** as fuel for the ovens, and his **wheat** he will joyously **gather into the barn** (v. 43).

A Grain of Mustard Seed (13:31-32)

31—Jesus utters yet another agricultural parable, concentrating entirely on the potency of good seed. **The kingdom of heaven is like** one single **grain of mustard seed!**

31—**It is the smallest of all seeds** (cf. Mishnah, *Niddah* 5:2; *Tohoroth* 8:8) but it becomes **the greatest of shrubs,** a veritable tree. Then, as if to drive home the impressive size of the plant sprung from the tiny seed, Jesus exclaims, **Birds of the air come and make nests in its branches!** Those climactic words echo Ezek. 17:22-24 and its picture of the glorious kingdom to which the nations flow in pilgrimage, like birds and beasts converging on a great tree to make their home in its branches and beneath its shade (cf. Ps. 104:12; Ezek. 31:16; Dan. 4:10-22). So the bad seed will yield only weeds burned in the oven (v. 30) but the good seed, apparently insignificant and so very vulnerable, will produce a mighty kingdom at last.

Leaven (13:33)

Another parable is twin to that of the mustard seed, even though the image shifts from raising wheat to baking bread. **Leaven** or yeast is a symbol of uncleanness (16:5-12; cf. 1 Cor. 5:6-8; Gal. 5:9) and may be used here by Jesus provocatively, in reference to his ministry as despised by his contemporaries or in reference to the outcast and suspicious character of the community attracted to him (cf. 9:11).

A woman took leaven and hid it (cf. vv. 35, 44) in **three measures of meal. Three measures** (cf. Gen. 18:16) means literally around 50 pounds of flour, and that translates into bread enough to fill 100 hungry people or more. Again, as in the description of the yield in the parable of the sower (v. 8), and as in the picture of the mustard tree sheltering all the birds (v. 32), the climax of this parable is a piece of wonderful exaggeration as though to say, "Here is something extraordinary! Meditate on this!"

On the one hand, something tiny (also symbol of things despised) is hidden, and its workings are unseen. It even appears to be swallowed up. But on the other hand that small and potent leaven transforms its environment and yields a great and boisterous feasting (food for 100). At present the **kingdom** is in the small and hidden and despised stage, and many are misled into imagining that there is nothing new under the sun.

Nothing without a Parable (13:34-35)

Jesus taught **in parables, to fulfill what was spoken by the prophet** (1:22). In this case the prophet turns out to be a psalmist (78:2-4; cf. Matt. 1:7-8; 20:43-44). For Matthew everything in ancient Scripture had anticipatory and prophetic value. But why is this Psalm quoted?

Jesus' speech and action may be parabolic in the sense of being provocative and puzzling. But his words and deeds are parabolic also in the sense of explosive and revealing. Jesus fulfills the hope of the psalmist for days of revelation, for the discovering of things long hidden (the same word is in vv. 33 and 44; cf. 10:26), for the publishing of secrets (v. 11; cf. 10:26). Jesus' words are genuinely revealing, stripping away veils. His is new speech for a new day.

Explain the Parable of the Weeds (13:36-43)

36—Jesus left the crowds and went into the house. It is sometimes asserted that this is the critical turning point in the structure of the Gospel. That is an overstatement, but at the very least these words are commentary on the saying in 13:12 and they illustrate how those who have (disciples) receive more and more, while those who have not (crowds) are in danger of losing even what little they have.

For the benefit of his disciples (and readers) Jesus expands on details in **the parable of the weeds.**

37-39—The explanation opens with a little dictionary of terms. The sower is **the Son of man** (8:20) who acts on the **field** which is **the world. The good seed** producing wheat means **the sons of the kingdom,** the people of God with whom the readers identify (8:12). **The weeds are the sons of the evil one,** and **the enemy who sowed them** (v. 28) is the **devil,** great antagonist of the Son of man from the beginning (4:1-11). The **harvest** (9:37-38) is **the close of the age** and the **reapers** are **angels** (cf. v. 49).

The phrase **close of the age** (*synteleia aiōnos*) is used only in Matthew (13:39, 40, 49; 24:3; 28:20), once in combination with Jesus' future **coming** (*parousia*, 24:3).

What happens in the history of **the world** and in every historical community including the church, all the way up to **the end of the age** is presented as the result of the working both of **the Son of man** and of **the devil.** Good and evil struggle to gain mastery over people and communities. Good and evil people live cheek by jowl in human communities.

In the Jewish apocalypse known as 4 Ezra (dated around the end of the first century A.D.), the seer asks the Lord about the presence of evil in the world and receives this answer: In the beginning a single grain of bad seed was sown into Adam's heart, and it will produce evil in the world up to the end and the time of harvesting. A new age will succeed the present evil age. Then good seed beyond number will be sown, so the final harvest of good will far outweigh that of evil (4 Ezra 4:28-32). In Jesus' parable the good seed is not sown after the bad seed has been harvested but both grow together. The new age has dawned, but the old for a time continues.

40—**As weeds are gathered and burned with fire, so will it be at the close of the age.** A terrible fate is stored up for **all causes of sin,** all who cause others to stumble and fall away from God (5:19; 16:23; 18:6-7), and for **all evildoers,** literally, all doers of lawlessness (cf. 7:23).

Throughout Matthew's Gospel Jesus warns of the fiery furnace (Daniel 3) or outermost darkness, where there is weeping and gnashing of teeth (8:12; 13:50; 22:13; 24:51; 25:30; cf. 3:10, 12; 6:30).

43—On the other hand, the final state of the **righteous** (v. 17; 10:41) will be as glorious as that of the evil will be dismal. **The righteous will shine like the sun in the kingdom of their Father** (cf. Dan. 12:3; Judg. 5:31; Sirach 50:7; Matt. 17:2). The present kingdom of the Son of man (v. 41; cf. 16:28) includes both good and evil, but at the end, the kingdom of the Father (v. 43) will dawn after the Son of man has acted as lord of the harvest to exclude all doers of lawlessness (cf. 10:23; see 4:17 on the vocabulary of kingdom).

It is regularly asserted that Matthew betrays a fascination with the last things, as though his Gospel contained an abundance of the sort of material found in the book of Revelation. But out of the complex of events which according to various strands of biblical tradition will occur in the final days of world history, Matthew here focuses on one only: judgment. And he uses judgment in a particular way. He does not teach it as though his readers had never heard of it. Rather, he seizes this one piece of tradition and bends it to his teaching of righteousness.

Judgment has always meant rewards for some and punishments for others. But who gets which? People are forever drawing lines to distinguish in-groups from out-groups. Matthew says that the basis of the final decree will catch many by surprise. The standard of judgment is not ethnic, linguistic, national, geographical, or even religious. What counts are deeds as the expression of the heart's condition. It is not enough to be children of Abraham (3:9) or to know Jesus and admire and confess him (7:21) or to do miracles in his name (7:22). It is not sufficient to bear the name "sons [citizens] of the kingdom" (v. 38).

All the many judgment scenes in Matthew reveal God's own hunger and thirst for good fruit, for human deeds of righteousness and mercy and love, and God's sharp criticism of lawlessness or indifference to the needs of the neighbor (3:10; 7:23, 24-27; 13:47-50; 21:28-32; 22:11-14; and especially 25:31-46).

What finally is the secret or private teaching to the disciples in the house? It is essentially a warning to the insider against the arrogance of judging outsiders and an encouragement to make good use of the privilege of being an insider.

Hidden Treasure, Pearl of Great Value (13:44-46)

Like the parables of mustard seed and leaven (vv. 31-33) these two short parables are twins, not identical but twins nevertheless. They are parallel stories of two men who know a thing of value when it stares them in the face and act decisively to possess it.

One was a hired hand guiding a plow across another man's **field,** the other a wealthy **merchant in search of pearls.** Both found a prize, one stumbling on it by chance and the other in the course of disciplined questing. In any case, having found a **treasure** or **one pearl of great value** (Prov. 3:15; Job 28:18; Matt. 7:6), they broke completely with their old patterns and in a surge of joyous energy did what they had to in order to seize the prize.

Hearers of these parables almost automatically applaud the good fortune of that hired hand and of that merchant and approve their quick thinking and decisive actions. But if so, then the question arises, should the hearers not likewise act with boldness born of the joy of discovery as they themselves are confronted with the treasure of the kingdom of heaven? Of course they should. They should reorder their lives (= repent, 4:17) with dramatic and joyous abandon. They should live under God with single-minded devotion (cf. 5:48).

Like a Net (13:47-50)

Both in vocabulary and theme the parable of the **net** closely resembles the explanation of the parable of the weeds (vv. 36-43). That explanation and this parable together stand like a pair of bookends embracing the two short parables of joyous finding (vv. 44-46). Those two intermediate parables (treasure and pearl) focus on people gladly sacrificing anything in order to seize the prize of the kingdom. They are celebrations of decisive, radical actions. But the bracketing parables (weeds and net) are stern warnings. Those who fail to seize the treasure and possess it will in the end have not joy but infinite sorrow. Whatever they have will be taken away. The bracketing parables speak the language of good and evil, of righteousness and lawlessness. They clearly imply that the joy of possession is the beginning and not the end of the matter. Possession brings a burden of responsibility. The joy of finding and possessing is set in a context of ultimacy and urgency.

47—The kingdom of heaven is like a net which was thrown into the sea. The net **gathered** (vv. 29-30, 40-41) **fish of every kind** and was **full** (cf. John 21:4-8). The fishermen dragged the net ashore and sat down and **sorted out the catch,** saving the **good** and discarding the **bad.**

An explanation follows immediately. It focuses not at all on the catching, not on the work of stretching the net from two boats, not on rowing out so that the net was stretched and then closed, not on dragging the net to shore, not on the joy of the fishermen at their great catch. The explanation has nothing to say about missionary action nor about the ecumenical fullness or variety of the catch (Luke 5:1-11; John 21:1-14; cf. Matt. 4:18-22).

Both fishing and hunting are old images of bringing people to justice (Jer. 16:16-18). So also here. **At the close of the age** (v. 39) **the angels** (vv. 39, 41; 25:31) **will come out and separate the evil from the righteous.**

The flourishing of evil people in any community is one problem, but another is the arrogance of the pious. Matthew records a number of sayings, noting on the one hand the uneasy coexistence of righteous and evil people, and warning on the other about the inevitable divine discrimination: two kinds of tree (7:17-19), two houses (7:24-27), wheat and weeds (13:24-30), good and bad fish (13:47-50), two sons (21:28-32), wedding guests with and without a proper garment (22:11-14), wise and foolish maidens (25:1-13), sheep and goats (25:31-46).

The accent in these words falls at different places, but all urge hearers to examine not others but themselves, and they both assure and warn that God will be the critic at the end (cf. Rom. 12:19). Good people, pious people, people who trust that they are God's people always are in danger of lapsing into false security or of falling into the habit of sniping at those deemed less godly. To the community is given the fundamental task of forgiving (chap. 18) and of making disciples (28:19). Forbidden to the community are judging, separation, fanaticism (cf. 7:1-5).

Every Scribe Trained for the Kingdom (13:51-52)

51—Have the disciples understood all this? They answer with an emphatic **Yes.** Understanding is a key word throughout the chapter (vv. 13, 14, 15, 19, 23) and is a hallmark of disciples. The following chapters will show that their **Yes** in response to Jesus' question is not only emphatic. It also may be somewhat optimistic and premature. They certainly are in a different class from scribes and Pharisees, and their understanding is impressive. Nevertheless, succeeding events will reveal the limits of their grasp. Matthew reports their confusion and impotence at the hunger of the 5000 (14:13-21) and the 4000 (15:32-38), at Jesus' walking on the sea (14:22-33), and in the discussion of the leaven of the Pharisees and Sadducees (16:5-12). What effect the execution of John (14:1-12) had on them we are not told, but it is clear that talk of crosses baffles and offends them (16:22-23).

52—But they have reached some understanding, setting them apart from leaders and from crowds. They understand that God is present and active in Jesus' ministry, working to bring ancient promise to fulfillment, gathering the scattered to do God's will before the day of judgment.

Who or what exactly is a **scribe trained for the kingdom of heaven?** After the return from Babylonian exile (538 B.C.) scribes as a class of legal experts began to arise in Judaism. They were lawyers or theologians, forerunners of ordained rabbis. But to whom does Jesus give the title? Who are these new scribes of the new age? Every person who knows the will of God as revealed in Jesus? Christian teachers (cf. 23:34)?

Every disciple or every Christian teacher, **trained** or apprenticed **for the kingdom of heaven,** is like a **householder** who opens his cash box and produces both **new** and **old** coins (cf. 12:35). The order **new-old** suggests that disciples, understanding and following Jesus (the new), do not destroy the old (5:17), but use it (the Law and the Prophets) in fresh ways. In this present context, however, **old and new** can be given even sharper content. The expectation of the coming of the Messiah to overthrow evil and to establish the reign of God, promised by prophets and righteous ones, is **old.** Jesus in the parables of chap. 13 has taught the hiddenness of the great power of God's rule in the present time and the consequent delay of the destruction of evil until the close of the age, bringing with it the dread possibility that God's people may miss the coming of the kingdom as it approaches in Jesus' ministry. This is **new.**

Matthew's Gospel seems to some readers to be the product of Christian scribal activity, and some see a kind of self-portrait of the evangelist in 13:52. The word translated **trained** is *mathē-teutheis* ("discipled" or "apprenticed"). It is related to *mathete* = "learn" in 11:29, to *mathēteusate* = "make disciples" in 28:19, and to *mathētēs* = "disciple," everywhere in the Gospel. Even Matthew's name (*Matthaios*) is similar to the Greek word meaning "apprenticed" or "trained."

The Carpenter's Son (13:53-58)

53—Matthew now ends the third of Jesus' sermons or discourses with the formula, **When Jesus had finished these parables** (cf. 7:28; 11:1; 19:1; 26:1).

Matthew launches into a narrative about Jesus' family, and so the paragraph concluding the chapter on parables is parallel in content to the paragraph immediately preceding the chapter (12:46-50). The parables of chap. 13 are thus bracketed by materials raising the question: Who is Jesus and who is his true family?

54—Jesus traveled to **his own country** (v. 57) and **taught them in their synagogues** (4:23), like a scribe discipled to the kingdom, bringing forth things old and new (13:52). They were **astonished** (7:28) and **wondered** about the source of his **wisdom** (*sophia*, cf. 11:19; 12:42) and **mighty works** (*dynameis*, 14:2; cf. 11:2-5; 21:23).

55-56—They could, however, penetrate no farther than seeing him as **the carpenter's son** with a **mother called Mary,** with **brothers** named **James and Joseph and Simon and Judas** and with assorted unnamed **sisters.** According to Mark (6:3) the townspeople call Jesus himself "the carpenter" (*tektōn*), a word meaning builder, craftsman, mason, or mechanic.

57—These statements about Jesus and his family indicate that Matthew has Nazareth in view (2:23) rather than Capernaum (4:12-13). People in his old hometown could not get past their old knowledge of Jesus and began to **take offense at him** (11:6; 17:27; 18:6-9). Jesus applied to himself the proverb that **a prophet is not without honor except in his own country and in his own house** (cf. Mark 3:21; 6:4).

58—Jesus did only a few miracles there **because of their un-belief** (cf. Mark 6:5). So the paragraph centers on Jesus as **the carpenter's son** and concludes with the word **unbelief.** Readers are being interrogated by this narrative. They are being asked not only whether they know who Jesus is but also whether they belong to his family.

These themes lead directly into chap. 14.

■ The Son of God and All the Children of God (14:1—15:39)

You Are the Son of God (14:1-36)

Chapter 13 concludes with the people of Jesus' hometown seeing him as nothing more than the carpenter's son and therefore taking offense at him in ignorance and unbelief. As chap. 14 opens, it seems that agents of unbelief are reacting more violently than ever against the messengers of God (cf. 11:12). Nevertheless, chap. 14 will not conclude before Jesus has trodden the waters underfoot and has been confessed as Son of God by his disciples (14:22-33).

The Head of John the Baptist (14:1-12)

1-2—The story of unbelief (13:53-58) continues and is painfully sharpened in the following famous account of the death of John the Baptist. **Herod the tetrarch** is Herod Antipas, son of Herod the Great (cf. 2:22-23), ruler of Galilee and of Perea, territory east of the Jordan River and the Dead Sea. Reports of Jesus' **powers** (*dynameis,* 13:54; see the introduction to chap. 8) filled him with dread: "Perhaps Jesus is really **John the Baptist raised from the dead,** coming back to haunt me!"

Previously Matthew has written only of John's arrest (4:12; 11:2) and of resistance to him (11:12) and has held back the news of John's execution until this point in the narrative, not far from the place where Jesus will begin to speak of his own arrest and dying (16:21).

3-4—John had thundered against Herod as an immoral man and an unworthy ruler because he had married **Herodias, his**

brother Philip's wife (Lev. 18:16; 20:21). Public denunciation of an autocratic ruler is a revolutionary act and Herod had John arrested and **put him in prison** at the fortress Machaerus on the eastern shore of the Dead Sea.

5—Matthew portrays Herod as unremitting in his hatred of John, while Mark shifts the burden to Herodias and speaks of Herod's respect for John. According to Matthew, Herod restrained himself from summary execution of John for one reason only: **he feared the people** (21:46). He did not want to alienate his subjects completely, and for their part they hailed John as a **prophet** of God (11:9; 21:25-27).

6-7—But **Herod's birthday** became John's death day. The tetrarch was in an expansive mood and began to show off his wealth and generosity to his cronies. He publicly promised to give to Salome, **the daughter of Herodias** and so his own step-daughter, **whatever she might ask,** because her dancing had so charmed his guests.

8—Herodias prompted Salome to request **the head of John the Baptist on a platter.**

9-11—**The king was sorry.** Matthew breathes not a word of Herod's regarding John as righteous and holy, or of his calculating that killing John would offend God and not only the crowds, or of his speaking with John gladly (Mark 6:20; cf. Luke 23:8; Acts 25:22). Herod is pictured as **sorry,** whether **sorry** to be manipulated by Herodias or **sorry** to be forced to take an extremely unpopular step is not said. But he had sealed his promise **with oaths** and had sworn it in the hearing of his guests. Rather than violate those oaths (5:33-37) or lose face with guests, or displease his wife and step-daughter (10:34-37), Herod ordered John **beheaded in prison,** and **his head was brought on a platter and given to the girl, and she brought it to her mother.**

When Herod Antipas first met Herodias, he was already married to the daughter of King Aretas of the Nabateans, an Arab kingdom with its capital at Petra (cf. 2 Cor. 11:32). Once Herod laid eyes on Herodias, he packed up his Nabatean wife and sent her back to her father. Offended, Aretas later declared war and defeated Antipas, an event interpreted by some ancient Jews as divine punishment for Antipas's execution of the prophet John (Josephus, *Ant.* 18.116).

Murder runs in Herod's family (2:16-18). Herod's family contrasts both with Jesus' natural family and then especially with the new community Jesus is calling into being (12:46-50; 13:53-58; 18:21-22).

12—The **disciples** of John (9:14; 11:2) pay their final respects to their master. Having **buried** John's body, they then go off and report to Jesus. So the forerunner completes his work, bearing witness to Jesus not only with his words (3:11-12) but finally also by his execution at the hands of Herod. In his dying, John foreshadows Jesus' own death and burial.

All Ate and Were Satisfied (14:13-21)

Themes of the previous paragraph continue in this new report. Like John, Jesus attracts a great following and is held in high regard by the people. But the most striking continuity has to do with feasting. As Herod gathered friends for a birthday banquet, so Jesus celebrates a great banquet in the wilderness, surrounded by crowds from all the villages and towns of the region.

13—When the forerunner died, **Jesus withdrew** (2:14; 4:12) **in a boat to a lonely place apart.** That movement underscores the sense of danger and rejection brooding over the narrative. But Jesus found no solitude in the wilderness, no quiet moments to contemplate John's martyrdom. **Crowds followed him on foot** from the towns ringing the sea. Herod feared the people because of John's standing with them (14:5; 21:26) and they are likewise intrigued with Jesus. They mob him, moths drawn to light.

14—And Jesus has by no means written them off as blind, uncomprehending, or hardened (13:14-15). In **compassion** (9:36) he receives them and heals their sick.

15-16—Late in the day, with the sun sinking towards the western horizon, the disciples suggest that Jesus dismiss the crowds and send them off to buy food for themselves. But Jesus will not have his disciples abandon the crowds to their own devices nor throw them onto provisions supplied by hereditary political leaders or by traditional religious leaders (16:11-12). Jesus commands, **You give them something to eat.**

17-19—The disciples examine their inventory with despair. **We have only five loaves here and two small fish.** But Jesus lives abundantly with little. In the presence of the crowds he takes in hand the **loaves and fish,** lifts his face to heaven, and blesses or praises God, giving thanks for those pitiful supplies. Then he **broke and gave the loaves to the disciples,** catching them into his own joyous movement of trust and love, and **the disciples gave them to the crowds.**

20-21—The great throng numbering some **five thousand men** plus **women and children** ate bread in the company of Jesus and were **satisfied** (cf. 5:6).

Herod's bitter banquet and Jesus' joyous feeding of 5000 stand side by side in awful contrast. Herod kills God's prophet, fearing that he will otherwise lose face or even lose his hold on power. Jesus acts out of deep compassion (9:36; 14:14; 15:32; 20:34) to satisfy the needs of ill and hungry crowds. Together the two meals foreshadow Jesus' last meal and execution. Jesus' path to kingship is not paved with slaughtered corpses but only with his self-offering on behalf of many (20:28).

Take Heart, It Is I (14:22-27)

Hearing news of Jesus, Herod feared that he was the ghost of John the Baptist (vv. 1-2). Jesus' own disciples struggle with similar notions (v. 26). Jesus struggles to lead them to understanding.

22-23—Jesus sends his disciples ahead to make a night crossing by **boat,** dismisses the crowds, and ascends the mountain (5:1; 15:29-31) **by himself to pray** (cf. John 6:15).

24—While Jesus prays (cf. 26:36-44), the **boat** bearing the disciples is out **on the sea beaten** (*basanizomenon,* literally "tortured"; cf. 18:34) **by the waves** with **the wind against them.** The entire scene conjures up the image of the church suffering torments of persecution amid doubts about the presence and power of the Lord.

25-26—At the height of the storm, in the depths of darkness during **the fourth watch of the night** (3–6 A.M.), Jesus comes to the disciples, treading on the waves (cf. Job 9:8; 38:16; Ps. 77:19; Sirach 24:5-6). The sight of Jesus **walking on the sea** fills the disciples with terror, and in **fear** and littleness of faith (v. 31) they scream, **It is a ghost!** (*phantasma,* cf. v. 2).

27—Immediately Jesus reassures them, **Take heart, have no**

fear! And Jesus identifies himself. But what precise encouragement does Jesus call to them? The RSV translates, **It is I.** However, Jesus' words are more than mere identification. They are really an awesome formula of self-revelation, literally "I AM" (*egō eimi*). Jesus presents himself to his disciples as the solid and saving presence of the eternal God (1:23; 18:20; 28:20; cf. John 8:58; Exod. 3:14; Isa. 43:10).

Peter Walked on Water (14:28-33)

A striking feature of Matthew's Gospel is the prominence accorded to Peter, especially here near the midpoint of the narrative in a series of scenes, most of which find no place in the other Gospels (14:28-33; 15:15; 16:13-20; 17:24-27; 18:21-22).

Here it is enough to note that the first of these scenes follows. At the conclusion of the scene, it will be necessary to ask about the significance of Matthew's focus on Peter.

28—Peter believes that in the presence of Jesus he himself can tread any storm under foot and asks to be summoned out onto the waves. Jesus says, **Come,** and Peter in perfect obedience (cf. 1:24-25) climbs out of the boat and begins to move across the face of the waters toward Jesus. Commanded by Jesus, the disciple dares anything.

30—But fear of the storm begins to overwhelm him, and **beginning to sink** he shrieks, **Lord save me!** (8:25; Ps. 69:11-3, 13-16), confessing at once both his impotence and his hope in words that continue to echo in the church's cry, "Lord have mercy."

31—Immediately Jesus reaches out his hand to catch him (cf. Ps. 18:16; 144:7), gently rebuking him as a man of **little faith.** Knocked off balance by the fury of the storm raging around him, Peter does not lose faith entirely, but he does waver (6:30; 8:26).

Readers disagree about the significance of Peter in Matthew's Gospel. Is Peter chief among the Twelve, holding a position of unique leadership among them? Or is Peter typical of the Twelve? The latter seems more likely.

Matthew sees the life of the post-Easter community mirrored in the experiences of the twelve disciples. But think how bizarre and how much less effective it would be if Matthew had not singled out one disciple (Peter) as representative but had instead always used all twelve simultaneously as mirror. Of course Matthew could have all twelve ask Jesus, "Explain the parable to us" (15:15; cf. 13:36; Mark 7:17). But it is difficult to imagine all twelve climbing out of the boat, attempting to walk on water, with Jesus then plucking them from the deep one after the other as they begin to sink (14:28-33).

Or think ahead to the great scene at Caesarea Philippi (16:13-20). In Matthew's portrait Peter combines in his own person both high confession and deep confusion. That is again far more dramatic and instructive about the character of the new community than it would have been if Matthew had ascribed those elements simply to "the disciples." If Matthew had followed this second course, readers might imagine that some disciples confessed while others were confused. But the reality concerning the Twelve and concerning the new community is more complex than that.

So the Twelve are presented in Matthew's Gospel as prototypes of the post-Easter community. To some extent, the life of the new community is played out ahead of time in the experiences of the Twelve, and among the Twelve, Peter is "first" (10:2) not as unique leader but as uniquely representative.

In the narrative of that wild crossing of the sea, Peter stands forth not as incomparable hero but as exemplar of varied facets of the community's life, all mixed and mingled in disciples of every age: boldness (even rashness) and obedience, fear and prayer, littleness of faith and confession. (More on Peter at 16:13-20.)

32—As soon as they climb into the boat, the wind ceases its blowing (Ps. 107; 28-29). The storm that seemed only to threaten life and limb proves to be vehicle of the presence of Jesus. Storm is often prelude to divine revelation, even chariot of the presence of God (Exod. 19:16-20; 1 Kings 19:11-12; Ps. 29; Ezek. 1:4).

33—Not Peter only but **all in the boat** worship him, confessing, **Truly you are the Son of God** (contrast 13:55). Jesus overwhelms the senses and the powers of the mind. Staggered by the weight of his presence, friends and foes struggle for understanding. Disciples progress from understanding to understanding (13:11-12) and ascribe to Jesus the highest name of all (cf. 3:17; 11:25-27; 16:16). The Gospel does not close, however, until people (and

Gentiles, at that!) speak that name, not of Jesus in his power, but of Jesus as the crucified (27:54).

Mark's portrait of the disciples in the parallel section (Mark 6:45-52) is strikingly different. In response to Jesus' walking to them upon the water, Mark says the disciples were utterly astounded, for they did not understand and their hearts were hardened. In Matthew's narrative the disciples, at least at this point, understand and confess.

They Recognized Him (14:34-36)

34-35—Jesus and his disciples land at **Gennesaret,** the fertile plain spreading out on the northwest shore of the Sea of Galilee. The local population **recognized him.** Knowing him and his compassion, they spread word of his arrival throughout the region, and people flock to him, bringing **all that were sick.**

36—They beg (8:5; 18:29,32) that they might merely **touch the fringe of his garment** (9:20-21; 23:5). So great is his power that the touch of the outermost edge of his garment suffices to heal (cf. Acts 19:11-12).

Leaven of the Pharisees (15:1-39)

Chapter 15 is actually a smaller unit set within a number of larger sections. First, it is part of the sequence of material in 15:1-16:12, which in turn is bracketed by two great moments of confession. Disciples hail Jesus as "Son of God" first in the boat on the sea (14:33) and then again at Caesarea Philippi (16:16). The enclosed material (15:1—16:12) begins (15:1-9) and ends (16:1-12) with treatments of the teaching or tradition of the Pharisees. So the twin themes of high confession of Jesus and deep opposition to Jesus, which loom so large in all of 11:1—16:20, are further developed here in chap. 15.

These Are What Defile (15:1-20)

At first it is a letdown to move from the awesome scene of walking on water to a scribal debate about clean and unclean. But the issue is weighty. God alone and not any human being had traced the sharp line between clean and unclean. And Jesus seems careless and cavalier about that boundary. Many react with revulsion to Jesus' free and easy contact with the unclean. Why does he permit himself and his garments to be pawed (14:36)? Why does he eat and consort with sinners (9:11, 14)?

All talk of clean and unclean is really talk about insiders and outsiders, who belongs and who is disqualified. So Jesus' debate with the Pharisees is really all about boundaries. How is the community of God to be defined and delimited?

1-2—Wind and water obey him, disciples confess, and the ill are healed, but Pharisees and scribes come to Jesus with complaint and accusation: **Why do your disciples transgress the tradition of the elders?** That his accusers come **from Jerusalem** has an ominous ring to it (cf. 3:5). That is the city of rejection and death (16:21).

By **the tradition of the elders** they mean the orally transmitted commentary on the Law, growing generation by generation. The Pharisees were its champions, assigning it an authority equal to that of the written Law (Torah), a position rejected especially by the Sadducees (cf. 22:23). Eventually the oral traditions were codified and deposited in writing as the Mishnah (ca. A.D. 200) and still later in the Talmuds.

3-4—Jesus and his disciples **do not wash their hands** in the prescribed ritual manner before eating, and so they transgress **the tradition of the elders.** But who in this debate are the real transgressors? Instead of equating tradition with God's will, Jesus sharply contrasts **the commandment of God** (Exod. 20:12) and the **tradition** (cf. 5:21-48; 19:3-9; 22:31). Nor does he dignify the tradition by connecting it with a long line of venerable **elders** reaching back to Moses. Instead he calls it **your tradition.**

Jesus presses his attack with an illustration. **God** gave the commandment, **Honor your father and your mother.** And Jesus adds that God underscored that command with threat and promise (Exod. 20:12; 21:17).

5—However, says Jesus, **you** in contrast to **God** have by means of your **tradition** found a loophole in the **commandment.** Your tradition permits pledging to donate property to the temple at some future time, while retaining the use of it and any income earned from it in the meantime. By such an arrangement a person could evade the responsibility of placing those material resources at the service of father and mother. So while the motive behind the evasion might be completely self-serving, the selfishness was disguised by a veneer of piety.

6—So the **tradition** ends up not as an expression of **the law of God** but actually as an attack upon it. **Tradition** in this case voids the word of God (cf. 5:17)!

7-9—Religious leaders easily become **hypocrites** (see commentary on 6:2; 23:13), inwardly divided, their integrity and wholeness splintered by their stubborn attachment to cherished ritual or doctrinal traditions. Jesus seals his attack with words of **Isaiah** (29:13), who distinguished between honor given by **lips** and praise issuing from the **heart,** thereby exposing the vanity of mistaking human **precepts** (tradition) for divine **doctrines** (the will of God).

10-11—The dispute spills over into public. Jesus addresses **the people,** unlearned and unwashed, calling them to ponder the Scriptures and the will of God: **Hear and understand** (13:13-15). As this second half of the section opens, Jesus begins to exploit the prophetic distinction between **lips** and **heart.**

What **defiles?** What pollutes and renders unclean and unworthy in the eyes of God? What is the source of transgression? Jesus says, **Not what goes into the mouth, but what comes out of the mouth.** This simple declaration is dangerous, since not only tradition but also Scripture contains vast quantities of material on things that defile by going into the mouth. Up to this point Jesus seems to uphold Scripture against tradition. But here he seems to brush aside rules of sacred Scripture. What is certain is that he is focusing on the defiling power of human traditions that cancel God's will (v. 6) and on the hypocrisy of pious noises made by lips when hearts are distant from God (v. 8).

12—The disciples alert Jesus that **the Pharisees** are offended (11:6) and they betray their own uneasiness (cf. 16:12) at Jesus' manner of speaking.

13-14—In phrases reminiscent of the parable of the wheat and weeds (13:24-30, 36-43) Jesus declares, **Every plant which my Father has not planted** (cf. 31:33; Isa. 5:1-7) **will be rooted up.** The disciples are warned to **let them alone** (13:28-30), not attack them in an effort to root them up. But they are to know them and mark them. They are **blind guides.** And in a word of warning to leaders and to the led Jesus says, **If a blind man leads a blind man both will fall into a pit** (cf. 23:16, 24; Rom. 2:19-20).

15-16—The warning about blind guides is plain enough. Indeed, Matthew's Gospel is full of warning about bad leaders (cf. 7:15-23; 24:11, 24, 45-51). When **Peter** asks Jesus to **explain the parable,** he seems to have in mind the words about defilement (v. 11). Here again (see commentary above on 14:28) Peter speaks for all the disciples, and for their part they mirror the posture of the post-Easter community. Even after the resurrection Jesus will remain in the midst of his community (28:20) mediating **understanding** to those gathered in his name.

17-18—Jesus launches into a lesson. What goes **into the mouth** does not strike the heart. Food hits **the stomach** and **passes on** through the digestive system. **What comes out of the mouth,** however, is more significant. It all **proceeds from the heart** and reveals **the heart** (v. 8). That is why Jesus says that **this**—rather than food—**defiles.**

19—**The heart** produces more than words: **evil thoughts, murder, adultery, fornication, theft, false witness, slander,** namely, the whole galaxy of attitudes and behaviors forbidden by the Ten Commandments (cf. 5:21-48). Behind **slander** is the Greek word elsewhere translated as "blasphemy" (cf. 9:3). All these have **the heart** as their launching pad.

20—**These are what defile.** These are what define a human being as clean or unclean. **But to eat with unwashed hands** (v. 2) **does not defile,** does not disqualify, does not render a person unfit for the presence of God. In the immediately following narrative a natural and yet astonishing conclusion is drawn from Jesus' argument.

A Canaanite Woman (15:21-28)

21—The scene shifts but the topic does not. Jesus now withdraws from Gennesaret at the shore of the Sea of Galilee (14:34) and travels far from the orbit of Jerusalem (15:1) toward **the district of Tyre and Sidon,** old pagan cities on the Mediterranean coast 30 and more miles to the northwest. These notorious cities have been named previously as more open to God than Chorazin and Bethsaida (11:20-22).

It is not clear whether Jesus actually leaves Galilee and enters Phoenicia. Perhaps the woman crosses the border from that region and enters northern Galilee. In either case, Jesus stands face to face with **a Canaanite woman,** a pagan and therefore unclean woman.

22—She addresses Jesus in the language of faith (cf. 9:18, 21; 12:23) and lays her need at his feet: **Have mercy on me, O Lord, Son of David** (cf. 9:27); **my daughter is severely possessed by a demon.** Her entire story closely parallels that of the Gentile centurion (8:5-13), while in her attitude she is the opposite of the authorities from Jerusalem (15:1-20).

23—Previously Jesus has exorcised demons in Gentile territory (8:28-34) as well as in Galilee (9:32; 12:22-23) but here he meets the woman's request with stony silence. **His disciples,** touched by the woman's plight, intercede for her and beg him to grant her request: **Send her away satisfied** (cf. 14:15).

24—Jesus' first words seem to be a chilling "No," both to the disciples and to the woman. **I was sent** (10:40; cf. 5:17) **only to the lost sheep** (9:36) **of the house of Israel** (10:5-6, 23). His mission, like that of the Baptist, is to turn Israel wholeheartedly to God, and only rarely and exceptionally does he have contact with Gentiles.

25—But the pagan woman approaches Jesus and kneels before him (cf. 8:2), renewing her plea: **Lord, help me** (cf. 14:30).

26—Jesus counters with a harsh little parable: **It is not fair to take the children's bread** (gifts for the people of God) **and throw it to the dogs** (Gentiles, cf. 7:6). Jesus brands the woman's request as simply inappropriate. His eyes and mind are fixed on the lost sheep of the house of Israel, and he will not abandon them.

27—In a statement remarkable for its humility and faith, the woman plays along with Jesus' harsh image and simply urges him to take it one step farther: **Yes, Lord, yet even the dogs eat the crumbs that fall from their master's table** (cf. 8:12). God's bounty is large enough for all creatures great and small, near and far, Israel and the nations!

28—Readers may be fascinated with that woman's wit or wisdom, but Jesus remarks on her **great faith** (8:10; contrast "little faith" in 14:31; 16:8). Responding to her faith, Jesus grants her request, so that **her daughter was healed instantly** (8:13).

The narrative is remarkable for the extent to which it extols both God's faithfulness to Israel and the power of boundary-crossing faith.

He Healed Them (15:29-31)

29—In a brief transitional piece, covering Jesus' move back along **the Sea of Galilee** (14:34; 15:1, 21), Matthew reports in summary fashion how Jesus **went up into the hills** above the lake and **sat down there** (cf. 5:1).

30—**Great crowds,** probably Jews and Gentiles alike (4:23-25), flock around him there. They have made no final decision about Jesus but remain fascinated with his authority over illness. They bring **the lame, the maimed, the blind, the dumb, and many others, and they put them at his feet.** He heals them all (cf. 11:4-5; 14:34-36). Coming immediately before the feeding of the 4000, this healing scene is remarkably like the one summarized so briefly at 14:14, prelude to the feeding of the 5000.

The great mixed **throng** of Jews and Gentiles **wondered** (9:33) at Jesus' good and mighty works, and they **glorified the God of Israel** (9:8; 11:6). Again God is defined as faithful to ancient promises made to Israel, even as Jesus heals both Jews and Gentiles, and even as Jesus breaks with hallowed traditions like ritual handwashing (15:1-20). As scandalous as it may appear to traditional teachers, what Jesus says and does brings glory to the God of Israel (see the comments on v. 28; cf. 5:16).

How Many Loaves Have You? (15:32-39)

Meals and bread play a role in much of the material in 14:1—16:12 (paralleling Mark 6–8): Herod's birthday banquet (14:1-2), feeding the 5000 (14:13-21), what and how people eat does not defile (15:1-20), crumbs from the master's table (15:21-28), feeding the 4000 (15:32-39), the leaven of the Pharisees (16:5-12). Bread is physical stuff to satisfy real hunger, but it is also a rich symbol for teaching and for salvation.

32—Seated on the mountain, surrounded by throngs glorifying the God of Israel (vv. 29-31), Jesus declares his **compassion on the crowds** (9:36; 14:14) and announces to his disciples that he is **unwilling to send them away hungry.** The crowds have spent three days in the presence of Jesus, and he worries lest they **faint on the way.**

33—In spite of their active participation in the distribution of loaves to the 5000 (14:19), the disciples are at a loss, and utter a poignant line voicing the dismay of the church faced with the immensity of human need in every age: **Where are we to get bread enough in the desert** (3:1) **to feed so great a crowd?** They see only impossibility, discouraged to have only **seven loaves** and **a few small fish** (cf. 14:17). But in the hands of Jesus that little is **bread enough.**

35-36—Jesus commands the crowds to sit like guests at his table. He seizes those **seven loaves and the fish,** and **having given thanks he broke them and gave them to the disciples** (14:19; 26:26), as aides or intermediaries, like waiters or servants (20:26-27) at a banquet, and they hand them round to the crowds.

37-38—**They all ate and were satisfied,** and they had **seven baskets full of broken pieces left over** (5:6; 14:20). That great crowd consisted of **four thousand men, besides women and children.**

39—Only when the crowds have been satisfied does Jesus dismiss them and cross by boat to the other side. The exact location of Matthew's **Magadan** is as unknown as Mark's Dalmanutha (Mark 8:10).

■ I Will Build My Church (16:1—18:35)

Upon This Rock (16:1-28)

The controversies of chap. 15 continue, but this section of the Gospel, which began all the way back in 4:17, will climax in the great confession of Peter (16:13-20). Peter's confession at Caesarea Philippi will echo the prior confession of all the disciples to Jesus, uttered on the sea made calm by Jesus' magisterial word (14:33).

Notes at 16:21 indicate how the narrative continues beyond the great turning point of Caesarea Philippi.

Signs of the Times (16:1-4)

1—Pharisees and Sadducees (an odd phrase, combining parties of opposing views as though they were one, cf. 3:7; 16:1, 6, 11, 12), approach Jesus, not as the crowds do, for feeding or healing, but **to test him** (4:3; 19:3; 22:18, 35). In some people Jesus' power rouses only apprehension or suspicion. They neither follow him nor hear him gladly. They probe his identity, demanding a **sign,** some authenticating signal **from heaven** (12:38). Does God really approve of this Jesus or not (cf. 21:23-32)?

2-3—Jesus replies that they can predict the weather and take appropriate action because they know how to read the sky (*our-anos*) and interpret **the face of heaven** (*prosōpon tou ouranou,* cf. Luke 21:54-56). Yet they do not know how to interpret **the signs of the times,** Jesus' words and deeds, and so they do not glorify the God of heaven, and their authority is not from heaven, no matter how pious they may appear (11:2-6; 15:30-31).

4—Not people of faith but **an evil and adulterous generation** (12:39; 17:17) scratches nervously for proofs, for guarantees, for a **sign. But no sign shall be given except the sign of Jonah** (12:38-42).

Leaven (16:5-12)

5-6—Bread provides the springboard for discussion once again (15:32). Jesus warns his disciples against **the leaven of the Pharisees and Sadducees.**

7-9—Like straight men in a comic routine, the disciples voice confusion, taking **bread** in a merely physical sense, setting up Jesus' response. Jesus first labels their misunderstanding an expression of **little faith** (14:31; contrast 15:28). Then he compels disciples and readers to ponder anew **the five loaves of the five thousand** and **the seven loaves of the four thousand** plus all the fragments which they later **gathered.**

Jesus prods them to see that they have received from his hand in abundant and even superabundant fashion all they need. In his presence the throngs, like sheep without a shepherd, harassed and helpless, and scattered on a thousand hills (9:36), were gathered as his table companions and they were satisfied (14:20; 15:37). And from his bounty he has begun to satisfy also the needs of the nations (15:21-28).

11—Those feedings were not merely a matter of literal bread filling literal stomachs. They were **signs of the times** (16:3), part of the proclamation of Jesus, hints and nudges from heaven. So he presses disciples and readers to **perceive** the larger dimensions of his distribution of **bread.**

12—Pressed mercilessly by Jesus, the disciples finally understand (15:16; 13:51; contrast Mark 8:21) that when he speaks to them of **bread** and of **leaven,** he is talking about his own life-giving **teaching** on the one hand and about **the teaching of the Pharisees and Sadducees** on the other. **Teaching** is to be taken broadly, not simply as a set of words but as an entire social and political and religious program, a way of life under God. Jesus declares his **bread,** his program of sustenance and life, to be sufficient. And in a statement that rounds out the unit beginning at 15:1, he declares his questioners to be guilty of defiling and corrupting God's people. Their teaching is not bread but **leaven. Beware,** he says, and cast it out (13:13; 1 Cor. 5:6-8; Gal. 5:9). It is ironic that Jesus will himself be cast out and killed at Passover time during the feast of unleavened bread (26:2).

You Are Peter (16:13-20)

13—Jesus again withdraws from the lake and moves about 25 miles north towards Mount Hermon and the headwaters of the Jordan River **into the district** (15:21) of **Caesarea Philippi** and the tetrarchy of Herod Philip (2:22; 14:3) on the border of Syria (4:24). Paneas, the chief city of the district, was rebuilt by Philip, son of Herod the Great, who named the renewed city **Caesarea** in honor of Tiberius Caesar (22:20) and added **Philippi** (= of Philip) to distinguish his city from the other Caesarea on the coast, constructed by his father (Josephus, *Ant.* 18.28).

The time has come for fresh understandings of Jesus and clarifications of the disciples' role. Jesus begins by asking his disciples, **Who do men say that the Son of man is?** Mark in his Gospel leads readers along until finally they are faced with the solemn declaration that Jesus is the mysterious "Son of man" (8:20) who goes to Jerusalem to suffer. For Matthew that is not the end but the beginning of the matter. He takes it for granted that readers know Jesus as **Son of man.** That title appears again at the end of this whole section (16:27-28) and so **Son of man** frames all the material between vv. 13 and 28. Matthew has constructed his narrative in such a way as to interpret that somewhat puzzling title by means of the confession of Jesus as **the Christ, the Son of the Living God** (16:16), and by means of the first passion prediction (16:12). Will the disciples (and readers) be able to understand the necessity of the cross both for the Christ and for their own mission?

14—People at large speculate that Jesus may be **John the Baptist** back from the dead (14:2), or **Elijah,** fabled helper of the weak and forerunner of the last times (17:10-13; 27:47; Mal. 4:5), or perhaps **Jeremiah,** great ancient critic of Jerusalem who suffered at the hands of the power brokers of his day (cf. 16:21; see 2 Macc. 15:12-16). If he is not one of these, they say, then he is some other in the line of God's **prophets** (cf. 21:11, 26, 46).

15—All that is high praise **but** is it high enough? That little conjunction **but** draws a sharp line between all those titles of popular approval named by the disciples and the surpassing high reality of Jesus.

Could Jesus be more than a renewer of ancient tradition? Could he be what the whole tradition was aiming at? Readers know already that Jesus and John are two and not one, that John plays the role of Elijah and is himself more than a prophet as the last of the prophets and forerunner to Jesus (11:7-14). And readers know that Jesus is greater than Jeremiah. The prophet Jeremiah, in days of old, saw in advance the coming of the days of Jesus (2:17) and proclaimed them from afar.

So far the disciples are speaking only for the crowds, reporting popular reactions to Jesus. **But,** says Jesus, to the chosen Twelve, **who do you** (plural) **say that I am?** As elsewhere (15:15, e.g.) it is **Simon Peter** who responds. Peter is not contrasted with the rest of the Twelve but speaks and confesses on their behalf, voicing their common conviction.

Nevertheless, Matthew is underscoring a contrast. All Twelve are contrasted with "men" and "some" and "others" (16:13-14) and especially with the Pharisees, Sadducees, and scribes (16:1-12; 15:1-20).

Peter confesses, **You are the Christ, the Son of the living God** (26:63-64). As the reality of the Son overwhelms mind and senses, people try to get a handle on him by fitting him into some convenient slot like **prophet.** However, **the Christ** or Messiah is not a prophet but the goal of prophecy, not another promiser but the inaugurator of the promised time (1:1, 17, 18). As **Son of the living God** he is the bearer of the presence of God and acts in the place of God (1:23), not as renewer of old traditions, but as agent of God's fresh creative work, bringer of new heavens and a new earth. (On "Son of God" see 2:15; 3:17; 4:3, 5; 8:29; 11:27; 14:33; 26:63; 27:40, 43, 54.) Peter does not say, "Show us the Father" (John 14:8), but confidently declares that he sees the face and heart of God in Jesus.

Living God is a traditional mode of speech but is not mere window dressing here. It underscores the fact that this Jesus, though crucified, is the Son living and present in the post-Easter community. He does not establish offices or appoint office holders to rule in his absence. He is never absent but ever in the midst (1:23; 18:20; 28:20).

17—Jesus' response to Peter's confession consists of three short verses, each of which has three parts: a thematic statement and a pair of parallel clauses expanding and expounding the theme. Jesus' first word to Peter is a beatitude (cf. 5:3; 11:6; 13:16) with the added clauses spelling out the grounds of blessing:

Blessed are you, Simon Bar-Jona!
(a) **For flesh and blood has not revealed this to you,**
(b) **but my Father who is in heaven.**

God's favor rests upon this confessor, the son of Jonah. In John 1:42; 21:15-17, Peter is called "son of John," and it is possible that "son of Jonah" is some kind of variant. However, Matthew's intention is probably to associate Peter and all the disciples with the prophet Jonah both in confessing and in experiencing death and resurrection (cf. 12:39-40; 16:4).

Simon is **blessed,** highly favored and roundly congratulated. TEV translates, "Good for you!" **Flesh and blood** (cf. Gal. 1:16) **has not revealed this.** The source of Peter's confession is neither human wit nor earthly intelligence **but** rather **my Father who is in heaven** (cf. 11:25-27). Peter's word is inspired utterance, heavenly gift (cf. 7:21; 13:11-12).

18—This verse is part two of Jesus' threefold response to Simon Peter's confession:

> **And I tell you, you are Peter,**
> (a) **and on this rock I will build my church,**
> (b) **and the powers of death shall not prevail against it.**

To him who said, **You are the Christ,** Jesus responds with a perfectly parallel **You are Peter.** Peter and Jesus trade compliments or confessions, insight for insight, title for title.

But what does it mean that **Simon** bears the title **Peter** or "Rock" (cf. Mark 3:16; John 1:41-42)? Interpreters regularly appeal to several different traditions which may lie behind Jesus' words to Peter and may possibly help to understand them:

1. Isaiah (51:1-2) had summoned Israel, "Look to the rock from which you were hewn and to the quarry from which you were digged. Look to Abraham your father [rock] and to Sarah who bore you [quarry]. He was but one when I called him, and I blessed him and made him many."

2. In rabbinic sources Abraham was sometimes viewed not only as the rock from which Israel was hewn but the rock on which God founded the entire world.

3. The Temple of Jerusalem was thought to rest on the great cosmic rock sealing the entrance to heaven and hell.

4. The Qumran community was governed by a council of twelve laymen and three priests, described as perfectly schooled in the Law. That council (or perhaps the entire community) is described as established on an unshakable foundation and precious cornerstone (1QS 8; 1QH 6:19-31; see Isa. 28:16), words which may be intended to describe the Qumran community as God's temple not made with hands.

5. Elsewhere in the New Testament, of course, Jesus (Matt. 21:42; 1 Cor. 3:11) or all the apostles together (Gal. 2:9; Eph. 2:20; Rev. 21:14) are described as the foundation of the new community.

Jesus bestows on Peter a new name, and immediately begins to expound the meaning of that name, as he declares, **On this rock I will build my church.** It is vital to note that the gift of the new name has nothing to do with any solid, rocklike, or unflinching features in Peter's personality. In fact Peter is fully capable of base misunderstanding as well as astonishing confession, so he is addressed in rapid succession both as foundation rock (16:18) and as stone causing others to stumble (16:23). The new name is his, not because he is a miracle worker or exorcist, not because he is visionary or prophet, not because he is the head or ruler of the new community, nor even because he is doer of charity or of deeds of righteousness. It is because he has the received faith and confession as gifts of heaven that Peter also receives his new name and its attendant promise.

Jesus looks at Peter, called, instructed, sometimes boldly treading the waters and sometimes sinking like a rock (14:28-31), full of understanding and often of little faith, but nevertheless at this point knowing and confessing. Peter stands forth among the Twelve as their representative, and on behalf of all he utters the good confession. And in him Jesus sees the whole future community of disciples and confessors. Jesus looks away from Pharisees and Sadducees and scribes (15:1-20; 16:1-12) and, gazing upon Peter and the Twelve, sees the **church** (only here and at 18:17 in the Gospels), the new community of the end times.

Jesus is "Son of the living God" (v. 16) and therefore not even the **powers of death** can conquer his community. Exactly what **powers** are meant? The phrase (literally, "the gates of Hades," *pylai hadou*) could mean Satan's evil power in general, or the apparently invincible power of the grave over all living things, or the deadly power of persecution (cf. 12:25-29).

Confession of Jesus involves saying no to other powers and other leaders, thereby opening disciples to their wrath and persecution. But Jesus, "Son of the living God," shares his own indestructible life with members of his community. Beyond all loss he promises a mighty harvest (13:3-8), beyond persecution and martyrdom, resurrection and shining like the very sun (13:43). All-devouring Hades will never consume and destroy the people of God. On the contrary, Hades will not be able to resist the power of heaven, liberating and resurrecting, at work in Jesus and the community.

19—The third and final unit of Jesus' word to Peter, like the first two, again consists of three parts:

I will give you the keys of the kingdom of heaven,

(a) **and whatever you bind on earth shall be bound in heaven,**

(b) **and whatever you loose on earth shall be loosed in heaven.**

To Peter (and the Twelve) Jesus gives **keys** (Rev. 1:8; 3:7; Isa. 22:22) here interpreted as authority to **bind** and to **loose.** In ancient rabbinic literature the terms **bind** and **loose** refer to "forbidding" or "permitting" actions, to the formulation of authoritative legal decisions, declaring that certain ordinances of the Law are or are not binding upon particular people in particular circumstances. So **bind** and **loose** refer to the regulation of the ethical life of a religious community by means of authoritative teaching, such as Jesus offered in the Sermon on the Mount (see especially 5:21-48; cf. 23:13). Binding and loosing therefore inevitably involve admitting people to or excluding them from the community. So, in response to Peter's confession, Jesus declares his intention to build a new community whose teachers will not be Pharisees and Sadducees and scribes (15:1-20; 16:1-12) and whose teachings will not be the traditions of the elders (15:2-3).

In fact, Matthew's Gospel is all about Jesus and the new community, how Jesus founds it, how its fellowship is entered and its life regulated. It is all about the secrets of its life, its standards, values, priorities, and style, what is permitted and what is forbidden, who is included and who excluded.

Who or what is custodian of all these secrets, standards, values, teachings, and decisions? Is Peter? Or a string of successors after Peter?

Everything in the Gospel points not to Peter and the disciples nor to any leaders or teacher trained and appointed by them but steadily and consistently to the living Jesus Christ alone (23:8-10). And how does Jesus instruct the community in the days after Easter? Through his words, the fullness of his teaching, deposited in the Gospel of Matthew. The Gospel of Matthew itself, as the treasury of the words of Jesus, addresses the community with authority, teaching how people enter the community (**keys**) and the standards and criteria for behavior within the community (**bind** and **loose**).

What then is the role of Peter in the community? Peter had a leading role among the Twelve (10:2) and apparently also in the founding of Matthew's community. The author assures his community, resting on the confession and labors of Peter, that it is well founded, not by human authority or ingenuity only, but by the exalted Jesus, Son of the living God. This Jesus is not a figure of the past alone. He is still present in the midst of the community, not as unseen observer only but with his authority and teaching. Therefore what is decisive for the health of the community is not any set of rules issued by the Pharisees of Jamnia nor even any teachings of contemporary Christian leaders claiming special inspiration but only the teaching of the exalted Jesus.

Matthew has collected the words and commands of Jesus, known from the disciples and Peter, and has recorded them with loving care in his book. This book contains "all that I have commanded" (28:19). These words of Jesus, full of blessing and encouragement, when written on the hearts of disciples, will ensure that the community is unshakable.

The successor of Peter is the Gospel of Matthew! It is grotesque to imagine that Matthew was interested in promoting any office, norm, or authority in addition to the words of Jesus (23:8-10; 28:18-20). Matthew reissued the words of Jesus because of confusion in the church resulting from the energetic and enthusiastic labors of prophets and teachers and leaders. It is Matthew's contention that anyone claiming to speak for the exalted Jesus should be tested by the norm of Jesus' own words, as enshrined in Matthew's Gospel.

20—But at this climactic moment Jesus suddenly calls for silence. The disciples are not yet ready. They have more lessons to learn, and they are passing hard.

Get Behind Me, Satan (16:21-23)

21—In 4:17 Jesus began **to preach.** Here in 16:21 Matthew says Jesus began **to show** (*deiknyein*), a word used of displaying visions and revelations on the one hand and of presenting arguments and evidence on the other (4:8; 8:4).

The content Jesus now reveals to his disciples is the hard news of the passion. He declares that he **must go to Jerusalem and suffer many things from the elders and chief priests and scribes, and be killed, and on the third day be raised.**

Death has cast its long hard shadow over Jesus' life from the beginning, when Herod sought the child's life (chap. 2). Early in his ministry religious leaders charged Jesus with blasphemy (9:3, cf. 9:11) and collusion with Satan (9:34; 10:25; 12:24), and soon they plotted to destroy him (12:14). The execution of John the Baptist (14:1-12), Jesus' forerunner, presages Jesus' own fate. The plot thickened as resistance to Jesus spilled over to include not only local leaders but also Pharisees and scribes who came down from Jerusalem to observe, to debate, to test (15:1-20; 16:1-4).

While all that was happening, Matthew repeatedly emphasized that Jesus' ministry consisted of teaching, proclamation, and healing (4:23; 9:35; 11:3-5). Those summary statements drew the readers' attention to Jesus as living up to his name as giver of life and salvation (1:21). But now a fresh set of ominous summaries begins.

For the first of several times (16:21; 17:22-23; 20:17-18) Jesus announces the necessity of his dying, summons disciples to take up their cross, and leads them forth on the narrow way to Jerusalem (16:20—20:34; cf. 19:1). There in the holy city (21:1—28:15) Jesus will be crucified and resurrected, and the Gospel will come to swift and stunning conclusion (28:16-20).

Jesus' prophecy of his death (17:12, 22-23; 20:17-19; 26:3) and the naming of Jerusalem as the goal of his journeying (16:21) distinguishes this new section from all the preceding.

Jesus does not merely foretell his passion, but says it **must** happen. That little word **must** (*dei*) means that the death of Jesus is sought not only by Jesus' enemies (21:14) but by God! The death of Jesus is deeply imbedded in God's own plan, hitherto kept secret.

Both the word **must** and the word **show** have about them the odor of apocalyptic, of things long hidden now being revealed because the right time, indeed the last time, has come. See the use of these two words in Rev. 1:1.

Jesus now begins to reveal that his rejection and death are in God's own plan, and his words also show that he freely accepts his allotted role in the divine plan.

22—As soon as **Jesus began to reveal** the passion, **Peter began to rebuke** or contradict him: **God forbid, Lord!** or "May God in his mercy spare you this!"

Peter and the others are shocked, disoriented, suddenly afraid. How can the death of Jesus be any part of God's plan? The Messiah, Son of the living God (16:16), should not die but live, that is, should satisfy a human agenda and fulfill human fantasies of success and glory. **This** (dying) **shall never happen to you!**

23—Now Jesus turns and speaks to Peter words absolutely the opposite of his earlier praise:

(a) **Get behind me, Satan.** Contrast, "Blessed are you, Simon Bar-Jona!" (v. 17);

(b) **You are a hindrance** (*skandalon,* cf. 5:29-30; 18:6), stone of stumbling, **to me.** Contrast, "You are Peter, and on this rock I will build" (v. 18);

(c) **You are not on the side of God but of men.** Contrast, "Flesh and blood has not revealed this to you but my Father in heaven" (v. 17).

Early Christian communities meditated on the select stone laid as a cornerstone in Zion (Isa. 28:16) and on the stumbling stone (Isa. 8:14-15) and saw that one and the same stone can function in two opposite ways. Sometimes those two images are associated with Jesus (Rom. 9:33; 1 Pet. 2:6-8; Matt. 21:42) but here they are applied to Peter.

The words of Jesus really contain two commands and not just one: **Get away,** Jesus says, since Peter's misunderstanding represents a Satanic blocking of the way of obedience, the way to the cross (cf. 4:10). Jesus would first of all clear him from the path, but then immediately adds a second command: **Behind me!** because he would also gain Peter once more as a follower on his way.

Discipleship includes the cross and indeed embraces the cross, because discipleship is a life of servanthood. Jesus' struggle to gain his disciples' acceptance of cross and service dominates the following chapters.

Come after Me (16:24-28)

24—Jesus treads the mysterious path of rejection and martyrdom with eyes wide open. His disciples hesitate, figuring the cost. Jesus speaks, encouraging them to **deny** themselves and to **take up the cross and follow** him. A harsh word, especially in a world where crucifixion was a familiar public spectacle, a dread and shameful torture reserved for slaves and foreigners. The cross was not yet an easy metaphor and had not yet been plated in gold.

Each of the three following verses offers a reason for cross-bearing, and each begins with the conjunction **for** or "because."

25—First, take up the cross (v. 24), **for** it is—paradoxically—the way of life. Life is precious and human beings at an early age begin learning how to preserve and expand it, enhance and protect it. What can be more important to any self than the life of that self? Fear and avoidance of anything life-threatening is deeply ingrained.

Jesus' word, however, seizes his audience by the jugular and shakes them, challenging their natural assumptions. His word consists of two antithetical clauses, each of which includes a pair of antithetical verbs (**save/lose** and **lose/find**).

> **Whoever would save his life will lose it,**
> **and whoever loses his life for my sake will find it.**

According to received wisdom, bearing a cross is revolting and disgusting. As he proceeds to contradict deep convictions about human life, Jesus does not bother to offer arguments or reasons. He simply shouts, "Halt!" He makes the most sweeping claims, as he summons to consideration of an absolutely opposite style.

By speaking of losing life **for my sake** he opposes their life with his life. He calls theirs a way of death, and whatever its surface appearance may be, he calls his own a way of life.

26—Second, he says to take up the cross (v. 24), **for** it is possible to **gain the whole world,** amass the most impressive stockpile of worldly wealth, and in the same instant lose one's life (see the parable of the rich fool in Luke 12:16-21). What does that **profit?** Or, to put it the other way around, is there any thing, any object, which a person would not gladly **give in return for his life,** that is, pay over in order to ransom or prolong life? Fear of loss prevents people from taking up the cross but Jesus promises strange gain: taking up the cross, in contradiction to the wisdom of the world, leads to saving, finding, and gaining one's life.

27—Third, take up the cross (v. 24), **for the Son of man** (8:20; 16:13) **is to come with his angels** (13:39, 41, 49; 24:31; 25:31) **in the glory of his Father** (19:28; 24:30; 25:31), far more splendid and enduring than the glory of the wealthy kingdoms of this world (4:8; 6:29). Then he will judge all nations, dispensing rewards and punishments, squarely based, as Scripture says (Ps. 62:12; Prov. 4:12) on **what** each **has done.** Literally, the Greek text reads, "He will repay each one" "according to his conduct" (cf. Rom. 2:6; 2 Tim. 4:14; Rev. 2:23; 20:12).

Matthew pictures Jesus in scenes of judgment sometimes as judge and sometimes as advocate or prosecutor (7:22-23; 13:41-43; 25:31-46), not because Matthew is harsh, demanding, or brooding and not because he is especially intrigued with the future of the world. On this topic see the introduction to chap. 24. Matthew by all means wishes to drive home the overriding value of very practical deeds of mercy and love. He struggled against trends in his environment, such as the elevation of ritual observance (12:1-14; 15:1-20) or boasting about spiritual endowments (7:15-23) or arrogance on the part of teachers and leaders (23:8-10). These and other currents threatened the vitality and centrality of mercy, and Matthew struggled against them. The immediate context of this saying (16:25-26) points to the nearly universal tendency to judge a person's worth on the basis of wealth. All that is excluded.

28—Then Jesus caps his summons to discipleship with the strong declaration, **There are some standing here who will not taste death before they see the Son of man coming in his kingdom.** In this difficult saying Jesus addresses not only Peter and the Twelve but the readers of every generation, pressing them to remember who they are and what time it is. They are his people, and he is coming at an unknown hour, breaking in to establish his sovereign rule (cf. 10:23; 13:41; 24:44). The Son of man (16:13) will appear at the end as judge or advocate-prosecutor and the ultimate question will not be one of titles and confession only (16:15-16) but of unselfish and cruciform living (16:21-27). Matthew everywhere praises that wholeness or integrity in which right confession is wed to right deeds.

Greatly Distressed (17:1-27)

The narrative of chap. 17, involving the inner circle of three disciples (17:1-13) and then the other nine (17:14-21) show once again how the disciples swing between faith and doubt, between understanding and misunderstanding in their response to Jesus. Only three are with Jesus on the mount of Transfiguration (vv. 1–13). They descend to discover the powerlessness of the nine in relation to the epileptic boy (17:14-21). That weakness is connected with the distress of all 12 at the announcement of Jesus' passion (17:22-23; cf. 16:21-28).

He Was Transfigured (17:1-8)

1—**Six days** lapsed after Peter's high confession and Jesus' first prediction of the depths of passion awaiting him and his disciples (16:13-28). Why this note about the precise time? The festival of Tabernacles or Booths comes six days after the Day of Atonement in the fall of the year at the beginning of the rainy season, and God spoke to Moses on the mount after six days (Exod. 24:16). But perhaps **after six days** is simply intended to focus attention on the fact that the transfiguration occurred on the seventh or climactic day.

Jesus summoned **Peter and James and John his brother,** an inner circle of three out of the Twelve (cf. 10:2; 20:20; 26:37; Gal. 2:9), and **led them up a high mountain apart.**

The adjective **high** is used also in connection with the mount of temptation (4:8). Awesome events occur on mountains in Matthew's Gospel: see 5:1; 14:23; 15:29; 24:3; 26:30; 28:16. In the biblical tradition, Mount Sinai is associated with theophanies to Israel (Exodus 19), Moses (Exodus 24), and Elijah (1 Kings 19). God was present with the people on Mount Zion (Ps. 68:16; Isa. 8:18; Joel 3:17), and Ezekiel promised (48:35) the renewal of the presence of God in a glorious future on a high mountain (Ezek. 48:35).

In spite of Matthew's apparent precision, efforts to locate the time on a calendar (festival of Tabernacles?) or the place on a map (Mount Tabor or Mount Hermon?) deflect us from Matthew's intent. When Matthew locates this moment of blazing incandescence between two solemn words on suffering (16:21-28 and 17:9-13) on an awesome height, in the company of two ancient worthies, he is not expounding ordinary geography. He is exploring the mystery of Jesus' sonship, and the mystery of discipleship. Jesus' sonship is defined by the path he travels. It commenced at baptism-temptation, leads through teaching and miracles, and climaxes in crucifixion-resurrection. This and no other is the way of the Son of God. But it is a path resisted by his closest disciples, and the transfiguration is part of God's own instruction to them and to the readers: "Listen to him!"

2—The cross had cast a harsh shadow on the path of Jesus and clouded the disciples' understanding (16:22). But now in response to their confusion and bleak mood, a great light (4:16) broke out and shone upon them. Jesus was **transfigured** (cf. 2 Cor. 3:18; Rom. 12:2) so that they were granted a foretaste of his coming glory (16:27-28). For one shining moment his present vulnerability was swallowed up by the brilliance of his coming majesty. **His face shone like the sun and his garments became white as light.** Moses, after speaking with God (Exod. 34:29-35), angels standing always in God's presence, and the righteous heirs of God's new world are elsewhere described in similar terms (13:43; 28:3; 22:12; cf. Dan. 10:5; 12:3; Rev. 1:16; 3:4-5; 7:9; 1 Enoch 14:20; 4 Ezra 7:97; 10:25).

3—Scales fell from the disciples' eyes, and they saw **Moses and Elijah talking with him.** Here Jesus is with Moses and Elijah; at the crucifixion he will be flanked not by two honored ancients but by two contemporary criminals (27:38). Where does Jesus really belong? In both places! The point of the transfiguration is that the downward way of Jesus is not only deep darkness but astonishing light. The path of service and suffering is hard but glorious.

In the eyes of Matthew, Moses and Elijah represent prophetic power, and in his view the prophets always suffered persecution (5:12; 23:29-35, 37). Nevertheless, neither of this awesome pair was thought by Jesus' contemporaries to be merely dead and gone. God had snatched them from an undeserving earth to his own bosom, and they were his lively agents still. Their appearance on the mountain is a sign of their approval of Jesus (even as he approves of them and has not come to cancel their work, 5:17; 7:12; 11:13; 22:40). They are for him and not against him. They affirm the hard path he walks as the path of deathless life.

4—Peter again (as in 16:16, 22) speaks for all as he volunteers to make **three booths** or tents, places of dwelling and abiding, one for Jesus and one each for Moses and Elijah. Peter places all three on an equal footing, thereby defining Jesus as a deathless prophet like Moses and Elijah. He also appears to think of himself with James and John as earthly counterparts of that heavenly triumvirate. Or does his outcry simply express his desire to embrace and freeze the glory of that moment, halting Jesus' forward march to the cross?

5—Peter's words, whatever their precise meaning, are inadequate, and his speech is rudely interrupted by the heavenly voice (cf. Acts 10:44). The entire scene with high mountain, awesome transformation, and cameo appearances by Moses and Elijah gets its proper interpretation when a **bright cloud** (Exod. 24:16-17; Ezek. 1:4; 1 Kings 8; Dan. 7:13; 2 Macc. 2:7-8; Sir. 24:4,8) **overshadowed them** (cf. Luke 1:35; Exod. 40:35) and **a voice from the cloud** solemnly intoned words spoken at Jesus' baptism, **This is my beloved Son with whom I am well pleased** (3:17; cf. 14:33; 16:16) and added, **Listen to him!** (Deut. 18:15).

To what are they to **listen?** Certainly to what Jesus has just said (16:24-28) and to the next words from his mouth (17:11-12) about suffering as the narrow way of sonship and the path of glory. That is Luke's understanding (Luke 9:31). But in the larger Matthean context disciples are called to listen to all that Jesus has commanded (28:19), to bend their necks to his yoke (11:24), to understand that the way of the cross and of servanthood is the way of sonship and discipleship. They are to listen to the crucified and resurrected Jesus as unique Son, greater by far than Moses and Elijah.

6—The disciples reacted by falling on their faces, a sure sign of **awe** before heavenly revelation (2:11; 14:33; 28:17; cf. Dan. 10:9; Ezek. 1:28—2:1; Rev. 1:17).

7—But then in a kind of parable of what always happens, Jesus did not grind their necks under the soles of his feet but **came and touched them** (8:3, 15; 9:25, 29; 28:18), lifting them into the joy of fellowship as members of his family (12:46-50; 28:9-10).

8—When the three disciples raised their eyes, Moses and Elijah had vanished, the bright cloud had disappeared, the apparition of shining face and gleaming garments had faded, and **they saw Jesus only,** as the abiding focus of their vision (cf. 28:20).

Elijah Has Already Come (17:9-13)

9—During the descent Jesus calls the experience on the mountain a **vision** and instructs his disciples to **tell no one until the Son of man** (8:20; 16:13,28) **is raised from the dead.** The vision, in other words, affirms the victorious character of the path Jesus is traveling toward the cross, and precisely for that reason the

story of Jesus is for the moment incomplete. He has still more
to say and do and especially to suffer. The shattering climax of
his way and the turning point of history lie ahead in his death
and resurrection.

10—The disciples are puzzled. How can Jesus promise resurrection? What about **Elijah? The scribes,** the theologians, teach
that **first Elijah must come** before the new world of resurrection
arrives.

11—Jesus interprets current events as final events. The tradition of the coming of **Elijah to restore all things** (Mal. 4:5; Sir.
48:10; Acts 1:6; 3:21) is not only correct but has been fulfilled.
Elijah has already come in the person of John the Baptist. However, people failed to recognize him and **did to him whatever
they pleased,** a euphemism for his hideous execution (14:1-12).
This **Elijah** by his suffering foreshadows the coming suffering of
the Son of man (v. 9). But because John the Baptist has come as
Elijah, he also fulfills all conditions for the turning of the aeons
and Jesus' resurrection.

13—Finally **the disciples understood** (cf. 13:51; 16:12). Unlike
outsiders, they grasp the identification of John the Baptist as
Elijah (11:9-14). In grasping that, they begin to see that John's
passion foreshadows Jesus' own suffering, and they see that rejection and death are not defeat but necessary prelude to the
resurrection of the Son of man.

As a Grain of Mustard Seed (17:14-21)

14—At least three of the disciples have been initiated more
deeply into the mystery of divine sonship (v. 13) but the others
still have miles to travel. **A man came up and kneeling before
him** (8:2; 9:18) laid a request at Jesus' feet. **Lord, have mercy**
(8:25; 9:2 14:30; 15:22) **on my son.** And he describes the lad as
an **epileptic.** Epileptics were thought to be under the evil influence of the moon because of his periodic seizures (the Greek
word is *seleniazetai,* from *selēnē = "moon").* Now and then, as
the moon waxes and wanes, he would sometimes act normally
and other times would throw himself into **fire** or **water** in a fit
of self-destruction.

16—The nine disciples have not yet reached the goal in Matthew's story. They **could not heal him.** In the whole section

13:53—17:23, all the disciples swing to and fro between understanding and inability. In both moods and modes they mirror the condition of the future church.

17—Jesus utters a complaint and a command. On the exalted mountain his commitment to the cross and to sonship as obedience has been marvelously affirmed. Now on the plain below he is assaulted by the old cry for miracles, for signs, for power. So he is exasperated, not so much at the disciples' inability, certainly not at the father's distress over his son's illness, but at the common thirst for marvels: **O faithless and perverse generation!** (12:39; 16:4; cf. Deut. 32:5). But exasperation yields to command: **Bring him here!**

18—Jesus saw **the demon** lurking behind the lad's illness (cf. 4:24) and **rebuked** him, and **the boy was cured** from that moment. Demons flee his presence (4:11).

19-20—**Privately** Jesus draws lessons for disciples and for readers. They are not faithless or perverse (v. 17), but they do waver dangerously. For the last time in his Gospel he calls them people of **little faith** (cf. 6:30; 8:26; 14:31; 16:8; cf. 28:17). As the narrative closes, Jesus uses a stunning image to encourage and exalt faith: **If you have faith as a grain of mustard seed** (13:31), you could move **this mountain** (17:1; 21:21; Isa. 40:4; 1 Cor. 13:2). Indeed, to men and women of faith, **nothing will be impossible** (19:26; 21:21-22).

Into the Hands of Men (17:22-23)

As they were gathering (some ancient manuscripts read, "living") **in Galilee,** Jesus uttered the second prediction of his passion, briefer than the first (16:21), omitting mention of Jerusalem and of the elders and chief priests and scribes. However, this one is cast into direct speech and Jesus clearly identifies himself as **the Son of man** (8:20; 16:13). While they do not reject Jesus' fresh declaration (cf. 16:22) or fail to understand it, as is the case in the reports of Mark and Luke, the disciples are **greatly distressed** (cf. 18:31; 19:22; 26:22, 37).

The Half-Shekel Tax (17:24-27)

Matthew once again punctuates his narrative with a paragraph featuring Peter (cf. 14:28-33; 16:13-23). This one bridges the gap between the passion prediction (17:22-23) and the discourse on the life of the new community (chap. 18). This passage is a bridge in the sense that it is a first commentary on the passion prediction, and at the same time it raises a question (about the meaning of "offending") which will be answered in chap 18. Chapter 18 contains much more than that, to be sure. As a whole it is a further, wonderful commentary on the implications of Jesus' passion prediction.

24—**Capernaum** was the center of Jesus' Galilean ministry (4:12-13) and in many ways functions as a symbol of opposition in the north (11:23; 17:24; but see 8:5) precisely as Jerusalem represents stubborn rejection of Jesus in the south (15:1; 16:21; 20:17-18; 23:37; but see 5:35).

The half-shekel tax was an obligation of every Jew 20 years old and up. Women and slaves were exempt, and some argued that priests and rabbis were also. The tax was due annually in the spring of the year and was earmarked for the upkeep of the temple in Jerusalem: for its supplies (wood, oil, incense), for offerings (birds, animals, meal), for the support of priests and Levites, for the care of the poor, for the maintenance of buildings, for vestments and vessels. (See Exod. 30:11-16; Neh. 10:32-33 [⅓ shekel] Josephus, *Ant.* 18.312; *War* 7.216-218; Mishnah *Shekalim.*)

On the 15th day of Adar, the 12th month of the year, tables were set up in Jewish communities beyond Jerusalem for the payment of the tax. Collectors approach Peter, asking, "Your **teacher** (8:19) pays **the tax,** doesn't he?" They seem to imply a further question, "He regards himself as subject to the temple and its authorities, doesn't he?" (12:6; 21:23-27).

25—Peter's **Yes** is at best only half right. Jesus speaks to him **at home** (8:14), introducing the topic with the formula, **What do you think?** This formula (cf. 18:12; 21:28; 22:17,44; 26:66) is an invitation not only to the person addressed but also to the readers to exercise care in mulling over the following question. Here the question calls for some meditation on a piece of ordinary human behavior: Do **kings of the earth** collect taxes, tolls, and tributes from their own children or from other people?

26—When Peter responds, **From others,** Jesus approves and draws conclusions: "You have correctly seen that the **sons** of earthly kings are **free!**" And Jesus implies the parallel: The Son of the heavenly king and all the sons and daughters of the king of heaven are likewise free. Since he is Son of God (16:16; 17:5), Jesus has no obligation to pay a tax in support of the temple, which is the house of God. He is free and so is the new community of his sisters and brothers (12:46-50).

27—Freedom is Jesus' first word, but it is not his last. In freedom he decides **not to give offense.** At 16:21 Jesus began to reveal to his disciples the divine necessity of his suffering and his own obedient and trusting acceptance of God's strange agenda. Furthermore, Jesus designed words and deeds aimed at helping his disciples to grasp the divine logic and everlasting rightness of the way of suffering and service. In the following section (18:1-35) Jesus will focus on the inner life of the community. He will speak of the horror of scandalizing little ones and of sinning against brother or sister. He will praise the grandeur of forgiveness that is freely, even infinitely repeated.

All along Jesus has freely provoked and scandalized opponents (9:1-13; 12:1-14; 15:12). Now suddenly he commands a submissive action and defends it by declaring that he wishes **not to give offense.** In earlier contexts "offense" has meant provocative statements or enactments of the new reality of the inbreaking kingdom. Jesus defends such offensive speech or behavior. But here in the present context (17:24-27 and chap. 18) "offense" means an action that causes a sister or brother to stumble and fall away from God. That is what Jesus forbids, calling for the free children of the kingdom to curb their freedom rather than to give such offense.

Jesus' words about voluntary renunciation of freedom and submission to sisters and brothers parallel his announcement of his voluntary commitment to the way of the cross (17:22-23a). But there is more here than giving up. The passion prediction includes also the promise of the miracle of resurrection, of glory beyond the passion, of triumph beyond all giving up (17:23b; cf. 17:2). So now Jesus instructs Peter to go to the sea and cast a hook, declaring that he will find a shekel (see commentary below on 26:15) in the mouth of the first fish that comes up—enough tax for the disciple and for the Master.

Both in the passion prediction (17:22-23) and in the strange paragraph on the shekel (17:24-27) Jesus is portrayed as submitting in obedience and service, while at the same time he remains mysterious Lord of all. Implicit in these passages is the promise that God will empower the disciples' every act of submitting and forgiving. These themes are carried forward in chap. 18.

■ FOURTH DISCOURSE: The New Community Practices Forgiveness and Reconciliation (18:1-35)

Chapter 18 features the fourth of the five discourses of Jesus in Matthew's Gospel. It begins with some familiar words, warmly urging disciples to become like children, and sharply warning against the failure to care for children and little ones (18:1-9; cf. Mark 9:33-48).

That opening serves as a kind of springboard or "text" for the remainder of Jesus' sermon or discourse (18:10-35). The chapter as a whole is all about the ordering of the internal life of the new community. The sermon extols the centrality of forgiveness as the community lives not simply after the great act of forgiveness (18:23-35) but in the presence of the one who went up to Jerusalem to offer his life on behalf of many (18:20; cf. 17:22-23).

Back in chap. 13 the Twelve emerged as genuine disciples. Jesus called them "Blessed" because of what they had been given to see and hear (13:16-17). Unlike merely curious crowds or openly hostile leaders of the people, the Twelve achieved understanding (13:51).

The subsequent chapters might have continued in that laudatory vein, offering rave notices of the Twelve and of the new community. Instead, Matthew has turned a critical eye on disciples and community.

Matthew notes (13:53-58) how inhospitable the hometown and family of the prophet could be, and he means not only Nazareth or Galilee or Judea. It soon becomes apparent that the Gospel is also raising questions in readers' minds about the church (16:18; 18:18), the new community, as the Messiah's "hometown." What kind of reception does Jesus receive here among those who like to style themselves his friends, his family? And what level of understanding is shown especially by those who are leaders in that new family?

In these chapters Peter is featured in three narratives unique to Matthew's Gospel (14:28-33; 16:17-19; 17:24-27; cf. 15:15). But not one of the disciples, including Peter, is glorified. The word "little-faiths" (cf. 6:30; 8:26) is applied to all of them and Peter's deficiencies are especially noted (14:30-31; 15:16-17; 16:8-11, 22-23; 17:19-20). Peter now plays a major role in chap. 18, although it has seldom been recognized. Peter's prominence in 17:24-27 is the occasion for the question controlling the first half of chap. 18: "Who is greatest in the kingdom of heaven?" (18:1). And according to Matthew (not so in Luke 17:4), it is Peter who raises the question which stands at the head of the second half of the chapter: "How often shall my brother sin against me and I forgive him?" (18:21).

Chapter 18 thus compels readers, presumably members of the new community, to ask themselves whether they are any more hospitable to Jesus than was Nazareth or Capernaum or Jerusalem (13:53-58). The question is put in particular to the leaders.

Were those leaders puffed up, imagining themselves to be indispensable links to the Twelve, privileged guardians of a holy tradition and its only true interpreters, magisterial doorkeepers at the threshold to the kingdom? Or could and did they offer signs and wonders as evidence of their legitimacy, or of their spiritual authority and intimacy with God, exactly the sort of proof Jesus refused to offer when it was demanded of him (4:7; 7:15, 21-23; 12:38-39; 16:1-4; 24:24)?

Did these latter-day leaders, successors of the Twelve, act as though they were the closest relatives of Jesus or the highest courtiers of the king? Did they imagine they were the "king's sons" (17:24-27), in some special sense not shared by other Christians? Chapter 18 roundly declares that all who believe in Jesus (18:6), including the "little ones," are full-fledged members of the community, and what they all owe is not any obedience from lesser to greater but forgiveness one to another.

Become Like Children (18:1-6)

1—At that time and in that same place (at home in Capernaum, 17:25), **the disciples came to Jesus** with a question. In Greek

(though not in the RSV) it includes the word "therefore." They
ask, "Who *therefore* is the greatest in the kingdom of heaven?"
The question grows out of reflection. If all Jesus has been saying
up to this point in the narrative about kingdom and community
is true, if Jesus is moving toward a universal dominion of righteousness, if Peter and the disciples have seen visions and received authority for solemn tasks, then what practical conclusions
for their shared life are the disciples to draw?

Who is the greatest, the most commanding, the highest rank-
ing? Is it Peter, who walks on water (14:28-33) and steps forth to
speak about Jesus and for Jesus (16:16-19; 17:4, 24-27)? How is
life in a really new community to be ordered?

Is it not a prime function of the Twelve and their successors
to sit on thrones and decide cases, dispensing justice at the gate
of the new community (cf. 19:28)? If chaos is to be avoided, must
not some have higher dignity, and titles equal to their more exalted rank (cf. 23:8-12)?

2—Jesus set **a child in the midst of them** (cf. 18:20) and solemnly declared, **Unless you turn,** unless your lives are trans-
muted by the alchemy of repentance (3:2; 4:17), **you will never**
so much as **enter the kingdom of heaven** (5:20; 7:21; 18:8-9; cf.
Mark 10:15), let alone rule there. Without an act of renunciation
and transfiguration, they will be too big, too bloated to slip
through the eye of the needle (19:23-24).

4—Having declared a principle in rather negative fashion,
Jesus underscores it in a positive parallel, echoing the words of
the opening question (v. 1): **Greatest in the kingdom of heaven**
are those who **humble** themselves **like this child** (cf. 5:19; 23:11).
To become an adult is to achieve independence, confidence, control over one's life. Is it possible or even good for people, once
they have achieved adulthood, to relearn the trusting language
of the child and open themselves to God, unashamedly crying,
"Abba, Father," depending entirely on the gifts and power of
another (cf. Nicodemus in John 3)?

5—Jesus defines power (17:19-20) and freedom (17:26) in the
kingdom by pointing to the child whom he embraces. Then Jesus
adds to the difficulty of the saying by identifying with the child,
the small, the powerless, the dependent, the marginal. With
alarming simplicity he declares that **whoever receives,** whoever

welcomes and holds dear, **one such child in my name,** for my sake, because I will it, **receives me** (cf. 25:31-46; 10:40-42).

If children hold the highest rank in the kingdom of heaven (see commentary below on v. 10), even if they are least in most human societies, then what?

6—Immediately Jesus broadens the principle by switching from talk of the literal **child** or **children** (four times in vv. 2-5) to more figurative speech of **these little ones** (18:6, 10, 14), meaning not just the young but people in general with essentially childlike traits. But which traits? And who exactly are **these little ones?** They may be recent converts, newcomers without any special standing in the community. More likely they are people who lack the special spiritual gifts flaunted by the leaders (10:42; 11:11). On the surface they seem to be thoroughly ordinary, unimpressive members of the community, and they are personally humble. Nevertheless, Jesus says, however deficient or insignificant they may seem to be, they can lay claim to one high qualification: they **believe in me** (cf. Mark 9:42).

Trust, openness to Jesus and his call, defines them. Only here and in the Markan parallel (Mark 9:42, not in Luke 17:2) do the Synoptic Gospels speak in this precise manner of "believing in Jesus." John's Gospel frequently uses this kind of language to define right relationship to Jesus.

That connection of faith is everything. Whoever severs that bond, **causes one of these little ones to sin** or stumble, to waver and have doubts about Jesus, is guilty of a capital crime.

In language of shocking severity, Jesus says it **would be better** to commit suicide by tying round one's neck **a great millstone,** the large kind cut from basalt and turned by ox or donkey—not the hand-held variety, which would be heavy enough—and to drown oneself in the depth of the sea, rather than to cause one of **these little ones** to stumble and fall. (The Greek word for offending, for setting stumbling blocks in another's path, is *skandalizō*. See 5:29-30; 11:6; 15:12; 16:23; 17:27; 24:10; 26:31-32.) Jesus' harsh words on offenses parallel his strong recommendations of righteousness.

Woe (18:7-9)

7—It is a fallen world and it is therefore **necessary** in the sense of inevitable **that temptations come.** It could be that temptations

are a necessary test of faith (cf. 1 Cor. 11:19) but see how the
same word "necessary" is used in 16:21 and 24:6.

Nevertheless, even if some sort of necessity or inevitability
attaches to temptations, that still does not excuse those in the
community who cause others to stumble. **Woe** (11:21; 23:13) to
those through whom temptations come! **Woe** to leaders in the
church who, instead of embracing the little ones, cause them to
waver in their faith in Jesus (cf. 5:18-19; 23:8-10; 24:10-12).

8-9—The hard sayings about cutting off a hand or plucking out
an eye are connected in the Sermon on the Mount with adultery
and sexual lust (5:28-30). Here the same images are applied to
sins of leadership: lust for power and rank and position, the tendency to treat little ones like second class citizens, sweeping them
into the corner, acting as though they were members of the community only by the grace of the leaders.

Whatever leads you astray in relation to sisters or brothers in
the community, even if it is as important as hand or foot or eye,
cut it off, pluck it out, throw it away.

Their Angels (18:10-11)

Whatever **the little ones** may be (see the comments on v. 6)
they are not insignificant. **Their angels** stand in the innermost
courts of heaven as angels of the Presence and so **always behold
the face of my Father who is in heaven.** They have immediate
access to God, and the well-being of those little ones therefore
is in God's unsleeping care. If teachers and leaders in the earthly
community wish to think in terms of rank, then they had better
remind themselves that the guardian angels of the little ones hold
the very highest rank. The Hymns of Qumran (1QH 5:20-22)
speak of angels as walking beside the meek, the lost, those eager
for righteousness (cf. Luke 16:22; Heb. 1:14).

11—This verse about the Son of man seeking the lost (cf. 20:28)
stands in some ancient manuscripts but was not originally part
of Matthew's Gospel. An ancient copyist knew it from Luke 19:10
and introduced it here as a relevant comment.

One Goes Astray (18:12-14)

12—Teachers and leaders are criticized elsewhere in the Gospel (5:19; 24:11) for endangering the lives of other disciples

through their teaching. In the present context leaders are warned against treating little ones with haughty contempt (18:10) and acting harshly or hastily to exclude them from the community. To such leaders, concerned for their greatness (18:1), impressed with their own prerogatives in the community (23:8-10), and convinced of their right to include or exclude, Jesus throws down a challenge, inviting them to draw spiritual conclusions from their observation of everyday conduct: **What do you think?** (cf. 17:25). **If a man has a hundred sheep, and one of them goes astray** (*planēthē*, cf. 24:4, 5, 11, 24), he just naturally leaves the 99 on the hillside and goes searching for the one, doesn't he?

13-14—When he finds the one, he is overjoyed. Just so, God rejoices not in culling the weak or deficient out of the community (cf. 13:24-30, 36-43) but in finding and embracing, healing and feeding.

It would ruin Matthew's point if the lost sheep were somehow the most valuable, most prized or largest (cf. Gospel of Thomas 107).

God's heart goes out to **these little ones** and it is not his **will** that any one of them should **perish** (cf. Luke 15:3-7). The Gospel of Matthew from start to finish is an exposition of the **will** of God to rescue from sin (1:21) and from the shadow of death (4:16), to touch the world and make it all right. The strategy for achieving that goal is for leaders to incorporate people into a community which practices discipleship in the presence of the resurrected Christ (4:19; 18:20; 28:19-20).

If Your Brother Sins (18:15-17)

At first this new paragraph looks like a set of by-laws for ousting a member who has broken the rules. It has about it the odor of the courtroom, of interrogation and prosecution, and in the history of the church has functioned chiefly as a set of minimum standards guiding judges in cases of excommunication. Comparable language appears in legal sections of the Hebrew Scriptures (Deut. 19:15) and in the constitution of the Qumran community (1QS 5:25-6:1; CD 9:2-4; 13:9-10). Closer in substance but differing in language is Paul's charge to the Corinthians regarding a sinner (1 Cor. 5:1-13; cf. 2 Cor. 2:5-11; 13:1; 1 Tim. 5:19).

The Essenes at Qumran aimed to establish a community in complete harmony with the laws pertaining to priesthood. Persons with moral and physical blemishes were rigorously excluded. Impurities and disabilities would offend the holy guardian angels of the community (1QSa 2:8-9; cf. Matt. 21:14).

The rules at Qumran about stages of rebuke leading all the way to excommunication seem designed to serve offended members as a safety valve, acting as a mechanism by which they might purge themselves of evil thoughts and so stay clean. The procedure in Matthew, so similar in outline, aimed at gaining the erring sister or brother.

Matthew recognizes the need for safeguarding the righteousness or integrity of the community (cf. 18:8-9) but carefully embeds this passage in a context of graciousness. Before the passage Jesus speaks of the one lost sheep (18:12-14) and after it of the unmerciful servant (18:23-35). Matthew has incorporated a tradition of his community but modified it by giving it this fresh context.

15—This section, like the last, is addressed especially to leaders and teachers. It describes how the spirit of the shepherd is to be implemented in cases where **brother** or sister **sins** or stumbles and so begins the long fall out of the community. That falling is a terrible thing (cf. 18:6-7) and leaders had better be working to catch and hold rather than to throw or push. Important ancient manuscripts lack the words **against you** after **if your brother sins** (cf. v. 21). Leaders are here reminded that the "little ones" are not their subjects or serfs but their sisters and brothers, not underlings but siblings.

Then a threefold procedure of reconciliation is defined: (1) privately, quietly (1:19) **between you and him alone,** tell him **his fault. If he listens** you have repaired the broken bond and restored wholeness to the community (cf. Lev. 19:7-18).

16—(2) But perhaps the fellow disciple is stubborn. Then **take one or two others** as **witnesses** and try again (cf. Deut. 19:15; 2 Cor. 13:1; 1 Tim. 5:19).

17—(3) That effort may also be in vain. If so, take the matter to **the church,** to the solemn assembly of sisters and brothers. The entire community is summoned to help regain the one straying sheep. The aim is to hold the straying within the forgiving

221

and ample embrace of the church. The word **church** (*ekklēsia*) never appears in the other Gospels, and its use in Matthew (16:18; 18:17) is one indication of Matthew's concern for the life of the post-Easter Christian community.

If even this effort fails, then **let him be to you as a Gentile and a tax collector.** It is odd to see this traditional name-calling surface here. These old terms describe from a pious Jewish perspective people whose vertical and horizontal relationships (relations with God and with neighbor) are fatally flawed (cf. 5:46-47). Elsewhere Matthew's Gospel notes how Gentiles and tax collectors by their simple and disarming faith put to shame pious Israelites (8:1-11; 9:9-13; 15:21-28). Sometimes it happens that the sinner **refuses to listen** and the mutual conversation among sisters and brothers breaks down.

The procedure outlined here undercuts any precipitous action on the part of leaders in the community. In fact the passage is remarkable for its silence on the matter of leaders or officers. How the Matthean community was organized we do not know. The Gospel, for all its keen interest in the life of the new community, breathes not a single word about bishops, elders, deacons, or any other offices or ranks. Yet it is hard to shake the suspicion that Matthew's rendering of the words of Jesus frequently has in view Christian leaders with a tendency to promote themselves at the expense of the little ones (see especially 23:8-10).

I Am There (18:18-20)

18—Leaders are forbidden to act unilaterally in expelling members from the community but must involve the whole assembly. And even the community as a whole must look beyond the total number of its visible membership. The primeval rift between heaven and earth is being overcome in the new community (see the comments on 6:10). When the church **on earth** acts **to bind** and **to loose,** to prohibit or permit (16:19), **heaven** actively participates, and **heaven** is all on the side of mercy and life (see v. 14). Heaven's participation functions both as promise and as threat.

Reconciliation is the goal of the procedures outlined for the community, and reconciled life has peculiar force. Hatred has terrible power to divide, disrupt, destroy. Reconciliation and loving community are even more powerful, especially when it is a community of humans and angels, of earth reconciled with heaven.

19—When **two** people, formerly estranged and warring, now **agree on earth** and offer a shared request to God, they tap awesome power.

20—And, says Jesus, **where two or three** (see vv. 16, 19) **are gathered in my name** (cf. 6:9; 7:22; 24:9; 28:19), not merely gathered, not merely together in human association but in the peace and power of **my name,** intentionally invoking my presence, **there am I in the midst of them.** And Jesus, enthroned on the prayers of the community, is the one leader absolutely necessary for the being and well-being of the church (cf. 23:8-10).

Jesus speaks of a community which asks not just what works pragmatically, or what we have always done traditionally. The new community focuses rather on God's will as Jesus has revealed and embodied it. And Jesus will be power surging up in the members to ensure that what they ask really is the will of God.

It was a conviction of ancient (as of modern) Jews that ten adult males were required to form a synagogue and hold a service. In a marvelous passage of the Mishnah, the question is raised whether the Shekinah, God's presence, would not rest upon an assembly of nine or of eight. What if only five were gathered, or three or two or one? Scriptural passages are quoted to support the confidence that the divine presence rests upon even the smallest number of persons, as long as they occupy themselves with the Law and meditate on the name of the Lord (Mishnah, *Pirke Aboth* 3:2-6).

Matthew's Gospel bears witness to the exalted Jesus rather than the Torah as the vehicle of the divine presence in the community (1:23; 18:20; 28:20; cf. 11:28-30), as it wrestles in prayer with doing the will of God on earth as it is done in heaven (1 Cor. 5:4; Luke 24:15; John 14:23).

Seventy Times Seven (18:21-22)

21—Once again **Peter** (contrast Luke 17:3-4) steps into the limelight (see the introduction to chap. 18). **Peter** correctly concludes that Jesus is exalting forgiveness as heavenly power able to maintain the health and wholeness of the community in the midst of a fallen world. But he makes the mistake of trying to count, to calculate, to quantify: **Lord, how often shall my brother sin against me, and I forgive him?** If my brother keeps on sinning, and will not stop, must I keep on forgiving? **As many as seven times?** These words of Peter, introducing the second half of the chapter, echo the language of v. 15.

22—If **seven** carries overtones of fullness or completeness, it is still not enough to express the radicality of Jesus' intention. He piles one seven on top of another: **I do not say to you seven times, but seventy times seven.** (Luke 17:3-4 neither features Peter as questioner nor does it move beyond seven to seventy-seven or to seventy times seven.) Perhaps the Greek is better translated "seventy-seven times," but in any case the dynamic at work in the new community must be totally opposite to that of which Lamech boasted. When a young man merely struck him, Lamech reacted violently and killed him, and then bragged of how he had been avenged seventy-seven fold (Gen. 4:15, 23-24). Forgiveness seventy-seven times or seventy times seven is unlimited, absolute, complete.

I Forgave You All That Debt (18:23-35)

In a supporting parable Jesus again tosses around awesome numbers designed to shatter all petty calculation and to prepare the mind for an exceeding righteousness (5:20) beyond all fussy quantification.

23—**The kingdom of heaven may be compared** (see commentary above on 13:24) to **a king** who declared that it was time to audit the accounts of all **his servants** (cf. 25:19).

24—The examiners discovered one servant who had lined his own pockets with **ten thousand talents** belonging to the king. **Ten thousand** is literally a "myriad," the largest number in the ancient Greek vocabulary, and **talents** were the heaviest weights or largest units of monetary value with one talent the equivalent of 6000 denarii (cf. 18:28).

Ten thousand and **talents** together signify the biggest stack of money imaginable. No individual servant, even if this were a high court official, could literally embezzle such a fabulous sum.

When the Romans first occupied Palestine in 63 B.C. they levied on the nation as a whole an annual tax of 10,000 talents, a sum so enormous, so impossibly burdensome, that Julius Caesar later reduced it.

25—The servant had no way to pay that crushing debt. Therefore **his lord** (*kyrios;* the parable pictures him as a typical oriental potentate) **ordered** that the servant himself, together **with his wife and children,** should be **sold** on the auction block as slaves, and all his property should be confiscated and liquidated with the proceeds to be applied toward the debt.

Only a fraction of the debt would be paid off, but the king's honor would be satisfied and other potential embezzlers would get the warning.

26—**The servant fell on his knees** (see commentary above on 8:2), threw himself face down, and begged his master: **Lord, have patience with me, and I will pay you everything.** His promise is preposterous. He could never pay off such a monstrous debt.

27—Nevertheless, the plea touched his master's heart. And moved to pity for him (cf. 9:36; 14:14; 15:32; 20:34) **the lord** not only **released him** (cf. v. 18; 16:19), rescinding his prior order, but actually **forgave him the** entire **debt** (6:12; 26:28), cancelling it with a magisterial wave of his hand.

28—**But that same servant** as he left the king's presence **came upon one of his fellow servants who owed him a hundred denarii,** no small sum, since it amounted to three months' pay for a day laborer (20:2). But certainly 100 denarii are paltry compared with 10,000 x 6000 = 60,000,000 denarii! (see the note on 18:24). In a gesture at once mean and ugly, totally at odds with the mercy he had just experienced, he grasped the jugular of his fellow servant and demanded, **Pay what you owe.**

The scene is full of irony. With nearly identical gestures and words (compare vv. 24 and 29) that second servant sought the same mercy which the first had just tasted.

30—But the first servant denied the plea of the second and hauled him off to **prison,** till his family or friends would ransom him by paying off the debt (cf. 5:25-26).

31—**His fellow servants, greatly distressed, reported to their lord.**

32-33—**His lord summoned him** and condemned him: **You**

wicked servant! (24:48; 25:26) **I forgave you all that debt because you besought me, and should not you have had mercy on your fellow servant, as I had mercy on you?** (5:7; 6:12, 14-15). The servant is not above the master, neither in suffering nor in serving and forgiving (10:24-25).

34—Pity (v. 27) gives way to anger: **His lord delivered him to the jailers,** literally, "the torturers," **till he should pay all his debt** (5:25-26).

35—Divine generosity is meant to empower hearty mutual forgiveness within the new community of sisters and brothers. Heaven and earth embrace and are no longer separated by a great gulf, when each one, forgiven by God, forgives the sister or the brother **from the heart** (cf. 22:37). Heartfelt generosity stands forever opposed to "hardness of heart," a sad virus affecting not only the unforgiving servant (18:28-30) but humanity in general (19:8).

Acting **from the heart** is the opposite of behavior carefully calculated to make an impression on one's peers (cf. 6:1-18) or designed merely to conform to some hallowed rule or tradition (cf. 15:2). It is certainly the opposite of life lived out of a selfish desire for reward or out of the fear of punishment. The phrase speaks of actions welling up spontaneously, joyfully, irrepressibly from lives touched by the life of God.

■ The Servant's Path (19:1—20:34)

On the Way to Jerusalem (19:1-30)

From 4:12 the action of the Gospel has centered in Galilee, but here in 19:1-2 a major geographical shift occurs. Jesus begins his march to Jerusalem, prophesied in 16:21 but only now actually set in motion. Jesus moves toward Jerusalem and toward his own death and resurrection. And as those events come closer, the full dawning of the kingdom also draws nearer (see commentary above on 4:17). So Jesus begins to address his disciples about life in the power of the kingship of God and how it differs from life as ordinarily lived and customarily experienced.

Chapters 19 and 20 deal with some fundamentals of human life: male and female, children and celibacy, marriage and divorce, rank and privilege and money.

Jesus struggles with the Pharisees (19:3-9) but even more with his own disciples (19:10-15; 20:1-26), with an anonymous young man who wishes to be a disciple (19:16-26), with Peter (19:27-30), and with the mother of James and John (20:20-21). So these chapters continue the drift of chap. 18, where it is insiders, not outsiders, who are the problem.

And what does Jesus teach? Not more rules and ordinances but a hard message about discipleship and the way of the cross. About the primacy of absolute love of the neighbor. Discipleship and love, learned in the company of Jesus, constitute a path both narrow and difficult (7:13-14). Passing difficult, it seems unreasonable and impossible to all Jesus' conversation partners in these chapters. Time and again the radicality of Jesus' call proves too much for insiders. But Jesus speaks not of human potential alone but of divine gifts, divine power, divine enabling, divine generosity and goodness.

Judea beyond the Jordan (19:1-2)

1—**Now when Jesus had finished these sayings** (the formula concluding each of the major sermons, 7:28; 11:1; 13:53; 26:1) he moved east and south out of **Galilee,** crossing **the Jordan** river, avoiding Samaria (10:5), and so approached **the region of Judea.**

2—As usual, **large crowds** follow in his wake, drawn by the power of his words and deeds. They bring to Jesus their sick and demon-possessed and he heals them all (4:23-25; 8:1; 9:35-36; 12:15; 14:13-14, 35-36; 15:30).

What God Has Joined (19:3-9)

3—**Pharisees** approach Jesus and put to him a controversial question. The legality of divorce was accepted on all sides, but ancient religious parties argued about grounds. Hence the accent in the question falls on the final three words: **Is it lawful to divorce one's wife for any cause? Any** old **cause** whatsoever? In other words, how does Jesus interpret the vague phrase, "some indecency," in the Law of Moses (Deut. 24:1)? Does he share the liberal view of gentle Hillel or the more stringent view of Shammai? The former thought that a man might divorce his wife if he did not care for her cooking while the latter judged that only infidelity was valid grounds for divorce.

4-5—Jesus does not play the game according to their rules. In his response he undercuts the ground on which his questioners stand. He moves back beyond the days of the Exodus and wilderness wanderings to the time of creation, a period boasting both chronological and spiritual priority. He moves back before Moses to God (cf. 15:4; 22:31; and see also the Antitheses in 5:21-48), back to **the beginning.** In **the beginning** we come into contact with God's primal, original intent. In **the beginning** (cf. 13:35) God made them male and female and said, **A man shall leave his father and mother and be joined to his wife, and the two shall become one** (Gen. 1:27; 2:4).

6—Jesus draws the conclusion, **so they are no longer two but one,** a single living being. **What therefore God has joined together let no man,** no human being, no human ruling or tradition, **put asunder** or separate. Not if you want to boast that you are living as God would have you live.

7—But **why then,** they protest, **did Moses command one to give a certificate of divorce?**

Jesus responds that Moses did not **command** divorce but only **allowed** it. Moses took a realistic view of human frailty and he compromised. Well acquainted with **hardness of heart** (cf. 18:35), with humanity's adamantine stubbornness, he made concessions.

But from the beginning it was not so. The original, primal intention of God expressed in the narratives of Genesis was that
marriage should be an indissoluble bond. And anything less, even
if condoned and regulated by Mosaic legislation, is evidence of
fallenness and of hardness of heart and stands in opposition to
the original vision of God.

9—Jesus concludes with words nearly identical to words in the
Sermon on the Mount. Trampling the marriage bond tramples
the will of God (5:31-32).

Eunuchs for the Sake of the Kingdom (19:10-12)

10—Jesus' disciples (not the Pharisees!) voice a shocked reaction. If marriage is such an inescapable obligation, a life sentence, then perhaps **it is not expedient** to marry. Perhaps it is
better to remain celibate. By their response the disciples reveal
that they share the view that men and women easily displease
one another, that marriage is difficult, that hearts are hard. The
only solution they can see to hardness of heart is not entering
into any deep and lasting relationship.

11—Jesus picks up on their comment and turns it over, examining it. Marriage, remarriage, and celibacy were live questions in the early church (see 1 Corinthians 7). Is there after all
some merit in the disciples' snap response? Is there a sense in
which indeed it is **expedient not to marry? Not all** can receive
this saying, says Jesus, but only those who have been given the
gift. **This saying** may be the disciples' word: it is expedient not
to marry. Or it may be Jesus' earlier word: What God has joined,
let no human put asunder. These words describe the two strong
choices: lifelong marriage or complete celibacy.

12—A harsh word, **eunuchs,** enters the conversation. Did opponents mock Jesus or some of his unmarried disciples as **eunuchs?** Marriage and begetting children were almost universally
regarded as a religious obligation. It is not clear whether celibacy
was practiced by the Essenes at Qumran. Temporary abstinence
from sexual relations was practiced, perhaps in accord with Ezek.
44:22, understood as marriage rules for the new age (1QSa 1:25;
2:11). In general, however, celibacy was regarded as disobedience
to the divine commandment to be fruitful and multiply.

Jesus takes that word **eunuchs** and uses the word at first literally and then figuratively of those who live celibate lives. He says that some may remain unmarried all their lives since they are literal **eunuchs** because of a birth defect or because of castration. That is a serious matter, since **eunuchs,** together with others suffering from physical deformation, were excluded from full participation in the life of the community (cf. 18:15; Deut. 23:1; Isa. 56:4-5; Acts 8:26-40; cf. Lev. 22:24).

But then some may be **eunuchs** in the sense that they voluntarily renounce marriage and sexual relations and the nurture of family (10:34-39). The disciples (v. 10) seem to say that such renunciation of marriage might spare a man a life of grief with a difficult partner. But Jesus has a renunciation of another sort in mind. It may be given to some to renounce God's creational gifts not out of selfishness, not from fear of being locked into a bad relationship, not from distaste for community and not because of a yen for solitude or peace, but **for the sake of the kingdom of heaven** (1 Cor. 7:26-34), because they hearken to a higher call, because God is calling them to serve a multitude of brothers and sisters in community.

In the space of a few short sentences Jesus defends both the indissoluble bond of marriage and the possibility of the celibate life without making a rule out of marriage or out of celibacy. He points not to old rules but to what each one is **given.** God is, through Jesus, dispensing fresh creative gifts, touching hard hearts, making the world all right again. And so he presses listeners to ask not what the rules and customs and traditions are but what their own gift may be. What powers and healings and renewings is God bestowing?

Let the Children Come (19:13-15)

14—The disciples are still captive to old traditions and old ways of thinking. People were bringing their children to Jesus for a blessing, but the disciples rebuke them and try to block their access. The disciples see wives (v. 7) and children only as burdens and liabilities, not as good gifts of the Creator who established the marriage union in the beginning (v. 4). But Jesus says, **Let the children come to me and do not hinder them, for to such**

belongs the kingdom of heaven (cf. 18:1-6). The saying has peculiar bite. Jesus offended people by receiving children, just as he offended by keeping company with tax collectors and prostitutes (9:11; 11:19; 21:32).

The childlike more readily travel the path to **the kingdom** than do the rich, the strong, the confident, the adult. Indeed, only those who turn and become like children can enter **the kingdom** (18:3-4). It is theirs.

"Little ones" of all kinds are innocent of the caution that comes with wealth and station (see 19:16-30) or the shackles of a learned tradition. Without a second thought or a moment's hesitation they eagerly receive the message of God's coming world as good news (11:25-26). Jesus **laid his hands on them** (9:18) in blessing, marking his oneness with them and sharing with them his life and health. And then he **went away.**

To Have Eternal Life (19:16-30)

The scene has shifted (v. 15) but audience and topic have not, as Jesus continues to challenge the traditional piety held by his disciples. He has just heaped extravagant praise on children as those who in their humility and poverty possess the kingdom (19:14).

Now, almost as if to confirm the profound truth of the preceding, Jesus is approached by a wealthy **young man** (v. 30), and they talk of riches and eternal life. The young man asks about **eternal life** (*zoē aiōnios*, 19:16-17), a phrase seldom met in the Synoptic Gospels but frequently seen in the Gospel of John. It is for all practical purposes the equivalent of **the kingdom** (19:14) of God or **of heaven.**

Over the centuries the report of this encounter has had an incalculably great effect on Christian attitudes to wealth and worldly power. Anthony in ancient Egypt (ca. 250) is not the only one to feel the force of Jesus' words to the rich young man.

The young man carries his wealth lightly, accepting it as a sign of divine favor and approaches Jesus in all seriousness and piety. He hails Jesus as **Teacher** (8:19, 21) and asks, **What good deed must I do to have eternal life?**—the ultimate blessing to top all earthly blessings. The RSV obscures the fact that the word **good** stands alone and unadorned in the Greek text, **What good** (*agathon*) **must I do?**

17-19—Jesus replies that the young man already has at hand all the moral instruction he requires. He points the young man to God who is absolutely **good,** and to God's will. Jesus makes no fresh demands, adds nothing to the Ten Commandments. He merely penetrates to their heart, in the process quoting five of the Ten Commandments, rounding them off with the word, **You shall love your neighbor as yourself.** It all adds up to self-giving and generous relations with the neighbor.

Mark and Luke also record this conversation between Jesus and the rich young man (Mark 10:17-22; Luke 18:18-23), but only in Matthew does Jesus sum it all up with the call to **love your neighbor** (cf. 5:43; 22:39; Lev. 19:18). This is one of Matthew's persistent themes. Other Matthean summaries of God's will stand at 7:12; 9:13; 12:7.

20—The serious young man replies, **All these I have observed** (some ancient manuscripts add "from my youth," as in Mark 10:20). **What do I still lack?** Jesus does not laugh at the young man's almost childlike naivete or expose him as hypocritical or hopelessly egotistical.

21—Jesus puts his finger not on any flaw in the young man's character but on the popular wisdom that regards wealth and power as infallible signs of God's favor. Jesus makes an alarming suggestion: how about great poverty as a sign of divine blessing and nearness to God (8:20)? **If you would be perfect** (5:48), undivided and whole, **go, sell what you possess,** and then **give** the proceeds **to the poor, and you will have treasure in heaven** (6:20). In 20:15 the landowner calls himself "good" and equates goodness with the sort of reckless, uncalculating generosity which Jesus here recommends.

Come, says Jesus, share my vulnerability, my weakness, my almighty trust in God. Enter my fellowship and **follow me** (4:18-22; 8:19-22), sharing freely with the poor and dispossessed (25:31-46).

22—Jesus' invitation strikes the young man as bad news. He does not receive the word with joy (13:20) but turns **sorrowful.** He does not **come** or **follow** but rather he **went away.** His attachment to his **great possessions** (13:22) finally dooms him to reject Jesus' invitation to real life, to God's new world, and to the practice of that new life ahead of time in discipleship and in the fellowship of the new community.

Jesus' words finally do expose the bedrock of the young man's life and it was not God after all, in spite of all the piety of the young man's speech. He claims to have his heart set on God and on eternal life, and to some extent he does want God, but his heart is divided (6:24), and he is not able to abandon his wealth. The narrative strikes hard at the readers and tests their sense of security.

23—Jesus then turns to his disciples with words summing up his encounter with the rich young man: **It will be hard for a rich man to enter the kingdom of heaven** (cf. 27:57).

This chapter seems to feature **hard** or difficult things: **hard** for a man to marry and not divorce (vv. 3-9), **hard** not to marry and to become a eunuch for the kingdom (vv. 10-12), **hard** to welcome and value children (vv. 13-15), **hard** to be generous like God who is unstintingly good (vv. 16-23), **hard** to be saved (v. 25).

24—How **hard?** Jesus paints an unforgettable picture. **It is easier for a camel to go through the eye of a needle than for a rich man to enter the kingdom of God.** The matter is far beyond human capacity, outside our reach, simply impossible.

25—But if it is that **hard,** and if we all have some property, some wealth, **then who can be saved?**

26—As the genealogy already indicates (1:1-17), the history of God's people did not produce salvation or the kingdom of God. Life or salvation are the product neither of individual nor of combined human efforts. As children and tax collectors and sinners perceive, it is not a human achievement or a human possibility at all. It is pure gift and comes from above (1:21; 19:11). As Jesus says, **With man this is impossible, but with God all things are possible.** Entrance into discipleship and a life of sharing are impossible if the final reality is hardness of heart. But the advent of Jesus opens the way to fresh possibilities as God through him begins to lay hands of blessing on the world, to renew, to save, to make it all right. Jesus thus concludes this portion of the passage (19:16-26) with a triumphant reminder of the power of God's goodness (cf. 18:27). Yet, the same passage clearly shows how difficult it is for the rich to part with any share of their possessions, how hard it is to trust the power of God (cf. 6:24; 22:21).

27—**Peter** now speaks up for the Twelve and for all who have made the kind of renunciation Jesus calls for. **We have left everything and followed you** (4:20-22). We have made sacrifices. We have exerted ourselves, spent ourselves, while others have not. **What shall we have?** Surely not just the same as all the rest! (This theme is developed in the following chapter in 20:1-16.)

Jesus' reply both acknowledges their discipleship and encourages discipleship on the part of the readers. **In the new world,** in the time of universal regeneration and renewal (*palingenesia*), when all nature is reborn and the dead are raised, when God's rule breaks out with unobstructed power and life will no longer be tarnished by the presence and pressure of sin and death, **when the Son of man** (8:20) **shall sit on his glorious throne** (10:23; 20:21; 24:30; 25:31; 26:64), when all Caesars and Herods place their necks beneath the soles of his feet, then **you who have followed me will also sit on twelve thrones, judging the twelve tribes of Israel** (cf. Luke 22:28-30; Rev. 3:21). Their leadership in the community, expressed in their discipleship, will never be forgotten. It will in fact be vindicated and celebrated in the new age.

The "time of rebirth" (*palingenesia*) first gained significance as a Stoic teaching: universal conflagration will be followed by the new world. Philo uses the word of the resurrection of individuals and of the restoration of creation after the flood, while Josephus uses it of the restoration of Israel after the exile. Later New Testament documents use the word of the restoration of the individual in baptism (Titus 3:5; cf. John 3:3-5). In the Synoptic parallels Luke 22:30 has "in my kingdom" and Mark 10:30 (cf. Luke 18:30) has "in the coming age."

29—Jesus broadens his promise: **Everyone** who has sacrificed possessions or family **for my name's sake** (10:22; 18:5) **will receive a hundredfold** (cf. 13:8,23) **and inherit eternal life** (cf. v. 16).

30—A proverbial saying of Jesus brings the present chapter to a close and strikes the note explicated in the following paragraph (20:1-16): **Many that are first will** in the future kingdom **be last, and the last** will be **first.** This saying, like the Beatitudes (5:3-12) and the woes (chap. 23), announces that all ordinary expectations are overturned in the presence of Jesus. The saying is repeated at 20:16, and the enclosed parable (19:30—20:16) casts light not only on the saying but on all the material in chap. 19 leading up to the saying. And then Jesus picks up that word "first" and continues to reinterpret it in the dispute about greatness (20:20-28).

Not to Be Served (20:1-34)

The parable of the laborers in the vineyard (20:1-16), by stressing the landowner's surprising generosity, continues themes of the preceding chapter (see the comments on 19:1) and in fact completes the section that began with the second passion prediction (17:22-23). Immediately following the parable, Jesus utters his third passion prediction (20:17-19). It sets the stage for the request of the mother of James and John, who comes seeking special status for her two sons (20:20-28). That passage about two uncomprehending disciples and their mother is designed to be read in closest connection with the following narrative, which features another pair in need of Jesus' healing touch: the two blind men of Jericho (20:29-34).

Laborers for His Vineyard (20:1-16)

This parable, unique to Matthew's Gospel, is bracketed by Jesus' words on the shocking reversal in store for **the first** and **the last** (19:30; 20:16). Matthew is intrigued by these ranks and their reversal, and he has set the parable precisely here so that it follows up on Peter's anxious question, **What then shall we have?** (19:27). What will we twelve **first** disciples receive? After all, we have left everything! And what will I, Peter, as **first** among the Twelve (10:2) get as a reward?

Jesus' praise of those Twelve is incalculably great (19:28-29) but the Twelve and all disciples after them must remember that **many that are first will be last and the last first** (19:30; 20:16).

The first are hard-working and long-suffering, faithful over the long haul (like the Pharisee in 19:3 or the rich young man of 19:16), while **the last** bear less and accomplish less (like the children of 19:13) and yet are treated as equals.

In another context the parable might have been told, like the parable of the prodigal son (Luke 15:11-32), to defend Jesus' warm embrace of tax collectors and sinners. Or it may have been used to interpret the incorporation of Gentiles (**the last**) into the ancient people of God (**the first**).

However, standing where it does in Matthew's Gospel, the parable is part of Jesus' response to Peter's outburst (19:27), and so is directed at church leaders of the earliest generation and at their nervous successors, anxious about rewards for their efforts and scratching for privileged positions. It is simply a fact that people regularly understand and appreciate God's strange calculus of grace as applied to themselves but fear and resent seeing it applied to others.

The parable, bracketed by that challenge to rethink and redefine the meaning of being "first," is at the same time an excellent introduction to the third passion prediction (20:17-19), to Jesus' words about the servant or slave as "first" (20:20-27), and to the ransom saying (20:28). This whole chapter in fact forms an excellent prelude to Jesus' entrance into Jerusalem (chap. 21) and his final days in that city.

1—The kingdom of heaven is like a householder (cf. 13:24, 45; 18:23), not an enormously wealthy absentee landlord (21:33) but an independent grower with a **vineyard** (a symbol of the people of God in Isa. 5:1-7; Jer. 12:10; John 15:1-6; cf. Matt. 21:28-32, 33-39) too large to work entirely on his own. He walks to the village square around six in the morning to **hire laborers.** Poor agricultural workers showed up in the **market place** each morning hoping to be hired. Hoping to exchange their energy and ability for a piece of silver to keep their families fed and housed and clothed.

2—The owner contracts with laborers for a denarius a day. The **denarius** was a small silver coin about the diameter of a dime but a bit thicker. A **denarius** was the minimum daily income required to sustain a small family (see the commentary on 18:28; 22:19; 26:9, 15; cf. Tobit 5:14-15).

3-5—Anxious about the harvest, the owner returns to the square to hire additional hands at 9 A.M. (**the third hour**) and 12 noon (**the sixth hour**) and 3 P.M. (**the ninth hour**). He promises to pay **whatever is right.**

6-7—It is astonishing that late in the day, around 5 in the afternoon (**the eleventh hour**), the owner sends still more workers into the vineyard. It is useless to ask how the owner had missed these last workers when he went to the village square earlier or why they were not working elsewhere. Were they lazy? Had they arrived late? Had they traveled from another village? And what is pressuring the owner? Why the rush? Is it harvest time, and does he fear damage to the crop from an early rain?

The parable itself concentrates rigorously on the exact number of hours worked and on the hope of payment cherished by those peasants as they compared themselves with one another. The elaborate details, the telling of the hours, and the mention of the denarius may be artificial but they effectively build a pattern of expectation.

8—At quitting time, around 6 in **the evening,** the workers line up in an order the absolute reverse of anything like seniority. The foreman or **steward,** acting on the owner's explicit instructions, pays out **their wages beginning with the last up to the first.**

9-10—When those who had worked only an hour each received **a denarius,** the others cheer the owner's generosity, swiftly calculating that they will receive proportionately more. **But each of them also received a denarius.**

Thin copper coins of less value than the **denarius** circulated in ancient Palestine (cf. Mark 12:42), so it would have been possible for the owner to pay the latecomers less if he had wanted to. To have paid less, however, would have doomed them to take home a pitifully small amount, less than a subsistence wage.

11-12—When the first, who had **borne the burden of the day and the scorching heat,** see that they received no more than the last, **they grumbled at the householder** (cf. Matt. 21:28-32; Luke 15:11-32).

13-14—One vocal laborer is pictured as representing all who came first, speaking up as Peter had in 19:27. To that one (and through him to all his companions) the owner responds, **Friend** (cf. 22:12; 26:50), **I am doing you no wrong.** He explains that he is giving to him and to all those hired early in the morning precisely what they had agreed on.

15—As to his liberality toward latecomers, the owner protests that he has the right to do as he wishes with his property. Then he asks, **Do you begrudge my generosity?** The sentence literally reads, "Is your eye evil [jealous or greedy, cf. 6:22-23] because I am good?" (cf. 19:16).

16—Jesus is not here announcing a set of rules to guide the economies of the nations all the way till doomsday. He is not attacking labor unions or the principle of equal pay for equal work, nor is he defending the right of owners and capitalists to run their businesses in whatever arbitrary fashion they choose. He is vividly describing two contrasting patterns of human conduct. On the one hand is behavior totally determined by a web of contractual relationships where everything is precisely weighed, recorded, calculated, and balanced. Such behavior may certainly be defended as a high and splendid achievement of people determined to build a dike against injustice and arbitrariness in human affairs.

But the parable contrasts such civilized calculations with shocking and undeserved generosity, with an unbounded and energetic goodness that simply reaches out in blessing.

The parable of the workers in the vineyard (20:1-16) concludes the long section that began with the second passion prediction (17:22-23). All the material in this section comments continuously on the hard and narrow road Jesus is traveling up to Jerusalem and death, nudging readers to see the path to the cross as the way of life. So this whole section summons disciples to pay the tax even though they are free and under no obligation (17:24-27), to become like children (18:1-4) and, far from offending any of the little ones, to do everything possible to seek and embrace and joyously include the little ones and the straying (18:5-20), to forgive 70 times 7 (18:21-22), to forgive one another from the heart (18:23-35), to live with wives as with a gift of God or to renounce marriage for the sake of the kingdom, whichever is their gift (19:1-12), to embrace and bless children (19:13-15), to share all they have with the poor (19:16-22), to give up everything and follow Jesus (19:23-29), to abandon calculation and practice wild generosity (20:1-16).

Going Up to Jerusalem (20:17-19)

17-18—Jesus has moved south from Galilee (19:1) to the area around Jericho, and is now poised and ready for his assault on

Jerusalem. Desiring his disciples to be ready also, Jesus utters the third "passion prediction" (cf. 16:21; 17:22). All three have much in common, but this third one strikes two new notes: Jesus will be handed over to the **Gentiles** (the Roman governing authorities), and he will be not merely killed but **crucified** (cf. 26:2).

Jesus sets his face **to Jerusalem** deliberately, provocatively, realistically. He sees the danger crouching in his path: **the Son of man** (8:20) **will be delivered** (*paradidōmi*), handed over by God's own plan even as he is betrayed by one of the Twelve. This passage and in fact the entire Gospel is pervaded by a sense that what we call good and evil are both in the hands of God (cf. 20:23).

The chief priests and scribes, the highest authorities among his own people, will judge and **condemn him** and then seek the collaboration of their Gentile oppressors, in putting him to death by crucifixion. For all its terror, the prediction climaxes with the ecstatic cry: **He will be raised on the third day!** Jesus does not attempt to escape but casts his whole existence into the abyss, confident that the hand of God will bear him up (4:5-8).

Matthew reports the saying not simply as a prediction of Jesus' personal fate but as encouragement to Jesus' followers in their life together as disciples.

Mark 10:32 reports the disciples' fear and trembling, and Luke remarks on their threefold and utter lack of understanding (Luke 18:34), but Matthew does not so much as hint at any negative reaction.

For Matthew this "passion and resurrection prediction" is the battle cry of the new community and its leadership. Jesus' words stand as though chiseled in stone, not simply as a summary of his historical path but as a perennial summons to the church to travel the narrow way of discipleship that leads to life. As the next paragraph reveals, the call to discipleship meets resistance in the community.

Whoever Would Be First (20:20-28)

20-21—Where Mark (10:35, 41) reports how James and John approached Jesus on their own, Matthew says **the mother of the sons of Zebedee** (4:21; 17:1; 27:56) threw herself at Jesus' feet (cf. 2:11; 8:2). She begs a favor of Jesus (cf. 19:13-15). This proud mother desires that her sons might sit, one at Jesus' **right hand** and one at his **left,** in the court of the coming glorious kingdom (19:28). She and her sons are firm believers in Jesus' coming triumph, but they mirror the popular and deficient view of the kingdom as a splendid and powerful oriental court, only grander (22:41-45). She is pictured in typical motherly fashion as ambitious for her sons, and she wants what her culture taught her to want, namely, prestige and honor.

The crucifixion has just been named for the first time (20:19) and it is ironic that she puts her request exactly at this moment and precisely in these words about sitting on Jesus' **right** hand and **left** hand. Two will indeed sit with Jesus at his **right** and at his **left** at the Good Friday gate of the kingdom (27:38), but that is not what this mother has in mind.

22—The mother now quietly fades from the scene as Jesus turns to address the sons directly. **You** (plural) **do not know what you are asking. Are you able,** strong enough in body and in spirit, **to drink the cup** of suffering which I am destined and ready to drink (cf. 26:39)? The brothers express unhesitating and enthusiastic confidence in their ability to share whatever Jesus faces: **We are able.**

23—Jesus replies, **You will drink my cup,** and in time they both did (cf. Acts 12:2 and Rev. 1:9). But Jesus continues by saying that granting places of special honor was God's own privilege. Jesus calls to discipleship.

24—Omitting all names (cf. Mark 10:41), Matthew simply says that **the ten were indignant** (cf. 21:15) **at the two brothers.** They react hotly at the implied threat to their own prestige and position. The disciples' hunger for honor, their flash of earthy indignation, their competitive spirit, their grumbling (cf. 20:11), is the springboard for sublime teaching.

25—The imaginations of the Twelve seem to be dominated by visions worthy of petty rulers of pagan states, surrounded by dazzling wealth, fawned on by their clients, heels resting on their enemies' necks.

26-27—But **rulers of the Gentiles** must not set the pattern for life and leadership in the new community. When the Twelve had asked, "Who is the greatest in the kingdom?" (18:1), Jesus had set a child in their midst. Here Jesus speaks of **servant** (*diakonos*) and **slave** (*doulos*) as model for those who would be **great** (*megas*, 18:1) or **first** (*prōtos*, 10:2; 19:30; 20:16) among the people of God. The slave, like the child, is a kind of nonperson. The child is at the disposal of parents, and the slave is at the master's beck and call. The slave's only value is in the work performed for the master. The slave has no independent personal worth.

28—Then in the stunning climax Jesus points beyond child or servant or slave to himself: **the Son of man** (v. 18; 8:20) **came not to be served but to serve,** and the service he offers is the free gift of his own **life as a ransom for many.** The entire existence of Jesus is summed up here in a single word: service. That service knew no limits and shrank not even from the cross.

The life's blood of a criminal poured out in execution had power to atone for his own sin (Mishnah, *Sanhedrin* 6:2). The shed blood of righteous martyrs was a powerful antidote to the sins of the whole nation (2 Macc. 7:37; 4 Macc. 6:28; 17:21-22). The outpoured life of **the Son of man** possessed awesome power as a **ransom for many.** The **many** (*hoi polloi*, 26:26) are all who labor and are heavy laden, staggering under burdens of old and inadequate visions, oppressive social systems, the tyranny of demonic powers. **Many** signifies not some small fraction calculated in advance or some tiny elite arbitrarily chosen, but rather stands for the vast uncounted multitudes of every time and place who will find in the service of the Son of man wellsprings of power for fresh creative life not bound to the old patterns of privilege and prestige.

Two Blind Men (20:29-34)

In the parallel, Mark tells the story of blind Bartimaeus, who threw off his beggar's cloak, jumped up and boldly approached Jesus, confident of healing. Matthew offers fewer vivid details and instead of one has **two blind men,** as also in an earlier healing, (cf. 8:28-34; 9:27-31). Is Matthew "catching up" after omitting Mark's prior account of the healing of the blind man from Bethsaida (Mark 8:22-26)?

29-30—Probably Matthew wants readers to see a close connection between "the two brothers" (20:24) and the "two blind

241

men" (20:30). Like **the two blind men,** the brothers need Jesus'
healing touch that they may see the truth.

The two blind men sit **by the roadside** begging alms of pilgrims
ascending from **Jericho** to the great feast at Jerusalem. Hearing
that none other than **Jesus** is **passing by,** they begin to raise the
chant, **Lord, have mercy on us, Son of David!** (see commentary
above on 9:27).

31—As the disciples had tried to shield Jesus from pestering
mothers (19:13), so now **the crowd rebuked** these blind men, in
their ignorance imagining that Jesus' progress to Jerusalem and
his worshiping there took priority over the needs of poor blind
beggars. Or did they think, like the mother of the sons of Zebedee, that Jesus was marching up to Jerusalem to establish his
sovereign rule there? In either case, Jesus has no more significant
business than to free (1:21), to serve (20:28), to heal (21:14).

32-33—Jesus summons the blind men and like a king dealing
with clients asks what favor they seek. Of course they ask that
their **eyes be opened.**

34—In pity (9:36; 14:14; 15:32; 18:27) and in royal power Jesus
touches them (8:3; 9:29), restoring their sight. He issues no ad-
monition to silence (as in 9:30) and the two join the throng gathered around Jesus as witnesses. They **followed him** up to Jerusalem, up to the temple, up into the stronghold of high priests
and elders of the people.

■ Teaching at Jerusalem (21:1—23:39)

Jerusalem and Temple (21:1-17)

Finally Jesus arrives at Jerusalem, his goal announced in 16:21,
target of his journeying since 19:1. But his connections with the
city are older and deeper than that. Jerusalem is the holy city
(4:5), and Jesus has called it the city of the great King (5:35), and
therefore it is his own royal city, for he is Son of David (9:27),
Son of God (3:17), king of God's people (2:2).

Jesus comes, publicly declaring his gentle kingship in provocative fashion, riding into Jerusalem mounted on a donkey and a
colt, not walking (21:1-11), and entering the temple not to worship

but actually to disrupt worship (21:12-13). The blind and the lame
will approach him for healing, and children will praise him as
"Son of David," while high officers of the temple will sputter
indignation (21:14-17). On the long day following his entry into
the city Jesus will teach in the temple (21:18—23:39) and on the
mount opposite (24:1—25:46).

All the City Was Stirred (21:1-11)

1-2—In the midst of festal throngs Jesus mounts the winding
road up from Jericho to **Jerusalem.** At **Bethphage** on the eastern
slopes of **the Mount of Olives** Jesus dispatches a pair of disciples
with orders to **go into the village opposite,** traditionally identified
as **Bethany** (21:17), and fetch for him not one animal as in the
other gospels but two: **an ass** and **a colt with her.**

3—Any objections to their untying the animals and leading
them off are to be met with the magisterial sentence: **The Lord
has need of them.** On **Lord** (*kyrios*) see 7:21, 22; 8:25; 12:8; 23:43-
45.

4-5—Jesus comes meekly and mounts up to his own destruction, and yet all creation is at his disposal (cf. 17:24-27). The
events of these last days will seem to rage out of control, to flay
and fell him, to tear and destroy him. And yet he here plainly
asserts mysterious authority. He hastens not only toward the dark
night of death but toward the perfect fulfillment of prophecy.
Behind the terrors of the passion the evangelist sees not a desolate
landscape occupied by demons of spite and envy but the heart
of Jesus consciously serving the will of God.

Matthew brings to bear on Jesus' entry one of his great fulfillment texts (see commentary above on 1:22). Matthew's quotation of Zech. 9:9 (introduced by words from Isa. 62:11) neglects
the words "just" and "saving" found in the original and by those
omissions stresses the word **humble** (*praüs,* translated "meek" in
5:5 and "gentle" in 11:29). Matthew is supremely interested in
Jesus' connections with salvation (1:21) and justice (or righteousness, 3:15) but here concentrates on the meekness of this **king.**
He will not Lord it over subjects, crushing them as the rulers of
the nations do (cf. 11:17-21; 20:25-28).

This king has his roots among the lowly and dispossessed and was himself a refugee (2:13-23) and wanderer (8:20). And here he now also mounts to kingship by means of lowliness and in the midst of deepest humility, without money or bribes, without arms or violence, without demagoguery or propaganda (cf. 4:1-11). National aspirations and communal resentments come to boil at the great ancient festivals (Passover, Pentecost, Tabernacles, Dedication), and Jesus flashes signals of kingship, and yet his is a kingship of peace (Isa. 11:1-9) attained by the power of deep humility. He is **king** (2:2; 27:11), but this **king** differs radically, crucially from all ordinary sovereigns (22:41-45).

6—Matthew stresses the way the disciples hurry to obey Jesus' command. They share Jesus' lowly approach to the city and to kingship (cf. 1:24).

7—They bring **the ass** and its foal. The **ass** is more than a beast of burden fit only for pulling the plow or the threshing sled. It is fit also for kings, especially for the king of the last times. That promised king will appear, riding on an **ass,** because he comes to inaugurate the age of peace and so utterly renounces chariots and horses, bows and swords (Gen. 49:11; Judg. 10:4; Zech. 9:9; Matt. 26:51-56).

They fetch two animals, throw their garments on two animals, and Matthew says Jesus enters Jerusalem riding on two animals! Has Matthew misunderstood poetic parallelism? Hardly. Playfully, insistently he portrays Jesus as the pluperfect fulfillment of prophecy. And he pictures Jesus the way ancient oriental gods and kings are frequently depicted: enthroned above a pair of animals. He comes meek but royal nonetheless.

8—The crowds make smooth his way (Luke 3:5; Isa. 40:4). Some **spread their garments on the road** (2 Kings 9:13) while **others cut branches from the trees and spread them on the road** (1 Macc. 13:51; 2 Macc. 10:7). Only John mentions palm branches (John 12:13), those ancient symbols of victory and glory.

9—Matthew has his own way of stressing the sublime royalty of Jesus: **the crowds** of pilgrims **went before him** and **followed** after him like a great honor guard, with shouts of **Hosanna,** "Save us, we beseech Thee, O Lord!" and crying out, **Blessed** (Ps. 118:25-26). Four times in the immediate context the crowds acclaim Jesus as **Son of David** (20:30-31; 21:9, 15). Here and everywhere in Matthew **Son of David** designates the one who ushers in not the old kingdom of David (cf. Mark 11:10) but a new kingdom of mercy and compassion (see commentary above on 9:27). **Blessed is he who comes** (11:2) to Jerusalem and its temple in piety and faith (cf. 23:29)!

10—**He entered Jerusalem** and **all the city was stirred,** literally, "shaken to its foundations" (*eseisthē*, cf. 8:24; 27:51; 28:2). Why and how was it **stirred?** With joy? With fear and trembling? With great foreboding?

It was a moment of decision. Who and what is Jesus? Why heed his criticism or trust his vision? What does he know about God or about being the people of God?

11—The inhabitants cry out, **Who is this?** And the pilgrims respond, this is the **prophet** (21:26, 46; 16:14) **Jesus from Nazareth of Galilee** (2:23; 4:13). By their acclamations they obey the ancient command to **tell** (21:5) **the daughter of Zion** (= the city of Jerusalem set on Mount Zion) who it is who comes. Not really adequate even for John the Baptist (11:7-15; 14:5), **prophet** is at least a decent start as compared with the attitude of their leaders.

That bolt of lightning, **Son of David, the prophet Jesus from Nazareth of Galilee,** now crackles in Jerusalem. And the city—with its lawyers and priests, its aristocrats and bureaucrats—faces something new in this upstart teacher with his fresh talk of God and his unbounded care for outcasts. Is he also more than a **prophet?** How much more? In what way more? What do **prophet** and **Son of David** mean when applied to him?

A House of Prayer (21:12-17)

12-13—Upon ascending the holy mount and entering the city of Jerusalem, Jesus heads directly to **the temple,** the goal of all pilgrimage. **Temple** (*hieron*, cf. v. 23) designates the entire sacred precinct. The temple complex at Jerusalem was the largest in the ancient world, covering more than 30 acres. Within its boundaries it enclosed concentric zones of increasing holiness: the court of the Gentiles, the court of the women, the court of Israel, and the court of the priests. In the very center stood the sanctuary proper (*naos*). Jesus leads his disciples up onto the sacred mount. But instead of submitting there to the authority of the priests, instead of piously sacrificing, instead of quietly observing ancient customs, he violently **drove out all who sold and bought** from the great platform of the temple mount.

As an aid to the throngs of international pilgrims converging on Jerusalem, money changers converted the coins of Greek, Roman, and Parthian mints into the shekels of Tyre, which were renowned for the purity of their silver and acceptable for payment of temple taxes (17:24-27), taking a small percentage commission for their service (Mishnah, *Shekalim* 1:6). The Jews themselves minted no silver coins except in the brief intervals of independence during the first and second revolts against Rome (A.D. 66–70 and 132–135).

Vendors of **pigeons** (cf. Luke 2:24) and other sacrificial animals also did a brisk business there. Merchants and changers had long been established on the temple mount in the outermost **court of the Gentiles.** Jesus expels them all, crying out in the words of prophecy, **My house shall be called a house of prayer** (Isa. 56:7) **but you have made it a den of robbers** (Jer. 7:11), a hideout to which bandits retire for safety and security after one of their raids.

Matthew's highly compressed report lacks Mark's note that Jesus did not permit anyone to carry any vessel through the temple courts (Mark 11:16) and John's description of Jesus' lashing the vendors with an improvised whip (John 2:15).

Nevertheless, Matthew clearly describes an act of forceful opposition to the ritual system as currently practiced. Jesus is not simply purging or renewing but rejecting. The clue to Matthew's understanding of the event has been given previously in two sayings of Jesus: "Something greater than the temple is here" (12:6), and "I desire mercy and not sacrifice" (9:13; 12:7). The latter saying is found in Matthew only. Strangely Mark and Luke have the embedding narrative but lack the saying. Having cleared vendors and money changers from the temple, and having brought sacrifice to a halt, Jesus now performs healings, showing what actions should replace sacrifice.

14—Jesus has previously offended scribes and teachers by receiving tax collectors and sinners and by eating with them (9:10-11). Now, on the holy mount and in the sacred precincts, **the blind and the lame** approach him boldly. Far from shunning them or excluding them because of their defiling imperfections (cf.

Deut. 16:16; 2 Sam. 5:6-8 LXX; Mishnah, *Hagigah* 1:1; 1QSa 2:5-22; 1QM 7:4-5), Jesus embraces them. And he exercises his authority as **Son of David** (v. 9) and heals them (cf. 4:23-24).

So Jesus turns the tables and reverses the order of things: vendors and changers are driven out, while the blind and lame are embraced. The first became last and the last first (20:16). And instead of the old system of purifications and sacrifices controlled by the priestly establishment, Matthew presents Jesus as meek yet forceful, defining mercy as the heart of holiness and the worship of God.

15—**Children** interpret the event for the readers. **Children** and the childlike (11:25; 18:2-6; 19:14) have strange clarity of vision. They see Jesus as God's movement into human history, fulfilling and healing and saving. They cry out (in a second acclamation found in Matthew alone), **Hosanna to the Son of David!** (see commentary above on v. 9; also 5:16; 15:29-31).

The chief priests and the scribes, however, are **indignant** (cf. 20:24). They do not fume simply because they perceive Jesus as a boisterous northerner violating the dignity of the sanctuary. Now are they outraged because he has launched a frontal attack on their carefully constructed system and their control of that system (cf. 15:9; 24:2; 26:61; 27:40). Matthew pictures them as objecting to mercy, objecting to healings, objecting to the praises of children. They do not at all regard the deeds of Jesus as **wonderful things** (cf. v. 42).

God's messenger has appeared suddenly in the temple, like a reformer's fire and a fuller's soap (Mal. 3:1-4). The blazing sun of righteousness has risen, with healing in its wings (2:2; Mal. 4:1-2; 4:16). For one shining moment he looks exactly like the one prefigured by John, cleaning his threshing floor and gathering his wheat (3:12). But those whom others called "wheat" reject him and those called "chaff" recognize him.

17—Jerusalem was impossibly crowded at Passover, and bands of pilgrims camped out on the hills or accepted hospitality in villages close by. Jesus with his disciples exits the holy city to lodge about a mile away at **Bethany** near Bethphage (21:1) on the eastern slopes of the Mount of Olives.

A Long Day in Jerusalem (21:18—25:46)

A new day begins here and extends all the way to the end of chap. 25. Within this body of material, unified in terms of time, a few breaks are obvious.

In 21:23—22:46 Matthew presents a series of polemical dialogs between Jesus and various authorities in the temple precincts. No shift in time or place marks the end of chap. 22 or the beginning of chap. 23, but the form of the material does change and so does the audience. In chap. 23 Jesus speaks a monolog about scribes and Pharisees instead of continuing in dialog with them, and Matthew specifies that the audience consists of crowds and disciples.

After that monolog or discourse of chap. 23, the scene shifts and the audience changes. Jesus leaves the temple, crossing to the Mount of Olives. He sits there opposite the temple mount, and speaks the words of chaps. 24–25 (about "the last things") to his disciples privately without any larger crowds surrounding them. The long day ends at the close of chap. 25, and chap. 26 picks up the story a day or two later with the start of Jesus' passion.

The cursing of the fig tree (21:18-22) is an altogether effective bridge between the preceding material and the new day. It is a piece of further reflection on Jesus' cleansing of the temple on the previous day (21:12-17) and it introduces the great themes developed in the course of the new day. The cursing of the fig tree is an astonishing and troubling demonstration of power, and it raises questions about the nature and source of Jesus' **authority.** The appearance here of the word **fruit** introduces the other major theme of this section.

The Fig Tree and the Mountain (21:18-22)

18—As the new day begins, Jesus makes his way back to the city from Bethany, and he is **hungry.** What is the nature of that hunger? Surely he hungers for something more than food for the stomach (cf. 4:2; 5:6; 16:5-12).

Approaching **a fig tree by the wayside** he finds **nothing on it but leaves only.** The **fig tree** with its lush growth of **leaves** is the picture of health and yet it bears **no fruit.** So the temple on its mount is splendid in appearance, impressing the senses with structures and ornaments, with clouds of incense and smoke of sacrifice, with sound of trumpet and chant of priest and Levite.

No fruit is a melancholy phrase in Scripture and particularly in Matthew (3:8-10; 7:16-20; 12:33; 13:8,23; 21:34,43; Jer. 8:13; cf. Luke 13:6-9). In curselike fashion (Mark 11:21) Jesus solemnly declares, **May no fruit ever come from you again!** At the word of Jesus the **fig tree withered at once.**

20—Not Peter (as in Mark 11:21) but **the disciples** comment: **How did the fig tree wither at once?** Their reactions serve both to underscore the instantaneous effect of Jesus' word and to provoke reflection on the source of Jesus' power.

In his answer Jesus does not point to any powers unique to himself. As in the healing of the epileptic boy (it also happened **at once,** 17:18), Jesus implies that the powers he exercises are available to all disciples, to all who have **faith** (17:20).

21-22—Faith is openness to God and reliance upon God, and Jesus praises it wherever he finds it, even in pagans (8:10; 15:28). Through **faith** and **prayer** people tap the power of God and become themselves sources of God's own healing and embracing, loving and reconciling. Faith with prayer is simply omnipotent (cf. 7:7-11; 18:19). **If you have faith and never doubt** (cf. 14:31), says Jesus, **you will not only do what has been done to the fig tree, but even if you say to this mountain, "Be taken up and cast into the sea,"** it will be done (17:20). When Jesus speaks of moving **this mountain,** he may be pointing across the valley to the holy hill of Zion (21:5), the mountain of the Lord on which the temple stood (Isa. 2:2-3).

But it would be wrong to imagine that the sayings on fig tree and mountain are attacks directed only at the old system of sacrificial worship on Mount Zion or at the Sadducean control of the means of redemption. Jesus' words blast any political or ecclesiastical structure, any national monument or religious establishment however splendid or weighty, which commands the awe of human beings and yet fails to produce **fruit.**

Here Jesus simply implies that **fruit** is the yield of people connected to God in faith and prayer. Many of the passages in the following section, climaxing in 25:31-46, discuss and define **fruit.**

By What Authority? *(21:23-27)*

The eight brief paragraphs of 21:33—22:46 and the long monolog of chap. 23 have at least two things in common: place and tone. All these words are spoken in the temple (Jesus' departure is noted in 24:1), and the tone is unremittingly combative and critical. All these debates and parables look like weapons tempered at an armorer's forge, but what is the warfare for which they were designed? Jesus is pictured debating with the chief priests and elders of the people (21:23), the chief priests and Pharisees (21:45), Pharisees and Herodians (22:15-16), Sadducees (22:23) and Pharisees again (22:34,41). Then the monolog of chap. 23, spoken to crowds and to disciples (23:1), flails Pharisees and scribes.

Through all these old controversies Matthew defines the source and character of Jesus' authority as model for the community of disciples. It is often said that Matthew's community was locked in mortal combat with synagogue communities and their leaders, and that Matthew applies to them the criticisms which Jesus had in an earlier generation leveled at priests and Sadducees, Pharisees and scribes. From the beginning, this commentary has been arguing that Matthew is criticizing not synagogue leaders but church leaders. Matthew takes up words spoken by Jesus against past leaders of God's people and applies those words to a new generation of leaders not outside but inside the church.

Jesus ascended the holy mount and **entered the temple,** the great sacred precinct (*hieron,* cf. v. 12). In the center, behind the court of the men of Israel and the court of the priests, stood the sanctuary proper (*naos*), with its dazzling porticoes and curtain (27:51). Only priests could enter its Holy Place and Inner Sanctum.

Somewhere in these sacred courts, **the chief priests and the elders** (= "the chief priests and the Pharisees" of 21:45), these representatives of the most powerful ecclesiastical and lay families, approach Jesus. Because of his growing influence or because he appears to place himself provocatively above rules and rulers, institutions and traditions (cf. 5:17-48; 12:1-14, 22-37), Jesus seems dangerous and upsetting.

The established leaders demand that Jesus produce his credentials. **Authority** (*exousia,* four times in this short paragraph) is a major theme in Matthew's Gospel and in fact sums up all that the Father has given to the Son (28:18; 11:27). They demand that Jesus tell them **by what authority,** by what right, with what backing he does **these things.**

What do they mean by **these things?** The carefully staged entry into Jerusalem? Cleansing the temple? Cursing the fig tree? Matthew (unlike Mark) focuses in particular on Jesus' **teaching,** and for Matthew that means Jesus' entire program for making disciples, including the cross and resurrection. The question is an excellent one: What is the nature of Jesus' credentials as he speaks and acts, and as he goes to the cross? Is God behind all that?

24-25—Jesus answers their question with a question of his own. He asks them for their verdict on **the baptism of John,** on the entire mission and ministry of John, summed up in his practice of baptizing at Jordan. Did it enjoy the backing of God? Was it **from heaven** and so have its source in God, or was it only **from men,** a merely human project?

They are stuck and they know it. If they answer **From heaven,** then Jesus will say, **Why then did you not believe him?** Why did you not trust God and receive his agent in faith (see 21:18-22)?

26—And they are afraid to say, **From men,** because **all,** the vast majority of the people, **hold that John was a prophet** (21:11, 46) sent from God.

The aristocratic rulers of Jerusalem had so long maintained peaceable relations with the dominant Roman power and retained their own positions of influence and prestige by practicing the arts of compromise and accommodation that they are simply incapable of making the sort of decision for which Jesus called.

27—They are reduced to answering, **We do not know.** Unable or unwilling to judge concerning the forerunner (the lesser), they are then written off as incompetent to judge the fulfiller (the greater): **Neither will I tell you by what authority I do these things.**

Neither priests nor readers get any easy answer. With the priests, the readers are cast back on the resources of the narrative as a whole and called to make choices. By what authority does Jesus salute the martyr John, call to discipleship, eat with tax collectors, heal the broken, enter the city, clear the temple, teach in public, endure rejection, and mount up to the cross? Can such a path really enjoy the backing of almighty God?

Two Sons (21:28-32)

28—A man had two sons, different from one another. (Luke 15:11-32, another parable of two sons, is like and unlike this parable in many intriguing ways!) He asks each son separately **to go and work in the vineyard today.**

29—The first begs off: **I will not.** However, he later **repented** (*metamelētheis,* cf. 27:3) and went as his father had asked.

30—The second son has the right words: **I go, sir** (*kyrie*), but he is all talk and does not actually **go** (cf. 7:21; 25:31-46).

Notice how the son winning approval is the first rather than the second. This suggests that Matthew is not interested in simplemindedly criticizing the Jews (those called at first) and extolling the Gentiles (those who come on the scene later). What does interest Matthew is obedience, whether it is offered by Jew or Gentile.

31-32—The relationship of the sons with their father might be studied from many different angles. But Jesus is master of the science of deeds and characteristically asks, **Which of the two did the will of his father?** (cf. 6:10). The priests and leaders are compelled to answer, **The first,** whereupon Jesus draws a conclusion. **The tax collectors and the harlots** (twice in vv. 31-32) seem on any ordinary analysis to have fallen far from God. Everything about their way of life looks like a very loud no to God. But their ears and hearts were open to John the Baptist. Officials and scribes, Pharisees and Sadducees, have the look of obedience, and they wear the mantle of piety. They appear to say yes to God, and to the Law, but they turned a deaf ear to John, to God's prophet, to the call for repentance. Therefore **the tax collectors and the harlots enter the kingdom of God** (*basileia tou theou,* seldom in Matthew; cf. 12:28) **before you.** The apparently unwashed, unqualified, and inferior masses do not simply squeeze in at the end but actually elbow their way in first (cf. 19:30; 20:16; 21:16).

32—John **came in the way of righteousness,** blazing the trail that leads to righteousness and the kingdom (3:15; 5:20; 6:33).

Whoever in any time or place repents and trusts in God and humbly seeks to discern and do the will of God is on the right path. Indeed, no other path will do. Rank and title, office and respectability by themselves are meaningless.

To Get His Fruit (21:33-46)

Jesus has previously spoken two other parables involving the owners of a vineyard, symbol of the people of God in Isa. 5:1-7. In the first (20:1-16) the owner hires workers at odd hours throughout the day. In the second (21:28-32) one of the owner's sons works in the vineyard while the other refuses. The present parable is linked especially with that immediately preceding parable of the two sons (see the introduction to 21:28). Here in this third vineyard parable Jesus speaks about a wealthy grower who supervises the layout of the vineyard, negotiates a contract with tenant farmers, and then departs to live in **another country** (cf. 25:14).

Finally, **the season of fruit,** the climactic time of harvest (9:37-38) toward which all prior working and waiting had tended, **drew near** (the Greek word *engiken,* is used of the drawing near of the kingdom in 3:2; 4:17; 10:7; cf. 21:1; 26:45). The owner **sent servants to the tenants to get his fruit** (cf. v. 19).

The tenants had bound themselves to the owner by solemn contract but now try to cancel the agreement and escape their obligations (cf. 20:11-15; 21:28-32). They seize two successive delegations of servants sent as agents from the owner, beating, killing, and even stoning them (cf. 22:4-5; 23:37). The owner then sends **his son,** thinking, **They will respect my son.**

The tenants, however, regard the son not with respect but with murderous cunning: "The son is **the heir.** Perhaps the old man has died. If we kill the heir, we have squatter's rights and will gain **his inheritance,** this entire vineyard, as our own."

39—So, seizing the son, they **cast him out of the vineyard and killed him** (John 19:37; Heb. 13:12-13).

40-41—Suddenly Jesus presses his hearers, the chief priests and elders (21:23), to render a verdict. **When the owner of the vineyard comes, what will he do to those tenants?**

Everyone knows the natural and inevitable consequence of

such behavior, and listeners respond without hesitation: **He will put those wretches to a miserable death, and let out the vineyard to other tenants who will give him the fruits in their seasons.** Here at the end, in words found in the mouths of priests and elders, the accent falls once more on the yielding of fruit (see the comments on 21:19).

42—Suddenly Jesus switches from parable to prophecy, from agriculture to architecture, and from talk of brutal murders and terrible deaths to the promise of new life: **The very stone which the builders rejected has become the head of the corner** (Ps. 118:22-23; Acts 4:11; 1 Peter 2:6-7; Rom. 9:23; cf. Matt. 16:18). This is the **Lord's doing,** and God's action cleanly contradicts all human cunning and human planning. It is **marvelous** (cf. v. 15), an unexpected and undeserved eruption of life in the midst of death.

43—The death and resurrection of Jesus lurk in the background of the parable (vv. 33-41) and the prophecy (v. 42), but the foreground is occupied by the drama of privilege taken from one group and given to another: **The kingdom of God** (v. 31) **will be taken away from you and given** to others, to new tenants, described as a **nation** (*ethnos*), and that nation is defined by a single phrase, **producing the fruits of it.**

44—Verse 44 is probably an early scribal insertion and not original. It strikes a note of sharp warning. The Lord will choose the rejected stone and make it the foundation for the new community and new world (16:18; 1 Peter 2:4-6), but that same foundation stone works cruelly in the lives of those who continue to reject it. Whoever **falls on this stone will be broken to pieces,** and **when it falls on anyone,** that person is crushed.

45—Hearing Jesus' words, **the chief priests and the Pharisees** (21:23) **perceived that he was speaking about them.** This application does not quite mesh with the parable. The parable (vv. 32-41) is sweeping and harsh: all the tenants of the vineyard conspire against the owner, and they will all die a terrible death. But the application (vv. 42-45) is restricted to the leaders, and they will merely be displaced, not killed.

The matter is not crystal clear, and commentators disagree on the use Matthew makes of this material: (1) Perhaps he is declaring Israel's sufferings at the hands of Rome are the awful consequence of rebellion against God, (2) and that the priestly and Pharisaic leaders of the people bear a particularly large burden of responsibility in that rebellion, (3) and that Israel's stubbornness has meant the opening of the kingdom to the Gentiles. But that is not all that Matthew is up to.

Matthew does more than simply spin out a theory of history and shifting fortunes within history. Jesus is pictured as speaking in this parable to priests and Pharisees (v. 45) or to priests and elders (v. 23) about the exercise of their authority or leadership under God. But why? Many think that Matthew repeats Jesus' parable in his own later generation in order to speak to Jewish leaders of his own day and paint them with Jesus' brush. But it is far more likely that Matthew is really addressing not Jews but Christians, especially Christian leaders. They feel secure as members of the new community which has inherited the kingdom (v. 43). And they pride themselves on being teachers and guides (23:8-10) in that community. Matthew thinks they need stern warning. It is not sufficient to hold membership in the correct people or community. Nor does it suffice to be counted as a leader or teacher. The Lord in fact scrutinizes leaders with particular care, seeking more than labels or slogans. The Lord desires **fruits in their seasons** (see 21:19 and 7:16-23).

It is not only possible but downright easy to read Matthew's Gospel as antipriestly and anti-Pharisaic, but it is a mistake to do so. Matthew uses the narratives about Jesus' past conflicts with Jewish religious authorities to press contemporary Christian leaders to critical reflection and self-examination. That is even clearer in the opening parable of chap. 22 (vv. 1-14).

46—The authorities would have arrested Jesus on the spot, so stung were they. But **they feared the multitudes** who continue to revere Jesus as a prophet (21:11, 26). Perhaps Matthew believes that the little ones (18:6) of the new community also grasp the essentials about Jesus more clearly than their leaders.

Royal Son, Yet David's Lord (22:1-46)

Chapter 22 consists of four scenes:
1. The Marriage Feast (22:1-14)
2. To Caesar the Things That Are Caesar's (22:15-22)

3. Sadducees Question the Resurrection (22:23-33)

4. Is the Christ the Son of David? (22:41-46)

These four scenes continue the sequence of sharp dialogs between Jesus and various leaders of Jerusalem which began in the previous chapter. The sequence as a whole begins at 21:18-22 with the narrative of the cursing of the fig tree. The report of that astonishing event is followed by three scenes rounding out chap. 21 and then the five scenes of chap. 22. These eight scenes are bound together into an impressive unity. All eight are played out in the presence of the same audience (disciples and crowds) in the same place (within the temple precincts) on the same day. The cursing of the fig tree introduces important themes developed in these scenes and stands as a kind of prelude to them and to all the following scenes of that long day that stretches down to the end of chap. 25 (see the notes on 21:18 and 21:23).

Matthew pictures Jesus embroiled in controversy with chief priests and elders, with Pharisees and Sadducees. Through these reports of old conflicts, on the eve of trial and crucifixion, Matthew presses both the leaders and the led in his post-Easter community to examine their own convictions and practices.

The Marriage Feast (22:1-14)

1—Chapter 22 opens with the parable of the wedding feast, the third in an intriguing series of three parables: (1) two sons (21:28-32), (2) wicked tenants (21:33-44), (3) wedding feast (22:1-14). These **parables** share important images: father and son or sons (1, 2, 3), vineyard (1, 2), the sending of two sets of servants (2, 3), murder of servants (2, 3), punishment of murderers (2,3). In one vital respect the three parables in the series are unanimous. All three paint vivid pictures of sharply contrasting responses to plain obligations, and in doing so they condemn disobedience or fruitlessness and summon readers to unflinching self-examination.

They have much in common, and yet they have been so arranged as to lead readers forward step by hard step. The first (21:28-32) yields the lesson that prostitutes and tax collectors (little ones) come more quickly to fruits and obedience than the leading lights in the religious community. The second (21:33-44) pronounces a verdict: unresponsiveness and disobedience deserve punishment (vv. 41, 43). The third (22:1-10) describes the execution of terrible punishment upon nay-sayers (v. 7). The appendix (22:11-14) to that third parable applies the lessons of the parable neither to ordinary members nor to leaders of the Jewish community but to the new Christian community and its leaders. In fact that surprising appendix (vv. 11-14) encourages reading all three parables as arrows fired at deficiencies inside the new community.

2-3—**The kingdom of heaven may be compared to a king** (cf. 25:34) **who gave a marriage feast for his son** (9:15; cf. Rev. 19:7-9; Eph. 5:21-33; John 2:1-11) **and sent his servants to call those who were invited.**

4—The guests spurned the initial invitation (cf. the wording of 21:29), whereupon the king **sent other servants** (21:36) with the urgent summons: **Everything is ready; come to the marriage feast!** (cf. Luke 15:23, 27, 30).

5-6—Some **made light of it** and without any further excuse simply went off to **farm** or **business** (contrast Luke 14:18). At this point the realism of the parable dissolves. In a bizarre reaction to a wedding invitation, some of those invited **seized his servants, treated them shamefully, and killed them** (21:35).

7—In response to the outrage the king dispatched **his troops** who **destroyed those murderers and burned their city.** Luke (14:16-24) tells how a man (not a king) gave a banquet (not a wedding feast) and sent his lone servant (not many) to call guests who made excuses, pleading extenuating circumstances, but they neither beat nor murdered the messenger (cf. also Gospel of Thomas 64).

Matthew's version of the parable with its excess of brutality on the part of invited guests and offended king sounds like a grim meditation on the history of Israel in the light cast by the fires of the Roman sack of Jerusalem in A.D. 70. It may be that, but it is more, and the parable continues.

8—The king draws a conclusion from the events narrated thus far: **The wedding is ready** (cf. v. 4) **but those invited were not worthy** (*axios*). The **worthy** (10:10-11, 13, 37-38; cf. 3:8) are further defined at the close of the parable as **chosen** (22:14).

9-10—The king wills that people fill the banquet hall and so again sends out servants, this time to the **thoroughfares,** to the edge of the city where the streets pass through the walls into the open country beyond. The servants scoured those **thoroughfares** and swept up **all whom they found,** so that finally the wedding hall was filled with a vast and motley throng.

Remarkably, **the guests** now crowding the hall are described in moral or ethical terms (contrast Luke 14:21, "the poor and maimed and blind and lame"). The hall is filled not with the good only but, shockingly, with **both bad and good** (cf. 5:45).

The new community in Matthew's view is a mixed body, both wheat and tares (13:24-30), good fish and bad (13:48), obedient and disobedient sons (21:28-32), sheep and goats (25:31-46). As Matthew pondered the strange make-up of the new community, he saw the grace of God in its odd assortment of people. God has acted with a marvelous disdain for all the old rules, all the old definitions of worthiness or acceptability and has filled the banquet hall to the rafters. Matthew loves to celebrate the surpassing depth and splendor of that grace. At the same time Matthew was painfully aware of sad tendencies among the good and the bad: (1) "Good" people in the community are tempted to embark on programs of purification, to weed out the tares or to cast out the erring. (2) And the "bad" are tempted to count on God's foolishness and to misconstrue grace as divine indifference to morality or behavior. So Matthew is tireless in warning that judging others is no business of the community, and equally ardent and insistent that history will end with God's judgment. Ever and again in Matthew's Gospel, Jesus spells out the terms of judgment, its criteria and standards, summoning to self-criticism, to self-examination, and to the timely yielding of obedience to God.

No Wedding Garment (22:11-14).   Verses 11-14 are without parallel in Luke's Gospel. This startling addition voices one of Matthew's deepest puzzlements: how can people, graced and embraced by God, actually do the will of God so tardily, so stingily, so grudgingly?

11-12—The king entered the banquet hall and spotted **a man who had no wedding garment.** That **garment** may be an especially splendid robe reserved for festivals (Luke 15:22) or an ordinary robe specially cleaned. In either case wearing **a wedding garment** to a wedding is simply as natural and right as a good tree bearing good fruit (21:41), and wearing ordinary, shabby, or soiled clothing signals an obvious defect and is an insult to the host.

13—The king ordered the offender to be bound hand and foot, and cast out into absolute **darkness** (see commentary above on 8:11).

14—For **many** (20:28; 26:28) **are called but few are chosen,** few stride forth to labor joyously in the vineyard, few yield good fruit willingly and abundantly, few have their lamps lighted and at the ready for the bridegroom's coming or the master's return. So the little additional paragraph (vv. 11-14) not only undercuts any Christian smugness at the fate of ancient Israel but also underscores the fact that the parable as a whole is not an example of sitting in judgment on others but is a goad to self-examination.

Verses 11-14 might fit better if those crowding the banquet hall were the originally invited guests. In that case it would make sense that most were properly garbed in festal robes, splendid and spanking clean, and that any guest in inappropriate clothing would provoke a shocked reaction. But since guests have been hastily and even forcibly assembled from streets and thoroughfares of a burning city, it should not be surprising that one is improperly attired. It is indeed a surprise that any do have wedding robes!

Nevertheless, what is quite clear is the way all three parables in this series (beginning at 21:28) climax in this picture of the king and the unworthy guest. Sharp warning to the new community! It is not sufficient to hold membership, to sit at table as invited guest, to have said yes instead of no. What is being promoted here is doing the Father's will, bearing fruit, being properly garbed.

Members of the new community all too glibly identify themselves with the bride clothed in fine linen, bright and pure (Rev. 19:8), boasting that they are clad in garments of salvation, the robe of righteousness (Isa. 61:10), imagining that only others, outsiders and unbelievers, lack a garment or have soiled their robes (Rev. 3:4-5). Matthew knows better.

Render to Caesar (22:15-22)

Matthew 22:1-14 concludes a series of three parables (beginning at 21:28) featuring fathers and sons, praising obedience (or the yielding of fruit or the wearing of a wedding garment) and threatening terrible punishment on disobedience. Without any change of place (temple) or time (same day) a new series consisting of four dialogs begins at 22:15:

1. Is it right to pay taxes to Caesar? (22:15-22)
2. Is there a resurrection? (22:23-33)
3. What is the central commandment? (22:34-40)
4. Is the Messiah the Son of David? (22:41-45)

Reasons will be offered in the comments below for identifying the theme of these passages as Jesus' own radical love for God. His oneness with God constitutes his authority, and his obedient and trusting love is a glorious example of the fruit God seeks.

15-16—The Pharisees (21:45) set a trap, hoping **to entangle him in his talk** (cf. Mark 12:13-17; Luke 20:20-26). Together with **the Herodians,** supporters of the political aspirations of the family of Herod the Great (see commentary above on 2:22; 14:1), they posed a trick question. The oily introduction with which they hoped to flatter Jesus and put him off guard ironically tells the truth: **Teacher** (19:16), **you are true and teach the way of God** (21:32; 7:13-14; Acts 9:2) **truthfully, and care for no man; for you do not regard the position of men.** He does not fear public opinion, and does not stand in awe of anyone's title, rank, or class. These words are a striking definition of moral courage.

17—Then they put their question: **Is it lawful,** is it right for our people and in accord with our people's faith and traditions, **to pay taxes to Caesar, or not?** (17:24-27). The Herods had always demonstrated their loyalty to their Roman patrons by energetic tax gathering, and the presence of **Herodians** is a strong reminder that some among the people did answer the question with a yes. The Zealots were the great nay-sayers. For them, payment of the tax was treason. Obedience to Caesar was the same as disloyalty to God. Pharisees differed among themselves on matters of taxation but are pictured here as raising the sensitive issue as a means of discrediting Jesus.

18—Jesus, fully aware that they put the question out of **malice**

(*ponēria*, "evil"), lives up to their own description of him (v. 16) and bluntly calls them **hypocrites** (6:2). Their sole reason for raising the thorny issue is to test and trap him. A yes will undermine his credibility with all patriots, while a no will only increase the suspicion that he is a firebrand and political agitator, intent on whipping up the flames of rebellion against Rome.

19—Jesus calls for a sample of **the money** for **the tax** (*kēnsos*, "poll tax"). His own purse, if he even had one (10:9-10), is clean, but his opponents unthinkingly reach down and readily produce the offensive **coin,** a silver Roman denarius (see 20:2).

20—Jesus inquires about the **likeness** and **inscription** (cf. Mark 15:26) on the coin. They can only blunder on, "It is **Caesar's** image and **Caesar's** legend." The silver denarii of Tiberius Caesar (A.D. 14–37) portray his profile and are inscribed with high political and religious claims. Coins were not only legal tender but were deliberately designed to serve as pieces of official propaganda. Tiberius's coins bear the graven image of his face, and they carry legends boasting that he is, for example, "son of the divine Augustus" or "highest priest" of the Roman Empire. Those small coins were loaded with material offensive to any sensitive conscience.

Jesus declares that his questioners should feel free to **render** or "give back" **to Caesar** that which bears his image and legend. And **to God** they should with an equal abandon **render** or give back that on which God has impressed the divine image (Col. 3:10) and inscribed the divine name (Rev. 3:12), namely, their own selves.

By no stretch of the imagination does Jesus make equals out of **Caesar** and **God,** nor does he retract his earlier declaration that it is impossible to be the slave of two masters simultaneously (6:24). Even if Jesus were speaking strictly literally, without a trace of sarcasm or irony, he would still be limiting the obligation to **Caesar** to the payment of a coin, while the obligation to **God** simply has no boundary at all.

22—His questioners **marveled** (21:15, 42). They were not merely outsmarted and Jesus' reply was more than simply clever. It is something for readers to stop at and ponder with care. His answer is much more than a piece of homely advice for disciples or a smart answer to critics. He here reveals in a memorable phrase his own platform, his program of obedient service, his own steady commitment to a life of doing the will of God (4:10; 26:39).

The words of Jesus throughout all these debates are certainly full of wit and intelligence, but the intelligence and wit are at the service of holiness. Jesus is not just flexing his intellectual muscles. Burning in his words is the hard gemlike flame of his own love for God and for the will of God, and precisely that connection is the source of his authority.

God of the Living (22:23-33)

On the surface, the connection between the preceding paragraph and the present one seems simple enough. Jesus' opponents are lining up to debate with him, each in their turn. And Matthew is merely reporting how Jesus cleverly confounds them one after the other, first the Pharisees and Herodians (vv. 15-22) and now the Sadducees (vv. 23-33). But the connection is deeper, and the issue is more interesting than the cleverness of Jesus.

23—Jesus has just spoken of abandoning one's entire life to God (v. 21), and it is therefore singularly appropriate that this next scene focuses on God's surprising gift of new life beyond death (cf. Mark 12:18-27; Luke 20:27-40). As the saying about "rendering to God" is a comment on Jesus' own platform, so his words about God's irresistible power also shine with the force of self-revelation.

Sadducees did not share the Pharisees' belief in **resurrection.** (See Acts 4:1-2; 23:6-10; Josephus, *War* 2.8.11-14; *Ant.* 18.1.3-5.) They did not find the doctrine in the Pentateuch, the oldest and for them the only authoritative Scriptures, and **resurrection** (*anastasis*) seemed to them not only an innovation but actually absurd.

24—They cite **Moses** (the Pentateuch) who said that **if a man dies** childless, **his brother** has a sacred obligation to **marry the widow and raise up** offspring for the deceased (Gen. 38:8; Deut. 25:5). This is a brief description of what came to be called "levirate marriage." *Levir* is a Latin word meaning "husband's brother." The institution of levirate marriage was designed to insure that families and family names would never die out. This familial or generational form of continuing life satisfied whatever desire the Sadducees may have had for immortality, and it was all they found in the Scriptures.

25-26—Having stated their own position, they then ask Jesus to imagine the case of a woman with seven (cf. 18:21) successive husbands, all brothers. Each in turn married her but dies without leaving any **children.**

27-28—Finally, they say, **the woman** also **died.** Gleefully they press on to their punch line: **In the resurrection, to which of the seven will she be wife? For they all had her.**

29—Jesus does not brush them off as frivolous but identifies the heart of the matter and responds with dignity and force. The Sadducees are quite simply **wrong,** and the source of their error is their ignorance of **the scriptures** and **the power of God.** They have set limits where no limits are possible. Jesus begins to speak of **the scriptures** as the self-expression of God, and of God as the everpresent and unlimited ocean of life.

30—**Resurrection** and eternal life (19:16) do not mean the endless extension of the same old existence we now live. The fact that **in the resurrection** people **neither marry nor are given in marriage** means that rich, on-going life with God will exist apart from restless generation and procreation, the mechanisms that Sadducees depend on for their "immortality." That people will be **like angels in heaven** means that human life will be utterly transformed (cf. 1 Cor. 15:35-50). And yet the transformation Jesus announces is not so much the conquest of time by timelessness or change by changelessness or materiality by spirituality but earthly mindedness by heavenly mindedness (16:23), so that the will of God is done by humans on earth as by angels in heaven (6:10). Divine, transfiguring energy aimed at that high goal is already at work, attacking the power of death and disobedience (12:28). (Jesus may have mentioned **angels** partly to needle the Sadducees, who denied their existence, Acts 23:8.)

31-32—It is **wrong** to deny **the resurrection of the dead,** to deny God's conquest of sin and Satan, and to deny God's everlasting embrace of the sheep of his pasture and the people of his hand (cf. 16:18).

Clinching his argument, Jesus quotes to the Sadducees a single unlikely verse (Exod. 3:16), chosen neither from the prophets (perhaps something like Isa. 26:19) nor from the psalms (say Ps. 16:10-11, for example) but from the Pentateuch, that one portion of Scripture which the Sadducees declared to be authoritative. From the Pentateuch, Jesus quotes not Moses but the Lord God (cf. 15:4; 19:3-9). And the Lord does not say, "Once upon a time I was in touch with Abraham and was his God." The Lord is the great I AM, the eternally living one, and says, **I am the God of Abraham, and the God of Isaac, and the God of Jacob.** The great I AM continues to live in relation to Abraham, and Abraham and all the other ancient worthies live in the presence of God. As in the genealogy at the beginning of the Gospel, so here also the listing of these ancestors serves in an argument designed to shift attention away from human solutions prepared by human efforts to God's surprising and irrepressible interventions. The Sadducees think only of men "raising up" children, but Jesus proclaims **the power of God** to "raise up" not only generation after generation in history but to "raise up" the dead at the end of all human history and all human striving. The verb used for "raising up" children (*anastēsei*, v. 24) has the same root as the noun for "the resurrection" (*anastasis*, vv. 23, 28, 30, 31).

33—Unlike their leaders, **the crowd** (21:8-11, 26, 46; cf. 26:5) heard Jesus gladly and **were astonished at his teaching** (7:28; 13:54; 19:25) not because he proved himself more clever than the Sadducees but because his words cast warm light on their own lives and strengthened them for love and joy and discipleship.

Furthermore, these words for a brief moment tear aside the veil from the mind of Jesus and reveal the source of his own authority and his own power to risk everything and to give everything. He has spoken eloquently about going to Jerusalem to suffer crucifixion (20:17-19). Here he reveals the source of the strength that sustains him in joy as he walks that hard and narrow way. Unlike opponents, he knows **the scriptures** and he rests secure upon the boundless depths of God's everlasting **power.** So he is strong to continue on his astonishing path of utter self-giving, not paralyzed by fear of being diminished or destroyed.

With All Your Heart (22:34-40)

34-36—Jesus has scarcely **silenced the Sadducees** when a **lawyer** or scribe (*nomikos* is used here, although *grammateus* is Matthew's usual word) approaches, sent by **the Pharisees.** Mark depicts this lawyer or scribe in warm and positive terms (Mark 12:28-

34; cf. Luke 10:25) but Matthew says only that **the Pharisees** are once again trying to spring a trap with their question: **Teacher** (22:16, 24), **which is the great commandment in the law?** What do you regard as the hub on which all the spokes turn, the fundamental principle underlying and illuminating everything in the entire complex body of inherited legislative material?

37-39—Jesus' reply is twofold: **You shall love the Lord your God** not simply with every atom of brain and blood and sinew but with your whole and undivided self, with the whole or totality (*holos*) of **your heart, your soul, your mind** (Deut. 6:4-9). **This is the great and first commandment.**

Immediately he continues, **And a second is like it,** bone of its bone and flesh of its flesh: **You shall love your neighbor as yourself** (cf. Lev. 19:18; Matt. 19:19). This second became deeply ingrained in the early church as the sum and substance of the will of God (Rom. 13:9; Gal. 5:14). It is the royal law (James 2:8), the law of the kingship of God, the law of Christ (Gal. 6:2).

40—**On these two commandments,** as inseparable as two sides of a single coin, as indivisible as body and soul, depend the entirety (*holos*, cf. v. 37) of **the law and the prophets** (7:12; 11:13), the will of God in its integral wholeness. These two commandments stand or fall together, and together they have absolute priority, in the sense that every other law, ordinance, or regulation is a refraction of the hard and holy light shining from this pair. Jesus resisted every effort to drive a wedge between love for God and love for neighbor (15:1-9), insisting graphically and forcefully on their inner connectedness (cf. 25:31-46).

An ancient scribal tradition taught that the Law contains not 2 or 10 but no less than 613 commandments. Some pious meditations then divided the 613 into 365 prohibitions (one for each day of the year) and 268 positive commands (one for each bone in the body), vividly and memorably declaring the Law's comprehensive application to all our times and all our movements. Scribes furthermore discussed the center or foundation of the 613. What unites them all into a single vital system? Jesus points unerringly to love (*agapē*). A deed deficient in love toward God or love toward neighbor, no matter how pious the deed may appear, is no real doing of the will of God (cf. 5:17-20; 1 Corinthians 13).

It is vital to note that these words are uttered in Jerusalem during Jesus' final days as he draws near to the cross. There he will quite literally yield up **heart** and **soul** and **mind** in loving obedience to God (26:39, 42), and there he will complete his loving service to the neighbor (26:26-28; cf. John 13:1). Thus these words stand not only as ethical instruction for the Christian community. They are that. But even more fundamentally these words are Jesus' own commentary on the narrow path he was treading toward Golgotha.

The false (Christian) prophets neither teach nor practice the entire Law and will of God (5:19; 7:15-23; 24:11-12), but Jesus, even though opposed as a blasphemer and deceiver (26:65; 27:63), does not cancel or annul so much as one iota of the Law but in his teaching and practice of love (*agapē*) brings **all** (*holos*) **the law and the prophets** to perfect and astonishing fulfillment (5:17-18; 7:12; 11:13).

This debate with the Pharisees over the central commandments focuses especially on fulfilling **the law** (v. 40). While the Pharisees are present and in a mood for scribal discussion on fundamentals of the faith, Jesus pursues with them the meaning of **the prophets** (vv. 41-48).

David Calls Him Lord (22:41-46)

41-42—In the eighth and climactic paragraph in the series (begun at 21:23) Jesus moves over to the offensive. (Mark has a different order and so a different climax, cf. Mark 12:35-37; Luke 20:41-44). The series began when chief priests and elders questioned Jesus' authority: What is its nature? What is its source? Here at the end Jesus poses an oddly parallel question about **the Christ: Whose son is he?** That is to say, Where does **the Christ** come from? What are his marks, and how will we recognize him when he comes?

They mouth the standard answer: "The Christ is by definition **the Son of David**." (cf. 1:1; 9:27). By that answer they mean not only that the Christ will come as David's descendant from the house and lineage of David, boasting of his pure Davidic blood, but that he will be like David, will resemble David, and will take up David's work, restoring David's kingdom using David's methods. The Christ, they insist, will be bone of David's bone and flesh of David's flesh, like him in every respect, only greater. He will be a man of valor, slaying his thousands and his tens of thousands, restoring the political and military as well as religious fortunes of his people.

43—Jesus challenges that orthodox conception: If all that is true, Jesus says, then how can it be that **David** uttered the words of Ps. 110:1?

The Lord (God) **said to my Lord** (the Christ or Messiah),

"Sit at my right hand, till I put thy enemies under thy feet."

This verse is quoted in the New Testament more frequently than any other passage of the ancient Hebrew Scriptures (e.g., 26:64; Acts 2:34; 1 Cor. 15:25; Eph. 1:20; Col. 3:1; Heb. 1:3, 13). Here Jesus focuses attention on this famous passage, conjuring up the picture of David in a moment of inspired prophetic foresight (cf. 13:35) greeting from afar the future advent of the Christ. And David in that inspired moment shrinks from calling the Christ his **son.** David is silent about any bond or likeness between himself and the coming Christ. Instead, **David calls him Lord.** Jesus is here arguing that David with his inspired choice of words acknowledges the fundamental otherness of the Christ, the otherness of his kingship, of his weaponry, of his methods, of his warfare.

Jesus is declaring that his contemporaries should not be shocked or surprised that the actual **Christ** sent by God far surpasses (cf. 5:20) prevailing opinions and expectations. Attention to Scripture, in this case Psalm 110, should have prepared them. Jesus is more than temple, more than a prophet, more than Solomon or Jonah (12:6, 41-42). In a sense he is indeed the Son of David (1:1) but here again he is also more.

The leaders of Israel missed the "more" and the otherness. And in Matthew's own day, leaders in the church easily made the same mistake. Church leaders were judging the action of Jesus and the passion of Jesus by the earthly standards of prestige and power (20:20-28; 23:8-10). But Jesus steadily calls for a new consciousness, a new and heavenly perspective, high and lifted up, which can see the way of service and suffering as the way of victory (16:23).

In fact the cross defines how much "more" this Jesus the Christ is than merely a larger or more potent version of old King David with exaggerated powers ruling over a bloated kingdom with expanded boundaries. This Christ in his terrible vulnerability is able to be misunderstood and betrayed, seized and tried, maltreated and crucified (26:25; 27:37). Yet strange and unlimited authority is bestowed upon him (28:18). He is the Son of David and yet he transcends everything Davidic.

46—Jesus left them speechless, not merely conquering them with cleverness but setting before hearers and readers a mind-boggling vision of the surpassing powers of the new age.

Woe to You (23:1-39)

Jesus' long harangue against scribes and Pharisees in Matthew 23 is deeply troubling. On the face of it Jesus appears to contradict his own summons to turn the other cheek and love every neighbor, including even—or especially—the enemy. In fact, part of what is disturbing to modern readers is the assumption that scribes and Pharisees are the enemy. Why are they painted with such dark colors? This is not description but cartooning, and cartooning of a dangerous sort. This chapter has contributed to the terrible equation, "Pharisee = hypocrite," and to slanderous caricaturing of ancient and modern Jewish religion generally.

The view adopted here, consistent with the approach taken everywhere else in this commentary, is that Matthew through these words of Jesus is addressing the Christian community, and especially the teachers and leaders of the community. Looking around in his own Christian community (perhaps in the 80s of the first century) Matthew is disturbed to find leaders exhibiting the behavior and attitudes criticized in Matthew 23.

Like strips of leather braided into a whip, Matthew has woven together sayings of Jesus uttered in criticism of the religious leaders of his day (back in the late 20s and early 30s of the first century). But Matthew seizes those sayings and with them whips Christian backs.

Key to this interpretation is the sudden switch in 23:8-12 from "they" (talking about scribes and Pharisees) to "you" (obviously addressed to Christians). In these verses Matthew tips his hand concerning his real interest. He is not reporting Jesus' opposition to Pharisees for the sake of the historical record. No. He recalls Jesus' sharp criticism of scribes and Pharisees in order to criticize the same or parallel faults in his own contemporaries. As Jesus struck out at leaders of the community of which he was a member, so Matthew uses the old words of Jesus in his own new situation a generation later, to castigate the leaders of his own Christian community.

This whole chapter is a dark mirror-image of the Sermon on the Mount. It sounds harsh in part because it turns everything on its head. Instead of beatitudes (5:3-12) we have woes (23:13-31). Instead of the high praise of righteousness, we have the castigation of hypocrisy and lawlessness. Instead of the promise of the divine presence, we confront the threat of the absence of God and of unrelieved desolation (23:34-36, 37-39).

What Matthew apparently intended here was to depict the kind of behaviors and attitudes condemned by Jesus.

Matthew found his opportunity in the Markan passage serving as skeleton for his own work. In Mark 12:38-40, almost at the end of his final teaching in the temple, Jesus utters one sentence critical of certain scribes. In Matthew that single sentence has become the nucleus of an entire discourse.

As it now stands, the chapter is full of vivid and memorable images. Unfortunately, when we shift our focus away from the "who" and fasten instead on the "what" that Jesus criticizes and "what" he values, the result is a list of virtues and vices which sounds abstract, bloodless, and trite when compared with the original images. Nevertheless, it is useful to attempt such a listing. It is a worthwhile exercise if it accomplishes nothing more than altering our ordinary anti-Pharisaic approaches to this chapter.

Condemned: preaching without practicing (v. 3), aggression towards pupils (v. 4), love of flattery and prestige (vv. 5-12), blocking and judging (vv. 13-15), evasive word games (vv. 15-22), superficial spirituality (vv. 23-24), posturing (vv. 25-28), resistance to the divine word (vv. 29-31). Valued: deeds in harmony with teaching (v. 3), enabling toward righteousness (v. 4), humility and a spirit of service (vv. 5-12), desire to enter God's kingdom and to open the way to others (vv. 13-15), simplicity and sincerity (vv.

16-22), justice and mercy and loyalty (vv. 23-24), generosity (vv. 25-26), integrity (vv. 27-28), attentiveness to the voice of God (vv. 29-32).

These lists are far less colorful than the original images of Matthew 23. Maybe readers can improve the lists, maybe transfuse or transfigure them. The basic point is that Matthew gathers traditional sayings of Jesus into a discourse aimed at undercutting certain kinds of behavior and certain attitudes exhibited by the Christian teachers and leaders of Matthew's own community.

Verses 1-12 are a general introduction to the chapter. It begins as an attack on the Pharisees (v. 2) but climaxes in direct address to leaders of the Christian community (vv. 8-10). In reissuing the traditional material collected in this chapter, Matthew is campaigning neither against the old Pharisees of Jesus' day nor against the new Pharisees of Jamnia in his own day but against leaders of his own Christian community. That is the key to the interpretation of this entire chapter.

Verses 13-31 contain seven (omitting v. 14) woes, seven denunciations of blind hypocrisy and lawlessness, warning Christian leaders to shun such behaviors and attitudes.

Verses 32-36 are all accusation and warning about the dread consequences of rejecting righteous blood and persecuting Jesus' envoys.

Verses 37-39 are a concluding lament over Jerusalem, lightened by the possibility of future repentance and blessing.

Moses' Seat (23:1-12)

1-3—The scribes and the Pharisees sit on Moses' seat (*kathedra*). From an early time, a real bench or seat, sometimes richly carved in stone, was reserved for the leader or teacher of the community at the front of the synagogue.

The point here of course is not architectural. The scribes are pictured as continuing the unbroken chain of tradition stretching back to Moses. Teachers and interpreters of the voice of God (Jewish or Christian!) are his descendants or successors and through them the genius of the great mediator continues to guide the people. So scribes and Pharisees seem to be praised, but the reference to the seat at the front of the synagogue already prepares for harsh criticism of the love of prestige (v. 6).

So therefore, Jesus says, and what follows is as odd and controversial as anything in this speech, **Practice and observe whatever they tell you** (cf. 28:19), **but not what they do.** Why not? **They preach** or talk *(legousin)* **but do not practice** (cf. 21:30). Two questions: How can Jesus be so positive, and how can he be so negative? Jesus has warned his disciples to beware the leaven (teaching) of the Pharisees (16:5-12), and he frequently contradicts positions they espouse (5:21-48; 12:1-14; 15:1-20; 19:3-9; 23:16-22). How can he now offer this sweeping recommendation that the crowds and disciples (23:12) should do **whatever** the Pharisees tell them? That is jarring.

What is going on here? Is this a little piece of rhetoric designed to grant opponents as much as possible? Something like: "Pharisees and scribes are widely respected as successors of Moses in our time, and in some respects that may be true." Or perhaps Jesus is saying, "I do not want to get bogged down in a quarrel concerning the credentials of the Pharisees, the niceties of doctrine, or the relative merits of the schools of Hillel and Shammai (cf. 19:3-9).

Or, most probably, the curious wording corresponds to Matthew's own situation in this way: Matthew recognizes that the resurrected Jesus himself instituted the teaching mission of the church (28:19), and Christian teachers hold an honored position in the new community. Matthew does not object. He is himself a teacher and places high value on the teaching mission of the church. He does insist, however, that teaching and teachers be evaluated critically in the light of the science of deeds, by the standard of the will of God, as taught by the one Teacher, Jesus (23:10).

When words do not issue in deeds, when high-sounding teaching and lofty slogans are contradicted by mean and low behavior, the result is hypocrisy (6:2). As the discourse goes on, Jesus will denounce in the most scathing terms that lack of integrity or wholeness.

4—Jesus offers examples of the fatal gap between word and deed. In the interest of making the ancient Law relevant to new conditions and of subordinating every aspect of life to the Law, ancient teachers developed an elaborate system of ordinances and obligations. And these they **lay on men's shoulders,** like **heavy**

burdens, hard to bear (cf. Acts 15:10). The professional scribe
had not only the inclination but also the education and the leisure
to master the web of requirements, but nonprofessionals, ordinary folks, were doomed to ignorance and infraction, left feeling
alienated and powerless. How different is Jesus' yoke and burden
(11:28-30).

5—A second reason (cf. v. 3b) for Jesus' blast against these
teachers: they are peacocks of piety, and perform in hopes of
attracting admiring stares (cf. 6:1-18; but see 5:16). For example,
they make **their phylacteries broad and their fringes long.** Mark
says they like long robes (12:38) but Matthew draws attention to
phylacteries, small leather boxes holding a fragment of parchment
inscribed with passages of Scripture. They were tied, ostentatiously in these cases, by leather thongs to forehead and upper
left arm, so that the words of the Law were more or less literally
on their mind and on their heart as they prayed (Exod. 23:16;
Deut. 6:8; 11:18). **Fringes** or tassels including a strand of blue
cord were commonly worn (also by Jesus, 9:20; 14:36) at the four
corners of a robe as a sign of being bound to the Law (Num.
15:38-39 and Deut. 22:12). Again, some ostentatiously enlarged
their **fringes.**

6—Furthermore, **they love the places of honor at feasts and
the best seats in the synagogues,** the seat of Moses (v. 2), for
example, and so exhibit an all too common hankering for prestige
(cf. 20:21; Luke 14:7-11).

7—Etiquette required that the inferior salute the superior and
that **salutations** should be more elaborate the higher that superior
ranked. The system suits them. They love **salutations in the market places.** They adore having people greet them with titles of
respect like **rabbi.** This last is the climax of the series and is
developed in curious and revealing fashion. It looks as though
Matthew has adapted Mark 12:38-40, omitting the enigmatic reference to devouring widows' houses (Mark 12:40), absorbing the
fascination with long prayers (12:40b) into the Sermon on the
Mount (6:7), and rearranging the remaining habits (Mark's sequence is: robes, salutations, seats) so that the climax comes in
the reference to **salutations.** (But it should be noted that the
sequence seats/salutations is found also in Luke 11:43.) **Rabbi,** a
term meaning "my master," was just coming into use in the first

century as a title for scribes. It is first seen in the New Testament where it is often used of Jesus.

8—Here Jesus switches from speaking about scribes and Pharisees and all they do and begins suddenly to say **you.** He looks at the disciples (v. 1) and through them speaks to the leaders of the young church concerning their behavior.

You leaders **are not to be called rabbi, for you have one teacher** (synonym for *rabbi*), namely, God (or Jesus?), and sitting at the feet of that one, no matter how your gifts or tasks in the community may differ, **you are all brethren** and equals. You must not set yourselves above others.

9—And to the little ones (18:6), tempted to yield to the conceits of the powerful and persuasive, Jesus speaks a parallel word equally as revolutionary as the preceding: **Call no man your father on earth** (cf. 3:9), **for you have one Father, who is in heaven** (5:45; 6:9). How easily people look to father figures and benevolent despots, begging to be told what to think and how to act in politics and religion. People in all times and places have displayed a depressing tendency to proud and destructive tribalism, calling themselves children (or followers) of some particular human ancestor or hero not shared by other peoples (cf. 3:9). The word of Jesus is a grand criticism of passive dependence and of petty tribalism.

10—A third and climactic saying, closest in form to the first (v. 8), looks beyond crucifixion to Jesus' exaltation: **Neither be called masters, for you have one master, the Christ. Master** (*kathēgētēs*) is a word derived not from the relationship of owner and slave or ruler and subject but is a piece of academic or educational jargon. It pictures Jesus as the one guiding mind of the new community. He is not an absence but a presence and therefore requires no surrogates to speak in his name, as does Moses (v. 2). He is not a dead figure of the past but is living evermore in the midst of his own (1:23; 18:20; 28:20).

11-12—The paragraph which begins with v. 1 climaxes in v. 10, and it remains only to round if off with a pair of thunderous declarations. The first seems addressed particularly to leaders, as Jesus turns ordinary understandings upside down: Whoever is **greatest among you shall be your servant** (20:25-28). In the second, Jesus cries to all: Those who **exalt** themselves **will be**

273

humbled, and those who **humble** themselves **will be exalted** (18:4)! These two verses press beyond the specific and detailed examples offered so far (vv. 2-10) and state fundamental principles, applying them especially to the leaders but also to the led.

Woe to You (23:13-31)

13-31—Of the seven woes (eight if v. 14 is authentic), all except the third (vv. 16-22) open with the same formula: **Woe to you, scribes and Pharisees.** Again, in each except the third the reason for the **woe** is introduced with **because.** Luke's Gospel contains a series of woes in Luke 11. Matthew's second and third woes (23:15 and 16-22) have no Lukan parallel.

The third and seventh woes are longer than the others, and the seventh gradually builds to a prophecy of punishment.

"Woe" is the opposite of "blessed." If the Beatitudes are a kind of wedding song celebrating the joy of God's presence with the people of the new age, the woes are a kind of funeral dirge, a lament for the dead (cf. 11:16-19). "Blessing" and "woe" are words of final judgment, spoken by the judge of the universe over the acquitted and the condemned, the sheep and the goats.

13—**Woe!** According to the Beatitudes (5:3-12), that grand fanfare of the Sermon on the Mount, the entire thrust of Jesus' program is to turn the key (*kleis*, 16:19; Luke 11:52) and fling wide the gates of the kingdom of heaven, especially to people judged unworthy or unlikely by the standards of prevailing piety. But **woe** is pronounced on spiritual leaders, be they Jewish or Christian, who **shut** (*kleiō*) **the kingdom of heaven.** They lock it up tight and render it inaccessible by their rush to judgment, their knee-jerk exclusivism, their misplaced priorities, their fussy systematizing, their ignorance of the way (7:13-14; 21:31-32), their love of their own position and authority.

14—This verse (cf. Mark 12:40) is not found in the best ancient manuscripts of Matthew's Gospel. The same theme surfaces in 23:25.

15—Both synagogue and church appealed to outsiders and made proselytes in the name of the God of heaven. The picture behind the word **proselyte** (*proselytos*, from *proserchomai* = "approach") is of one who once lived as a stranger outside but now has come the whole distance into the bosom of the family. How terrible, if the energy expended in making **a proselyte** turns the outsider into a **child** not of God and heaven but of **hell** or gehenna (5:22; 23:33). Again, this hard word is directed at the church and its leaders (cf. 7:21-23).

16-22—This third **woe,** alone of the seven, addresses not "scribes and Pharisees" but **blind guides** (cf. 15:14), **blind fools** (v. 17, cf. 5:22), **blind men** (v. 19). The strange little paragraph, repeating the teaching of 5:33-37, is full of old legal jargon. The word **swears** appears ten times in seven verses and **oath** occurs twice. Jesus criticizes sophisticated word games, employed by some ancients to evade responsibility (cf. 15:5). It was considered clever and permissible to leave oneself a loophole, swearing by **the temple** or **the altar,** for example. Then if necessary one could later break the **oath** with the following argument: Certain parts of the temple are especially holy (the **gold of the temple,** vv. 16-17, or the **gift that is on the altar,** vv. 18-20) and they have binding power in an **oath.** However, **temple** and altar by themselves have no such power in the tradition. Therefore an **oath** naming them alone is deficient and breaking such an **oath** leaves one guiltless.

Jesus attacked the casuistry of such argumentation, denouncing it as **blind, blind** to the presence of God in whose presence all deeds are acted and all words spoken. He sought truth before God and love in relation to the neighbor as a full-time, not just a part-time, matter.

23—The fourth **woe** blasts the habit of majoring in minor matters. Ancient opinion was divided over questions of tithing. It was certainly agreed that the great basic crops of grain, wine, and oil were subject to tithing together with the firstlings of the flocks (see Num. 18:12-14; Deut. 12:6; 14:22-23; Lev. 27:30-32). However, zealous individuals insisted on paying tithes even on such trifling "crops" as the herbs **mint and dill and cummin.**

Jesus does not fault that rigorous practice in itself and even seems to commend it (but see 9:13; 12:7). However, something is dead wrong when those same fussy rigorists neglect the weightier things of the Law (cf. 22:36), and here Jesus names a second trinity as more important than the trinity of herbs: **justice and mercy and faith.** Luke 11:42 has "justice" and "love of God," and Mic. 6:8 and Zech. 7:9-10 offer comparable summaries.

Nothing on God's earth is praised more highly in this Gospel than a thirst for **justice** or righteousness (5:6), a generous spirit in dealings with one another (5:7), simple honesty and trustworthiness in matters great and small (23:16-22).

24—The ancients used strainers every day, sometimes just a cloth thrown over the spout of a pitcher or the mouth of a jar, to filter out foreign matter from their wine and water. The pious were especially on the lookout for anything unclean and contaminating. But how easy it is in moral and spiritual matters to end up practicing the strangest form of sanitation, **straining out a gnat** but blindly **swallowing a camel.**

25-26—The fifth **woe** contrasts **the outside** and **the inside of the cup and of the plate.** Some **cleanse the outside** only, while **the inside** remains not simply unwashed or unclean, as might be expected in a nicely balanced phrase, but **full of extortion and rapacity** (Mark 12:40; Amos 2:6-8). Jesus diagnoses the uncleanness as ill-gotten gain, the result of injustice, plunder, avarice, actions directly opposed to justice, mercy, and loyalty (v. 23). The hottest water will never cleanse such cups. Luke reports the cleansing process in interesting terms: Give to the poor what is in your cups and plates and then everything will be clean for you (Luke 11:39)!

26—What is called for is not just the cleansing of the inside of cups and plates but the purifying of persons in the depths of their inner being. In fact this must be done **first** (cf. 15:11, 17-20). The result will be wholeness and integrity, **inside** and **outside** equally clean. No more false appearances and fatal disjunction.

27—The sixth **woe** continues to play on the theme of inside/outside. **Hypocrites** are **whitewashed tombs, outwardly beautiful** or at least brilliant, but **inwardly they are full of dead men's bones** (cf. the fig tree, 21:19). Corpses defile, and so touching a tomb or walking on a grave renders a person unclean (Luke 11:44). Therefore in the spring of the year as the time for the Passover pilgrimage drew near, the damage to roads caused by the rains of winter was repaired and tombs were whitewashed, as part of the annual program for easing the way of pilgrims in their ascent to the holy city and warning them of the presence of tombs lest they unwittingly defile themselves and so be disqualified from the feast (Num. 19:16; Mishnah, *Shekalim* 1:1).

28—The outside of these fatally flawed persons is described as beauty and righteousness, but inside they are all **hypocrisy and iniquity.** Behind this latter is the word "lawlessness" (*anomia,* cf. 7:23).

The theme of a splendid or innocent facade masking an inner decay or rapacity or a fundamental uselessness surfaces repeatedly in Matthew's Gospel (cf. the fig tree, 21:19; other trees in 7:16-20; 12:33; wolves in the guise of sheep, 7:15; disobedience under a "yes" in 21:30).

29—The seventh and final **woe** is again the dark side of bright beatitudes (5:6, 10-12). It continues in a fresh form the talk of **tombs** and righteousness begun in the sixth woe (vv. 27-28).

Here the charge against the **hypocrites** is that they **build the tombs of the prophets** and **adorn the monuments of the righteous** (cf. Acts 2:29) and so display studied public respect for the ancient messengers of God. But their devotion is fatally flawed.

30-31—The tomb builders, in speaking of those who murdered the prophets, describe them as their **fathers.** Jesus picks up on that and presses it, accusing the new generation of being **sons** of the old indeed, made of the exact same stuff as those murderers. The fathers killed, and the sons build tombs (Luke 11:48). They are partners in crime. The **sons** in fact continue the old rebellion of the **fathers** against God's emissaries.

All the Righteous Blood (23:32-36)

32—Jesus utters a cry, dripping with sarcasm, urging those leaders to go ahead and do their worst: **Fill up the measure of your fathers** = bring to a head the ancient pattern of resistance to the messengers of heaven.

33—But he warns that a terrible fate is prepared for those who show themselves to be such **sons** of such **fathers.** Words first found in the Baptist's mouth echo here once more (3:7; 12:34): **You serpents, you brood of vipers! How are you to escape?** Unless they repent, they are wriggling their way towards **hell** or gehenna (5:22; 23:15), even though they fantasize that they are marching straight to the kingdom of heaven (5:19-20).

34—They stand exposed as rebellious sons of rebellious fathers.

Jesus says, **I send you** emissaries and envoys. The **I send** is emphatic, and the first person language dominates from here to the end of the chapter (cf. 5:21).

Jesus is uttering a magisterial claim, not found in the other Gospels: I, not the Eternal God or the Immortal Wisdom of God but **I** as Divine Wisdom-in-your-midst (see commentary above on 11:19; 1:23), **I send you prophets and wise men and scribes** (cf. 11:25-27; Wisdom of Sol. 7:27). That is what has been happening from the beginning and what continues to happen. **Prophets and wise men and scribes** (cf. 13:17) signify not only the messengers of old whose words were written in scripture (cf. Luke 24:44) but also and especially the Lord's servants in the contemporary church (cf. 10:41-42), both wandering missionaries and proclaimers (**prophets**) and settled teachers (**wise men and scribes,** cf. 13:52). Neither here nor elsewhere does Matthew hint at any organization in terms of apostles, elders, deacons, pastors, or bishops.

Jesus as Lord of the church sends proclaimers of the way of righteousness (13:17; 21:32), but the history of the world also is the story of unrighteous and murderous resistance. Some messengers they **kill and crucify** (20:19; 27:22-23) and others they **scourge** (10:17) and **persecute from town to town** (10:23).

35—This tale of God's patient speech on the one hand and of humanity's thirst for **righteous blood** (cf. 27:4) on the other began in primordial times and is rushing to its awful climax. This miniature history of the world (vv. 34-35) should be compared with other little histories in Matt. 1:1-17; 21:33-43; 22:1-14 (cf. Acts 7; Hebrews 11). Unlike the genealogy, which reaches back to Abraham and then focuses on kings, this history stretches all the way back to Abel and fixes attention on **prophets and wise men and scribes,** bringers of a word from above.

The murder of **innocent** (or "righteousness," *dikaios*) **Abel** is recorded in the first pages of the Bible (Gen. 4:8; Heb. 11:4). Then 2 Chronicles, the last book in the sequence of the Hebrew Bible, reports the murder of a priest named **Zechariah** in the courts of the Lord's house (2 Chron. 24:20-22). So the history recorded in scripture both opens and ends with murder. Human history runs from a story of the spilling of innocent blood to an account of blood defiling a holy place.

And that scriptural story is not a closed book. For Jesus suddenly announces, **All this will come upon this generation.** This sad story will reach its climax in **this generation.** These verses prepare the way for Matthew's unique report about the spilling of Jesus' righteous blood and the defiling of the temple by Judas's return of the blood money (27:3-10). That report connects the murder of Jesus to the whole long history of disobedience to God's agents.

As a Hen Gathers Her Brood (23:37-39)

37—Jesus suddenly cries out, **Jerusalem, Jerusalem** (Luke 13:34-35), addressing not merely the ancient city but also the comtemporary religious community.

How terrible it is that religious communities, not benighted pagans, are guilty of **killing the prophets and stoning those who are sent to you.** Jesus continues to speak in first person language as the one who has through all the ages **sent** those bearers of the divine word and continues to send them. In a stunning image Jesus portrays himself as attempting in every generation to gather God's people to himself and through himself to God, **as a hen gathers her brood under her wings.** But religious authorities can be as persistent in resistance as he is in sending and speaking. And religious people are easily misguided by false authorities (23:9).

38—Echoing Jeremiah (12:7) Jesus declares, **Your house,** the temple at Jerusalem, sign of the presence of God, **is forsaken and desolate.** Indeed, the sacred center of any community resisting God is heading for ruin, for desolation, for the very opposite of the great promise of this Gospel: the presence of God (1:23; 18:20; 28:20).

39—Sharp denunciation and savage warnings fill the chapter, and yet the last word is an invitation to repentance, a call to life. The one thing needful is that people and leaders turn from killing and crucifying, from scourging and persecuting, from resisting and stoning the messengers. The final word is a call to turn and greet the Messenger, **Blessed is he who comes in the name of the Lord** (21:9; Ps. 118:26)!

■ FIFTH DISCOURSE: The New Community Readies Itself for the Coming of the Son of Man (24:1—25:46)

Especially because of this fifth and final discourse of Jesus (chaps. 24-25), it is often said that Matthew and his community burned with feverish curiosity about the last things, the signs of Jesus' future advent, the ticking of the cosmic clock, the blowing of the last trumpet, and the final judgment.

Multitudes of readers are taught to match clues in these chapters with current events in order to calculate how close we have come to the end of human history.

Obviously these chapters are loaded with bizarre images, familiar from ancient Jewish and Christian apocalyptic writings: a great tribulation more terrible than anything previously known, false prophets with lying oracles preying on people's fears, crude idolatries energized by the sudden appearing of the desolating sacrilege, an epidemic of apostasy infecting the faithful, history stuttering to an end in the midst of trumpeting angels and screaming eagles, the earth shaking and the stars falling from the sky, the whole clamor silenced as God's final word of curse and blessing thunders, fires for the wicked and bliss for the elect.

This kind of language welled up irrepressibly in the first century, as Jews and Christians alike felt the earth and its old eternal rocks shifting and melting beneath their feet. The end of the temple and the end of the world, the breakup of Jerusalem and the breakdown of the cosmos merged in their imaginations. The chaos of history was seen as a sign of the imminent end of all things.

No one disputes the heaping up of apocalyptic imagery in Matthew 24–25. But what does Jesus intend by it?

Jesus does not merely repeat the tradition, insisting that its odd details are correct. Nor does he simply reveal fresh details, filling in a few old blanks. He does not provide a more accurate and timely calendar of future events. He is not expounding a timetable at all and clearly says so (24:36).

Jesus uses apocalyptic but teaches compassion. The discourse opens with the disciples talking about the splendor of sacred buildings (24:1-2) and closes with Jesus speaking of the unsurpassed splendor and holiness of compassion toward the little ones (25:31-46).

Between that beginning and that end Jesus focuses on the transitoriness of all things. What endures? What can stand when the power of divine judgment shakes every foundation? Will the temple or any other religious institution provide shelter from the blasts of angelic trumpets? Can connection of race or nationality (cf. 3:9)?

We are finally confronted (25:31-46) with a new version of the old commandment of love. Compassion or care for the needy is the most splendid and only really durable work of the human community. Here, as in the Johannine farewell discourses (John 13:31—16:33) and in Paul's hymn on love (1 Corinthians 13), traditional apocalyptic rhetoric is stretched to its limits and made to carry the message of the everlastingness of love.

Not One Stone upon Another (24:1-3)

1—**Jesus left the temple and was going away.** He had been in the temple since 21:23, but this poignant sentence conveys more than simple information about change of locale. It brims with foreboding and the sense of abandonment (cf. 23:38).

His disciples interrupted his flight with a backward glance, commenting on the many **buildings of the temple,** on their beauty and impressive size, their holiness and indestructibility. The temple complex (*to hieron*) included the sanctuary itself (*ho naos*), set on its own stepped platform surrounded by its railing with signs warning Gentiles against proceeding any further. At the outer edges of the Court of the Gentiles were covered porticoes or stoas dominated by the great Royal Stoa at the south end of the temple mount. There too were the great staircases for pilgrims and monumental entrances. Herod the Great had lavished rich attention on those buildings, and they were impressive (John 2:20; Josephus, *War* 1.401; *Ant.* 15.380-425).

2—In response to his disciples' enthusiastic outburst, Jesus solemnly repeats that terrible destruction is drawing near, and even that which seems most sacred and most stable will not be exempt (26:61; 27:40).

3—Jesus **sat** to teach (5:1) on **the Mount of Olives** across the Kidron Valley, opposite the city, overlooking the temple. **The disciples** gathered about him privately, as representatives of the new community. The topic of his teaching, **your coming and the close of the age,** is one thing and not two. **Coming** (*parousia*, 24:3, 27, 37, 39; Acts 3:20; Heb. 9:28) is a technical term for the sudden manifestation of a deity or a state visit by an emperor or other high dignitary. Jesus' **coming** or final epiphany will itself mark **the close of the age** (*synteleia tou aiōnos*, 13:39, 40, 49; 28:20; Heb. 9:26), the conclusion to the old aeon and the opening of the new age of God's unopposed sovereignty.

But is it true? Is he the coming one? (11:3). And where is the world really headed? Is it winding down to death and awful destruction? Or are all the varied strands of history weaving a complex and secret pattern which one day will be complete and furnish all of history with a fitting conclusion (*synteleia*)? The disciples inquire, **When** will all these things happen? and **What will be the sign** or signal that you and that ending are drawing near?

The Structure of the Discourse

The two questions voiced by the disciples in 24:3 govern the arrangement of material in most of chaps. 24 and 25: **When will this be?** (24:36—25:46), and **What is the sign of your coming?** (24:4-35).

I. **What sign? (24:4-35)** Matthew 24:4-14 describes the whole period all the way up to the end. As history approaches its close, tribulation will arise, and many will be overcome by anxiety or led astray from love.

The section 24:15-31 looks again at the identical time and does two things: (1) It sharpens the focus on the coming great tribulation and describes the desolating sacrilege and the propaganda of false Christs and false prophets (vv. 15-28). (2) It reveals that tribulation is not the last word spoken over human history, and nails the reader's attention to the final epiphany of the Son of man (vv. 29-31).

Then 24:32-35 summarizes the chapter up to this point. Terrors in history and nature are signs that he is near.

II. **When? (24:36—25:46)** Matthew 24:36-41 announces one of the keynotes of this whole section: No one knows when that day will arrive.

Two more characteristic notes of this section are introduced in
24:42-44: **Watch and be ready,**

- like the servant managing wisely his master's household
  (24:45-51),
- like the five wise maidens with oil in their flasks (25:1-13),
- like the faithful servants who invested the talents entrusted
  to them (25:14-30).

Then the section 25:31-46 with its vision of the sheep and the
goats forms the majestic conclusions to this pair of chapters and
to the entire body of the teaching of Jesus as presented by Matthew.

I. What sign? (24:4-35)

The Beginnings of the Sufferings (24:4-14)

4-6—Jesus does not give them the assurances they desire. He
points to what is essential: **Take heed that no one leads you
astray,** and **see that you are not alarmed.**

5—**Many** false messiahs with deceitful signs will rise up and
say, **I am the Christ,** I am the leader to salvation. Powerful leaders
and authorities within the community (cf. 7:21-22; 23:8-10) will
claim to speak and act for the Christ and even as the Christ. **And
they will lead many astray.** To lead astray (*planaō*, 18:12-13;
22:29; 24:4-5, 11, 24; Jesus as *ho planos*, 27:63; *planē*, 27:64) is
not merely to teach a few wrong ideas about the world's clock or
to misread events in nature or history but is to lead others down
paths of uncaring, of treachery, and of hate (vv. 10-12).

6-7—**Wars** will erupt and **rumors of wars** will strike fear in
human hearts. **Nation will rise against nation** and **kingdom
against kingdom** in civil and international strife. **Famines and
earthquakes** will tear apart the fabric of nature and society. Yet
all this **must** happen. That word **must** (*dei*, cf. 16:21) describes
these terrible things both as inevitable (cf. 18:7) and as still subject
to God's ultimate control.

8—**All this is but the beginning of the sufferings** (*ōdines*,
"birthpangs"), the beginning of the labor pains of the new age
(John 16:20-22; Rom. 8:22; Isa. 26:17; 66:7; Hos. 13:3; 1QH 3:9-
10). They have no finality but are inevitable preliminaries on the
way to the new world. It is easy to make too much of them and
of signs like them.

9—Calamity breeds fear and suspicion, and tottering societies look for scapegoats. **They will deliver you up to tribulation** (*thlipsis*, v. 21) **and put you to death. And you will be hated by all nations,** the same nations that the community calls to discipleship (28:18-20). And that hatred will burn against them, Jesus says, **for my name's sake,** because they act on his authority and follow on his way (cf. 10:22, 39).

10—But what forms the climax to this catalog of apocalyptic terrors? What could be worse than wars and rebellions, famines and earthquakes, tribulation and persecution to the death? The paragraph concludes with unique words probably hinting at the actual situation in Matthew's own community.

When the hammer blows of persecution fall on the community, many will stumble and **fall away** from the path of faith (cf. 18:6) and begin to **betray** and **hate** one another within the community.

11—Danger from outside is bad enough. Danger from insiders is more horrible still. **Many false prophets** (5:19; 7:20) **will arise** from within the new community and **lead many astray** (v. 4).

12—**Wickedness** (*anomia*, 7:23), outright indifference to the Law of God and the will of God, will increase, and **love** (*agapē*, 22:37-38) will shrivel and **grow cold.**

13—Horrors fade, and the paragraph concludes with a challenge and a promise. Jesus summons his followers to hold out **to the end** (*eis telos*, cf. 10:22), to the highest degree and till the last moment. One who **endures** in the faith and on the way in the midst of history's terrors will be scorned as hopelessly naive and foolish, but Jesus promises that only such a one **will be saved** (10:22; cf. 1:21; 6:13).

14—A further promise: The terrors may seem to herald the invincible power of hate and death. But **this gospel of the kingdom** (4:17; 10:17), the news of God's approaching rule, **will be preached** irrepressibly and against all odds, throughout **the whole world** (28:19). Persecution will scatter preachers and preaching to the four corners of the world. Then **the end** (*to telos*, 24:6; cf. *synteleia*, v. 3), the God-appointed goal, **will come.**

The Desolating Sacrilege (24:15-28)

The preceding section (vv. 5-14) surveys the entire period from the present all the way up to **the end** (v. 14), describing it as a time of **tribulation** with terrible possibilities of apostasy and hate.

In what follows, Jesus speaks not of a different and susequent period but of different features of that same time.

15—In the coming evil days **the desolating sacrilege spoken of by the prophet Daniel** (Dan. 9:27; 11:31; 12:11) will suddenly stand **in the holy place.** By the New Testament period **the desolating sacrilege** had become a stock item in the inventory of horrors expected in the last days. **The desolating sacrilege** means a shocking intrusion into **the holy place** by some object or power, at once hideous and polluting. The sacred center of things, the place of contact with God and source of blessing and purification, is trampled on, defiled and utterly corrupted, jeopardizing connection with God and with health.

Daniel's prediction was inspired by the crudities of Antiochus IV, the Syrian ruler at whose order (168 B.C.) an altar and image of Olympian Zeus were erected in Jerusalem's temple and pigs were slaughtered there in sacrifice (1 Macc. 1:54-64; 2 Macc. 6:2). Lurking behind the image and adding to its force are memories also of other moments: Herod set a great carved eagle above the facade of the temple; Pilate displayed legionary eagles in the holy city; the Emperor Caligula threatened to erect his own image in the sanctuary (A.D. 37–40) (Josephus, *Ant.* 17.151; 18.55, 261; cf. *War* 6.316).

Difficulties abound, as indicated in the cry, **Let the reader understand!** What should readers **understand?** That the sign of **the desolating sacrilege** had been fulfilled already, perhaps in the destruction of the temple in A.D. 70? Perhaps they should understand that if such a foul presence could find room in the heart of Jerusalem, the holy city (5:35; 27:53), then it could also arise at the heart of the new community. If the new community was to be the dwelling place of the divine presence (1:23; 18:20; 28:20), then it is the new shrine or sanctuary, and that means it is the place where the desolating sacrilege should never stand, and yet it is also precisely the place which defiling powers will want to attack and occupy.

One strand of Christian interpretation came to identify the **desolating sacrilege** as the antichrist and to think of the sudden, awesome eruption of evil at the center of power in the church. One thing wrong with that tradition is that it has usually imagined that the evil was erupting or would erupt in someone else's church, while Matthew calls readers to vigilance about their own behavior, their own style of leadership, and their own community.

The end will be a time of cataclysms, probing, and revealing what people are made of. All the old securities including the most sacred strongholds will be shaken. Nothing earthly will be immune.

16-20—Then Jesus utters four odd little statements. On the surface it looks as though he is counseling people how to handle the breakup of the universe! But no matter how much they sound like it, his words are not really advice. Jesus paints a picture. The sudden eruption of **the desolating sacrilege** (v. 15) and of **the great tribulation** (v. 21) will be like the furious onslaught of an invading army, catching the population unawares and throwing them into panic.

16—It is the kind of time when refugees from cities and towns will **flee** for their lives **to the mountains.** Eusebius (*Ecclesiastical History* 3.5.3) records a tradition that the Christian community of Jerusalem fled not to the mountains but to the city of Pella in the Jordan valley when Jerusalem came under siege in A.D. 66–70.

17—In such a time people are lost if, instead of fleeing immediately and unencumbered, they try to rescue **what is in** their **house.**

18—Peasants **in the field** are lost, if they hesitate and **turn back** (Luke 9:62) to retrieve their **mantle** or cloak left at the edge of the field or back in the house (Mark 13:16). Better to flee away naked (Mark 14:52; Amos 2:16).

19—Pregnant women and nursing mothers cannot keep up and may fall behind in the rush to escape.

20—Flight to safety is rendered more perilous if it happens **in winter,** when streams are swollen and roads turn to mud and chill creeps into the air, or **on a sabbath,** when the pious can in good conscience travel no more than 2000 paces (cf. 12:1, 10).

21—The description uses terms borrowed from the long experience of humankind with invasion and warfare. But the days immediately preceding the end will be even worse, and the wars of human history are only weak parables. The topic is **the great tribulation** (v. 9), the final trouble, **such as has not been from the beginning of the world until now.**

22—A tramping army moves over a landscape like reaper over a field cutting everything in its path. But wars do leave some survivors in their wake. Out of the ferocity of those last days some will be **saved** (v. 13). **For the sake of the elect** (see commentary below on v. 31) the number of **those days will be shortened,** namely, by God. This means that history, even when the most monstrous forces seem to have their way, never fully slips out of God's control or eludes God's purpose. God is always greater and has the power and the will to bring people safely through (6:13; 26:41).

23-24—Now comes counsel and advice. The warning about **false Christs and false prophets** (vv. 5, 11 and cf. 7:15-23; 1 John 4:11; 2 Peter 2:1) is renewed and expanded, reminding readers that the real concern of Jesus' discourse is not the fate of Jerusalem and temple but of the new community as shrine of holiness. By displays of **great signs and wonders** (7:22; Rev. 13:13-14), they will try to **lead astray** (vv. 4-5, 11) **even the elect** (v. 22).

25—The community is forewarned and so forearmed.

26—**Do not go out,** says Jesus, when the rumor spreads that **he is in the wilderness,** the traditional place of the sudden appearance of prophets and national saviors, both true and false (3:1; 4:1; 11:7; Acts 5:36; 21:38; cf. the wilderness community of Qumran and later Christian monks).

Do not believe it, when you hear **he is in the inner rooms. The wilderness** carries overtones of social and political revolution, aggressive, even violent action in public on behalf of a radically new order. **Inner rooms** sounds a different and opposite note, a quiet turning inward (cf. 6:6). To the present time prophets continue to arise proclaiming that the kingdom will be fully realized and Christ will establish his rule if only we adopt a new social-political program or a new psychological technique, and also acknowledge these teachers as themselves our "Christs" (24:5). How does the kingdom come? By violence in the public arena? Or quietly as fresh inner light?

27—Hidden, obscure, unrecognized in his ministry, apparently absent or powerless in the present (giving false Christs and false prophets their opening), Jesus will at the end be revealed to all, and no mistake about it. **As the lightning** cracks open the dark cauldron of the sky all the way from east to west, just so public and obvious will be **the coming of the Son of man** (v. 3).

28—This word may be a kind of afterthought, relating not to v. 27 but to vv. 24-26. When church and society become rotten, more like a corpse than a living body, then **eagles** or vultures, namely, false Christs and false prophets, see their opportunity and gather. Or, if the verse is to be connected to v. 27, it means that Jesus and his angels coming to execute judgment are like **eagles** or vultures.

29—**The tribulation of those days,** portrayed in terms of social and historical cataclysms, is now pictured as a cosmic convulsion. **Sun** and **moon** fail to shine. **The stars will fall from heaven** and **the powers of the heavens** (the planets) will be shaken off course and dart in erratic fashion. Everything stable and dependable, by which humans set their clocks, arrange their calendars, and navigate their ships, the first creatures of God to be hung in the sky to mark the steady and reliable sequence of night and day (Genesis 1), begin to dissolve and fall apart. Creation begins to return to chaos as history ends. But where does it all end? At the feet of the Son of man. That is the point of all this talk.

30—**Then,** at the moment when chaos and terror seem to have the upper hand, **there will appear the sign,** and the **sign** is nothing other than **the Son of man** (8:20; cf. 12:38-40). The **sign** is not simply the earthly Jesus, the one who speaks. The **sign** is the crucified and resurrected Jesus, with nailprints in his indestructible hands. It is Jesus, neglected or nourished in the little ones (25:31-46). That one is the coming **Son of man,** and no one will mistake his coming.

All the tribes of the earth will mourn (Zech. 12:10-12; cf. John 19:37 and Rev. 1:7) to see how wrong they were, to see victorious the one they wounded, to see alive the one they took for dead, to see the greatness of the one they ignored in little people. They shall see **the Son of man** no longer homeless, obscure, or weak but **coming on the clouds of heaven,** on the storm of God's presence, with power and great glory (16:27).

31—With **trumpet** fanfare (1 Cor. 15:51; 1 Thess. 4:16; Rev. 8:1-2; Isa. 27:13) he will dispatch **his angels** (13:41) with a single charge: **gather** (9:38) **his elect** (24:22, 24) **from the four winds, from one end of heaven to the other** (cf. John 11:51-52), from all the places to which they were hounded (9:36; 10:23; 24:16).

Commentary   Chapter 24

He Is Near (24:32-35)

32—Everyone can read the evening and the morning sky, and speak confidently of fair weather or storm (16:2-3). And everyone can read the **fig tree** (21:18-20) and note in branch and bud and leaf the signs that **summer is near.**

33—But it is hard to **see all these things,** these convulsions of nature and history, and to read them as signs of hope. Yet they mean that the Son of man **is near, at the very gates** (cf. *parousia,* v. 3, means a royal visit to a city; cf. Ps. 24:7-9).

34-35—Surprisingly, Jesus asserts, **Truly I say to you, this generation will not pass away till all these things take place. Heaven and earth will pass away, but my words will not pass away** (cf. 5:17-18). Is Jesus promising the end of the world during **this generation?** Or is he declaring that all these preliminaries, all these premonitory signs, will have their dread start during this generation? This passage has certainly troubled the generations and still refuses to yield a single and certain sense. Was Jesus mistaken? Or should we defend Jesus' omniscience by torturing the text? Perhaps **this generation** means the people of God. Or **all these things** means the destruction of Jerusalem (A.D. 70).

That ancient generation of first hearers and first readers saw all that they needed if not all that they wanted: Everything foretold in the Law and the Prophets (11:13-14; 13:16-17), the shifting of the eons (27:51-53), and the sovereignty of God elbowing its way into the midst of the kingdoms of this world (4:17; 12:28). All these things were taking place and are taking place. The long-awaited coming one has drawn near, is present, and is locked in mortal combat with resisting powers in the midst of human history (12:24-28).

In every generation people confront the signs of war and rumors of war, of famine and earthquake, of social and historical and cosmic collapse. These are not the exclusive property of any one time. And their usual effect is to strike fear in hearts and inspire feelings of dread.

Into the teeth of the whirlwind Jesus throws a word of hope. **All these things** will **take place** starting right now (cf. 16:28) but **all these things** will also **pass away,** just as the totality of **heaven and earth,** the whole historical and created order, **will pass away.** But, he promises, **my words will not pass away.** His **words** are

words of hope, of the power of God and the love of God, of victory over Satan, of the triumph and everlastingness of mercy.

His **words** are the great treasure of Matthew's Gospel, the reason this book has been prized through successive generations. They have endured and have enabled readers to endure, by placing them squarely within a structure of love: loved by God in the mercy of the Christ and summoned to yield an answering love toward every neighbor and toward God, no matter how evil waxes and no matter how foolish compassion appears to be.

II. When? (24:36—25:46)

Jesus' rhetoric has been conjuring up scenes of terror: marching armies and masses of refugees, falling stars and veering planets. Now the talk seems to switch to gentler scenes of weddings, plowing, milling, and sleeping. But all these happy times and normal occupations are interrupted, almost savagely.

So unlike the preceding paragraphs, this new section breathes not a word of awesome signs heralding the approaching end. Quite the contrary. The end will come without sign or warning, precisely when people everywhere are absorbed in the most peaceful and ordinary routines.

If the Householder Had Known (24:36-44)

36—That day and that hour (cf. 26:45) will remain unknown right up to the end. A three-member assertion underscores the futility of every attempt to calculate in advance the time of his coming to close the age (v. 3): **no one,** no human being, **knows, not even the angels of heaven, nor** even **the Son.** Jesus' apparently artless declaration of his own ignorance of the time of the end probably was designed to undercut assertions by Christian prophets. They claimed to speak in his name (7:22) and to know the exact time of the last hour (24:5, 23-26), and they manipulated Christian communities with their prophetic utterances.

The end is known and it is under blessed control. Only **the Father knows,** and that is sufficient. In this context Jesus speaks of God as **Father,** that intimate and family name (cf. 6:9), thereby centering hearts on God's own loving care for those caught in the cruel jaws of history.

37—**The coming** (*parousia*, v. 3) **of the Son of man,** contrary to talk of the distant early warning signals of deep rumblings in the world's basement (vv. 15-20, 32-33), will be like the flood in **the days of Noah,** like sudden death (vv. 40-41), like a thief in the night (v. 43).

38-39—**In those days before the flood** (Genesis 6–9) people ate and drank (sc. 24:49; Luke 21:34) and entered into marriages (cf. 25:1-13) as though life would forever continue its smooth course. **They did not know** anything different right up **until the day Noah entered the ark and the flood came and swept them all away.** Just so sudden and unannounced will be **the coming of the Son of man.**

40-41—A matched pair of homely scenes offers a second picture of the suddenness of the coming of the Son of man. **Two men,** alike in every respect, walk out at dawn to work **in the field** side by side as they had for years. But that day **one is taken** by sudden death and only **one is left** alive to return home in the evening.

Two women, practically twins, leave their houses carrying grain. They spend the morning chatting while **grinding at the mill** as they had done dozens of times before. But that day **one is taken** without warning and only **one is left** alive.

These brief and realistic stories of men and women are sometimes taken out of context and used in the service of the so-called rapture, the theory that the elect will be physically caught up to safety in heaven out of the coming tribulation. It is possible that "taken" means the ingathering of all the elect by the angels of God (24:31). But these stories have nothing to do with rapture. They have everything to do with vigilance in the time before the sudden advent of the Son of man (cf. Luke 12:16-21). These biographies of Noah's generation and of peasants and housewives are intended to do nothing more complicated than make the case for unrelenting watchfulness, as the conclusion (v. 42) plainly shows:

42—**Watch therefore, for you do not know on what day your Lord is coming.** As the term **Father** (v. 36) sounds the good news that even the worst of times are in the best of hands, so **Lord** is a trumpet call to duty and fidelity. The nature of that fidelity will be defined soon enough. But first a third picture of the suddenness of the advent of the Son of man.

43—Breaking and entering, by actually digging through the mudbrick wall of a house (see 6:19), is an ancient problem. Obviously it would never succeed **if the householder had known** exactly **in what part of the night the thief was coming** (1 Thess. 5:2; 2 Peter 3:10). **He would have watched** with friends at his side and a weapon in hand and **would not have let his house be broken into.** But the thief is careful not to broadcast his coming.

44—Jesus breaks off, draws a line and adds up the score. He directly addresses the community of disciples. The answer to the question of when he will come to bring the age to a close (v. 3) is twofold: (1) **The Son of man is coming at an hour you do not expect,** and (2) **You must be ready** always. Vigilance and readiness are the themes of what follows.

Most readers would probably agree that vigilance and readiness are good things. Nevertheless, Jesus tells three further stories (24:45-51; 25:1-13, 14-30) in part defining and in part defending vigilance (watchfulness) on the one hand, and readiness (described as fidelity, wisdom, or goodness) on the other.

All three stories have similiar casts of characters: a master or lord and one or more servants or attendants. And the plots are also similiar: the lord assigns tasks (or tasks are clearly defined by tradition); the master or lord leaves for an indefinite period of time; the servants or attendants perform their tasks well or badly; suddenly the lord returns, and the servants are called to account; some are praised and others blamed.

A fourth scene, that of the great judgment (25:31-46), is similar in cast of characters and plot, but speaks less parabolically, less obliquely. It stresses the final elements in the plot outline, and functions as climax not only of the series beginning in 24:45 but of the entire discourse (24:1—25:46). Indeed, it is the capstone of all five of Jesus' discourses in the Gospel of Matthew.

Faithful and Wise Servant (24:45-51)

45—In the first case the **master** before departing appoints one **servant** to manage his household and supervise the entire staff of servants, seeing that they have what they need for their varied tasks and for their own sustenance (cf. 10:10). That servant will be called **blessed** (cf. 5:3; 25:34) if **his master** upon returning finds him fulfilling his job faithfully and wisely in accord with instructions.

47—In fact, that servant will be promoted and **set over all his possessions.**

48—On the other hand, a **servant** designated as manager may in the interim forget that he has a master (23:8-10) and may start acting as though he were himself owner and master. **He begins to beat his fellow servants,** lording it over them (20:25). And he abandons himself to carousing and drunkenness, using the master's food and drink in wild self-indulgence (24:38; 25:42). The whole paragraph is a warning especially to leaders in the church.

50—**The master of that servant will come on a day when he does not expect him and at an hour he does not know** (24:36, 39, 42, 44).

51—A trusted **servant** may turn out to be wicked (v. 48). In that case the master will not simply **punish** but literally "cut him to pieces" or "cut him off" from the faithful. He will be lumped with **the hypocrites** (6:2; 23:13), treated as the impostor he is. On that day wicked servants will know the truth, and with weeping and gnashing of teeth (8:12) will cry out in belated anguish and regret.

Ten Maidens (25:1-13)

1—This parable, unique to Matthew (but cf. Luke 12:35-38), presents the final revealing of **the kingdom of heaven** in terms of wedding customs (cf. 9:15; 11:17; 22:1-14; 24:38). The **ten maidens** are the bride's attendants. **The bridegroom** would come with his companions to take the bride from her parents' house to his own. When he approached, the maidens would go out with lighted **lamps** and **meet** him and his party.

2-4—Now **five** of the maidens were **foolish** (7:26; 24:45) and **five were wise** (7:24; 24:45). **The foolish had lamps** but no extra **oil,** while **the wise took flasks of oil with their lamps.**

5-6—**The bridegroom was delayed** (24:48) so long that all ten, not just five, finally **slumbered and slept.** Suddenly **at midnight** (Luke 12:38) they woke to the cry: **The bridegroom! Come out to meet him.**

7-9—**All those maidens rose and trimmed** the wicks of their oil **lamps. The foolish** realized that their lamps were flickering out and pleaded with the wise, **Give us some of your oil. But**

the wise haughtily advised the foolish (at midnight!), **Go to the dealers and buy for yourselves.** And apparently the foolish ran off to make purchases.

10—While the foolish were gone, **the bridegroom came** and the wedding festivities continued. **Those who were ready** (cf. 24:44) **went in with him to the marriage feast** (22:4, 8) **and the door was shut.**

11-12—The foolish arrived tardily and cried, **Lord, Lord,** (cf. 7:21), **open to us** (Luke 11:5-7; 13:25). The answer is solemn and severe: **I do not know you** (7:23; Luke 13:27).

It is neither necesary nor particularly helpful to interpret each detail in allegorical fashion, even though it would be easy to equate the bridegroom with Christ, the delay with the strange tardiness of the second coming, the ten maidens with the Christian community, and the exclusion of the foolish with eternal punishment. Once launched on such a course, readers can hardly be blamed for asking what the lamps and the oil or the dealers signify. As it stands the parable is a story of a wedding told in bold and stylized fashion, realistic except for a few details (shopping at midnight and the bridegroom's refusal to open the door). And it has been supplied with an unadorned conclusion (v. 13).

13—The leaders and ordinary members of the community **know neither the day nor the hour** (24:36, 42, 50). Therefore they are urged to watchfulness (24:42), here defined as a form of wisdom (vv. 2-9) and readiness (v. 10).

Talents (25:14-30)

A further parable reinforces the preceding, undergirding its assertions on the suddenness of the master's arrival, the necessity of watchfulness and the dread consequences of being foolishly unprepared: This last is now spelled out in terms of fear, sloth, infidelity, and downright wickedness.

14-15—**A man going on a journey** summoned three **servants and entrusted to them his property** (24:45). **To one he gave five talents, to another two, to another one.** A talent was the largest monetary unit of the ancient world (see commentary above on 18:24), and therefore these are no ordinary slaves. They are trusted administrators, and the parable is directed especially at leaders in the Christian community.

16-18—Two servants **traded** with their **talents,** each doubling the original **five** and **two. He who had received the one talent** did not drink it up with carousing or make a run with it to the big city or the nearest border (24:49; Luke 15:13; Philemon 16). **He dug in the ground and hid his master's money** (cf. 13:44). It lay idle, saved for the day of the master's return.

19-21—**After a long time** (24:48; 25:5) **the master** returned home and **settled accounts.** One after the other the three servants appeared. The first had doubled the talents entrusted to him. His master praised him as **good and faithful** and promoted him: **You have been faithful over a little, I will set you over much.** He is taken even more fully into his master's confidence and drawn closer to his master's side: **Enter into the joy** (cf. Heb. 12:2) **of your master.**

22-25—The whole scene is repeated in the case of the second servant. Finally the slave **who had received the one talent came forward.** In addressing his master, he sketches him as a **hard** and unscrupulous man: **reaping where you did not sow and gathering where you did not winnow.** Afraid of losing the one talent and suffering the consequences, he had anxiously hidden it in the ground and now rather proudly produces it with a little flourish: **Here you have what is yours.**

26-27—**But his master** denounced him as **wicked and slothful.** The master accepts the unflattering character sketch drawn by his slave (v. 24) and concludes: **You ought** at least **to have invested my money with the bankers,** so that **I should have received,** if not double, then at least the original plus a little **interest.**

28-29—That third servant is stripped of his lone talent, and it is given to the servant who had doubled five. To the faithful more will be entrusted, while the faithless will lose everything they ever had. Powers and privileges are used or lost. The lesson is not new (13:12). The lesson is straightforward: Readiness is described not as a passive posture but as fidelity at work in assertive action. (A different version of the parable occurs in Luke 19:11-27, where it is told to quash the expectation that the kingdom in all its glory was set to appear immediately.)

30—**The worthless servant** was **cast into the outer darkness** where existence is all regret, all weeping and gnashing of teeth (see commentary above on 8:12).

You Did It to Me (25:31-46)

Compared with the talk about the sudden arrival of a thief in
the night (24:43), the tardy approach of a bridegroom (25:1-13),
or the sudden return of a pair of absentee masters (24:45-51;
25:14-30), the new scene appears less parabolic and indeed almost
painfully straightforward.

This parable or vision of the nations, separated like sheep and
goats, is astonishing, and yet it is the perfectly apt climax to the
series of scenes beginning at 24:36, to the discourse starting at
24:1, and to all the teaching of Jesus enshrined in the Gospel of
Matthew as a whole.

Like the farewell discourse of John 13:31—16:33, it sums up
the life of Jesus, comments on his death, and addresses the church
quite directly about its own life situated between his lowly ministry and his glorious coming epiphany.

It picks up and develops the theme of the coming of Jesus as
Son of man to bring the age to a close (24:3) and the theme of
separation found in the preceding talk of those going astray contrasted with those enduring (24:11-13), tribes of earth full of regret
contrasted with the elect (24:30-31), Noah rescued but others
swept away (24:37-39), one taken and the other left (24:40-41),
blessed and wicked servants (24:45-51), wise and foolish maidens
(25:1-13), faithful and slothful servants (25:14-20).

The questions **When?** and **What sign?** have entirely faded from
sight, and every phrase is concentrated on describing as literally
and nonparabolically as possible the meaning of preparedness and
watchfulness. Or, the question of **When?** is given a different and
surprising answer: The Son of man is coming now, in the lowly.
And what is the **sign** of his coming? The poor and needy are
themselves odd and often unwelcome signs of his presence.

31-32—No one knows when, but finally **the Son of man** will
come (24:3) **in his glory** with power over every enemy and **all
the angels with him** (13:39, 41, 49; 16:27; 24:30-31). He will sit
on **his glorious throne** (19:28; 20:21; 26:64), and **all the nations**
(28:19) will be gathered before him, indicating that he will come
not simply as a witness (see commentary above on 7:23; 10:32-
33) but as the world's judge.

A powerful moral and spiritual imagination has framed this

scene. It is as idle to inquire where as it is to ask when such an event will occur. The point is that the last word in history (24:35) belongs to the Son of man who, like every refugee, once had no place to lay his head (2:13; 8:20) and, like every condemned prisoner, tasted hatred and abuse in his own body (17:22; 20:18-19). Once an innocent victim, once an itinerant herald of divine love, he will be given all authority in heaven and on earth, and he will sit as Judge. Hence his life and teaching, full of the divine righteousness, possess unsurpassable urgency and ultimacy.

He will separate the nations **as a shepherd separates the sheep from the goats. Sheep** and **goats** mingle and graze together each day. But when they are moved to fresh pasture or when sheep are due for shearing or goats for milking, or when evening falls and the goats must be sheltered against night's chill, then they are separated. **And he will place the sheep at his right hand** (22:44; 26:64), **but the goats at the left.**

34—The lowly speaker, on his way to lonely crucifixion, sitting unknown and unnoticed on the Mount of Olives (24:3), will in the end be universal **king** (*basileus*) and will invite those **at his right hand: Come, O blessed** (contrast v. 41) **of my Father** (6:9; 24:36), **inherit the kingdom** (*basileia*, 4:17; 5:3; 6:10; cf Luke 23:42-43) **prepared from the foundation of the world. The kingdom** is God's own surpassing gift, planned and readied by God from the first moment of the world's history, and it is quite unlike any earthly realm (cf. 20:12).

Who are these **blessed** ones (*eulogēmenoi*, cf. *makarioi* in 5:3), and why do they receive this thundering and eternal word of congratulations?

35-36—The heart of the matter is expounded in six simple sentences. With only the slightest variation, these sentences ring out four times in the next ten verses: (1) **I was hungry and you gave me food.** (2) **I was thirsty and you gave me drink.** (3) **I was a stranger and you welcomed me.** (4) **I was naked and you clothed me.** (5) **I was sick and you visited me.** (6) **I was in prison and you came to me.**

37-39—These sheep at the right hand are now called **the righteous,** and their behavior, commended by the king at the final judgment, in the final paragraph of Jesus' public teaching in the entire Gospel, is a final concrete definition of that righteousness which Jesus urges and teaches everywhere in this Gospel (cf. 1:19; 3:15; 5:6; 10:41; 13:17; 23:29, 34).

The righteous will be surprised: **Lord, when did we see thee?** Three times they ask **When?** New meaning is attached to the question. The old question, **When** will all these things take place? (24:3), is utterly transformed. The question is not, When will the end come? but, When will the nations start living in accord with the righteousness which God in Christ gives and requires?

40—To their question, **When?** the king (v. 34), identifying with the lowly, will solemnly respond, **As you did it to one of the least** (10:42; 18:10, 14) **of these my brethren** (12:48-50; Heb. 2:11), **you did it to me.**

Differently from Peter and the first disciples, differently from fabled saints and miracle workers, differently from brilliant thinkers and teachers, **the least of these my brethren** have been appointed by Jesus as his representatives in the world. Jesus identifies with them in their need (10:40; 18:5). He demands nothing for himself but faith only (18:6). He summons his disciples to mercy, to love. Yet finally love for neighbor is not something separate from love for the Lord (22:39).

41—The second half of the narrative darkly mirrors the first. Those **at his left hand** are not **blessed** but **cursed** and he will say not **come** but **depart from me** (7:23). They enter not the **kingdom** but **the eternal fire** (13:42, 50) **prepared for the devil and his angels.**

42-43—The reason is no longer any surprise. He was **hungry, thirsty, a stranger, naked, sick,** and **in prison.** And they simply did nothing.

44-45—**When** (v. 38), they ask, **did we see thee?** The answer is clear and devastating: **As you did it not to one of the least of these, you did it not to me.**

46—The final verse is a thunderclap, summing up both halves: **And they will go away into eternal punishment, but the righteous into eternal life.**

So the fifth and final discourse, saturated with talk of the end of human history and God's coming triumph, draws to a close in this vision of righteous deeds. Nothing about golden streets, jeweled foundations, or gates of pearl. Nothing about high honors bestowed on miracle workers or exorcists, on gifted visionaries or prophets, on stunning speakers in tongues human or divine (7:15-23). Nothing about an everlasting hierarchy of teachers and leaders exalted in higher and higher ranks according to the splendor of their eloquence or knowledge (23:8-10). This awesome vision shines with the same fire that burns in Paul's hymn of love in 1 Corinthians 13.

These words of Jesus, identifying with the world's outcasts, stand immediately before the narrative of his own betrayal, arrest, torture, and execution.

As the vision ends, everything is ready for the Passion Narrative to begin.

Indeed that great and final vision (25:31-46) prepares readers for the Passion Narrative (chaps. 26–27). In his vision Jesus speaks about being identified with the world's outcasts, and in his passion he actively and actually identifies with them. The Son of God (27:40, 43) stands deliberately and voluntarily in the shoes of the powerless, the weak, the defenseless, the hated, the tortured. He began as a refugee and he ends as a condemned criminal. He gave his blood for them and for many (20:28; 26:27).

■ The Passion of the Son of Man (26:1—27:66)

Delivered Up (26:1-16)

The Son of Man Will Be Delivered Up (26:1-2)

1—Jesus entered the city of Jerusalem at the beginning of chap. 21 and soon began to teach among the crowds in the temple (21:23—23:39) and then to instruct his disciples privately on the Mount of Olives in a fifth and final discourse (chaps. 24–25).

Matthew here marks the conclusion to that last discourse with very nearly the same words he had used to close the previous four (cf. 7:28-29): **When Jesus had finished all these sayings.** New here is the use of the little word **all.** The addition of that one word signals that the formal teaching of Jesus is now at an end.

But Matthew's narrative does not yet end. As a member of the Christian community, Matthew inherited a rich body of material about Jesus: reports of Jesus' words and deeds and sufferings. In addition Matthew learned a traditional framework holding all those materials together in a continuous narrative stretching from birth to resurrection and from Bethlehem and the Jordan River to Nazareth and Capernaum and from there to Jerusalem.

Matthew has set the discourses into that traditional framework so that words of Jesus, on the one hand, and the deeds and sufferings of Jesus, on the other hand, complement and interpret one another. He will show how this teacher of the higher righteousness, who will sit on a throne judging all nations (25:31-46), is himself tried and condemned by earthly judges and authorities. By means of the five discourses Matthew has unforgettably portrayed Jesus as teacher. But by weaving the discourse into the great traditional framework of Jesus' whole life, Matthew shows that Jesus still far surpasses the category of teacher in more ways than one.

Jesus is a teacher in whom words spoken and deeds enacted form an undivided and perfect unity. Yet even that accomplishment does not say nearly enough. This teacher is the crucified and resurrected one. Of course, other teachers and sages suffered martyrdom but this one has also been raised to life by God's mighty power and exalted high above all heavenly and earthly authorities. Not teacher only, this Jesus is Lord, coming judge, unique Son of God, Emmanuel.

At the end Matthew will once again bind the words of Jesus to the narrative of the death and resurrection. He will conclude his entire account of Jesus with that great and final scene in which the crucified and resurrected one stands on the mysterious mountain and refers disciples and readers back once more to his teaching (28:16-20). Jesus lives forever in the community of disciples as exalted teacher (cf. 23:10).

2—Matthew begins his narration of Jesus' passion and resurrection in phrases at once solemn and ironic. Jesus has just broken off talking about **the Son of man** as judge of all peoples (25:31-46) and now abruptly begins to sketch a grim picture of people as judges of that same **Son of man** (cf. 16:13). He announces that **he will be delivered up** (*paradidotai*) **to be crucified** (cf. 16:21; 17:22-23; 20:18-19). And Jesus declares, irony upon irony, that all this will happen during **the Passover,** festival of freedom and faithfulness (cf. vv. 4-5).

Arrest and Kill Him (26:3-5)

3—His words not only predict this fate but unleash the forces arrayed against him. Set loose by the word of Jesus, **the chief priests and the elders of the people** (see the commentary on 2:4; 16:21; 21:15; 28:11-12) solemnly **gathered** (2:4; 22:34, 41; 26:57; 27:17, 27, 62; 28:12; Psalm 2; Acts 4:26) **in the palace of the high priest,** a post held by Caiaphas A.D. 18–36 (cf. John 11:49; Luke 3:2; Acts 4:6).

4-5—The plan was to **arrest Jesus by stealth** and **kill him** quietly. They agreed to avoid acting **during the feast** or in the presence of festal crowds (see v. 55). Jesus enjoyed a popular following as a prophet (21:46), and the authorities stepped lightly lest they spark a **tumult among the people.** Riots in the city would provoke a Roman intervention and result in the curtailing of their own privileges. But the word of Jesus has already determined that he will be executed during the Passover. This is not the worst time, as the priests think, but the absolutely right and fitting time (cf. 16:11-12).

In Memory of Her (26:6-13)

Sandwiched between the two installments of the priests' plotting against Jesus (26:3-5, 14-16) and contrasting sharply with it is the story of the nameless woman's act of costly devotion. In similar fashion the story of the magi approaching Jesus with their gifts (2:7-12) is embedded in the account of Herod's murderous scheming (2:1-6, 16-18). (In fact, numerous motifs of the birth and infancy narrative are echoed here at the end of Matthew's book.)

6-7—Jesus, like the Baptist (11:8) and unlike his enemies (26:3), is not to be found in an aristocrat's palace. He was **at Bethany** (21:17) **in the house of Simon the leper** (cf. 21:14), where suddenly **a woman,** in an extravagant gesture of devotion and respect (Ps. 23:5; Luke 7:46), broke open **an alabastar jar of very expensive ointment** and **poured it on his head.**

8-9—**The disciples** (Mark has only the vague "some people" and John points the finger at Judas) were **indignant** (20:24; 21:15) and condemned the act as a **waste.** Usually Matthew offers a more positive picture of the disciples than Mark does (cf. 20:20) but here Matthew says **the disciples** object, saying that the **ointment might have been sold for a large sum** (Mark 14:5 mentions 300 denarii; see the comments on 18:28 and 26:15) and the proceeds could have gone to **the poor** (cf. 19:21).

10—The disciples' thinking seems to be right in line with Jesus' own powerful words about care for the poor uttered in the preceding chapter (25:31-46), and yet Jesus vigorously defends the woman. What they call **a waste** Jesus describes as **a beautiful thing** or "good deed" (*ergon kalon*, see 5:16).

Matthew gives no hint that he reads the woman's act as one by which Jesus is anointed as Messiah. Jesus was called to his ministry of righteousness at his baptism and was there at the Jordan anointed with the Spirit (3:13-17). The woman's prodigal outpouring confesses her perception of the singular and surpassing worth of this Jesus who has just now announced his impending passion.

That woman sees what the disciples fail to see. They want a Jesus who is rich and powerful Lord, one who from time to time reaches into his purse and dispenses gifts upon the poor. However, far from distancing himself from the world's weak and vulnerable, Jesus here and everywhere absolutely identifies with them. He declares that the disciples will in the future have ample opportunity to demonstrate whether they really understand Jesus and his program. As he says, **You always have the poor with you.**

The woman acknowledges his path and hails him in this quiet moment immediately before his crucifixion. Unlike the Twelve, she sees with stunning clarity into the heart of Jesus' purpose, and she confesses it with her gesture. Her breaking of the stem of the flask and her pouring out of ointment mirror and acknowledge his breaking of bread and pouring of wine, the breaking of his body and the pouring out of his life, his unbounded love for God and neighbor.

12—Jesus acknowledges her insight. **In pouring this ointment on my body she has done it to prepare me for burial.**

13—Neither Mark nor Matthew knows her name, but both record Jesus' high and solemn praise and tell her story **in memory of her.** Indeed, her story deserves unending repetition. She was herself an uncalculating giver, and she saw and celebrated the rightness of his self-giving love.

Judas Iscariot (26:14-16)

14—From the nameless woman Matthew returns to men with infamous names. **Caiaphas** was named in v. 3, and now **one of the twelve who was called Judas Iscariot** approached **Caiaphas** and **the chief priests** to cut a terrible bargain.

15—Unlike the nameless woman, Judas is no giver. He asks, **What will you give me if I deliver** or betray (*paradidōmi*, 26:2) **him to you?** They happily paid out money into his hand (cf. 28:12), giving him exactly **thirty pieces of silver** (Zech. 11:12; see the comments on 27:3-10). Most likely these were silver shekels, each worth four drachmas or denarii. The total amount (120 denarii) was roughly equivalent to four months' wages for a day laborer (20:1-16).

The succession of paragraphs presents an awful contrast. At Bethany the woman honors Jesus, lavishing upon him ointment worth a large sum. All twelve misread Jesus' purpose and so object to her action. Judas is singled out as one who cares nothing for the poor or for Jesus. He breaks utterly with Jesus' commission to messengers of the new community about taking no coins in their purses (10:9). Indeed, he has a thirst for silver.

16—Money in hand (cf. 10:9), Judas **from that moment sought an opportunity** (*eukairia*, cf. *kairos* in v. 18) **to betray him.** What precisely would he **betray?** Did he pass to the priests details of Jesus' teaching, perhaps twisting Jesus' words and providing a basis for bringing charges (cf. 26:59-61)? Did he simply reveal Jesus' movements so that authorities might arrest him quietly without any public fuss (vv. 5, 47)?

And why did Judas betray? Was he disappointed that Jesus did not lead a popular uprising against the Romans? Matthew displays little interest in the what or why. He concentrates instead on the mystery of contradictory responses to Jesus.

The marvelous abandon of the woman's self-giving (cf. 2:11) contrasts sharply with the calculations of the disciples and especially with the obscene greed of Judas and the murderous intent of the priests (cf. 2:16).

I Will Keep the Passover (26:17-30)

At Your House (26:17-19)

17—The Passover meal was eaten in the early evening as the 15th of Nisan began, and the Feast of Unleavened Bread officially ran from Nisan 15 to Nisan 21 (or 22 in the Diaspora) according to Exod. 12:15-20. By the time of Jesus, custom dictated clearing the house of all leaven on Nisan 14, the Day of Preparation for the festival of Passover–Unleavened Bread, and so Nisan 14 became in effect **the first day of Unleavened Bread.**

On the first day of Unleavened Bread, numerous traditional tasks had to be performed by those desiring to **eat the Passover:** clearing the house of every crumb of leavened cake or bread (cf. 13:33; 16:6, 11-12), purchase and preparation of herbs and spices and other Passover foods, selection of a lamb, the ritual slaughter of the lamb at the temple and its roasting at home or at a community oven, the furnishing of a room. But all these details are banished from view, as Matthew concentrates once more (cf. v. 2) on Jesus' mysterious control of events.

18—He directed disciples to enter Jerusalem, find a certain inhabitant, and simply announce, **The Teacher** (8:19; 23:8) **says, My time is at hand; I will keep the passover at your house with my disciples.**

His **time** or season (*kairos*, 8:29; 16:3; cf. "the hour," 26:45) is not his alone but is the climax of long ages (1:1-17), and what is now **at hand** is not only the time of his execution but the hour of the dawning of the kingdom (3:2; 4:17; 24:3).

19—Brief as it is, the paragraph in impressive fashion displays the majesty of Jesus. He commands, and for once his disciples respond with unblinking obedience. In contrast to the authorities in Jerusalem and in contrast to Judas (vv. 3-5, 14-16), they **did as Jesus had directed them** (cf. 1:24; 21:6).

At Table (26:20-30)

Matthew (like Mark and Luke) portrays two scenes and two only at the one table, focusing in turn on two participants: Judas (vv. 20-25) and Jesus (vv. 26-30). The two scenes present two ways, one leading to terrible death as inexorably as the other leads to indestructible life (cf. 7:13-14).

The precise reason behind Judas's act remains obscure, but what should be clear is that he commits the sin of offering up a fellow human being to death for monetary gain. He reclines at table as one who eats up brother and sister, consuming their lives.

Jesus at the same table seeks life for every sister and brother and offers all that he is and has to renew and replenish their lives.

The one eats and eats up, devouring, while the other feeds with the stuff and substance of his own being, bread from heaven.

Is It I, Lord? *(26:20-25).*   **20-21—Evening** marked the beginning of a new day, the 15th of Nisan, when the pious not merely **sat** but reclined (*anakeimai*) at table, signifying their status as free people under God and lighted their lamps to celebrate the Passover.

Jesus gathered **the twelve,** nucleus and mirror of the new community of women and men of all times and all places. Suddenly he punctured the bittersweet joy of the festivities with the pronouncement: **One of you will betray me** (cf. vv. 2, 15).

23—With fragments broken from large flat loaves, guests scooped food from common bowls and dishes spread before them on the table. Jesus paints a terrible picture: **He who has dipped his hand in the dish with me will betray me.**

Sharing a meal was a profoundly spiritual act, a declaration of kinship and trust, and so betraying a table companion was a byword for mean and hideous behavior (Ps. 41:9). Jesus had defined betrayal as a sign of the shocking horror of the last times (24:10).

24—To the new community, struggling with hatred and betrayal in its very bosom, Jesus makes two comments: first he declares, **The Son of man** (v. 2) **goes as it is written of him.** God's gracious plan proceeds in spite of human treachery. In fact God takes treachery in hand and turns it till it serves the plan that the Son of man will ascend to authority by way of rejection and suffering.

Second, Jesus defines just how shocking and awful a thing betrayal is: **Woe** (18:7; 23:13) on every traitor; it would have been better if he had not been born (18:6). Judas came to share that judgment on his own existence (27:3-10).

22, 25—One by one the disciples react in horror, "I am not the one, am I, **Lord?**" Last of all, calling Jesus not **Lord** but **Master** or rabbi (cf. v. 49; see the comment on 8:19), Judas speaks up, "I am not the one, am I, **Master?**" But Jesus answers, **You have said so** (v. 64; 27:11).

For the Forgiveness of Sins (26:26-30).   The shadow of possible betrayal haunts every gathering of the community past and present (vv. 20-25), but after that sober warning the narrative moves to talk of overwhelming mercy.

26—At table **Jesus took bread** and **blessed** (*eulogeō* = "praise God," 14:19) and **broke it** and **gave it to the disciples** (14:19; 15:36), saying, **Take, eat; this is my body.**

27-28—Then, almost perfectly mirroring and paralleling his action over the bread, **he took a cup,** gave **thanks** (*eucharisteō*, 15:36) and **gave it to them,** with words of command and interpretation: **Drink of it, all of you** (20:22-23); **for this is my blood of the covenant** (Exod. 24:8), **which is poured out for many** (20:28) **for the forgiveness of sins.**

Jesus identifies himself with bread, dark and wholesome, staff of life, gift of God. And with Passover wine, red in the cup, warm on the lips, rejoicing the heart, loosening the tongue in confession and praise.

Bread and wine, so basic but by no means simple. They share a kind of history of violence. Bread comes from grain, sickled and winnowed, from the heads of the wheat finely ground between millstones. Wine is from fruit plucked from the vine, crushed underfoot, the blood of the grape (Gen. 49:11).

Bread on the shelf quickly grows mold, and wine in a jug turns bitter and spoils. Their one true destiny is to be eaten up and swallowed down. Only so do wheat and grape achieve their destined purpose. Only so do they fill and warm and satisfy.

So bread and wine define Jesus' passionate living and his violent dying as a miracle of self-giving and satisfying.

28—This loaf and cup, this eating and drinking, link his living and dying to Passover (26:2, 5, 17-19), to slavery and peoplehood, to oppression and freedom. His **blood,** his outpoured life, is the foundation and ground of **the covenant** (Exod. 24:8), fresh and new (Jer. 31:31-34), in a new time, newly open and universal, **for many** (20:28). Its yield is nothing less than **the forgiveness of sins** (1:21).

Jesus' words over bread and wine as Matthew records them seem shaped by liturgical use, as they fall more neatly into parallel lines than the wording found in Mark. But more significant is the unique connection forged by Matthew with **forgiveness.** That particular linkage is lacking in the other evangelists and in Paul when they quote the words of Jesus at the supper.

It seems so right in Matthew. The destiny inherent in his name (1:21) is about to be accomplished. People, his people, **many** people, will find in his outpouring of his life release from the crippling tyranny of **sins** (9:2, 5, 6), liberation from the grip of the evil one (6:13), freedom and energy for God's kingship and righteousness (6:10-12,33). This is Matthew's focus.

From the beginning Matthew declares the presence of God in Jesus (1:22) and the presence of Jesus in the community (18:20; 28:20). He is no absent Lord. Here in the words over loaf and cup Jesus invites participation not in bread and wine alone, not in ritual act alone, but in his own present power and being. And the sign of his presence and being is not ecstasy and spiritual intoxication, nor increase of prophetic or thaumaturgic power (7:15-23). His being is carefully defined as a passion for giving and forgiveness (6:12, 14-15; 9:8; 18:23-35).

29—This meal has finality written all over it. It is the end as climax of all that precedes, and its fellowship will be renewed **in my Father's kingdom,** at the close of the age (8:11; 28:20).

30—Passover ritual includes the singing of Psalms 115–118, called the Hallel or "praise" (cf. "hallelujah" = "praise Yahweh!"), by those gathered at the festal table. The earliest Christians sang the traditional psalms and soon also composed new hymns for use in their celebrations (Acts 16:25; Eph. 5:14; Col. 3:16; Rev. 5:8-10; 14:3).

Jesus and his disciples concluded the meal by raising their voices together in **a hymn** to God. Then they **went out** beyond the city wall and crossed the Kidron Valley to the western slope of **the Mount of Olives** (21:1; 24:3).

All Fall Away (26:31-56)

I Will Not Deny (26:31-35)

31—Jesus predicts that **all**, not Judas only, will fail him: **You will all fall away** (forms of the Greek word *skandalizō* appear frequently in Matthew: 5:29, 30; 11:6; 13:21, 57; 15:12; 17:27; 18:6, 8; 24:10; 26:31, 33) **because of me this night.** Betrayal and falling away are signs of the last times (24:10). Judas alone betrays, but all abandon or **fall away.** But once again, even this dread event is taken up and woven into God's design. **It is written, I will strike the shepherd** (9:36; 25:32) **and the flock will be scattered.** God utters that awful sentence (Zech. 13:7) and so somehow stands behind and works through the frenetic efforts of Caiaphas and Pilate and all the others, overruling their designs.

32—Precisely because God is in that striking down, it will not spell finish, as Jesus' enemies hoped. **After I am raised up** (16:21; 17:9, 23; 20:19) to indestructible life, **I will go before you,** march triumphantly ahead of you, **to Galilee** (28:7, 10, 16). The resurrected shepherd (Heb. 13:20) will resurrect the flock. Fortunes of shepherd and flock rise and fall as one.

33-34—For the first time in the passion narrative **Peter** steps forward. He is named and speaks, and tries to separate himself from the others. But he is pictured as sadly typical in his boast: **Though they all** abandon you and **fall away** (v. 31) **I will never fall away.** To him and through him to all, Jesus responds solemnly, **This very night,** before the stars set and the rooster crows (vv. 74-75), almost before your boast has ceased echoing from hill to hill, **you will deny me** (10:33; 26:70, 72) **three times** (cf. v. 44), and that means utterly, completely, terribly.

35-36—**Peter** insists that he would happily drink the bitter cup of death (10:22, 32-33, 37-39; 16:22, 24-28; cf. 20:22) rather than **deny** him. And **all the disciples** echo Peter's confidence.

Gethsemane (26:36-46)

36—They arrive at **a place** (*chōrion;* John 18:1 calls it a garden, *kēpos*) named **Gethsemane** ("oil press") on the lower slopes of the Mount of Olives (v. 30) opposite the Temple Mount. Ancient olive trees still grow on the spot but none is as old as the time of Jesus. A generation after the death and resurrection of Jesus the Roman legions assaulting Jerusalem (A.D. 70) cut down all the original olive trees, using them as firewood to cook their food and as lumber in the construction of siege engines. It was here that Jesus had sat a few days earlier, on these same slopes opposite the Temple Mount (24:3ff.), predicting the events that now begin.

37—Having posted eight disciples in one place, he takes **Peter and the two sons of Zebedee** (4:21; 17:1) a short distance farther. There he begins **to be sorrowful and troubled.**

The early church saw in the torments of Jesus the plight of the pious in every age (Ps. 42:5-6, 11) and drew strength for its own trials from his deep sorrows and struggling, signs of a shared humanity and a common vulnerability (Heb. 2:10-18; 4:15; 5:7-8; John 12:27).

38—In the grip of crushing sorrow, his heart ready to burst and he to die (Jonah 4:8-9; Sirach 51:6), Jesus seeks the supporting presence of friends and appeals to them, **Watch with me.** These words about the hour of the Son of man and the necessity of vigilance echo themes from Jesus' speech uttered on this same hill a scant few days earlier (24:36-25:13). Those predicted final times begin already.

Matthew here places highest value on community, as he portrays Jesus' desire to be surrounded by friends, by companions, by the new family (12:46-50).

39—Going on **a little farther,** he throws himself face down upon the earth, footstool of God, and then the one who is the presence of God (1:23) himself prays to God, seeking the will of God. The bond of oneness with God can be snapped not by death but only by infidelity and disobedience.

Struggling to stay attuned to God, Jesus cries out, **My Father.** Matthew pictures Jesus with the phrases **my Father, our Father,** and especially **your Father** on his lips frequently. These forms of address are never used in Mark, but Mark once has Jesus address God with the familiar "Abba" (14:36), which is parallel to Matt. 26:39 and is the equivalent of **my Father.** The Aramaic word "Abba" ("Father") was used in prayers by some sectors of the early church (Gal. 4:6; Rom. 8:15) but Matthew avoids it, using instead the Greek translation.

Jesus prays: **If it be possible** (19:26), without derailing your secret purpose, **let this cup** of suffering (20:22-23; John 18:11; Isa. 51:17, 22) **pass from me; nevertheless, not as I will but as thou wilt** (see the comments on v. 42).

40-41—Returning to the disciples, he finds them not alert, not vigilant, not participating in his struggle, but **sleeping,** like sentinels snoring at their posts (cf. 1 Thess. 5:6-7), like wicked servants (24:45-51) or foolish maidens caught off guard (25:1-13).

Jesus speaks the name of **Peter** but rebukes them all (warning also the readers). **Peter** is of course singular but the verbs here are all plural. (The TEV translators think the word is addressed only to Peter, James, and John: "How is it that you three were not able to watch?")

Jesus rebukes them and renews his exhortation: **Could you not watch with me one hour? Watch** and **pray,** that you may not **enter into temptation.** The final terrible conflict between God and Satan (cf. 4:1) is approaching. Only vigilance and prayer will prevent their being overwhelmed in the coming time of trial. Jesus adds, **The spirit is willing but the flesh is weak.** The **spirit** is the human being as child of God, endowed with the Spirit of God, **willing** and eager for combat with evil, full of confidence, indeed often overconfident. How easy it is for the children of God to forget that they are also **flesh,** clay of the earth in the hand of the potter, frail and flawed, and therefore **weak.** How easy it is to feel above the need to pray, "Deliver us! Lead us not to hard testing!" (6:13).

The disciples are the very picture of athletes of piety of every era. They pride themselves on having the spiritual resources for every emergency (26:22, 35). They imagine they are more faithful than Judas (v. 25) and greater than the little ones (18:6), apparently so much poorer in spiritual endowments than they themselves! Jesus' word gently warns them of the pitfalls of spiritual pride and of criticism of weaker sisters and brothers.

42—Jesus then withdraws once more and repeats the substance of his first prayer but in words exactly expressing Matthew's own fundamental concerns. **My Father** (v. 39), if I must drink this cup, then so be it. **Thy will be done!** (see the comments on 6:10; 7:21; 12:50; 18:14; 21:31; cf. John 5:30).

43-44—Returning, he finds the disciples asleep again. Once more he goes away and prays **for the third time** (cf. v. 34; 2 Cor. 12:8), uttering **the same words.**

Gethsemane displays Jesus' threefold struggle for clarification and the perfect triumph of his consecration.

45—Incredibly, the disciples sleep, even though **the hour** has struck (v. 18) for **the Son of man** to be delivered into the hands of sinners (v. 2).

46—Fresh from prayer, Jesus rouses his disciples and strides forth to confront the **betrayer** (v. 21).

He Kissed Him (26:47-56)

47—Sadness tolls in Matthew's identification of **Judas** as **one of the twelve** (v. 23). While the eleven slept, Judas had been busy. That betrayer now leads **a great crowd** (cf. John 18:3) armed with **swords and clubs** and with authority granted by **the chief priests and the elders of the people** (26:3, 14).

48-49—They had arranged a signal. **The one I shall kiss is the man; seize him.** Judas had betrayed the sanctity of table fellowship (v. 23) and now puts to obscene use the custom of saluting one's friend with the kiss of peace (Luke 7:45; Rom. 16:16; 1 Cor. 16:20). As he approaches, Judas sings out, **Hail, Master!** (v. 25) and **kissed** Jesus.

50—Jesus responds, **Friend** (20:13; 22:12; cf. 11:16), **why are you here?** Or the words could be translated as an imperative: "Do what you have come for!" That would accord with the way Jesus is portrayed throughout this section as himself setting the dread events of his passion into motion. So TEV has "Be quick about it, friend!" Still others translate, "I know why you have come." The signal given, **they laid hands on Jesus and seized him.**

51—Suddenly one of Jesus' companions (John 18:10 names Simon Peter) **drew his sword** or dagger **and struck the slave of the high priest and cut off his ear.** Finally the disciples rouse themselves from their slumbers. But since they have not entered prayerfully into Jesus' struggles, the action they now undertake is totally at odds with Jesus' resolve.

52—**All who take the sword will perish by the sword,** as violence begets violence. Jesus himself walks the gentle way of meekness (5:5; 11:29; 21:5), renouncing violence (see commentary above on 4:1-11; 5:39; cf. Gen. 9:6).

311

53—If force of arms were the royal road to the kingdom, Jesus would **appeal to my Father** (v. 39) and receive at once **twelve legions of angels,** a mighty host, since each legion of the Roman army consisted of 6000 troops. But Jesus seeks the hearts of twelve disciples and the repentance of twelve tribes, not the swords of twelve legions, whether of humans or of angels.

54—Swords in any number, with their attendant bloodshed, would frustrate and not further the plan of God declared in **the Scriptures.**

55—**At that hour** (v. 45) Jesus addresses the mob pressing in on him: Do you take me for an outlaw, a revolutionary, a terrorist (*lēstēs*), armed and dangerous? Are **swords and clubs** (v. 47) necessary **to capture me? I sat** (5:1) daily **in the temple teaching** (21:12). He had not led crowds into the wilderness, forming them into companies and battalions, nor had he hatched plots behind closed doors (24:26). Jesus is a teacher, whose words are a matter of record, set down by Matthew in five great discourses (see commentary above on 5:1). He is no rebel intent on the violent overthrow of Jewish or Roman governments.

56—The new community will not be one more nation united by common boundaries, race, and flag, but will be a new people bound by his teaching. He does not read **the scriptures of the prophets** as a blueprint for rebellion against Rome, and he rejects that fanatical nationalism which breeds a religious devotion to the sword. Instead he consecrates himself to walking in obedience and meekness, in love and compassion, even though the end of that path is the cross, dread instrument of political repression, terrible tool of Rome's program of "pacification" of subject peoples.

Confronted by Jesus' radical interpretation of scriptural hope and in contradiction to their own solid declaration (v. 35), **all the disciples forsook him and fled.** He came to save his people (1:21) and gather them as a new community (vv. 28, 132), but to accomplish those ends he first must stand utterly alone.

On Trial (26:57-75)

He Has Uttered Blasphemy (26:57-68)

In a trial we expect issues to be clarified, motives to be revealed, points of view and values to be exposed, facts to be uncovered. Reports of trials invite readers to weigh issues, take sides, render their own verdict. The trials of Jesus were early pondered and used as a basis for exhortations (cf. 1 Tim. 6:12-14; Rev. 1:5).

57—His captors lead Jesus to the palace of **Caiaphas** (v. 3), where **the scribes and the elders had gathered** (cf. 2:4; 16:21; 20:18).

58—**Peter followed,** but only **at a distance,** not daring to identify with Jesus as he and all the others had boasted they would (vv. 33-35). Arriving at the high priestly palace, Peter finds a spot for himself among **the guards** and servants in the large **courtyard** open to the sky around which the palace was built. But Peter follows not in perseverance (24:13-14), not to testify on Jesus' behalf, not to witness any new beginning but simply **to see the end.** In his unfaith he does not realize he is actually present at the new creation.

59—Peter sits passively, but inside the palace **the chief priests and the whole council** (10:17), guardians and guarantors of justice, pervert justice by actively seeking **false witness against Jesus, that they might put him to death.** But even though many stepped forward, they can not discover sufficient grounds for a legal verdict of condemnation.

60—**At last two came forward.** The rules of evidence required the agreement of at least two witnesses in order to convict a prisoner accused of a capital crime (Deut. 17:6; 19:15).

61—Their testimony is not described as false. These witnesses accuse Jesus of having said, **I am able to destroy the temple of God, and to build it in three days** (cf. 27:40; John 2:19).

Matthew differs from Mark in several points: in saying the priests actively sought false testimony, in eliminating Mark's reference to the temple as "made with hands" (i.e., a merely human institution), and in including the phrase **I am able,** so that the saying is a declaration of Jesus' power over the temple rather than a threat to destroy it.

The keepers of the temple are certainly portrayed as stung by Jesus' teaching (21:45). And Christians of Matthew's day, looking back on the Roman siege of Jerusalem (A.D. 70), may have begun interpreting the destruction of the temple as God's judgment on the city for the crucifixion of Jesus.

Matthew does record tough words spoken by Jesus against

scribes and Pharisees (chap. 23), the sons of the kingdom (8:12), the towns of Israel (10:15; 11:21-23), and the city of Jerusalem (23:37-39). Nevertheless, it is both false and dangerous to imagine, as many readers have, that Matthew singles out temple or priests or Pharisees or Israel as Jesus' special target.

From the beginning Matthew makes it clear that the stern warnings issuing from the mouth of Jesus are directed against smug insiders (of Israel or the church), the rich, the first, the privileged, and the powerful, all who are careless about the will of God, all who neglect love and fidelity and justice.

Those who will receive the kingdom are not simply Gentiles in place of Jews but little ones and children, tax collectors and harlots, the meek, the peacemakers, the penitent, those with a hunger and a thirst for righteousness.

What is true about the charge at his trial is that Jesus did steadily announce that he came with power to effect shocking and tumultuous transformation. Priest and prophet, law and ritual, temple and sacrifice, calendar and Sabbath, tradition and venerable institution, without love of God and love of neighbor do not and cannot suffice to make the people whole and save them. All these, without love and mercy and righteousness, are nothing (cf. 9:13; 12:6-7, 8, 9-14; 15:2).

62-63—The high priest (v. 57) questions Jesus directly about the substance of the charge. But Jesus remains fearlessly (10:28) and serenely **silent.** He does not anxiously stammer (10:19) or babble in his own defense or express outrage or malign his accusers. But he does not deny the charge, either. By his silence he rests his case with God (27:14).

Then **the high priest,** piously invoking the name of **the living God** (16:16), places Jesus under solemn oath and demands a plain and unambiguous response: **Tell us if you are the Christ** (1:1; 27:22), **the Son of God** (3:17; 4:3; 27:40, 43). This question is frequently regarded as inappropriate, not following from the preceding sentences, but **the Christ** or Messiah was expected to come and establish a new temple in a new age of holiness. Temple and Christ belong together, and references to the identity of Jesus and to the temple appear together frequently from the entry into Jerusalem onwards.

64—Jesus affirms, **You have said so** (v. 25). It seems incredible, even laughable, and the words of the priest are not the ones Jesus would choose to describe himself. Nevertheless, Jesus says, **I tell you,** from this time forward, if only you have eyes touched by the hand of God (11:6; 13:16-17; cf. 8:29), **you will see the Son of man** (8:20) **seated at the right hand of Power** (22:29; Luke 1:35; Acts 4:7) and **coming on the clouds of heaven.** Jesus conjures up traditional pictures of God's agent coming to earth, riding the clouds, enthroned, glorious, triumphant (19:28; 20:21; Dan. 7:13; Ps. 110:1; 104:3). What is shocking and marvelous is that Jesus points to himself, a prisoner on his way to the cross, as that ultimate agent of God.

65—**The high priest tore his robe** in a traditional ritual gesture of shock and horror. **Blasphemy,** he cries. All Jesus' judges are pious men of God completely convinced that they are engaged in a hard but necessary task designed to safeguard the honor of God. Their duty as they see it may be unpopular with the crowds but they take the long view and see their work as ultimately God-pleasing. The irony is that the one they condemn as blasphemer and deceiver is the one who really, deeply, and finally pleases God and delights God (3:17; 17:3).

They put their question, and Jesus gives his answer. The court may now dispense with witnesses, since the accused stands condemned out of his own mouth.

It is not necessarily **blasphemy** (cf. 9:3; 27:39) for a human being to call himself Messiah or Christ. What makes Jesus' utterance **blasphemy** is the fact that he is so powerless. This poor, bedraggled Jesus, defenseless and at their mercy, dares to style himself Christ and Son of God! In the thinking of the high priest he is dragging the Divine Name down into the mud of vulnerability and suffering, thereby dishonoring God, tarnishing the bright glory of God.

66—Immediately the high priest presses for a vote, and the court delivers the verdict: **He deserves death.** So the Son of man, great final judge of the universe (25:31), is himself judged deficient and condemned by a human court. Jesus has come to grant true life (1:21) and he is now handed over to cruel death.

Jesus has lived his life on the edges of death and violence from the beginning (2:13; 11:12; 12:14; 14:2-11; 17:12), and his words are full of poignant references to sheep in the midst of wolves

(10:16), to sword and division (10:34-35), to foes in one's own household (10:36), to seed trampled underfoot or swallowed by birds (13:3-8), to prophets rejected and heirs killed (21:35-39), to servants slaughtered (22:6) and to prophets and sages, scribes, and the righteous murdered (23:29-35).

67—And that great healer, the stiller of storms and raiser of the dead has foretold and embraced his own death as part of God's design as fulfilling Scripture. And he offers no resistance, not even a word (v. 63), as captors and guards **spat in his face and struck him.**

68—**Some slapped him** (5:39) and taunted him: **Prophesy to us,** use your powers (24:24) of clairvoyance, **you Christ!** See if you can tell us our names and identify us. Ironically, at the very instant when they mock, denying that he has prophetic power, his prophesies are coming true in their own cruelty towards him inside the palace and in Peter's denials outside. At the precise moment when they ask, **Who was it that slapped you?** Peter speaks denials that cut more terribly than physical blows.

I Do Not Know the Man (26:69-75)

69—While Jesus offers his testimony inside, **Peter** is sitting **outside in the courtyard** (v. 58). **A maid,** a young whisp of a servant girl, frightens him with her comment: **You also were with Jesus the Galilean.**

70-71—Before witnesses, Peter utters a denial (v. 35) and moves off to the gate at the entrance way. There another girl says **to the bystanders, This fellow was with Jesus of Nazareth** (2:23).

72-73—Peter utters a second denial, this time **with an oath** (5:34, 36; 26:63): **I do not know this man** (7:23; 10:32-33). Then **the bystanders** themselves say to Peter that his Galilean accent (v. 69) proves that he is **one of them,** a member of the community of disciples.

74—Peter then solemnly invokes a curse upon himself if he should lie and with a solemn oath denies Jesus yet a third time. **And immediately the cock crowed,** signaling the dawn of the day and the beginning of the end.

75—Then **Peter remembered.** His actions have precisely mirrored Jesus' terrible warning. He leaves the palace and weeps bitterly in his own private outer darkness (24:51).

Innocent (27:1-26)

Matthew's narrative nears its conclusion, as Jesus stands accused before Pilate (vv. 1-26), is taken out to be crucified (vv. 27-44), and then dies and is buried (vv. 45-66).

The trial before Pilate (27:1-26) contains significant material unique to Matthew: the suicide of Judas, the dream of Pilate's wife, Pilate's handwashing, and several references to the power of Jesus' blood. The material may be divided into three subsections: Jesus is handed over (vv. .1-2), Judas's end (vv. 3-10), trial before Pilate (vv. 11-26). The first and third sections bracket the second (cf. 26:3-5, 6-13, 14-15). Together the three sections offer a meditation on guilt and innocence and on the power of Jesus' blood.

They Delivered Him to Pilate (27:1-2)

1—The trial of Jesus in the palace of the high priest (26:57-68) lasted through the night and resulted in a verdict of guilty (v. 66). At daybreak **all the chief priests and the elders of the people** confirm the verdict and agree on procedure. Since only the Roman authority can carry out a sentence of death, they bind Jesus and betray or deliver him up (*paredōken*) **to Pilate the governor** (10:18), thereby setting themselves with Judas under the word uttered by Jesus: Woe to that one by whom the Son of man is betrayed (26:14). In the following section (vv. 3-10) Judas will actually dissociate himself from them.

When Herod's son Archelaus (2:22) turned out to be an unsatisfactory puppet, the Romans deposed him in A.D. 6, and with few interruptions thereafter they ruled Judea directly. Pilate was **governor** or prefect of Judea (A.D. 26–36) and subordinate to the imperial legate of Syria.

Innocent Blood (27:3-10)

In his account of Judas's end, told so differently from Luke in Acts 1:16-20 (see also Papias, fragment 3), Matthew emphasizes the innocence of Jesus and the power of his blood. (Luke is especially interested in the Spirit's choosing of Matthias, thereby bringing the number of the inner circle of disciples once more up to twelve. Furthermore, Luke describes the death of Judas differently from Matthew, interpreting the name of the "Field of Blood" as referring to the bloody death of Judas rather than to blood money.)

3-4—Judas repented, took **the thirty pieces of silver** (26:15), and went to **the chief priests and the elders,** declaring **I have sinned in betraying innocent blood** (*haima athōon;* cf. *haima dikaion,* 23:35; 27:24). People argue about whether Judas really **repented** and suggest that he merely felt remorse or despair, but the word used here is the same as the one used in the full and positive sense in 21:30 (*metamelētheis*). Furthermore, Matthew is lining up witnesses to the innocence of Jesus prior to his crucifixion, and Judas, even though he betrayed Jesus, is taking his place as one such witness.

5—He rid himself of the money, casting it down **in the temple** (*ho naos;* see the comments on 24:1). Then he went and **hanged himself,** as Ahithophel, traitor to King David, had done (2 Sam. 17:23).

6-8—The chief priests now despise the silver as **blood money** (*timē haimatos,* "the price of blood"), and hence unclean. They believe it would pollute the holy place if mingled with other offerings (cf. Deut. 23:18). So they purchase **the potter's field.** The money, deemed unfit for the temple and holy place, is used instead to buy a field for use as a burial place for **strangers,** presumably Gentile visitors to Jerusalem.

Matthew has pondered the power of the blood of Jesus (26:28; 27:24-25) and sees a strange truth in the use of that blood money. That purchased ground for **strangers** to the covenant, **strangers** like Rahab and Ruth (1:5), **strangers** like the magi (2:1), **strangers** like the centurion and his squad (27:54), or like the nations (28:19). **Strangers** (and not they alone) benefit from the **blood,** from the dying of Jesus (20:28; 26:26-29).

That place bears the name **the Field of Blood** (*agros haimatos;* Akeldama, Acts 1:19) **to this day** (28:15). Tradition locates that field on slopes just south of the old city of Jerusalem at the eastern end of the Valley of Hinnom (cf. 5:22). But Matthew is not interested in geography. He sees the action of the priests in purchasing that field as ironic testimony to the truth about the benefits of the death of Jesus.

9-10—Furthermore, Matthew views the priests' action, full of disdain for Judas's repentance and indifferent to that innocent blood, as the fulfillment of a prophecy, here ascribed to **Jeremiah** (cf. Jer. 18:2-4; 19:1-13; 32:6-9; but actually found in Zech. 11:12-13), and introduced with a solemn formula (see the comments on 1:22; see also 2:17-18).

The Governor Wondered (27:11-14)

The Roman capital of Judea was at Caesarea on the seacoast, some 60 miles from Jerusalem. Passover fanned the embers of nationalism among Jews, and Roman governors prudently strengthened the garrison at Jerusalem and took personal command. Leaving Caesarea, they resided temporarily in Jerusalem, using as their headquarters the grand palace constructed by Herod the Great at the western edge of the city, adjacent to the present Jaffa Gate (Josephus, *Ant.* 15.317-318).

It is less likely that the fortress Antonia, at the northwest corner of the Temple Mount, served as praetorium.

11—The high priest had asked Jesus whether he was "the Christ, the Son of God" (26:63). **The governor** asks essentially the same question, with "Christ" understood in a political sense: **Are you the King of the Jews?** (cf. 2:2). With the same words he had used twice before (26:25, 64) Jesus affirms the substance but not the precise form of the question: **You have said so.**

12-14—To further charges and accusations brought by members of the Sanhedrin, Jesus makes **no answer. Pilate** urges him to respond, but Jesus gives **no answer, not even to a single charge.** Because of that dignified silence, sign of Jesus' knowledge of God's plan and his acceptance of it (Isa. 53:7), so different from the ranting and babbling of other prisoners (cf. 26:62-63), **the governor wondered greatly.** He was both astonished and confused.

Barabbas or Jesus (27:15-26)

15—The custom of a holiday amnesty with the release of a prisoner in celebration of the festival of freedom is not known apart from the Gospels. By means of this report, Matthew focuses once again, as in vv. 3-10, on the innocence of Jesus and the power of his blood, the might of his outpoured life.

16—Just then the dungeon held **a notorious prisoner.** Matthew does not specify his crime, but Mark (15:7) and Luke (23:19; Acts 3:14) say that he had committed murder during an insurrection, indicating that he was some kind of rebel or freedom fighter. That prisoner's name was **Barabbas,** which means "son of Abbas" or "son of the father," and some ancient manuscripts actually give his name as "Jesus Barabbas."

17—So crowds gather, ready to shout the name of their favorite. Pilate asks which one they want, **(Jesus) Barabbas or Jesus who is called Christ?** In Acts 3:14-15 Luke says they had a terrible choice: Do you prefer the murderer or the Author of life? In Matthew the choice between the one who in violence spills the blood of others and the one who gives his blood on behalf of others lies just below the surface. Apparently as a warning to his readers, Matthew focuses on the strange contrast between outsiders (Pilate and his wife) attempting to heed divine revelation and insiders (priests and crowds) struggling against God. It happened before and it can happen yet again.

18—Ancient sources outside the Scriptures portray Pilate as corrupt, cruel, and decisive (Philo, *Leg. ad Gaium* 38; Josephus, *Ant.* 18.55-62, 176-178), but Matthew pictures him here as cautious, fair, and vacillating. Pilate hesitates, because he sees that Jesus' accusers were acting **out of envy,** jealous of his popularity with the masses (21:11, 46; 26:5). And Pilate counts on those same masses taking Jesus' side and relieving him of the necessity of making a hard decision.

19—Furthermore, at the precise moment when Pilate was **sitting on the judgment seat** (*to bēma*, his tribunal or rostrum; cf. John 19:13; Acts 19:12), weighing the evidence, he receives word from heaven via his wife. Because of **a dream** (1:20) she calls Jesus **righteous** (*dikaios*, 1:19) and communicates that to her husband. So Pilate's reading of human nature (v. 18) is matched by his wife's reading of heavenly signs. Early Christian legends give her name as Procula Claudia, embellish Pilate's efforts to free Jesus, and transform both of them into Christian saints. Matthew's interest is in reporting how heaven and earth join forces to testify to the innocence of Jesus at the exact hour when Jesus appeared before his Roman judge.

20—Meanwhile, the religious leaders are not idle, but provoke

the people, literally "the crowds" or "the masses" (*hoi ochloi*), to demand freedom for **Barabbas** and death for **Jesus.**

21-23—In spite of the obvious bias of the accusers, and in spite of the revelation of heaven's favorable verdict on Jesus, Pilate abdicates responsibility and puts his fateful question to the crowds: **Which of the two do you want me to release for you?** And they all cry, **Barabbas.** Still hoping to find a popular basis for doing the just thing, Pilate asks, **Then what shall I do with Jesus who is called Christ?** Their response: **Let him be crucified.** In a final effort to spare Jesus, Pilate says, **Why, what evil has he done?** They name none but cry all the louder, **Let him be crucified.**

24—Pilate had come up to Jerusalem to ensure public order, and his delaying tactics were beginning to produce the one result he most wanted to avoid: **a riot** among the populace.

Ostentatiously Pilate **took water and washed his hands,** a traditional gesture signifying noninvolvement in a crime (Deut. 21:6-9; Ps. 26:6). And he piously declares, **I am innocent of this man's blood.** (Some ancient manuscripts add the word "righteous" and so the phrase would be, "I am innocent of this righteous blood," or "I am innocent of the blood of this righteous man"; cf. 23:35; 27:4.) But it is not so easy to wash out a crime.

25—Pilate served notice that the crowds would be responsible for an enormous injustice. **And all the people** (*pas ho laos*) answered, **His blood be on us and on our children!** (23:35). An awful cry, and not easily understood. It is almost always taken to mean that Matthew here pictures the Jewish people (*ho laos*) of that generation as readily taking the guilt of the death of Jesus upon themselves and upon all their descendants after them. It is interpreted as part of Matthew's alleged displacement theory, according to which the church of Jews and Gentiles (or even the church of Gentiles alone) displaces Israel as people of God, and is connected with 21:43 and 28:19. And this passage has unfortunately provided a biblical basis for anti-Semitism.

But the cry is by no means lacking in ambiguity and subtlety. Throughout the passion narrative Matthew meditates on the power of the blood of this righteous one. Can it be that the people in crying out express a fundamental truth in ironic fashion? The blood of Jesus is indeed upon them and their children, for good or for ill. The blood of Jesus is intended by God for a new covenant of forgiveness for "many" (20:28; 26:28), and the "many" are both strangers (27:3-4) and the people of Israel (27:25). His blood speaks more graciously than the blood of Abel (23:35; Heb. 12:24), and yet it is necessary to open our ears to hear what it says (13:13-17).

To his readers Matthew says that Jesus' blood, meant by God for blessing, may yet be a terrible stain accusing God's own people (even the readers) of unbelief and disobedience, if they should refuse the offered blessing.

26—In the end Pilate freed **Barabbas** but **scourged Jesus** and **delivered him** (*paredōken*, 26:2) **to be crucified.** Scourging meant flailing a prisoner's back with a heavy whip made from leather thongs with bits of stone or metal tied to the end of each thong. Scourging alone was often enough to kill a man.

Crucified, Dead, and Buried (27:27-66)

In reporting the crucifixion, Matthew fixes attention on the royalty of Jesus. Jesus is mocked as king (27:27-31), crucified as king (27:32-38), and then mocked yet a second time as king and Son of God (27:39-44).

They Mocked Him (27:27-31)

27-29—Inside the **praetorium,** headquarters and residence of the Roman governor (see 27:2, 11), the entire cohort (*speira*, a tenth of a legion or 600 soldiers; cf. John 18:3) gathers to toy with Jesus. They deck him out with a soldier's **scarlet robe,** fashion a make-shift **crown of thorns** with the spikes mimicking the radiate form of real crowns, stick it on his head, and place in his right hand **a reed** or staff (*kalamos*, v. 48) as a make-believe scepter. With extravagant mockery they kneel before him and cry, **Hail, King of the Jews!** (27:11; see Philo, *Flacc.* 5-6).

30—The soldiers then show their contempt for the pretensions to power and authority in that title by spitting on their prisoner and by grabbing the reed out of his hand and striking him on the head with it. Their actions are a cruel parody of the homage paid by the magi (2:1-12), by humble suppliants (8:2), and by awestruck disciples (14:33). Ironically, some of these same soldiers will themselves soon confess Jesus as Son of God (v. 54). They will be converted to recognizing in Jesus a strange authority, but for the moment they are blind to every authority and every power except that of swords and spears and legions.

31—Eventually they tire of their little game, strip off the scarlet, replace it with his own peasant's cloak, and lead him away **to crucify him** (20:19).

They Crucified Him (27:32-38)

32—**Marching out,** the squad of soldiers detailed to crucify Jesus press into service (5:41) **a man of Cyrene, Simon by name.** The distance from the inner court of the praetorium at Herod's palace (v. 2) to Golgotha (v. 33) was only a few hundred yards, but Jesus has been brutalized and weakened by scourging. They therefore compel Simon to carry Jesus' **cross,** probably only the horizontal beam of the cross, since the upright posts for crucifixions were permanently installed at places of execution.

33—Jesus was executed at **a place called Golgotha (which means the place of a skull).** The Gospels never call the place a hill and never offer any explanation for its name. Since early in the 4th century in the days of Constantine, a Christian church (Anastasis or Church of the Holy Sepulchre) has marked the traditional place of crucifixion, now well inside the old city, but outside the walls in the time of Jesus. Matthew merely remarks that this life-giving place bears the name of **skull** and has the look of death, challenging readers to penetrate the surface and get behind appearances.

34—It was customary to offer condemned prisoners a drink of **wine** as a kind of sedative. According to Mark (15:23), the soldiers tried to give Jesus wine mingled with tranquilizing myrrh. Matthew, however, reports that they offer Jesus wine mixed not with myrrh but with **gall,** a bitter acidic substance. Matthew views that act as a further piece of cruel mockery and hears in it an echo of Ps. 69:21. The underlying Hebrew word in the Psalm actually means "poison."

35-36—The soldiers finish the grim task of crucifixion, and then settle down as guards (cf. vv. 62-66) at the foot of the cross. They begin to gamble to see who will walk away with Jesus' clothing

(Ps. 22:18), to trade those poor garments in the market for a few small coins.

37—Custom dictated fixing to the cross a placard specifying the crime for which a prisoner was condemned. Over Jesus' head was the notice, **This is Jesus the King of the Jews.**

That placard tells the truth, but the truth in it is by no means simple. Matthew insists that Jesus really is "son" of David "the king" (1:1, 6, 17), king of the Jews (2:2), royal Son of God (3:17; 17:5), and that in Jesus the kingship of God is dawning (4:17; 10:7; 12:28). At the same time, Jesus cracks the Davidic mold and breaks with the pattern of Davidic kingship (21:41-45) by coming in meekness (11:29; 21:5), renouncing pomp and privilege and earthly power (20:25-26).

Jesus both envisions and enables a divine-human society founded not on arrogance or violence, but on meekness, forgiveness, and service. But that meekness is a reproach to the arrogance of ideologies based on purity of blood (3:9) or power of sword (26:52-53).

To the exponents of ordinary visions of human society Jesus appears offensive or dispensable. They find it easy and necessary to sweep him away, branding his vision of God's sovereignty as blasphemous or mocking it as mad or simply shaking their heads and dubbing it naive.

So the one title above the cross reveals at least three different truths. The guardians of the purity of blood and sanctity of tradition call that title true in one sense: this weak Jesus is guilty of the crime of blasphemy (26:65) for calling himself Christ, Messiah, Son of David, Son of God.

To Romans, trusting superiority of arms, the title speaks a different truth: Jesus is some kind of rebel and therefore a menace to the public order. His real offense against the native authorities may be his popularity among the masses, but in the end Romans find it convenient to brush Jesus aside. So the title on the cross expresses Roman contempt for the Jews and their hopes of freedom, and speaks a warning to every potential freedom fighter.

For Matthew the title proclaims the truth of the mysterious and contrary kingship of Jesus who rose to "power" among his people not by means of the sword nor through appeals to race or blood but through lowly service, through total commitment to the will of God and love of neighbor, through acts of mercy and justice and loyalty. The cross declares that Jesus' sovereignty contradicts (and is contradicted by) the powers and authorities that ordinarily govern human life and society. The cross spells meekness and gentleness, the renunciation of violence as the basis of community, the abdication of arrogance in social relations.

38—Strange kingship. This king is pictured as enthroned upon the cross with **two robbers,** not petty thieves (*kleptai*) but outlaw bandits or rebels (*lēstai,* cf. 26:55), one on his right hand and one at his left (note the desire of James and John in 20:21-23) as his only honor guard.

Save Yourself (27:39-44)

Mocking follows, so that the crucifixion (vv. 32-38) is set between two scenes of mocking (vv. 27-31 and 39-44). All three scenes focus on Jesus as King of Israel and Son of God.

39-40—Passersby **derided him** (Ps. 22:7), kept on slandering, insulting, and blaspheming him (*eblasphēmoun,* cf. 9:3). Their words echo accusations leveled at the end (26:61) and temptations posed at the beginning (4:1-11):

  a: **You who would destroy the temple and build it in three days,**

    b: **save yourself!**

  a': **If you are the Son of God,**

    b': **come down from the cross!**

The *b* lines are clearly parallel. Less obvious but no less real is the parallelism between the two *a* lines. What makes these two lines appropriate here is not simply their connection with accusations and temptations. These two lines have an inner connection. **Temple** is place of the presence of God, place of unique connection between God and God's people. From beginning (1:23) to end (28:20) Matthew presents Jesus as Son of God and presence of God. If Jesus really is Emmanuel and Son of God, then indeed something greater than the temple is here (12:6; John 2:19-22).

41-43—**The chief priests with the scribes and elders** join in the mockery, and for the second and third times (vv. 40, 42) in this scene the word **save** appears: **He saved others,** healed others; **he cannot save himself.** The truth of the matter is not that he cannot but that he will not save himself. He will not serve himself, will not spare himself, will not abuse the power of God by preserving himself (26:52-54). His opponents, and oftentimes also his friends, cannot understand that he saves others by spending himself, by yielding up his life and substance (20:28; 26:26-28). Yet that is precisely the way he fulfills the promise of his name (1:21), and it is no accident that the name **Jesus** occurs 38 times in chaps. 26–27 in the course of Matthew's narration of his passion.

In mockery his enemies cry out, **He is the King of Israel; let him come down now,** without dying, **from the cross and we will believe in him.** The **now** is emphatic and is repeated: **He trusts in God; let God deliver him now,** before death, **if he desires him** (Ps. 22:8); **for he said, I am the Son of God** (26:64; cf. Wisdom of Sol. 2:12-20). Jesus will be delivered but not short of death, not before the cross. He goes all the way to the most bitter end in trust and love, rejecting the temptation to tread a more comfortable path (4:1-11; 16:22-23).

44—Even **the robbers** (v. 38) executed with him join in reviling him. At that moment he is almost completely alone, abandoned by friends and foes, by the rulers of his own people and by Roman authorities, by his powerful judges and even by his fellow condemned.

Forsaken (27:45-50)

Three scenes bring the narrative to a close. The first two round out the report of the events of Good Friday, and the third belongs to the next day: (1) his death on the cross (vv. 45-56), (2) his burial (vv. 57-61), and (3) the setting of the guard at the tomb (vv. 62-66).

45—In the passion narrative the action slows to a crawl, and Matthew, notes the passing of morning and evening and even individual hours. **From the sixth hour** till **the ninth hour** (noon till three) unnatural **darkness** (24:29; Amos 8:9; Exod. 10:22) shrouded **all the land** (or all the "earth," *gē*).

46—Then Jesus cries aloud, addressing God in Hebrew and continuing in Aramaic, **Eli, Eli, lama sabachthani?** which means, **My God, my God, why hast thou forsaken me?** These words are the first line of Psalm 22, and the early church saw in the sufferings of Jesus a perfect fulfillment not of the one line only but of that entire psalm.

47-49—Some imagine he is calling for help to the prophet
Elijah (16:14; 17:3). One of the bystanders soaks a sponge in cheap
wine ("vinegar" in RSV), fixes it to **a reed** or staff, and begins to
hoist it up to Jesus' lips (v. 34; 25:35; Ps. 69:21). But others prevent
it: **Let us see whether Elijah will come to save him.**

50—But Jesus is not appealing to Elijah to rescue him. He is
not begging for his life (see v. 11), and in fact neither Elijah nor
God will spare Jesus. With a final cry (Ps. 22:2, 5, 24) and a final
act of trust, Jesus **yielded up his spirit** to God.

The Earth Shook (27:51-54)

51—So far in the course of Jesus' passion, God has been silent
and either distant or inactive. But at the precise moment of Jesus'
dying, God sends powerful signals of divine approval upon the
crucified. God does indeed "desire" him (v. 43; cf. 3:17; 17:5).
Matthew tells how **the curtain of the temple was torn** or split
(*eschisthē*). This was most likely the **curtain** between the Holy
Place and the Holy of Holies (Exod. 26:31-33; Josephus, *Ant.*
8.75) rather than the curtain at the entrance (Exod. 26:36-37;
Josephus, *Ant.* 8.75), and its tearing at this precise moment signifies its end (cf. 24:2) and the opening of a fresh approach to the
throne of grace through the crucified (Heb. 6:19; 9:3; 10:19-22).
Not the curtain and the temple, not sacrifices and rituals, not the
priests and their leadership (9:13; 12:6-7; 21:12) but the crucified
and resurrected one will save God's people from their sins (1:21).

Furthermore, **the earth shook** (8:24; 24:7; 28:2; Ps. 68:8) and
the rocks split (*eschisthēsan*). The earthquake signals a great exchange: as Jesus dies, the dead revive. **Tombs were opened,** and
many bodies of the saints (*hagioi,* Rev. 18:20, 24) who had **fallen
asleep,** many holy people of old, **were raised** from death (cf.
Ezek. 37:12; Zech. 14:5; 1 Thess. 3:13; 4:14). Jesus' death is the
great consummation of the promises of God, and the rising of
ancient holy ones celebrates that fact. But his death is inseparable
from his resurrection, and so the vivified saints enter **the holy
city** (4:5), but only after he quits his own tomb on the third day.

The narrative involves a curious chronology. It appears that
the holy ones awaken in their tombs on Good Friday but do not
leave them to enter Jerusalem until Sunday. Matthew's intention,

of course, is to declare that in the earth-shattering moment of Jesus' death-and-resurrection, considered as a single complex event, God touches the universe with creative hands here at the end of ages as at the beginning and the old world with its old patterns and institutions starts to crack apart and the new world begins to emerge from the dust and ashes of the old. And a new community of old saints (v. 52) and new believers (v. 54) emerges in that hour.

The entire picture is astonishing. These are events of the sort expected for the day of judgment. In fact, to this day the slopes of Zion and of the Mount of Olives converging on the Kidron Valley just outside the temple mount in Jerusalem are covered with graves of Jews and Muslims and Christians. All three faiths contain the tradition that the day of resurrection and judgment will begin precisely at that spot.

All these extraordinary signs narrated by Matthew mark "the beginning" of the end times (24:8) and not yet the moment of the coming of the Son of man as judge. But they do clearly signal that this lowly Jesus is that coming judge. The last times have drawn dramatically nearer, and people are summoned urgently to take their stand for or against Jesus and his authority.

Splitting and quaking and rising were signs from God, and **the centurion and those with him were filled with awe** and exclaimed, **Truly this was the Son of God.** (The RSV footnote has "a Son of God," but *huios theou,* lacking the definite article in Greek, stands before the verb "to be" and should be rendered as definite in English.) The crucified Jesus is the Son of God. That acclamation by a Roman centurion and his squad of legionnaires parallels the confession of the disciples (14:33) and Peter (16:16), contradicts the mockery of Jesus' opponents (4:1-11; 27:40, 43), and agrees perfectly with the voice of God (3:17; 17:5). The mission to the Gentiles has begun, and the elect are being gathered from the four winds (24:31).

Many Women (27:55-56)

55-56—For the first time Matthew records that **many women had followed Jesus from Galilee, ministering to him** (*diakoneō,* cf. Luke 8:2-3). Among them were **Mary Magdalene, Mary the**

mother of James and Joseph, and the mother of the sons of Zebedee (20:20; Salome in Mark 15:40). They do not abandon Jesus (cf.26:56) but endure to the end as friends and witnesses (v. 61; 28:1; cf. 26:6-13), **looking on from afar.**

His Own New Tomb (27:57-61)

57—For the first time **Joseph of Arimathea** (a few miles north of Jerusalem) enters the narrative. He is described in two odd phrases: **he was a rich man** (Isa. 53:9), and he was **a disciple of Jesus** (cf. John 19:38). That combination, while odd, is not impossible (19:21-26). Mark calls him a member of the council (Sanhedrin) who was looking for the kingdom of God (cf. Luke 23:50-51). Joseph petitioned Pilate for the body of Jesus, **wrapped it in a clean linen shroud, and laid it in his own new tomb hewn in the rock.** Those details may reflect pious Christian preoccupation with the cleanness of shroud and tomb as befitting the majesty of Jesus, or meditation on that tomb in the **rock** (*petra*, 16:18), receptacle of the corpse and place of resurrection, as the historical place of the rise of the new community.

61—**And Mary Magdalene and the other Mary** (28:1), **sitting opposite the tomb,** witness these things.

Sealing the Stone (27:62-66)

62—Matthew alone of the evangelists tells of post mortem anxieties and machinations on the part of Jesus' opponents. Those champions of the sanctity of the Sabbath (12:1-14) profane the Sabbath by meeting with Pilate to conduct a piece of business.

63-64—They address Pilate respectfully as **sir** or Lord (*kyrie*, 8:2) and speak of Jesus as **that impostor,** that deceiver (*planos*; cf. 24:4-5, 11, 24; Test. Levi 16:3). They recall Jesus' prediction, **After three days I will rise again** (16:21; 17:23; 20:19). They suspect his disciples may steal the body (28:15) and then may spread the word, **He has risen from the dead** (28:6-7). If that should happen, they say, **the last fraud** or deceit (*hē eschatē planē*), namely, saying that Jesus has been resurrected, **will be worse than the first,** namely, calling Jesus a prophet (21:46). At least the Pharisees in that delegation believe in resurrection (cf. 22:23), and they know that resurrection means divine approval or vindication. They most emphatically deny that God would resurrect and thereby vindicate this Jesus, placing the stamp of divine approval upon all his outrageous words and deeds.

They therefore petition Pilate that **the tomb be made secure until the third day.** And Pilate grants their request.

65—Whether Pilate dispatches a squad of Roman soldiers or merely gives the petitioners permission to take their own precautions is beside the point. Matthew pictures the tomb not only as closed with a great stone (Mark 15:46; 16:3), but also officially sealed and guarded by an armed company. The apocryphal Gospel of Peter (ca. A.D. 150) embellishes this tradition in several details. It names the centurion (Petronius) and describes how Pharisees, scribes, and elders helped the soldiers roll into place a great stone across the mouth of the tomb and seal it with seven seals. Then they pitched a tent before the tomb and settled in to prevent any tampering or deception (Gospel of Peter 8:28-33).

Matthew pictures the opponents of Jesus as speaking piously but acting profanely, Jewish and Roman authorities with their heads together on the Sabbath, rushing about to take what they regard as realistic precautions, all in vain.

The soldiers, the stone, and the seal on the stone will be no more effective in the case of Jesus than in the case of Daniel when Darius threw him to the lions and sealed their den (Dan. 6:17). Matthew mocks all the efforts of Jesus' enemies as hopeless and almost humorous, for the earth has already been shaken, splitting the rocks (v. 51), and it will shake yet again (28:2).

And through everything Matthew mocks the notion that the resurrection of Jesus is the final deception (*eschatē planē*) and that Jesus is the great deceiver (*planos*), leading God's people astray. He appeals to his readers' imaginations in this paragraph, and is ready now to present the resurrection as the highest truth and Jesus as final and legitimate Teacher and Lord of the people of God (cf. 23:8-10).

■ All Authority in Heaven and on Earth (28:1-20)

This concluding chapter consists of three sections. The first (28:1-10) focuses on events at the tomb on Easter morning and has parallels in the other canonical Gospels, even though Matthew certainly surprises readers with his fresh accents and incidents more than once.

The second scene (28:11-15) concludes Matthew's unique report regarding the guards at the tomb (27:62-66; 28:4).

The third scene (28:16-20) is the stunning end of the chapter and climax of the entire Gospel, the peak to which all the action has been ascending from the beginning: the pronouncement of the exalted Jesus of his own incomparable authority, his charge to the community, and his promise of enduring and unending presence.

By his death and resurrection Jesus fulfills the promise of his name (1:21) and begins to bring life and freedom to God's beleaguered people. By resurrection he is manifested as Emmanuel (1:23), the presence of God shining in the midst of the new community. He is there in the midst, as Savior and as Teacher of God's people (23:10), with creative power and with his words, establishing the community in the way of righteousness.

The death and resurrection of Jesus are not only the climax of Matthew's narrative. In Matthew's mind they are the turning point of world history and are revealed as such by the quaking of the earth (27:51; 28:2).

He Has Risen (28:1-10)

1—Where Mark (16:1) says that women arrived at the tomb early on Sunday morning "to anoint the body," Matthew says that **Mary Magdalene and the other Mary** (cf. 27:56,61) went out some time between the dark and the daylight **to see the sepulchre** (cf. 27:61). Matthew does not so much as hint that the women could have entered the tomb to anoint the body. In contrast to Mark, Matthew describes them as coming to pay their respects from a distance, prevented by the guards from approaching closely. Access is denied them, and the emptiness of the tomb cannot possibly be their doing!

2—The tomb is empty and the world is full, and that is the

work of God alone. **A great earthquake** signals the action of God as at Exodus and Sinai and as promised for the end of the old age and the beginning of the new (see the references in the comments on 27:51). Signs in the earth beneath now match the sign in the heavens above at Jesus' birth (2:1-12).

Not the mysterious "young man" of Mark 16:5, nor the disciples (27:54), nor any human agency whatsoever, but **an angel of the Lord** (Exod. 3:2-6; Acts 7:30) **rolled back the stone and sat upon it.** Satan tempted Jesus to win a following by performing stunts, with angels as a kind of safety net (4:6), but Jesus steadily and deliberately refused to use angelic power to avoid the way of cross and righteousness and service (26:53). Nevertheless, the hand of heaven can be traced in Jesus' origins and in his destiny. He came not as the culmination of the procreative power of human generations but as pure gift of God, and that gift lives beyond the grave by the same creative power of God.

3—In appearance the angel is blinding and bright, **like lightning,** and his garb **white as snow,** pictures recalling the splendor of the transfigured Jesus (17:2) and his promise that the righteous will one day shine like the sun in the presence of their God (13:43; Dan. 12:2-3). The angel descends from the world of light where God's will is ever obeyed (6:10) and comes clothed in the burning purity of the heavenly world (Isa. 1:18; Ezek. 1:4; Dan. 7:9-10; 10:6; Rev. 1:14). In Mark the "young man" acts primarily as teacher of good news, sitting on the right hand within the tomb and proclaiming the Easter gospel, but Matthew portrays the angel as apocalyptic figure, shattering presence, throwing the stone aside and opening a new age in cosmic history.

4—**The guards** collapse. On Easter the dead and defenseless one comes to life and brings saints to new life (27:51-53) while the mighty of the earth faint dead away. They lie like trophies at the angel's feet, and the angel speaks to the women, declaring to them and to the readers the dawn of the new age in Jesus.

5-7—They had come to see a tomb, a house of death, to pay their last respects to a dead friend, to keep a vigil and chant a dirge, but the angel speaks of new life: **You seek Jesus who was crucified. He is not here; for he has risen, as he said** (12:40; 16:21; 17:23; 20:19).

In the first place, Easter is a message about Jesus. He was

crucified, done to death by powerful enemies shocked or frightened by the claim that he heard God's voice clearly calling him to identify in meekness with outcasts and to share the burdens of the oppressed (3:13-17; 8:14-17; 11:25-30; 21:5; 26:36-46). He was **crucified** by religious and political leaders, full of mocking at his silence and his weakness. He was **crucified,** but God did not let Jesus drop. God intervened, so that **he has risen.** The resurrection is the divine verdict on Jesus with all his works and words. His enemies lifted him to the cross; God lifts him to fresh and indestructible life.

And Easter is a message about the new human community. Therefore the angelic message continues: **Tell his disciples that he has risen from the dead, and behold, he is going before you to Galilee; there you will see him.** The resurrected one is shepherd of the flock (9:36) and immediately he begins to gather the scattered (26:31-32; Heb. 13:20).

8-10—The women receive the angelic announcement **with fear and great joy,** and they begin running from the tomb. Suddenly Jesus confronts them. At first his appearing seems to add almost nothing to what they know from the angel. But Matthew makes it clear that the impulse behind discipleship and the foundation of the new community is not a vision of angels, not some ambiguous sign like an empty tomb, nor some spectacular event like the magi's star, certainly not ecstatic seizure or prophetic inspiration of Christian leaders. It is the presence and word of Jesus himself.

The women fell at his feet and **worshiped** him (2:2, 8, 11; 14:33), acknowledging him as their exalted Lord (contrast the behavior of priests in 26:65-68 and of soldiers in 27:27-31). Christian devotion to the resurrected Jesus is certainly the awestruck and grateful response of the beneficiaries of divine grace, but it is not slavish obeisance to an oriental despot. Jesus lifts the women with his words, telling them to lay aside their fear and to speak to his **brethren.** He is creating not a harem and an army but a new family under God (12:46-50; 25:40; John 20:28; Ps. 22:22), a family in which he is the firstborn among many sisters and brothers (Rom. 8:29; Heb. 2:11-18).

This Story (28:11-15)

Sandwiched between the worship of the women in Jerusalem (vv. 9-10) and the worship of the eleven in Galilee (vv. 16-17) is the scene of the bribers and the bribed who deny Jesus' resurrection. Choices are set before the readers.

The brief scene is reminiscent of the gathering of the magi before Herod the Great inside his palace at the beginning of the Gospel (2:1-12), and it is in stark contrast to the scene on the mountain (28:16-20). All three scenes are dominated by authorities wielding impressive power and holding high office. Before them stand people who have seen signs or heard reports and who arrive as suppliants and seekers. The authorities dispose of matters, issuing instructions and offering assurances.

11—Not one but two reports of the events at the tomb arrive back inside Jerusalem. The women carry their message to Jesus' disciples, and the guards report the same events to the chief priests, telling them **all that had taken place.**

12-14—Once again the enemies of Jesus hatch a plot (26:3) and pay out money to ensure cooperation (26:14-15). Once they sought out false testimony (26:59-60), and now they pay **a sum of money** (cf. 26:15) to suppress the truth and spread a lie. Incredibly the soldiers agree to include as part of their story the confession that they had fallen asleep. They thus destroy both their credibility as witnesses and their reliability as guards. Furthermore, the council promises to shield them from the wrath of Pilate.

15—The soldiers pocketed **the money** (cf. 26:15) and did as they were told. The next scene (28:16-20) pictures Jesus with his disciples, instructing them to teach (*didaskontes*) all nations. Here the soldiers are being pictured as disciples of the priests and elders, "taught" or "instructed" (*edidachthēsan*) by them. The RSV obscures the connection between these two scenes by using the word **directed.** The readers are being asked, Whose disciples do you want to be? And who is your teacher (*didaskalos*, cf. 23:8)? This paragraph is a sharp call to make and hold a right decision.

Make Disciples (28:16-20)

A great final scene in Galilee caps Matthew's Gospel and brings it to fitting conclusion. How fitting it is may be gauged by imagining the much different ending Matthew could have penned.

He might have concluded by picturing the enthronement of Jesus along the lines of Dan. 7:13-14, with the presentation of the resurrected Son of man before the Ancient of Days, his solemn investiture with power and dominion over all nations, and the declaration that his kingdom would never be destroyed.

Or Matthew might have portrayed Jesus as an awesome figure with face like shining sun, with eyes like flames of fire, wearing robes richly decorated with royal, priestly, and military emblems (Rev. 1:12-20). Or again, the Gospel might have closed with a Christian hymn celebrating the movement of Jesus through obedient death to glorious triumph over things in heaven and on earth and under the earth (cf. Phil. 2:6-11) or one on the all-embracing reach of his epiphany and sway (1 Tim. 3:16).

Or Matthew might have closed his Gospel as Luke did, with the intimacy and warmth of the meeting with two disciples on the road to Emmaus, dialoging about hopes and fears, breaking bread together (Luke 24). Or Matthew might have recorded how Jesus wooed faith from a reluctant disciple, submitting hands and side to rude inspection, coaxing faith into full flame (John 20).

But in perfect harmony with his presentation of Jesus in all the preceding pages, Matthew has chosen to close his Gospel not with a visual or pictorial representation of Jesus' assumption of power, and not with sharing bread or touching his body, but with a deceptively simple scene featuring the words of Jesus, the church's one teacher and master (23:8-10).

16—The narration of the meeting of Jesus with his disciples is a marvel of reserve. No attempt is made to describe the resurrected one or to draw his portrait. Matthew says nothing about Jesus' posture or gestures: nothing of whether he is walking, standing, sitting, taking food, displaying hands or feet or side. Not a single word about the time, whether the meeting occurred in the morning or evening, on Sunday or a weekday, on Pentecost or at some other season. Nothing about Peter, Thomas, Cleopas, Mary Magdalene, or any other individual disciple.

Matthew is almost as reticent about the setting or circumstances of the encounter. It is not described as having happened on a road, at table, in an upper or lower room, or in a village or town. Matthew stresses that in obedience to Jesus' instructions, **the eleven disciples** left the city of Jerusalem and assembled in

Galilee, where Jesus had uttered his initial proclamation (4:17) and had called his first disciples (4:18-22). There in the north they gathered on a **mountain.** It is not clear whether they went **to the mountain to which Jesus had directed** (*tassō,* cf. 1:24) **them** (to go), or to the mountain "where Jesus had set their lives in order," that is, the place of the Sermon on the Mount, where Jesus had given their lives new shape. In either case Matthew once more (4:8; 5:1; 14:23; 15:29; 17:1) conjures up an unnamed and mysterious mountain as place of revelation, and what is revealed is the most authoritative ordering of the life of the new community.

17—The **eleven** gathered before him with faith and unfaith. **When they saw him, they worshiped him** (v. 9), **but some doubted** or hesitated. To the close of the age, the church is a mixed body consisting of good and evil (22:10), wheat and tares (13:24-30, 36-43), sheep and goats (25:32-33), and even "the good" are sometimes people of "little faith" (6:30; 8:26; 14:31; 16:8).

18a—In spite of their imperfections, Jesus approached and spoke to them. Matthew shows no interest in proving Jesus' physicality (Luke 24:36-40) or in interpreting his wounds (John 20:24-29). Matthew says nothing of Jesus' moving unhindered through doors (John 20:19, 26), of eating at table (Luke 24:30, 41-43), or of any miraculous provision of fish (John 21:4-8). Matthew concentrates exclusively on the words Jesus speaks.

18b-20—Jesus had been betrayed and abandoned, slandered and condemned, whipped and crucified. But now he lives and speaks from a throne higher than that of any mortal ruler, summoning his band of followers to a mighty task, universal in space and time. In form and substance his speech is an imperial decree. In contours and even to a certain extent in content his speech strangely resembles the edict of Cyrus the Persian that permitted and encouraged Jewish exiles to return to Judah from Babylonian captivity and to rebuild their temple in Jerusalem (2 Chron. 36:22-23).

The decree of Jesus has three parts: claim to authority (v. 18), commission or command (v. 19), and motivation or promise (v. 20). The decree is a mere handful of words (50 in the Greek text), and yet nothing more and nothing greater could be expressed with a thousand words.

18b—Jesus declares the universal reach of his sovereignty. **All**

authority in heaven and on earth has been given to me. No creature whether visible or invisible is beyond his care, beneath his notice, or past his knowing or reaching. He is the one through whom God will make all things all right.

From the beginning of his Gospel Matthew has been defining the **authority** (*exousia*) of Jesus. That same word is translated elsewhere in the New Testament as "power" or "freedom" or "right." The word is rich and provocative in connotation.

Authority is what Hellenistic religion promised to its adherents (Acts 8:19; 1 Cor.6:12; 8:9; 10:23; 2 Cor.10:8; 13:10), and it is a word used in Judaism of teachers qualified to judge legal matters. In Matthew's Gospel the **authority** of Jesus is bound especially closely to his teaching (compare Matt. 7:29 and Mark 1:22).

That Jesus has **all** authority is explained in part by the other three uses of **all** in 28:18-20: "all nations," "all I have commanded," "all the days." The writ of councils, kings, and governors is severely limited (10:17-18, 28). But the wide expanse of heaven is the throne of God, and the length and breadth of the earth is his footstool (5:34-35). Jesus claims **authority** running to the outer edges of the universe, summons all nations to discipleship, commands obedience to all his orders, and promises to be present to the end of all days.

All that teachers and scribes saw in Torah or Wisdom—existing before the foundation of the world, seated on the lap of the heavenly King, the principle by which the world hangs together and makes sense, guide and light for the life of God's people—Matthew sees in Jesus (5:21-48; 11:28-30; 16:12; 18:20; 23:1-36). And all that priests saw in the temple—great ancient focal point and public symbol of God's presence and provision and of Israel's devotion and identity—Matthew likewise locates in Jesus (12:6; 21:12, 23-27).

But most especially this magisterial claim of Jesus undercuts the petty and pompous claims of all the leaders of the Christian community, whether renowned for learning (23:8-12) or for their spiritual endowments (7:15, 22; 24:11, 24; cf. Rev. 3:22). Against any Christian leaders boasting of sanctity or authority or spiritual gift, and tempted to set themselves above the little ones in the community, the word of Jesus rings out clearly and most emphatically: "You have one teacher, one master" (23:8-10).

Jesus, identified by all he taught, all he did, and all he suffered in the preceding chapters of the Gospel, and nothing or no one else, is the foundation for the life of the new community, and he is the touchstone for assessing all the speech and silence, all the action and passion of the church. He has neither peer nor successor.

19—The little word **therefore** at the beginning of v. 19 means that the command enshrined in v. 19 flows directly out of the claim of v. 18. In fact the point of all that authority and the nature of that authority comes into clear focus in the command. The command begins to unveil the meaning of the authority.

Because of the word of command, the entire saying (vv. 18-20) bears the traditional name, "The Great Commission." And the commission has been understood primarily in terms of a summons to missionary and evangelistic activity. But caution is needed here. The saying lacks the usual early Christian words for sending, apostleship, or mission. Also missing are the customary words for gospel, preaching, proclaiming, repentance, and forgiveness (contrast 10:7). Lacking also is any explicit reference to charismatic activity: exorcism, healing, raising the dead (contrast 10:8), or prophecy (7:22).

Furthermore, the word usually translated into English as **go** functions in the original as an auxiliary. That means that it does not describe a separate action alongside of making disciples but rather underscores the urgency of making disciples.

Jesus issues orders, and they may be translated: "Be busy constantly making **disciples of all nations.**" Discipleship is the heart of the matter. And the charge to **make disciples** is aimed at telling the church not only what to do about people outside but especially what to do with the people inside the new community. This is a command about the integrity of the church.

Matthew reminds readers that Jesus wills not a numerically large community, not an efficient and well-organized community, not a learned community, not even a community intoxicated with the gifts of the Spirit. Perhaps the vision of Jesus includes some or all of these, but his gaze is fixed steadfastly on discipleship.

In the end **all nations** will be gathered before the Son of man in his glory, and they will be divided into sheep and goats (25:31-46). That vision of the last times operates with the widest possible horizon, embracing all humanity without exception. So also the summons to make disciples has all humanity in view (24:14). The vision and the will of Jesus is that people from **all nations** become a new community of **disciples.**

That happens in two ways; first, by **baptizing them in the name of the Father and of the Son and of the Holy Spirit.** That means by incorporating people of all classes and kinds into the community and its life. The making of disciples occurs in the second place by **teaching them to observe,** to obey, **all that I have commanded you.**

Baptism was widely regarded in the early church as the moment when the Spirit was first poured into the life of the believer. After baptism, the same Spirit seized particular individuals and bestowed on them special powers. In some parts of the early church, and apparently in Matthew's community also, the Spirit was understood primarily as divine energy producing ecstasy, visions, prophecies, speaking in tongues, and miracles.

When Jesus speaks of Spirit and baptism here at the conclusion and climax of the Gospel, he is silent about all such popular gifts and powers. And he is emphatic and vocal about the connection of Spirit and baptism with discipleship. Jesus' own baptism, as described by Matthew (3:1-17), was above all else Jesus' first step on the way of righteousness (3:15; 21:32). All Jesus' charismatic energy and prophetic power—he was conceived by the Spirit (1:18, 20) and at baptism the Spirit descended upon him (3:16)—was focused on executing the Father's will and standing against demonic forces and obstructionist human authorities. The power of the new creation is at work in Jesus (1:1). He conquers evil and overthrows its rule (4:1-11; 21:28). The rule of God and of righteousness is now breaking in (6:33).

So here at the close of the Gospel, baptism and the Spirit are named not in connection with ecstasy, or freedom from the bonds of tradition, or pyrotechnic display of charismatic endowment. However highly Matthew may have respected and cherished all these, he held righteousness and discipleship even more dear.

The way Matthew has linked the Spirit in a series with the Father and the Son leads in the same direction. Baptism is **in the name of the Father and of the Son and of the Holy Spirit.** The use here of the triune formula has provoked a wealth of discussion, but two points seem especially important. In the first place, the formula proclaims the presence of God in the Son and in the Spirit, thereby confessing God to be not an abstract principle but a saving (1:21) and re-creating (12:28) personal power, reaching into human history to establish a new community of persons out of all the nations.

In the second place, the Spirit is reined in. Previous passages tie the Spirit to the Father (3:16; 10:20) or to the Son (12:18, 28) but now all three are bound as closely as possible. And the three constitute one name. The Spirit has no fresh mission separate or distinct from that of Father and Son, contrary to what some inspired leaders in the community may have believed. Baptism is an act of the community, setting a person onto the way of discipleship, onto the path of righteousness as a person in the possession and under the authority of the single reality **of the Father and of the Son and of the Holy Spirit.**

20—Disciples are to be made by baptizing people and by **teaching them to observe all that I have commanded you.** The gravitational center of this **teaching** is not theories or doctrines. Throughout Matthew's Gospel Jesus proclaims that all the Law and the Prophets add up, not to some speculation about God or angels or heaven, not to a schematization of history into successive aeons, but to the higher righteousness (5:20). That is what the Law and Prophets point to, and that is what Jesus taught and **commanded.** That is what he insisted on from beginning to end, from the Sermon on the Mount (chaps. 5–7) all the way down to the vision about the sheep and the goats at the conclusion to his final discourse to his disciples (25:31-46).

So God's movement into the world in Jesus has as its goal a community of disciples, gathered from among Jews and Gentiles, initiated through baptism into the community and onto the way of righteousness, practicing the will of God as Jesus has interpreted it.

Yet another stream springs from the authority of Jesus and further defines its awesome character. The words describing it are connected to the preceding and given prominence by the solemn introduction: **And lo!**

The authority of Jesus extends over time as well as over the space in which all nations live. He is not confined to the past.

Jesus is not merely the revered founder of the community. He has not cast his mantle upon successors, and he does not need to create a corps of elders, shepherds, priests, bishops, or other leaders to govern the community in his absence. Jesus is neither dead nor absent.

He is Emmanuel, the place of the presence of God, and he continues with the community, indwelling the community, wherever two or three gather in his name and lift their voices in prayer (see commentary above on 1:23; 11:28-30; 18:20).

I am with you is Jesus' solemn promise to be with the people of the new community, guiding, helping, protecting and empowering them in all their historic struggles.

Jesus' disciples need not look for any other teacher or teaching, any fresh revelations or new instructions, any supplementary energizings or powers above or beyond what they have in him, their Master and Teacher, the Son of God. Easter means the ongoing life of the one Teacher, Jesus, in the time of the church.

Always, as long as the stars hold their place and sun rises and sun sets, as long as the seas rush in and out, as long as the heavens above and the earth below endure, the disciples are well supplied, with gifts and teachings to suffice them, for he himself continues with them as Lord and Teacher with his word. His disciples have all they require—all the blessings and rescuing and also all the commands they need—for all the days **to the close of the age** (cf. 13:39).

SELECTED BIBLIOGRAPHY

Research Reports

Daniel Harrington. "Matthean Studies since Joachim Rohde," *Heythrop Journal* 16 (1975) 375-88.

R. G. Hamerton-Kelly. "Matthew, Gospel of." *IDB* 5: 580-583.

Joachim Rohde. *Rediscovering the Teaching of the Evangelists*. London: SCM, 1968.

Donald Senior. *What Are They Saying about Matthew?* New York/Ramsey: Paulist, 1983.

Graham Stanton. "Matthew's Gospel: A New Storm Centre," in *The Interpretation of Matthew*, ed. G. Stanton. Philadelphia: Fortress, 1983. Pp. 1-18.

Commentaries

Robert H. Gundry. *Matthew: A Commentary on His Literary and Theological Art*. Grand Rapids: Eerdmans, 1982.

John L. McKenzie. "The Gospel according to Matthew," in *Jerome Biblical Commentary*, ed. R. E. Brown, J. A. Fitzmyer, R. E. Murphy. Englewood Cliffs: Prentice Hall, 1968.

Daniel Patte. *The Gospel according to Matthew: A Structural Commentary on Matthew's Faith*. Philadelphia: Fortress, 1987.

Eduard Schweizer. *The Good News according to Matthew*. Atlanta: John Knox, 1975.

Krister Stendahl. "Matthew," in *Peake's Commentary on the Bible*, ed. Matthew Black and H. H. Rowley. London: Thomas Nelson, 1962. Pp. 769-798.

Herman Waetjen. *The Origin and Destiny of Humanness*. San Rafael: Omega, 1976.

Selected Bibliography

Studies

B. W. Bacon. *Studies in Matthew.* New York: Holt, 1930.

Gunther Bornkamm, Gerhard Barth, and Heinz J. Held. *Tradition and Interpretation in Matthew.* Philadelphia: Westminster, 1963.

Raymond Brown and John P. Meier. *Antioch and Rome.* New York: Paulist, 1983. Meier treats Matthew in "Part One: Antioch."

W. D. Davies. *The Setting of the Sermon on the Mount.* Cambridge: Cambridge University Press, 1964.

Richard A. Edwards. *Matthew's Story of Jesus.* Philadelphia: Fortress, 1985.

Peter Ellis. *Matthew: His Mind and His Message.* Collegeville: Liturgical Press, 1974.

Robert H. Gundry. *The Use of the Old Testament in St. Matthew's Gospel.* Leiden: Brill, 1967.

Douglas R. A. Hare. *The Theme of Jewish Persecution of Christians in the Gospel according to St. Matthew.* Cambridge: Cambridge University Press, 1967.

George D. Kilpatrick. *The Origins of the Gospel according to St. Matthew.* Oxford: Clarendon, 1946.

Jack Dean Kingsbury. *Matthew As Story.* Philadelphia: Fortress, 1986.

John P. Meier. *Law and History in Matthew's Gospel.* Rome: Biblical Institute, 1976.

——————— . *The Vision of Matthew.* New York: Paulist, 1979.

Benno Przybylski. *Righteousness in Matthew and His World of Thought.* Cambridge: Cambridge University Press, 1980.

Graham Stanton, ed. *The Interpretation of Matthew.* Philadelphia: Fortress, London: SPCK, 1983.

Krister Stendahl. *The School of St. Matthew and Its Use of the Old Testament,* rev. ed. Philadelphia: Fortress, 1968.

Georg Strecker. "The Concept of History in Matthew (1967)," in *Interpretation of Matthew.* ed. G. Stanton. Pp. 67-84.

Christology

J. D. G. Dunn. *Christology in the Making.* Philadelphia: Westminster, 1980.

L. Gaston. "The Messiah of Israel as Teacher of the Gentiles: The Setting of Matthew's Christology," *Interp.* 29 (1975) 25-40.

F. Hahn. *The Titles of Jesus in Christology.* London: Lutterworth, 1969.

David Hill. "In Quest of Matthean Christology," *IBS* 8 (1986) 135-142.

J. D. Kingsbury. *Jesus Christ in Matthew, Mark, and Luke.* Philadelphia: Fortress, 1981.

——————— . *Matthew: Stucture, Christology, Kingdom.* Philadelphia: Fortress, 1975.

_____ . "The Figure of Jesus in Matthew's Story: A Literary Critical Probe," *JSNT* 21 (1984) 3-36.

Barnabas Lindars. *Jesus: Son of Man.* Grand Rapids: Eerdmans, 1984.

M. Jack Suggs. *Wisdom, Christology, and Law in Matthew's Gospel.* Cambridge: Harvard University Press, 1970.

Structure of Matthew

H. J. B. Combrink. "The Macrostructure of the Gospel of Matthew," *Neotestamentica* 16 (1982) 1-20.

Edgar Krentz. "The Extent of Matthew's Prologue: Toward the Structure of Matthew's Gospel," *JBL* 83 (1964) 409-414.

J. D. Kingsbury. *Matthew: Structure, Christology, Kingdom.* Philadelphia: Fortress, 1975.

C. Lohr. "Oral Techniques in the Gospel of Matthew," *CBQ* 23 (1961) 403-435.

F. J. Matera. "The Plot of Matthew's Gospel," *CBQ* 49 (1987) 233-253.

Marianne M. Thompson. "The Structure of Matthew: An Examination of Two Approaches," *Studia Biblica et Theologica* 12 (1982) 195-238.

Additional Bibliography by Chapter

Matthew 1–2

Raymond E. Brown. *The Birth of the Messiah: A Commentary on the Infancy Narratives.* New York: Doubleday & Co., 1977.

_____ . "Gospel Infancy Narrative Research from 1976 to 1986: Part I (Matthew)" *CBQ* 48 (1986) 468-483.

Marshall D. Johnson. *The Purpose of the Biblical Genealogies,* 2d ed. Cambridge: Cambridge University Press, 1988.

Brian M. Nolan. *The Royal Son of God: The Christology of Matthew 1– 2 in the Setting of the Gospel.* Göttingen: Vandenhoeck & Ruprecht, 1979.

G. M. Soaves Prabhu. *The Formula Quotations in the Infancy Narrative of Matthew.* Rome, 1976.

Krister Stendahl. "Quis et Unde? An Analysis of Mt 1-2" (1960), in *The Interpretation of Matthew,* ed. G. Stanton. Pp. 56-66.

Chapter 3

John P. Meier. "John the Baptist in Matthew's Gospel," *JBL* 99 (1980) 383-405.

Walter Wink. *John the Baptist in the Gospel Tradition.* Cambridge: Cambridge University Press, 1968.

Selected Bibliography

Chapter 4

Birger Gerhardsson. *The Testing of God's Son*. Lund: Gleerup, 1966.

William O. Walker Jr. "The Kingdom of the Son of Man and the Kingdom of the Father in Matthew," CBQ 30 (1968) 573-579.

Wilhelm Wuellner. *The Meaning of "Fishers of Men."* Philadelphia: Westminster, 1967.

Chapter 5

D. C. Allison Jr. "The Structure of the Sermon on the Mount," *JBL* 106 (1987) 423-445.

G. Barth. "Matthew's Understanding of the Law," in Bornkamm et al., *Tradition and Interpretation in Matthew*. Pp. 58-164.

Hans Dieter Betz. *Essays on the Sermon on the Mount*. Philadelphia: Fortress, 1985.

W. D. Davies. *The Setting of the Sermon on the Mount*. Cambridge: Cambridge University Press, 1964.

R. Guelich. *The Sermon on the Mount*. Waco: Word, 1982.

―――――――――― . "Interpreting the Sermon on the Mount," *Interp.* 41 (1987) 117-130.

R. A. Horsley. "Ethics and Exegesis: Love Your Enemies and the Language of Non-Violence," *JAAR* 54 (1986) 3-31.

L. E. Keck. "Ethics in the Gospel according to Matthew," *Iliff Review* 40 (1984) 39-56.

George A. Kennedy. *New Testament Interpretation through Rhetorical Criticism*. Chapel Hill: University of North Carolina, 1984. Pp. 39-72 (on the structure of the Sermon on the Mount).

W. Kissinger. *The Sermon on the Mount: A History of Interpretation and Bibliography*. Metuchen: Scarecrow, 1975.

Luise Schottroff et al. *Essays on the Love Commandment*. Philadelphia: Fortress, 1978.

Robert Tannehill. *The Sword of His Mouth*. Philadelphia: Fortress, 1975. Important studies of the rhetoric of Jesus' sayings.

Disciples

Richard A. Edwards. "Uncertain Faith: Matthew's Portrait of the Disciples," in *Discipleship in the New Testament,* ed. F. Segovia, Philadelphia: Fortress, 1985. Pp. 47-61.

Ulrich Luz. "The Disciples in the Gospel according to Matthew" (1971), in *Interpretation of Matthew,* ed. G. Stanton. Pp. 98-128.

J. D. Kingsbury. "The Verb 'Akolouthein' ('to follow') as an Index of Matthew's View of His Community," *JBL* 97 (1978) 56-73.

Paul Minear. "The Disciples and the Crowds in the Gospel of Matthew," *ATR* 2 (1974): 28-44.

Prayer

Philip Harner. *Understanding the Lord's Prayer.* Philadelphia: Fortress, 1975.

J. Jeremias. *The Prayers of Jesus.* Philadelphia: Fortress, 1978.

E. Lohmeyer. *Our Father.* New York: Harper & Row, 1965.

On prayer in the Old and New Testament periods see also C. W. F. Smith, *IDB* 3:857-867; H. Greeven and J. Herrmann, *TDNT* 2:775-808.

Chapter 7

J. E. Davison, "Anomia and the Question of an Antinomian Polemic in Matthew," *JBL* 104 (1985) 617-635.

D. Hill, "False Prophets and Charismatics (Matthew 7:15-23)," *Biblica* 57 (1976) 327-348.

P. Minear. "False Prophecy and Hypocrisy in the Gospel of Matthew," *Neues Testament und Kirche,* ed. J. Gnilka. Freiburg: Herder, 1974. Pp. 76-93.

E. Schweizer. "Observance of the Law and Charismatic Activity in Matthew" *NTS* 16 (1970) 213-230.

Chapters 8–9

G. Bornkamm. "The Stilling of the Storm in Matthew," in G. Bornkamm et al. *Tradition and Interpretation in Matthew.* Pp. 52-57.

Birger Gerhardsson. *The Mighty Acts of Jesus according to Matthew.* Lund: Gleerup, 1979.

H. J. Held. "Matthew as Interpreter of the Miracle Stories," in G. Bornkamm et al. *Tradition and Interpretation in Matthew.* Pp. 165-299.

Howard Clark Kee. *Miracle in the Early Christian World.* New Haven and London: Yale University Press, 1983.

J. D. Kingsbury. "Observations on the Miracle Chapters of Matthew 8-9," *CBQ* 40 (1978) 559-573.

Chapter 9

John Donahue. "Tax Collectors and Sinners," *CBQ* 33 (1971) 39-61.

Chapter 10

Schuyler Brown. "The Mission to Israel," *ZNW* 69 (1978) 73-90.

Morna Hooker. "The Prohibition of Foreign Missions (Mt. 10:5-6)," *ExpT* 82 (1971) 361-365.

L. Sabourin. "You Will Not Have Gone Through All the Towns of Israel" (Matt. 10:23), *BTB* 7 (1977) 5-11.

Selected Bibliography

Chapter 11

M. J. Suggs. *Wisdom, Christology and Law in Matthew's Gospel.* Cambridge: Harvard University Press, 1970.

Marshall D. Johnson. "Reflections on a Wisdom Approach to Matthew's Christology," *CBQ* 36 (1974) 44-64.

H. D. Betz. "The Logion of the Easy Yoke and of Rest (Matt. 11:28-30)," *JBL* 86 (1967) 10-24.

Chapter 13

L. Cope. *Matthew: A Scribe Trained for the Kingdom of Heaven.* Washington: Catholic Biblical Association, 1976.

John Donahue. *The Gospel in Parable.* Philadelphia: Fortress, 1988.

J. D. Kingsbury. *The Parables of Jesus in Matthew 13.* London: SPCK, and St. Louis: Clayton, 1977.

Chapter 15

Janice Capel Anderson. "Matthew: Gender and Reading," *Semeia* 28 (1983) 3-27.

Chapter 16

G. Bornkamm. "The Authority to Bind and Loose in the Church in Matthew's Gospel" (1970), in G. Stanton, *Interpretation of Matthew.* Pp. 85-97.

_____ . "End-Expectation and Church in Matthew," in Bornkamm et al. *Tradition and Interpretation in Matthew.* Pp. 15-51.

R. E. Brown, P. Donfried, J. Reumann, eds. *Peter in the New Testament.* Minneapolis and New York: Augsburg and Paulist, 1973.

J. Burgess. *A History of the Exegesis of Matthew 16:17-19.* Ann Arbor: Edwards, 1976.

R. H. Hiers. "Binding and Loosing: The Matthean Authorizations," *JBL* 104 (1985) 233-250.

J. D. Kingsbury. "The Figure of Peter in Matthew's Gospel as a Theological Problem," *JBL* 98 (1979) 67-83.

R. J. McKelvey. *The New Temple.* New York: Oxford University, 1969.

Chapter 17

Terence Donaldson. *Jesus on the Mountain.* Sheffield: JSOT, 1985.

Chapter 18

D. Patte, ed. *Kingdom and Children* (Semeia 29, 1983).

E. Schweizer. "Matthew's Church," in *Interpretation of Matthew,* ed. G. Stanton. Pp. 129-155.

Matthew

B. B. Scott, "The King's Accounting: Matthew 18:23-34," *JBL* 104 (1985) 429-442.

William G. Thompson. *Matthew's Advice to a Divided Community: Matthew 17:22-18:35.* Rome: Pontifical Biblical Institute, 1970.

Chapter 23

D. Garland. *The Intention of Matthew 23.* Leiden: Brill, 1979.

B. Lategan. "Structure and Reference in Mt. 23," *Neotestamentica* 16 (1982) 74-87.

S. Van Tilborg. *The Jewish Leaders in Matthew.* Leiden: Brill, 1972.

Chapters 24–25

F. W. Burnett. *The Testament of Jesus-Sophia.* Washington: University Press of America, 1981.

L. Cope. "Matthew 25:31-46—The Sheep and the Goats Reinterpreted," *NovT* 11 (1969) 32-44.

J. Lambrecht. "The Parousia Discourse: Composition and Content in Matt. 24-25," in M. Didier, ed. *L' Evangile selon Matthieu.* Gembloux: Duculot, 1972. Pp. 309-342.

J. R. Michaels. "Apostolic Hardships and Righteous Gentiles. A Study of Matt. 25:31-46," *JBL* 84 (1965) 27-37.

D. O. Via. "Ethical Responsibility and Human Wholeness in Matt. 25:31-46," *HTR* 80 (1987) 79-100.

Chapters 26–28

A. Matthew's Passion Narrative

Nils Dahl. "The Passion Narrative in Matthew" (1955), in *The Interpretation of Matthew,* ed. G. Stanton. Pp. 42-55.

J. Fitzmyer. "Anti-Semitism and the Cry of 'All the People' (Matt. 27:25)," *TS* 26 (1965): 667-671.

Frank Matera. *Passion Narratives and Gospel Theologies.* New York: Paulist, 1986.

Donald Senior. *The Passion of Jesus in the Gospel of Matthew.* Wilmington: M. Glazier, 1985.

Hans-Rudi Weber. *The Cross: Tradition and Interpretation.* Philadelphia: Fortress, 1977.

B. Eucharist

Joachim Jeremias. *The Eucharistic Words of Jesus.* New York: Scribner's, 1966.

I. H. Marshall. *Last Supper and Lord's Supper.* Grand Rapids: Eerdmans, 1980.

Selected Bibliography

C. Crucifixion

Joseph Fitzmyer. "Crucifixion in Ancient Palestine, Qumran Literature and the New Testament," *CBQ* 40 (1978) 493-513.
Martin Hengel. *Crucifixion in the Ancient World and the Folly of the Message of the Cross.* Philadelphia: Fortress, 1977.
John Reumann. "Psalm 22 at the Cross," *Interp.* 28 (1974) 39-58.

Chapter 28

G. Bornkamm. "The Risen Lord and the Earthly Jesus: Matt. 28:16-20," in J. M. Robinson, ed. *The Future of Our Religious Past.* London: SCM, 1971.
S. Brown. "The Matthean Community and the Gentile Mission," *NovT* 22 (1980) 193-221.
D. Hill. "The Conclusion of Matthew's Gospel," *IBS* 8 (1986) 54-63.
B. J. Hubbard. *The Matthean Redaction of a Primitive Apostolic Commissioning.* Missoula: Scholars Press, 1974.
J. D. Kingsbury. "The Composition and Christology of Matt. 28:16-20," *JBL* 93 (1974) 573-584.
Bruce Malina. "The Literary Structure and Form of Matt. 28:16-20," *NTS* 17 (1970) 87-103.
Otto Michel. "The Conclusion of Matthew's Gospel" (1950), in *The Interpretation of Matthew,* ed. G. Stanton. Pp. 30-41.
Robert H. Smith. *Easter Gospels: The Resurrection of Jesus according to the Four Evangelists.* Minneapolis: Augsburg, 1983.

ABOUT THE AUTHOR

Robert Smith has taught at Pacific Lutheran Theological Seminary in Berkeley, California, since 1983; he serves also on the doctoral faculty of the Graduate Theological Union. Previously he taught New Testament at Christ Seminary-Seminex in St. Louis and at Concordia Theological Seminary, also in St. Louis. Prior to teaching he served as pastor in Chappaqua, New York.

Dr. Smith has written commentaries on *The Acts of the Apostles* (1970) and on the letter to the *Hebrews* (ACNT, Augsburg, 1984). He is the author also of *Easter Gospels: The Resurrection of Jesus according to the Four Evangelists* (Augsburg, 1983) and the coauthor of *The Lutheran Church in North American Life, 1776-1976.* He edits "Preaching Helps," a bimonthly supplement in *Currents in Theology and Mission.*

He and his wife, Emita, live in El Cerrito, California.